Agency and Ownership in Reconciliation

Agency and Ownership in Reconciliation

Youth and the Practice of Transitional Justice

CAITLIN MOLLICA

Published by State University of New York Press, Albany

© 2024 State University of New York

All rights reserved

Printed in the United States of America

No part of this book may be used or reproduced in any manner whatsoever without written permission. No part of this book may be stored in a retrieval system or transmitted in any form or by any means including electronic, electrostatic, magnetic tape, mechanical, photocopying, recording, or otherwise without the prior permission in writing of the publisher.

For information, contact State University of New York Press, Albany, NY
www.sunypress.edu

Library of Congress Cataloging-in-Publication Data

Name: Mollica, Caitlin, 1986– author.
Title: Agency and ownership in reconciliation : youth and the practice of transitional justice / Caitlin Mollica.
Description: Albany : State University of New York Press, [2024]. | Includes bibliographical references and index.
Identifiers: LCCN 2023039242 | ISBN 9781438497440 (hardcover : alk. paper) | ISBN 9781438497457 (ebook) | ISBN 9781438497433 (pbk. : alk. paper)
Subjects: LCSH: Truth commissions. | Youth in peace-building. | Transitional justice.
Classification: LCC JC580 .M65 2024 | DDC 323.4/9—dc23/eng/20240112
LC record available at https://lccn.loc.gov/2023039242

10 9 8 7 6 5 4 3 2 1

For mum

Contents

ACKNOWLEDGMENTS ix

INTRODUCTION
Hearing and Seeing Young People in Peace and Conflict:
Lessons from and for the Practice of Reconciliation 1

CHAPTER 1
Contextualizing Transitional Justice for Meaningful
Youth Participation 31

CHAPTER 2
Locating Young People in Peace and Conflict:
The Development of Scholarship for Children and Youth 53

CHAPTER 3
Establishing Visibility: A Human Rights Approach to the
Involvement of Young People at the TRC in South Africa 85

CHAPTER 4
Claiming Ownership? Contrasting Narratives of Agency and
Participation at the Sierra Leone and Timor-Leste TRCs 121

CHAPTER 5
Seeing and Hearing Youth: The Solomon Islands Truth and
Reconciliation Process 159

CONCLUSION
Considering the Legacy of Young People's Participation
and Adopting a Way Forward 201

NOTES	219
BIBLIOGRAPHY	261
INDEX	283

Acknowledgments

Firstly, this book would not have been possible without the deep love and support of my parents Jane (dec.) and Joe. I am forever grateful to them and appreciate their commitment to nurturing my love of books and learning. This book is for you. I also want to thank my brother Lachlan, my sister-in-law Gabbi, my niece and nephew (Olive and Ernie), Nonna (dec.), and the G'ma for being my number one cheer squad as I worked to finalize this manuscript.

I am fortunate to be surrounded by a community of exceptional female scholars who have provided years of mentorship and support during my research journey. Particularly I would like to thank professors Renée Jeffery, Sara Davies, Kate Lee-Koo, and Bina D'Costa, as well as assistant professors Jana Tabek, Bridget Harris, and Erin O'Brien. I also extend an extra special thank you to Dr. Helen Berents for "talking youth" with me and for your wisdom, mentorship, collaboration, and friendship. To Séverine Autesserre, professor at Columbia University, thank you for encouraging me to pursue my PhD and for introducing me to interpretive research methodologies, without which I would not have been able to tell the stories in this book. I also extend my sincere appreciation and warmest thanks to those who reviewed this manuscript both formally and informally. I offer my gratitude for the thoughtfulness, care, critical eye, and respect they showed this work.

During my academic career I have been lucky to receive support from exceptional research centers that show an extraordinary commitment to nurturing empirically grounded scholarship. I extend my sincere thanks to Professor Melissa Bull and the QUT Centre for Justice and to my colleagues at the Griffith Asia Institute and Centre for Governance and Public Policy, as well as my current institution: Newcastle Business School.

Finally, chapter 5 of this book would not have been possible without the support of the Solomon Islands community, specifically the young people. I am grateful to all those who spoke with me and trusted me with their stories. In particular, I would like to thank Florence for inviting me into her home and for showing me the best of Solomon Islands culture and community.

Introduction

Hearing and Seeing Young People in Peace and Conflict: Lessons from and for the Practice of Reconciliation

> Young people around the world are striving for peace, justice, inclusion, gender equality and human rights. Their aspirations, views and demands need to be heard . . . and their plight addressed.
>
> —UN Security Council, Resolution 2250

Strolling down a street in Honiara, Solomon Islands, one sunny afternoon in November 2015, I hear the pounding of drums and the strums of electric guitars begin to fill the air. As I follow the upbeat and melodic rhythms, I come across the National Art Gallery precinct, which today is adorned with bright colored banners announcing and welcoming the Solomon Islands community to the monthly youth markets. Surrounding the stage, where a band of youth artists are playing original soft rock tunes, reggae, and pop hits, are stalls selling arts and crafts, food, and magazines. Established by Youth@Work, a local organization hosted by the secretariat of the Pacific Community until it was handed over to the Solomon Islands government in 2019, these markets and Youth@Work programs are led largely by youth and for youth. As such, they reflect of model of substantive participation where youth demonstrate not only agency but ownership over their stories and community interactions.

The precinct is filled with people young and old, dancing joyfully, eating, talking, and laughing, all while watching local youth artists complete their masterpieces and their livelihoods. Responsibility for these stalls, the business plans that established them, and the markets themselves reside with Solomon Islander youth. Brightly colored knitted bags, homemade beauty and bath products, and printed T-shirts are displayed and sold with pride by youth who self-identify as entrepreneurs, business owners, and productive stakeholders in the (re)building and development of the Solomon Islands following the Tensions.[1] These markets, and the opportunities they enabled for substantive participation, illustrate the realm of the possible with respect to the political and public engagement of youth in the reconciliation and restoration of a nation following violence and instability.

Following my initial visit, I returned several more times to observe the interactions and to speak with youth about the role these markets played in their lives. Among the most notable insights provided by youth was the varied perspectives on how these markets contributed to their capacity to recast their role in the community following the Tensions. As Nelson Robridge Legua, a youth entrepreneur who sold his printed shirts at the markets, explained, these public spaces are an important opportunity for Solomon Islander youth to "take a shot, showcase our talents." A "time to open up"[2] to the community. As such, for many these youth markets, and the possibilities for economic empowerment they enable, illustrate the significance of thinking beyond simply institutional settings for the realization of inclusive justice. Within transitional communities still grappling with the legacies of past conflict, and youth's participation as key stakeholders to the violence and subsequent attempt to pursue peace and justice, it is critical that mechanisms and strategies for justice and peacebuilding are spaces where youth can challenge perceptions of their capacity and claim ownership of their experience via visibility, storytelling, and community participation.

Many young people I spoke with highlighted the importance of the markets for development and economic opportunity. In addition, they stressed that the outcomes from these markets could potentially act as a panacea for entrenched interpersonal and intergenerational challenges. As Sandra Barlett, program director of Youth@Work, explained, this program when coupled with Graduate Youth Entrepreneurship "gives youth a start . . . training them in business skills and providing them with startup capital" during a time when the community has "run out of jobs."[3] The association with interpersonal reconciliation is similarly reflected in the theme of the 2016 markets, "solidarity through culture,"[4] which highlighted the importance of creating substantive opportunities for *all* Solomon Islanders to come together across generations and youth's leadership role in the activities central to this pursuit of solidarity.

During my visits, youth's ownership over their stories and their participatory capacity was on full display. While busy selling, many also took time to interact, learn, and narrate their experiences of being young in the Solomon Islands (the opportunities and the challenges), not just with peers but with elders and visitors. What was immediately evident was that their stories had been profoundly shaped, both inadvertently and directly, by the Tensions and subsequent efforts to pursue reconciliation and justice. As one young stallholder explained: The Tensions "was very bad for young people . . . but I am doing ok now . . . slowly rebuilding, although the Trauma it is still there. But you must take these opportunities . . . as time to show what you can do, where you are from."[5] A similar story was shared by a young musician who reflected that following the Tensions "the country is still finding its feet and figuring out where youth fit within the system. Progress is being made but there is conflict between the old system and the new development culture. But the more training, the more opportunities to show I am participating, means I get respect from 'big men' (older generations: Chiefs) in my community."[6]

Notably, these markets were essential sites for bonding and (re)building interpersonal relationships between youth and the wider community. This sentiment was highlighted by a participant in the 2015 Graduate Youth Entrepreneurship program: "The Solomon Islander youth, we work hard to be in this program. It is for the whole community, and the community likes to be involved with us, providing us with work placements and supporting our fairs and stalls. It is an opportunity to show our skills."[7] Through substantive participation at these markets youth publicly demonstrated their capacity to take ownership of their livelihoods and thus to contribute to the community. What was immediately evident was that exposure to youth's substantive participatory capacity was instrumental for the realization of interpersonal reconciliation. As Bartlett explains, "The big success, the social change success, is that we've put youth development on people's minds. In Solomons, it was always, youth are a problem, youth are a time bomb . . . but now they see that youth are doing things."[8]

The importance of seeing youth must not be overstated. As illustrated by the example of the youth markets in the Solomon Islands and across the various interactions of young people with Truth and Reconciliation Commissions (TRCs) throughout this book, inclusive justice necessitates processes where youth are not merely seen and heard. Communities emerging from conflict and grappling with the legacies of human rights violations through transitional justice processes must also create spaces where youth's experiences, and the meaning they ascribe to them, are taken seriously. As such, for transitional justice practices to be substantively inclusive of youth as autonomous political agents they need to acknowledge and create opportunities for youth empowerment.

Indeed, as one youth entrepreneur suggested, "Youth can either be empowered to help healing and problem-solving or they can continue to be influenced and disenabled by the effects of the conflict, such as disruption of education and family problems. We promote local culture through youth products and local *kaikai* and the use of village structures to incorporate and promote youth."[9] Agency and ownership were visible and taken seriously because of the youth's participation and leadership in the development and implementation of these markets. As such, their actions in this public, noninstitutionalized space challenged deeply embedded, marginalizing perceptions of youth that resonate throughout the community. These markets and youth's stories and experiences that emerge from them are reflective of the tension and synergy surrounding substantive youth participation in transitional justice contexts. Before turning to the stories of youth in reconciliation, and their substantive participation, it is important to situate their storytelling agency within broader discourses of engagement with youth themselves as autonomous political agents.

Situating Youth as Substantive, Autonomous Political Agents

On December 9, 2015, the United Nations Security Council unanimously adopted Resolution 2250 on Youth, Peace and Security (YPS). This landmark resolution reflected a turning point in how the international community understood its relationship with young people, institutionally acknowledging their contributions as active stakeholders in the outcomes of post-conflict practices.[10] Central to this discursive evolution was the affirmation that youth play an "important role . . . in the prevention and resolution of conflicts and the sustainability, inclusiveness and success" of post-conflict practices; thus they should be empowered to lead and make decisions on their development.[11] Resolution 2250 compelled international actors, states, and youth to establish partnerships for the development of inclusive post-conflict practices. While this resolution was the first to codify recognition of the importance of young people's engagement for sustainable peace, the normative discourse has been slowly evolving since the 1990s. This evolution is due in part to the on-the-ground advocacy of young people, which has sought to challenge the status quo and reframe their interactions with practices in the peacebuilding and transitional justice fields.

Ideational evolution does not occur in a vacuum; it is informed by the external environment in which it exists, namely the social, political, and cultural conditions that create the milieu. Recognition that young people are active agents striving for peace and justice is the result of decades of youth advocacy and leadership in the development of informal peacebuilding practices. In addition, recognition of their political agency and their role as knowledge producers is informed by the stories young people share during reconciliation practices. These stories and the processes for telling them are central to the ideas presented in this book.

UN Resolution 2250 and subsequent YPS Resolutions 2249 (2018) and 2535 (2020) affirm what two decades of evolution in the relationships between young people and formal TRC processes revealed. Both demonstrate that young people "should be actively engaged in shaping lasting peace and contributing to justice and reconciliation" within the formal peace architecture. Also evident is the importance of informal reconciliation practices designed and implemented by youth to pursue justice alongside these formal institutions. Restoring trust and ensuring meaningful accountability through acknowledgment requires interactions between formal and informal sites of agency. This is particularly instrumental when the formal (often institutionalized) practices perpetuate conditions that limit the manifestation of agency and deny opportunities for ownership. Recognizing young people's capacity as political agents is critical for meaningful reconciliation. Attempts to end the culture of impunity within post-conflict states have a greater chance of lasting success when youth are empowered to substantively participate, as their contributions can produce a peace dividend.[12] In 2022, there were 1.85 billion young people (individuals between the ages of ten and twenty-four years old) in the world. Of these, 90 percent lived in developing countries and one in four have experienced violence and instability. Inclusive practices, therefore, that promote ownership amongst this diverse and expansive community are critical for lasting peace and meaningful reconciliation.

Reconciliation facilitated through TRCs is increasingly viewed by the international community as expected practice for states emerging from violence and instability. This approach acknowledges the link between rebuilding trust within and between conflict-affected communities and the pursuit of justice and sustainable peace. Emphasizing the restoration of trust and interpersonal connections within society facilitates an expansive and forward-looking approach, and transitional justice aims for more than retributive (criminal) accountability for past violence. This approach to reconciliation recognizes the embeddedness of transitional justice practices within broad approaches to peacebuilding. Looking beyond the relationship between the perpetrator and the state when seeking justice for mass human rights violations is also critical to attaining sustainable peace because it acknowledges the widespread impact of conflict. As previous research surveying youth-inclusive practices suggests: "We pay so much attention to those who fought, and not enough to those who did not. This complicates reconciliation. Those who did not fight have to be recognized and appreciated but they are often ignored."[13] Valuing the experiences of a cross section of stakeholders within reconciliation acknowledges the importance of ownership and agency for sustainable peace. When young people's conflict stories are taken seriously, and they feel heard, there is more political will and buy-in for reconciliation and thus a greater likelihood of sustainable peace. Where young people are concerned, how post-conflict practices manage inclusion often determines the legitimacy of the process and their motivation to meaningfully engage.

Principles of inclusion are increasingly used by the international community and transitional governments as a marker for determining the success of reconciliation practices. Inclusive practices that center the decision-making capacity and leadership of traditionally marginalized individuals promote ownership amongst diverse stakeholders; thus they are integral for ideas about justice to be embedded within communities. They are also essential for the restoration of interpersonal relationships following violence and instability as they can facilitate greater trust of institutions and between individuals. Despite normative consensus that broader inclusion produces more responsive reconciliation practices, and the positive gains made toward greater visibility, the relationship between young people and TRCs is often fraught with challenges and missed opportunities.

While the institutional discourses that inform the creation of TRCs have evolved over time to normalize the participation of young people, implementing meaningful engagement and exercising care over their stories has proven to be a persistent challenge. As the cases in this book demonstrate, these challenges are informed by constantly shifting political and social struggles that exist within post-conflict communities around attempts to define the character of young people's participation. The legacy of this tension between normative evolution and implementation is further reflected in attempts to operationalize the UN Resolution 2250 mandate for substantive inclusion. As the secretary general noted in 2020, despite evidence that meaningful inclusion facilitates transformative and sustainable peace agreements, youth continue to be left out of the room and excluded from decision-making.[14] Discussions of participation, therefore, need to consider more than just visibility or tokenistic representation.

Creating Substantive Participation

Advocacy for the creation and adoption of UN Resolution 2250 as a codified global framework was driven by civil society, particularly youth-led organizations.[15] In calling for an institutionalized approach to inclusion, youth advocates urged Member States to empower their substantive participation in formal post-conflict practices, including dispute resolutions strategies, peace agreement negotiations, and transitional justice mechanisms. This form of inclusiveness is understood as widespread involvement in leadership and decision-making for a cross section of post-conflict communities, including women and young people. Key to this form of inclusion is autonomous decision-making as well as the implementation of efforts that facilitate widespread youth participation. This therefore goes beyond the tokenistic "add youth and stir" approaches common to technocratic inclusion.[16]

Notions of substantive participation codified within Resolution 2250 promote an active and expansive role for young people, which draws on their leadership capacity and centers their voices in decision-making. It requires that Member States "consider ways to increase the inclusive representation of youth in decision-making at all levels in local, national, regional and international institutions and mechanisms for the prevention and resolution of conflict."[17] Characterizations of participation that emphasize engagement with decision-making structures challenge long-standing discourses of passive involvement for young people, where their inclusion is piecemeal, selective, and mediated by powerful actors.

In the context of formal reconciliation, substantive participation should be determined by how the stories of young people are used within the conflict narrative. Furthermore, the character and location of young people throughout TRC processes is also instructive for assessing claims of meaningful participation. Creating networks and conditions for substantive participation has been a constant challenge for peace and conflict practices, including TRCs. Visibility, while important, denotes shallow participatory parameters and creates a cycle of exclusion that has the potential to undermine the institutions aims. Youth-led research reveals that to be meaningfully inclusive, practices within the peacebuilding and transitional justice fields must undergo "a paradigm shift in how [they] design and implement" strategies for peace and justice, "partnering with young people from the outset."[18] Youth advocates suggest that central to this idea is the notion that institutions within the formal peace architecture must work "*with* young people as critical partners . . . as opposed to inviting [them] as an add-on or to tick the box of participation."[19] Practices within the transitional justice field must undergo a similar discursive and practical shift.

Two decades of sporadic and piecemeal evolution in the character of young people's engagement with TRCs demonstrates what the secretary general affirmed in his report on the YPS agenda, that still "more needs to be done to create an enabling environment for young people in which they are seen and respected as citizens with equal rights, equal voices and equal influence."[20] As such, the development of an enabling environment that is responsive to young people's needs and experiences requires not only that we are mindful of local contexts but also that we learn from previous interactions between young people and formal institutions. The chapters in this book provide opportunities to reflect on how young people's engagement with TRCs has changed over time. More broadly, the stories of young people's interactions with these TRCs offer insights into the internal and external beliefs, traditions, and experiences that have informed how we understand notions of substantive participation today.

Understanding how young people's experiences are constructed in times of transition provides insight into the priorities of post-conflict communities. Within the peace and justice architecture of these states, actors often ascribe meaning to the conflict experiences of children and youth without considering the implications on their agency. Young people's stories have become central to the popular discourse on peace as they offer aspiration and a "promise of a progressive future" in times of instability and transition.[21] However, the stories of youth leadership in practices that seek to deal with legacies of past violence are often missing from these formalized tales as they challenge or complicate the political narrative agreed upon by governments and powerful stakeholders.

Absent also are the stories from young people that reflect a diverse and complex tapestry of conflict experiences. Instead, their voices in reconciliation practices are often imbued with political meaning to maintain the simplistic binaries that have long determined how political communities interact with them, namely as either victims or perpetrators (discussed further in chapter 2). This binary has permeated the popular frameworks of formal justice institutions and facilitates the maintenance of marginalizing technocratic processes based on traditional hierarchical power structures. By using young people's stories to construct a false binary, these power structures "erase and deny the multiple experiences" of those who exercise agency through their negotiations of "complex systems of risk and oppression" to act for peace and justice within their post-conflict communities.[22]

Calls by young people for institutions to recognize, represent, and take seriously the diversity of their conflict stories have grown increasingly loud. This advocacy is underpinned and supported by an emerging body of empirical youth-led research, which demonstrates that young people "play a critical role in the implementation" of post-conflict practice "due to their inevitable engagement in (re)building societal trust, social cohesion and leading reconciliation across generations."[23] Young people therefore must be empowered to exercise agency over their own stories. Exclusion from formal justice practices or managed practices that mediate their participation in the rooms where reconciliation narratives are created perpetuates a silence that impacts youth participation. This exclusion has the potential to generate deep mistrust amongst young people in the legitimacy of TRCs and the capacity of reconciliation processes to fulfill their potential for restoring substantive and positive relationships between young people and the transitional community.

Since its emergence the YPS agenda has focused attention on the importance of centering young people, letting them tell their stories and empowering them to explain what their experiences mean for them. Cycles of exclusion from peace and justice processes are endemic for young people; young people are consistently spoken about rather than spoken to, which leads them to pursue other avenues of engagement outside these institutions. As noted in the 2018 assessment of youth's engagement with peace and security practices, "structural and collective dimensions of young peoples" victimization, vulnerabilities, and grievances must sit at the epicenter of strategies for addressing the marginalization young people experience when engaging with formal institutions.[24] Recounting young people's experiences within formal transitional justice practices therefore can either enable continued vulnerabilities or help to meaningfully resolve them.

Attention must be paid to children and youth's participation in transitional justice because the character of this engagement is central to the legitimacy of the institution for young people, their willingness to buy into and support the narratives constructed, and thus the capacity of these institutions to promote an enabling environment. Young people must be empowered to participate in these institutions and supported in attempts to create peace and justice practices that exist alongside them in informal spaces. While understanding how young people's stories evolve across formal institutions (such as TRCs) offers critical insights into strategies for substantive inclusion, these stories do not exist in a vacuum. As youth advocates explain, young people also "need to be recognized for the value of their informal contributions, as a critical bridge to formal peace" and justice processes.[25] Reconciliation practices occurring by and with young people on the margins are also important sites of agency and voice. While not exhaustive, the following examples offer opportunities to reveal the significance of youth-led justice strategies for meaningful reconciliation.

Young People Working for Reconciliation Outside Institutions

Advocacy efforts by youth in informal spaces demonstrate their potential to substantively contribute to formal reconciliation. It is increasingly acknowledged that young people occupy a significant role as transmitters of historical memory to fulfill the "never again" promise of acknowledging past human rights abuses, a key mandate of transitional justice practices.[26] Informal spaces offer more opportunities for public engagement and thus facilitate collective buy-in for the aims of reconciliation. An emerging body of youth-led empirical research demonstrates that the initiatives developed by young people for reconciliation contribute substantively to the restoration of interpersonal relationships and accountability through acknowledgment in post-conflict communities.

In Colombia for example, young people have been instrumental in pursuing social acceptance and healing between the community and the guerrilla soldiers of the Revolutionary Armed Forces of Colombia (FARC). Following the failure of the referendum on the peace deal in 2016, due in part to the divisive nature of a proposal to reconcile with and reintegrate FARC soldiers, a group of young people began the Cartas por la Reconciliación (Letters for Reconciliation) campaign. This campaign, which "encouraged young people and the broader public to send welcoming letters to FARC guerrilla fighters," aimed to reestablish productive and positive interpersonal relationships.[27] In doing so, this initiative sought to break the cycle of violence and mistrust that had developed within the community and thus promote a culture of healing through acceptance. Letters for Reconciliation gained significant momentum and visibility throughout Colombia, with nearly seven thousand ex-combatants receiving letters welcoming them back into society.[28] By promoting shared dialogue and stories this campaign empowered young people to exercise ownership and agency over their participation and enabled active buy-in to the reconciliation aims of Colombia.

Similar efforts to promote reconciliation through dialogue on the periphery are evident in Rwanda. Here, young people have worked collectively to create a forum for acknowledging the traumas of the past. Founded by students, Never Again Rwanda (NAR) is a youth-led peacebuilding organization that pursues sustainable peace through discussions that acknowledge the root causes of past violence. Youth engagement is the cornerstones of NAR's work, which it facilitates through the creation of spaces where youth "from survival, ex-perpetrator and returnee backgrounds" can gather to tell, own, and share their conflict stories.[29] In groups of twenty to thirty, young people meet to have their voices heard, to receive support for trauma, and to think critically about what the stories of their experiences mean. Communal spaces, like the one established by NAR, that enable and empower young people to share their views on conflict and its implications for the future provide a model for substantive inclusion that formal reconciliation practices could learn from or engage with.

Youth-led community building initiatives that foster dialogue and enable the socialization of reconciliation norms contribute substantively to interpersonal reconciliation efforts in post-conflict countries. The 2016 National Ethnic Youth Conference in Myanmar, for example, sought to cultivate trust between ethnic groups through youth-led constitution-making dialogues and debates on peace and reconciliation issues.[30] Likewise, in Cameroon the Cercle International pour la Promotion de la Création uses theater and intercultural activities, as well as interreligious dialogue, to empower young people's participation in reconciliation.[31] Attempts at reconciliation that mobilize young people have the capacity to rebuild interpersonal relationships within communities by offering fresh perspectives on the root causes of violence and instability. When young people are empowered to lead and act as knowledge producers the potential for change is transformative. As these examples demonstrate, young people have the capacity and political will to develop strategies that both acknowledge past cultures of violence to promote healing and look forward, reframing cultures and traditions in order to overcome and prevent violence.

Youth-led approaches in countries such as Cote d'Ivoire have been instrumental in revealing the importance of partnerships within reconciliation practices for sustainable peace. For example, the Réseau Action Justice et Paix (RAJP) joined with UNICEF to create capacity building programs with young people and to provide recommendations for the reparations policy of the National Commission for Reconciliation and Compensation for Victims. Independent youth-led initiatives such as these that pursue engagement with formal structures through partnerships create further visibility and opportunities for young people to assert ownership over their reconciliation experiences. As Ladisch and Rice suggest, "The catalytic effect of [these] projects matter more than any final product" because the act of engaging in dialogue where a tool was produced by youth for youth establishes a productive legacy for advocacy and rebuilding relationship.[32] Within informal spaces, young people's pursuit of partnerships offers viable avenues for inclusion, as well as prospects for greater coordination between formal and informal reconciliation practices.

The peace and justice work of young people in informal spaces has also contributed significantly to shifts in the discourse regarding their relationship with human rights norms. As their advocacy work becomes more visible in formal peace architecture and their stories are increasingly heard, young people have revealed themselves to be critical rights defenders rather than simply passive rights holders. This shift is significant as it informs how their role in the pursuit of accountability for human rights violations is understood and acknowledged within social and political spaces. The Youth Transparency and Building Foundation in Yemen, for example, has established a network for young people to document the human rights violations in Taiz. This youth-led process that centers their stories reveals the value of these approaches, allowing young people to own and possess agency over their stories. As one young activist explains, documentation processes facilitated by young people are "important to grant fair transitional justice."[33] As such, when young people have ownership over their stories it heightens their willingness to engage with the politics of transition.

Keeping Pace with Evolving Identities and Classifications for Young People

The constantly evolving character of young people presents both challenges and opportunities for their engagement with transitional justice practices. Increasingly, scholarship and practice has advocated for greater recognition of the complexity associated with developing clear guidelines for conceptualizing young people, driven in part by the growing recognition that they are not a homogenous demographic.[34] Definitions of young people remain highly contested as notions of youth in particular are "allusive, yet meaningful" in their intent, particularly when seeking to distinguish their experiences and political agency from children.[35] Understanding classifications of young people is further complicated within institutional spaces by the porousness of references to children and youth. An examination of young people's reconciliation narratives (chapters 3, 4, and 5) reveals this complexity as the prolonged nature of TRC processes often results in a slippage between these classifications in the formal conflict narratives produced in the final reports of TRCs.

To manage this complexity, I have used the term *young people* throughout this book to denote a distinction from adulthood. The term, used in this way, includes children, youth, and adolescents and seeks to acknowledge and capture the vast and complex ways that individuals in peace and conflict practices describe their own identities, as well as how institutions conceive them (discussed further in chapter 2). Thus, the use of young people often signals the presence of both children and youth. It is also used to denote instances where the distinction between who is being talked about is unclear, although this also warranted constant critical reflection throughout the chapters. Where TRC dialogues, reports, and stories have explicitly used the terms "child" or "youth," I have retained these descriptors, yet this also required searches for more detailed descriptors of the intent behind the classifications (as describe in chapters 2–5).

I apply a critical lens to reveal and analyze the discursive slippage and overlap between these classifications. Pathways between childhood, youth, adolescence, and adulthood cannot be predetermined and are not universal. The analysis in this book seeks to be mindful of this by respecting first the voices of young people. To that end, where young people self-identify as youth in their stories, this is reflected in the analysis.[36] This is particularly important when talking about TRCs, as the prolonged process associated with this justice means that for many individuals temporalities are complex and shifting. The definitional frameworks used throughout, echo the one outlined by the 2005 World Youth Report, which casts youth as "an important period of physical, mental, and social maturation" where they "are actively forming identities and determining acceptable roles for themselves."[37] Within this approach, the "for themselves" is critical as it makes space for their subjectivity and ownership in the representation process. It also recognizes youth's capacity as competent social agents whose perspectives offer valuable insights. Framing the experiences of youth this way acknowledges their uniqueness and their capacity to evolve into and out of youthhood at different paces and in TRC contexts across temporalities. Applying a critical lens to classifications of young people also serves as recognition of the power structures that inform definitional decisions within institutions, particularly when conceptualizing their relationships to these structures.

Yet understanding young people's engagement with TRCs also requires an examination of how those interacting with these practices conceive and cast young people. Pragmatic considerations, such as resourcing, statistics gathering, and timing, impose constant pressure on institutions to establish consistent and replicable parameters for guiding interactions with and between young people in social and political spaces. Özerdem and Podder offer a useful starting point for classifying young people in peace, justice, and conflict contexts. These classifications are informed by three positionalities: one that prefers age-defined categorization, one that highlights the social embeddedness of identities, and one that emphasizes the physiology that informs an individual's situatedness.[38] Together these discourses provide a comprehensive scaffold for representing young people and their interactions with reconciliation practices. A note of caution, however: when used on their own, these discourses perpetuate barriers to young people's engagement. This is in part due to their failure to consider how self-identification informs young people's unique experiences and how their diverse voices are represented and imbued with meaning.

Of the three discourses, the numerical classification, which underpins the age-defined perspective, governs institutional understandings of young people. Within these classifications, variations exist across and within institutions, creating a nuanced, fluid, and complex framework for guiding interactions with young people. Notions of childhood and the classification of child remain static and apply for individuals under the age of eighteen. Yet this numerical boundary is complicated by overlapping ideas for classifying youth and adolescents. UN Resolution 2250 on YPS, for example, defines youth as individuals between the ages of eighteen and twenty-nine, while the UN General Assembly definition uses the age range of fifteen to twenty-four.[39] Among the most important development to emerge from recent attempts to numerically classify youth is the recognition that "variations of definition . . . may exist on the national and international level."[40] Acknowledging this, for each of the cases examined in this book I have provided the local numerical classification used by each state to guide its understanding of and interactions with young people.

Young people's inevitable transition into adulthood indicates a need to create viable succession planning. It also highlights the importance of preserving institutional knowledge about youth leadership and their advocacy efforts, as well as their approach to participating in mediation dialogues and reconciliation processes. While there is no unified model for youth participation, looking ahead to how engagement is maintained and strengthened represents a critical imperative for both formal and informal transitional justice processes.[41]

A Place for Young People in Reconciliation

The acknowledgment of youth as a demographic distinct from children is relatively new and underdeveloped in the transitional justice field. In practice, youth are increasingly recognized as political actors with diverse interests and the capacity to own their autonomous decision-making. Despite this, institutional representations of their participatory capacity are derived from persistent, disproven perceptions that are incomplete and pejorative.[42] Understanding the diverse ways that youth engage in post-conflict contexts and their contributions to reconciliation practices is of critical importance because there is often a high-density youth population in these contexts. There are approximately 600 million individuals between the ages of fifteen and twenty-four living in transitional countries today.[43] In the Solomon Islands, for example, the median age of the population during the conflict was nineteen, and in 2012 (the year the TRC report was handed over to the Solomon Islands government) youth constituted 31 percent of the population.[44] Given this, it is unsurprising that youth were named thematic stakeholders in the reconciliation process.

The Solomon Islands, however, is not unique in its demonstration of this demographic dividend; this trend is also evident in the other cases examined throughout this book. For example, in Sierra Leone at the time of the TRC report's publication youth made up 55 percent of the population, and in Timor-Leste during the conflict one in five individuals were between the ages of fifteen and twenty-five.[45] The prevalence of youth in these post-conflict communities makes their voices and stories essential to the reconciliation process and for broader attempts at sustainable peace through reconciliation. Without these stories, the conflict narratives that TRCs produce remain incomplete and their reconciliation mandates go unfulfilled at the community level. As Karen Brounéus observes, "reconciliation is a societal process" that involves not only "mutual acknowledgment of past suffering" but also "the changing of destructive attitudes and behaviors into constructive relationships towards sustainable peace" that enable productive futures.[46]

Fulfillment of the goal of reconciliation, therefore, requires widespread recognition of the stories of youth, as told from their perspectives, to build and restore authentic relationships.

The exclusion of these stories from the formal TRC conflict records has social and political implications, as the silencing of youth hinders the capacity of the post-conflict community to meaningfully rebuild relationships with the transitional society's largest demographic. Simply put, the reconciliation stories of youth are an essential yet often unacknowledged factor in the pursuit of accountability. Despite several notable bodies of work that investigate the relationship between youth and peacebuilding, youth contributions, particularly their engagement with reconciliation processes, have been overlooked in transitional justice.[47]

The participation of children in conflict, transitional justice, and peacebuilding practices, however, is well defined and globally acknowledged. Since the almost unanimous ratification of the United Nations Convention on the Rights of the Child (CRC) in 1989, the needs and experiences of children have become an increasingly central part of the reconciliation narratives of post-conflict communities. This was due to a shift in the dominant perceptions of childhood that occurred during the drafting of the CRC as states sought to create a universal classification of the *child* that would transcend culture, nationality, gender, and race.[48] Perceptions about children shifted from dominant beliefs that they are passive objects of their parents to seeing them as social agents with rights, defined broadly as entitlements.

The concept of agency is central to the discussions within this book, as displays of agency denote meaningful and substantive participation by young people. Although a detailed discussion of agency is included in chapter 3, it is necessary to provide a working definition up front. Throughout the book, Norman Long's notion of agency is adopted. This definitional approach is significant for understanding the importance of young people's voices and ownership over their stories as it "attributes to the individual actor the capacity to process social experiences and to devise ways of coping with life." Long continues by qualifying how displays of agency are embedded within and informed by context and interactions. He explains that "within the limits of information, uncertainty and other constraints that exist, social actors are 'knowledgeable' and 'capable.' They attempt to solve problems, learn how to intervene in the flow of social events around them, and monitor continuously their own actions, observing how others react to their behavior and taking note of various contingent circumstances."[49] This definition provides expansive and flexible parameters for discussions of youth and their political participation. The emphasis on learning and problem-solving is essential to considerations of youth agency because it allows for an acknowledgment of individuals capacity to critically engage with events and devise strategies as independent knowledge creators. As such, it recognizes the important yet complex need for autonomous decision-making in youth's pursuit of agency and ownership.

Centering understandings of agency when examining the actions of youth provides us with opportunities to reveal how these individuals navigate and own their roles within the social and political world. Finally, this definition provides a useful starting point as it recognizes and helps explain the constantly evolving capacity of young people that is informed by their interactions with other actors, institutions, and social structures. To that end, this conceptual framing of agency echoes the emerging dialogue on young people within peace and conflict, which acknowledges their evolving capabilities. While discursive notions of political agency have evolved within the peace and conflict fields, in practice challenges remain with respect to the pragmatic realities of the notion of evolving capabilities. National and international policymakers often fail to take seriously how evolving capabilities, determined by external parties, inform changes in the character of political interactions. This tension goes some way toward explaining why young people's diverse experiences and stories continue to be marginalized within formal practices of transitional justice.

The discourse on young people is framed by the institutionalized beliefs of states about their relationship to this demographic, which are embedded in the CRC. As Anna Holzscheiter observes, "The CRC enshrined for the first time in international law, the right of the child to express his or her own views,"[50] thus giving children a voice. In doing so, the CRC provided a framework for guiding the interactions of children with the social and political world. Building upon the norms established in the CRC, the *Graça Machel Report* (1996), the *Cape Town Principles* (1997), and the *Paris Principles* (2007) offer further foundational parameters for the inclusion and recognition of children's voices in post-conflict practices. Graça Machel's report, *The Impact of Armed Conflict on Child*, which was presented to the UN General Assembly in 1996, made visible for the first time the broad range of roles that children occupy in conflict zones and highlighted patterns of abuse experienced by child soldiers.[51]

Following this, in 1997 the policies of the *Cape Town Principles and Best Practices* were adopted to manage and prevent the recruitment of children into the armed forces and to address the issues of "demobilization and social reintegration of child soldiers in Africa."[52] The principles were the product of a symposium conducted by UNICEF and the NGO Working Group on the CRC, which brought together experts to create practical strategies for governments to eliminate the recruitment of child soldiers. Building on the developments from *Cape Town*, the *Principles and Guidelines on Children Associated with Armed Forces or Armed Groups* (also known as the *Paris Principles*) were adopted alongside the *Paris Commitments to Protect Children from Unlawful Recruitment or Use by Armed Forces or Armed Groups* at the international conference Free Children from War in February 2007.[53] These two documents aimed to provide more detailed guidance for states and NGOs looking to implement strategies for the prevention and reintegration of child soldiers.[54] Taken together, these institutional reports "have significantly contributed to the advancement of children's rights in conflict zones" by ensuring that their needs and interests are not only visible but addressed by states in their post-conflict practices.[55] While well-intentioned, this dialogue laid the foundations for classificatory slippages between children and youth within the formal justice architecture. The universal framing of young people who fought as child soldiers created a narrow image of their participation and obscured opportunities for individuals to claim agency outside this institutionalized discourse.

Despite this normative shift, the capacity of youth to be heard in these contexts is constrained by social perceptions and liberal philosophical notions of what constitutes *childhood*.[56] These views of childhood emphasize the innocence and vulnerability of children and conceive them as predominately apolitical, thus ascribing a distinct character to their experiences.[57] When young people are represented post conflict, it is often from the perspective of external stakeholders who assign political meaning to their experiences. This is particularly prevalent in the reconciliation discourse, as young people are often talked about rather than spoken to.

Representations of young people reproduced and disseminated by NGOs and think tanks illustrate the broader challenges with public discourses on young people constructed within formal institutions without their voices. These stakeholders are an essential part of the stories of young people, as they advocate for their needs and interests. Yet their reporting, while well-intentioned, often fails to reflect a holistic representation of how young people experience conflict and engage with reconciliation practices. This is due in part to their reliance on emotive representations and Western liberal assumptions, which fail to represent young people's unique conflict experiences and thus silence displays of agency in their participation in post-conflict practices.[58]

In this sense, representations of young people in these contexts are highly selective and prioritize narrow understandings, which relegate youth as a distinct demographic to the periphery. As a result, child soldiers remain the most visible and widely represented group of young people in transitional justice discourses.[59] Within the reconciliation discourse, the prioritizing of the child soldier narrative has had significant impact on the capacity of formal mechanisms such as TRCs to reflect young people's distinct voices. By prioritizing and universalizing the soldier experience this discourse has inadvertently contributed to institutional slippages between children and youth within formal reconciliation narratives.

Representing the stories of youth and young people who occupy roles distinct from the soldier narrative in the post-conflict contexts, therefore, is a complex endeavor because it requires a challenging balancing of expectations across a wide range of stakeholders. This has resulted in an oversimplification of young people's stories, particularly in the institutional narratives created by TRCs. Youth experience conflict, violence, and instability in diverse and at times surprising ways. They are victims, perpetrators, advocates, peacebuilders, political leaders, and spoilers with the capacity to inform our understandings of the political and social world through their speech and their actions. Historically, however, post-conflict processes have excluded their unique voices, framing their experiences and interests as the same as children and women. This socially constructed framing of youth emphasizes who they are not, situating their identity within the broader context of attributes typically assigned to children, adults, and the elderly.

The increased visibility of children in the conflict environment has resulted in a rapidly expanding scholarly field devoted to conducting empirical research on their experiences. These studies focus on describing and assessing the rights, needs, and motivations of children during and after conflict.[60] Despite a few notable exceptions, a critical examination of the relationship between youth and formal reconciliation practices is largely absent from this research.⁶¹ Indeed, scholarship has yet to extensively consider how young people's needs and experiences are reflected in the conflict narratives of post-conflict states and the impact of these representations for notions of substantive inclusion. As demonstrated throughout this book, youth are a group of individuals distinct from children and adults. However, the complexity of the storytelling process during times of transition often creates institutional slippages that impact how we understand their interactions with reconciliation practices. Youth experience conflict and contribute to reconciliation in ways that are different from children and from adults due to different ideas about their conflict experiences and their reconciliation needs. They also have a unique stake in the outcomes of reconciliation due to their status as youth. As such, youth are uniquely positioned to contribute to reconciliation in ways that are innovative and future-orientated when enabled and empowered to substantively participate.

THE EVOLUTION OF YOUTH ENGAGEMENT IN TRCs

Beginning with South Africa, a small but growing number of TRCs have incorporated programs that encourage the participation of young people and facilitate the inclusion of their voices into the reconciliation narrative. The nature and extent of this engagement has steadily evolved to allow for considerations of their needs in the mandates and recommendations of TRCs.⁶² Since the landmark South African case, TRCs in Guatemala, Peru, Timor-Leste, Sierra Leone, Liberia, and the Solomon Islands have conducted hearings on the experiences of children to collect and engage with their stories. Finding the voices of youth, however, in the TRCs of transitional states is a more complex process. Apart from the TRC in Sierra Leone, the child classification is often used to represent the stories of all young people, particularly in the final reports. When examining the evolution of young people's participation in transitional justice, therefore, we must be mindful of the impact of these institutional slippages on our understanding of substantive inclusion.

The *Truth and Reconciliation Commission of South Africa Report* contains a chapter dedicated to the experiences of children. This TRC was one of the first to directly engage with the needs of children in its recommendations and through its reparations program.⁶³ In Peru, the *Comisión de la Verdad y Reconciliación* (CVR) was released on August 28, 2003.⁶⁴ Like South Africa, this report contains a dedicated chapter on the human rights violations committed against children during the conflict, as well as targeted recommendations to address their post-conflict needs. Two years later, in October 2005, the conflict stories of children were documented in the final report of the Timor-Leste TRC. The final report, entitled *Chega! The Final Report of the Commission for Reception, Truth, and Reconciliation* (CAVR), contains a dedicated chapter on children that reflects their direct testimony obtained through statements and public hearings.[65]

Following this, in 2010 a children's version of *Chega!* was published in comic form by the Asia Justice and Rights (AJAR) center and the Secretariado Tecnico Pos-CARV (STP-CARV).[66] Developed as an educational resource to assist teachers in explaining the conflict and the TRC process, this version of the report aimed to make the stories of conflict accessible to young people in Timor-Leste. The production of accessible reporting both in Timor-Leste and Sierra Leone denotes a turning point in the reconciliation discourse. Notably by reproducing the conflict narrative for young people, these reports empower them to disseminate knowledge and interpret truths. In doing so, they enable young people to play an active role in the maintenance of stories for the pursuit of meaningful accountability and to occupy a stake in the realization of the never again mandate that underpins the pursuit of reconciliation through TRCs.

Reporting for the Sierra Leone TRC also demonstrated a discursive turning point in the institutionalization of the stories of young people as it was the first to acknowledge the distinct experiences of youth. *Witness to Truth: Report of the Sierra Leone Truth and Reconciliation Commission* was presented to the government on October 5, 2004, and contained the direct testimony of both children and youth, separated into distinct chapters.[67] Alongside the official report UNICEF published, in consultation with the TRC, the *Truth and Reconciliation Commission Report for the Children of Sierra Leone*.[68] Sierra Leonean youth successfully advocated for the development of this child-friendly report and played an instrumental role in its creation, highlighting not only the visibility of young people throughout this process but also the impact of their political agency. The goal was to produce an easily accessible document for "the children of Sierra Leone . . . and others outside Sierra Leone [to] better comprehend what the children of Sierra Leone experienced during war."[69] The distinction between the experiences of children and youth is represented at all stages of the Sierra Leone TRC process and throughout the final report. Broadly speaking, the reporting and engagement of Sierra Leonean youth (examined in chapter 4) suggests an evolution in the discourse related to the relationship between youth, reconciliation, and transitional justice.

Finally, the *Solomon Islands Truth and Reconciliation Commission Final Report: Confronting the Truth for a Better Solomon Islands* was presented to the prime minister at the time, Gordon Darcy Lilo, in February 2012.[70] Although obligated by an act of parliament requiring that the TRC report be made available to the public, successive governments have failed to officially release it.[71] Despite this, an unofficial version was made available online in April 2013 by the report's editor Bishop Terry Brown.[72] What is notable about the Solomon Islands case is that tension between stories by and stories for youth remains prominent and that this discourse impacts the ownership and political agency within the formal TRC structure. Illustrated in chapter 5, youth have a complex relationship with reconciliation, which is exacerbated by the persistence of classificatory slippages in the public representations of their stories.

Among these reconciliation practices, the Sierra Leone TRC is widely considered a model for the direct engagement of children, as it was the first to establish guidelines for taking statements from children.[73] The contributions of children to TRCs have helped shape more holistic reconciliation narratives that reflect not only their conflict experiences but the changing nature of childhood within international politics. Missing from many of these reconciliation processes, however, is a nuanced understanding of youth's place in the reconciliation process. Indeed, Sierra Leone is unique in its decision to formally represent youth as a distinct demographic with its own reconciliation narrative. The Sierra Leone TRC was the first to institutionally acknowledge the diverse experiences of youth through a dedicated chapter that centers their voices and acknowledges their capacity to assign meaning to their own experience. In doing so, this TRC established a framework for the institutional engagement of youth as a separate demographic in truth-telling practices. Furthermore, it highlighted the importance of recognizing and engaging with the complex and distinctive experiences of youth. The engagement of youth with reconciliation practices, however, is a story of ebbs and flows, as the Sierra Leone case remains the only TRC to reflect the distinct experiences of youth at the institutional level. As demonstrated in the final chapter, efforts to operationalize this discursive shift within formal transitional justice practices have been fraught with challenges and stymied by the maintenance of traditional power structures.

Far more common are cases such as the Solomon Islands, where despite the active participation of youth in the reconciliation process, their stories, when institutionalized, reflect a narrow understanding of their capacity, needs, and experiences. In the Solomon Islands case, youth played a substantive role in the investigative proceedings of the TRC, which when revealed challenge the institutionalized discourse of the final report. At the outset, the TRC's operating framework seemed to suggest that youth would formally participate in the TRC as political agents. Moreover, the nature and extent of their engagement indicated that, for the first time, youth's role in both the conflict and throughout the reconciliation process would be meaningfully acknowledged.

As the evolving narrative of young people's public representation presented here demonstrates, it is the process associated with conducting TRCs (the hearings and submissions), rather than the end point (the report), that is important for understanding how youth in particular own and interpret their potential contributions to the pursuit of accountability. Their participation in the process provides an opportunity to claim ownership over their conflict experiences and to reframe their relationships with the broader community. In addition, the open forum facilitated by the TRC process allows youth to demonstrate their capacity to act as political agents and to positively contribute to reconciliation and sustainable peace.

Interpreting Youth Representation in Transitional Justice

Broadly speaking, scholarship has overlooked the substantive participation of youth in reconciliation processes. Rarely does their actual engagement fit the prominent institutional narratives and norms that guide our interactions and understandings of their experiences. This book, therefore, uses an interpretative approach to examine the narratives surrounding young people's engagement in TRC processes. TRCs were chosen as the focus of this discussion because claims that they are open and inclusive due to their nonprocedural nature and their restorative approach to justice (discussed in chapter 1) ensures that they should be perfectly positioned to provide a space for young people to be visible and to potentially have their voices heard. The community-driven, narrative style of TRCs provides individuals typically excluded from retributive approaches a forum to actively participate in post-conflict justice. As advocates observe, "Truth telling can provide space for members of marginalized groups to perform publicly as citizens, perhaps for the first time in their lives."[74] That is, TRCs allow individuals the opportunity to exert agency and claim ownership over their conflict experiences as political actors. In doing so, the process lends legitimacy to the conflict experiences of the individuals traditionally left on the margins of transitional societies.

Where youth are concerned, scholars suggest that the process of storytelling encourages agency, empowers, and facilitates participation.[75] When young people are substantively included in TRCs, they are enabled to claim ownership over their transitional justice experiences and to participate in ending the culture of impunity. The interactive and collaborative nature of storytelling also provides youth with a forum to reframe their relationships within the broader community, demonstrating their capacity to act as political agents. By providing submissions to TRCs either in writing or at open or closed hearings young people are given the opportunity to speak for themselves, rather than having others speak for them. Yet substantive inclusion extends beyond being able to speak or be seen. Mandates for substantive inclusion in reconciliation require attention to how the stories are embedded within the reconciliation process and the pursuit of strategies that allow young people to assign meaning to their own experiences as knowledge producers.

Understanding young people's political agency requires an individualized approach that centers their voices. This acknowledges the value of a stakeholder's firsthand stories, rather than using these stories to inform a collective social narrative. Truth telling as a process provides a potential space for youth to claim agency when they are enabled and empowered as knowledge producers. As the cases in this book demonstrate, when young people's narratives are heard and they are allowed to assign meaning to their stories, reconciliation, and restorative justice more broadly, enables youth to reframe how they participate in the formal justice architecture. This has implications for young people's engagement in the formal structures of post-conflict states because it ensures that youth are included in the decision-making and implementation process of TRCs.

The findings in this book have broader implications for how we understand the contributions of TRCs to the goal of reconciliation. They illustrate that measures of success should be reappropriated to emphasize the importance of reconciliation processes rather than the outcome. Looking at the process rather than the outcome (the final report) creates space for young people's agency. In addition, emphasizing the process of reconciliation allows for greater consideration of the contributions of informal practices led by youth in the pursuit of reconciliation. By spotlighting the process, scholars and practitioners are better able to determine whether the reconciliation process meets its primary goals of inclusion and acknowledgment.

Centering Agency as a Key Variable for Analysis

Agency is reflected and produced through the stories people tell and their impact on the social and political community. As McEvoy-Levy explains, considerations of youth agency recognize that they have the capacity to "shap[e] their own and other's social conditions" and thus to meaningfully participate as political agents.[76] The opportunity to speak, be heard, and most importantly be listened to is central to establishing an inclusive reconciliation process that considers and values the contributions of youth. Agency is fundamental to the true nature and extent of youth's engagement with transitional justice practices. Lee-Koo observes with respect to children that "for participation to be meaningful, [they] must have the capacity to be politically transformative . . . their contributions to peace must be understood and respected."[77] The same is true for youth and their distinct voices and ideas. When youth are enabled to exercise agency and to tell their stories in formal processes, they demonstrate the capacity to positively influence their communities. Indeed, capturing the voices of youth in the reconciliation narratives produced by TRCs not only contributes to the production of a more inclusive and holistic conflict narrative but also allows for the development of recommendations that are future-focused, innovative, and directly target the post-conflict needs of youth. Language and stories allow traditionally marginalized individuals to exert political agency and to challenge dominant and marginalizing representations of their experiences.

To better understand the spaces within which social representations of young people and their engagement evolve we need to consider the beliefs and traditions that inform these stories. Beliefs and traditions are revealed in speech and in silence. Therefore, to understand different representations of youth it is necessary to deconstruct and analyze the language stakeholders use to construct narratives about their engagement. The analysis in this book contributes to an emerging body of empirical scholarship that reveals the value of narrative methods for exposing voices and revealing how stories are used to create meaning. In doing so, it looks to highlight the experiences of individuals typically excluded from the retributive (legal) approaches to justice.

Central to this exploration are stories about youth and stories by youth, in particular their role in conflict and transitional justice practices. Stories when heard and taken seriously provide significant insights into the reconciliation needs and interests of young people, whose stories are often excluded from transitional justice. It is through stories, and more specifically the process of storytelling, that we form a connection between the lived experiences of individuals, their relationships, and their interpretations of the world around them. As Robert Atkinson concludes, "We think in story form, speak in story form and bring meaning to our lives through story."[78] All individuals navigating the social and political world are therefore knowledge producers. To that end, the analysis contained in this book uses an interpretative approach to reveal the stories of young people. In particular, it looks to reveal tensions between different public representations of young people, which are created based on how young people's stories are used, and the actors managing the narrative.

Narrative-driven methodologies and interpretative analysis contribute to a more nuanced and holistic understanding of those traditionally marginalized or excluded from the research process. They provide researchers with an opportunity to hear the stories of a wide range of stakeholders, as well as a means for understanding how these voices interact with each other and the broader contexts in which they are situated. Taken together, the cases in this book demonstrate an evolution in young people's engagement with and representation within TRCs. By exploring how the stories of young people in reconciliations practices are "constituted by and form webs of belief" made up of "theories and assumptions" as well as social, historical, and political facts, we can reveal the opportunities for and challenges to more inclusive reconciliation.[79]

Taking seriously the voices of children and youth is essential to the development of stories that reflect the heterogenous, firsthand experiences of all young people. Yet young people's stories are also rarely heard through the prism of young people's experiences; they are often embedded within political structures, which presents challenges to their agency and substantive inclusion. Narratives that tell stories only about individuals are problematic because they reproduce and promote marginalizing stereotypes. As such, it is essential that when discussing young people's experiences, we locate their stories within the broader context in which they are situated. The purpose of TRC reports is to provide a narrative of the conflict by collecting and collating the stories of individuals.[80] As the goal of the truth commission process is to restore relationships through acknowledgment and documentation, the product of this process provides an obvious entry point into the conflict stories of young people.

Given the widespread recognition that youth are key stakeholders in the aftermath of conflict, their stories must be taken seriously for their contributions as individuals rather than seeing their voices as purely part of a collective political narrative. When young people's voices are used as tools for external agendas their contributions as political agents are mischaracterized or ignored. As the cases presented in this book demonstrate, youth have been increasingly visible in transitional justice practices. TRCs are the primary mechanisms responsible for facilitating this visibility by seeking testimony from young people and through their inclusion in the mandates and recommendations of the various commissions. Through thematic hearings, written submissions, and artwork commissioned by the TRCs, young people have increasingly been afforded the opportunity to tell their stories firsthand in a range of creative ways. Rarely, however, are these stories institutionalized in a nuanced manner that reflects their complex and diverse relationships with conflict and reconciliation.

Simply put, this book considers whether TRC processes, which are widely recognized to be inclusive and representative, truly see young people and their experiences. It does so through an examination of the different representations of young people that have contributed to the reconciliation narratives of TRCs from the 1990s onward. It highlights the political processes, desires, and beliefs that inform depictions of youth in the final reports of TRCs. In doing so, it provides a critical exploration of the relationship between youth, reconciliation, and engagement. Taken together, the cases in this book demonstrate that the evolution of young people's engagement with formal reconciliation practices ebbs and flows and that public reflections of their capacity to substantively participate do not exist in a vacuum. Rather, representations of young people that are responsive, pragmatic, and mindful of the uniquely transitional nature of this demographic allow for more meaningful engagement and more responsive inclusion. Furthermore, this form of representation produces a more holistic and inclusive narrative of the experiences of young people in transitional context. Until we can see youth, the acknowledgment mandate of TRCs will remain incomplete.

Conclusion

Despite the increased engagement of young people in TRC processes, institutional representations of their experiences often remain static and are overly reliant on the binary classifications of victims and deviants. While youth and children are increasingly visible in transitional justice, their distinct voices and agency continue to go unheard as the beliefs of external actors about the roles they occupy in conflict crowd out the self-reflections, particularly in the case of youth's engagement at the institutional level. This tension between external reflections and self-reflections produces a dilemma for states engaged in reconciliation processes.

While the international dialogue on young people embedded in the CRC acknowledges their evolving capabilities, the stories told in the formal narratives of conflict reflect the belief that youth share similar experiences to children, and as such their stories should be represented alongside them. This is problematic because these narrow representations create and propagate restrictive participatory boundaries that deny young people agency and ownership over their experiences. Overreliance on truths constructed using these binaries also fails to reflect institutional slippages, where the stories of youth and children become difficult to separate, either through organization rules and norms or the prolonged nature of conducting transitional justice practices. These representative complexities hinder the capacity of youth to substantively participate and to exercise agency and ownership over their conflict stories and their role in post-conflict practices. In addition, the overreliance on these victim/perpetrator classifications obstructs the reconciliation process by perpetuating inaccurate, unhelpful, and marginalizing narratives about young people that do not acknowledge the uniqueness of their conflict experiences or their motivations for participating in conflict and post-conflict practices.

In place of these characterizations, this book offers an alternative agent-centered account of young people, which starts from the position of "youth as themselves."[81] Creating meaningful reconciliation narratives that hear and take seriously the experiences of young people requires TRCs to capture in their final reports the broad range of stories told during the collection process. By using an agent-centered approach, the analysis throughout this book demonstrates the unique and productive relationship that youth and children have with the reconciliation process. Furthermore, the agent-centered approach allows us to consider the impact of institutional slippages between classifications of young people and explain the persistence of binary representations when describing the experiences of youth. Chapters 3 to 6 construct a narrative of young people's engagement with TRC processes that reflects and assesses the ways in which key actors have interpreted the role of young people in conflict and its implications for meaningful, lasting reconciliation.

Taken together, the arguments in these chapters suggest that representations of youth should be fluid and reflect the multitude of roles they occupy, both in conflict and reconciliation. Explorations of young people's experiences illustrate that they are both victims and perpetrators but that these roles do not exclude them for asserting active political agency or from asserting leadership in the pursuit of reconciliation. Rather, these experiences and the meaning they assign to their stories during reconciliation offer opportunities for more responsive reconciliation practices. When formal reconciliation practices such as TRCs engage with young people as political agents, they reveal unique and diverse ideas about reconciliation, sustainable peace, and development. This has broader implications for how we understand the contributions of TRCs to the goal of reconciliation in transitional contexts. Notably, youth's historical experiences with TRCs demonstrate that it is the process associated with conducting TRCs, rather than the outcome, that should determine the success and contributions of TRCs to restorative justice.

Chapter 1

Contextualizing Transitional Justice for Meaningful Youth Participation

> The priority for youth was to have their voices heard. They know it is important to be a part of the national [reconciliation] narrative.
>
> —Interview A, Solomon Islands, Oct. 2015

In 2008 the Solomon Islands parliament passed legislation establishing a Truth and Reconciliation Commission (TRC) in an attempt heal deep-seated community rifts through storytelling.[1] Central to the TRCs mandate was the investigation and revelation of the causes and circumstances surrounding the civil conflict known as the Tensions. This violence erupted in 1998 and continued until 2003 when the Regional Assistance Mission to the Solomon Islands (RAMSI) intervened at the request of the government. At the time of RAMSI's intervention, an estimated 200 people had died and 11,000 had been displaced from their homes. In addition, between 1998 and 2003, approximately 5,700 human rights violations were committed, including 1,412 instances of torture, 212 abductions, 95 cases of arbitrary detention, and at least 62 cases of sexual violence.[2] Instances of widespread human rights violations as such necessitated a process whereby individuals' experiences of these harms could be heard and legitimized through acknowledgment.

Alongside these physical violations, the Tensions left 1,856 public buildings destroyed and looted. The Solomon Islands experienced widespread institutional collapse as schools, hospitals, police stations, and court houses closed and international donor agencies and businesses evacuated the country. The immediate impact of the violence and displacement was felt predominately by the communities of Guadalcanal, Malaita, and in the capital, Honiara; however, the instability associated with the Tensions had a ripple effect throughout the Solomon Islands.

For youth, alongside the immediate effects of the violence they experienced, the socioeconomic and structural consequences of the conflict were far reaching. Interruptions to their education due to school closures and the abandonment of government efforts to implement the National Youth Policy, which proposed practical measures for their increased political participation, left youth further isolated and marginalized. Their stories as such were an integral piece of the reconciliation puzzle for the Solomon Islands, and as indicated by the above quote, youth recognized that to be heard their participation was critical.

For youth, the lack of job opportunities in Honiara during and in the immediate aftermath of the Tensions meant that those who had moved to the capital to pursue work either returned to their home provinces or loitered around the streets smoking and chewing beetle nuts.[3] Indeed, the instability of the Tensions led youth to pursue "a collective solution to their marginalization" and the aimlessness brought about by the closure of schools and lack of work during the conflict.[4] These responses by some youth to the violence and instability also informed public beliefs surrounding youth, perpetuating deeply rooted cultural notions of youth as *Masta Liu*, a term used to describe people, usually men, as loitering, hanging around, or wandering aimlessly.[5] Cultural sentiment that cast the youth of the Solomon Islands as *Masta Liu* emphasized their delinquency and positioned them as subordinates to the "big men" during the conflict.[6] As Matthew Allen observes, the relationship between youth and "governments, media and think tanks" was heavily impacted by the *Masta Liu* classification.[7] This was problematic for youth in the Solomon Islands as their interactions with the community during the conflict and throughout the transitional justice process were influenced by this narrow representation.

Recognition of the Tension's impact on the youth of the Solomon Islands was built into the conflict's core transitional justice mechanism, the TRC, which was launched by South African archbishop Desmond Tutu on April 29, 2009. In principle, the TRC recognized that opportunities were needed for youth to tell their stories and have their conflict experiences publicly acknowledged. In addition, the participation of Solomon Islander youth in the implementation of the TRC allowed them to demonstrate agency and thus challenge the cultural stereotypes that informed beliefs about youth prior to and during the conflict.

The stated aim of the commission was "to restore the human dignity of victims and promote reconciliation" by investigating and reporting on the nature and extent of the human rights crimes committed during the Tensions.[8] The process sought to facilitate "national unity and reconciliation" by providing an inclusive environment for "all stakeholders" to contribute to the outcomes of the TRC.[9] To that end, the TRC made special provisions to allow for community-wide engagement and acknowledgment. Central to this mandate was an effort to secure testimony from groups and individuals typically excluded from transitional justice practices. Specifically, the commission identified that youth were a key "thematic" group for targeted investigation, alongside women, ex-combatants, and children.[10] This thematic focus consisted of a dedicated program for youth in which their experiences were conceived and cast as complementary to, yet distinct from, those of children. The objective of these youth-focused initiatives was to facilitate a level of participation that would "break the culture of silence" often associated with the conflict experiences of youth.[11] Designations between children and youth serve as an institutional acknowledgment of the heterogeneity of young peoples' conflict experiences, thus creating space for increased ownership over their stories.

A further significant development toward the meaningful engagement of youth in TRCs was the inclusion of their voices throughout the formal consultation and planning process. The participation of youth in the activities and events associated with the creation and implementation of the TRC saw them stand out as "productive citizens" with a unique stake in the outcomes of justice and reconciliation.[12] From its inception, the Solomon Islands TRC cast youth and children as distinct and thus enabled a reconciliation process more open to the diverse contributions of these demographics. This level of inclusion marked a significant development in the way youth participate in transitional justice processes.

Despite this undeniable progress, when the TRC handed down its final report in 2012, a dedicated discussion of youth was conspicuously absent. While women, children, and ex-combatants were all afforded chapters and institutional consideration, youth were not. Rather their stories were incorporated under the category of children and characterized as either victims or perpetrators of the violence. These public representations and the institutional slippage between children and youth present significant challenges for substantive inclusion as they fail to reflect the diverse ways youth experience and attribute meaning to conflict. Moreover, this institutional slippage denies youth agency in the reconciliation process because it limits their capacity to demonstrate their contributions to post-conflict reconciliation and to provide reflections on the meaning assigned to their stories. While this institutional slippage provides pragmatic opportunities to construct a unified conflict narrative, it also has the capacity to alienate and homogenize young people who are key stakeholders due to their diverse contributions. When stakeholders are excluded from transitional justice practices, they are less likely to buy into its aims or legitimate its mandate, which further perpetuates cycles of exclusion that restorative justice approaches seek to avoid. For restorative processes such as TRCs to fulfill their mandates of reconciliation through acknowledgment, young people must be valued as knowledge producers.

The case of the Solomon Islands TRC illustrates the key discord, which informs young people's engagement with transitional justice processes. On the one hand, the past two decades have seen increasing recognition of the importance of including all young people in transitional justice processes, particularly TRCs. On the other hand, ideas about and representations of the roles youth occupy in post-conflict processes often remain superficial. Further complicating these discourses within the transitional justice field are persistent institutional slippages that fail to distinguish between children and youth. Storytelling during TRCs, despite best intentions, is limited in its capacity to represent complex and multifaceted narratives. As a result, when young people's stories are told, they often perpetuate politicized notions of their place within these communities, which manifests as simplified and institutionally defined movement between classifications of children and youth. In the past, contestation has occurred between public representations of youth and the political reflections of youth due to a lack of critical reflection of the fluid and dynamic relationship between youth, reconciliation, and community-focused restorative justice. Transitional justice scholarship has yet to investigate the impact of young people's diverse engagement or to consider how we might effectively separate the experiences of children and youth within reconciliation practices.

At the same time, national and international policymakers have been slow to center young people's voices in transitional justice processes, preferring to talk about them and for them rather than with them. With this in mind, this book examines the evolution of young people's engagement with TRC processes. To do so, it explores how TRCs, which publicly identified young people as key actors, have interacted with their voices and their stories. Focusing on the cases of South Africa, Sierra Leone, and the Solomon Islands, this book considers the development of young people's representation within the reconciliation discourse and assesses the impact of youth participation on the final reconciliation narrative produced in each context.

Despite significant developments in the nature and scope of youth participation in TRC processes, a tension persists between the stories told by youth and their representation in formal narratives of conflict. This presents a significant challenge to the pursuit of meaningful reconciliation, which is broadly acknowledged to be a process that pursues healing and an end to the culture of impunity through acknowledgment. The ways young people are represented during formal institutionalized transitional justice processes informs our capacity to understand their experiences of conflict and to address their post-conflict needs. While youth are increasingly visible, their voices continue to go unheard, particularly in transitional contexts where the beliefs of external stakeholders perpetuate deeply rooted institutional norms regarding the roles of young people in conflict.

This chapter outlines the developments in the transitional justice field that have sought to facilitate a more inclusive justice environment. Creating enabling environments for the pursuit of meaningful reconciliation requires formal practices to hear and take seriously the needs and experiences of marginalized groups, in particular young people. To illustrate this claim, this chapter examines the emergence of restorative and holistic approaches and evaluates their capacity to facilitate the participation of individuals traditionally marginalized by retributive justice. Next, this chapter considers the literature on reconciliation and the capacity of TRCs to facilitate an inclusive and responsive process that acknowledges the harms experienced by individuals and the broader community. To that end, it discusses the importance of the widely acknowledged "turn to truth" for the increased engagement of a diverse range of stakeholders in the justice process of transitional states. Finally, this chapter considers the relationship between the character of reconciliation and the capacity of mechanisms to ensure substantive inclusion. To that end, it suggests that where young people's participation is concerned, pursuing interpersonal reconciliation offers more opportunities for engagement than political reconciliation.

Transitional Justice

Since the political transitions of the 1980s and 1990s, states have increasingly sought to pursue justice for human rights violations.[13] These transitions brought about and reflected an increased focus on accountability within international human rights discourse, heightening the focus on individuals, particularly the most innocent and vulnerable. The decision by post-conflict states to pursue justice for human rights crimes indicated a strengthening of norms related to international and humanitarian law, as well as individual criminal accountability.[14] During this period, states employed a variety of mechanisms in the search for accountability including trials and truth commissions, reparations and institutional reforms, apologies, exhumations, vetting, memorialization, and ceremonial justice practices. These mechanisms denoted the logistical parameters for transitional justice, which today has become a defined field of study and practice.[15] Yet the inclusivity and substantiveness of these frameworks remains a central challenge for which young people's stories offer important lessons.

While each of these tools is varied in its nature and approach to justice, they share the underlying common aim of providing redress to victims of human rights violations. To that end, they seek to facilitate an end to the "culture of impunity" that has historically plagued states experiencing violence and instability.[16] The increased prominence of transitional justice measures in post-conflict communities has contributed to what has been termed a "revolution in accountability" or "the justice cascade."[17] Transitional justice, as such, provides states with an opportunity to engage with the past in order to avoid repeating the conditions that produced the violence and instability.

Over the past three decades, transitional justice has evolved into "a global project," with states across all regions employing mechanisms to deal with the legacies of past violence.[18] More recently transitional justice practices have been utilized to promote the rule of law, reconciliation, development, sustainable peace, and human rights as notions of accountability and justice have evolved in both nature and scope.[19] These developments in the practice of transitional justice have inspired an expansive body of research on international jurisprudence, as well as the politics of accountability. Indeed, scholars have engaged extensively with debates about the nature, purpose, scope, and sequencing of transitional justice processes.[20] With the evolution of transitional justice, the practice has become an expected and normalized process in which states no longer grapple with whether to pursue justice for human rights crimes but rather which combination of measures would be most appropriate to the justice needs of the local community. Well-worn debates about peace versus justice and truth versus justice have been replaced with more nuanced discussions about how justice is achieved and who contributes to the process. Given this, the analysis herein contributes to this new sub-field of inquiry by providing an assessment of the capacity of TRCs to include the voices and experiences of youth. Broadly speaking, it examines the evolving relationship between youth, reconciliation, and the practice of transitional justice.

Since its emergence as a defined field, scholars have engaged in a long-worn debate regarding the definition of transitional justice.[21] Rather than revisit this, I adopt Renée Jeffery and Hun Joon Kim's expansive definition, which concludes that transitional justice is "the pursuit of accountability for, and attempts to make right, the wrongs of human rights violations committed in the past associated with major political shifts, including movements from authoritarian rule to democracy, or ruptures, such as those that mark the end of violent conflicts."[22] In adopting this wide-ranging definition, I hope to reflect not only the range of contexts where transitional justice is now used but also the diverse array of mechanisms (and more importantly the combinations of mechanisms) implemented in transitional contexts. Furthermore, this inclusive definition allows for the consideration of the constantly evolving array of actors who actively contribute to the practice of transitional justice. It does so by recognizing that fluidity is essential when pursuing justice for human rights crimes in diverse and evolving contexts.

Transitional Justice as an Evolutionary Process

While states have been using the mechanisms of transitional justice since the time of the ancient Greeks, it was not until the third wave of transitions to democracy in Latin America and Eastern Europe that it found form as a defined field of study and practice.[23] Nevertheless, the early precursors to transitional justice provide valuable insights about the processes and practices pursued in the search for accountability. The transitional justice practices employed in ancient Greece and in the aftermath of the French revolution demonstrate that transitional justice processes are "shaped by the memory of earlier transitions."[24] That is, transitional justice is evolutionary in nature and scope, as it is responsive to the successes and failures of prior attempts to hold individuals accountable for crimes committed during past transitions and conflicts. For example, in ancient Greece "the measures taken after the second restoration of Athenian democracy were shaped by what was perceived as excessive severity in the first."[25] In this way, the practice of transitional justice is highly reactionary, as changes to the ways in which transitional communities pursue justice are informed by the emergence of new precedents, norms, discourses, and behaviors.

The evolutionary nature of transitional justice remains integral to its capacity to provide recourse for human rights abuses. The ability of transitional justice approaches to adapt to changing norms, and more importantly social structures, has allowed a wider range of stakeholders to participate meaningfully and substantively. Furthermore, the evolution of youth engagement presented in the following chapters demonstrates the same capacity to respond to lessons learned. While the representations of youth presented in the final reports are nonlinear, the ways in which each engages with youth is shaped by the practices of prior TRCs. Engagement with young people as children that begins in South Africa evolves with each new TRC established that acknowledges the importance of young people's participation. As evident in the following chapters, each TRC grapples with the discursive implications of young people's participation and with casting their identities as either children or youth. Central to this are revelations about the implications of young people's stories, and the meaning ascribed to them, on our understanding of youth's capacity for substantive participation. Transitional justice approaches have the capacity to respond to changing norms and adapt to the needs of transitional communities, ensuring their longevity as expected practice following conflict. Yet overcoming enduring silences requires that we take seriously how politics informs meaningful interactions between stakeholders during these processes.

Classical Transitional Justice

Classical transitional justice prioritized responses to human rights abuses that were retributive and legal in nature, and thus it was restrictive in scope. The legalistic focus of early transitional justice approaches was a by-product of developments in international humanitarian and human rights law. These developments occurred in response to the systemic and horrific nature of human rights violations committed during World War II, which necessitated "a new vocabulary for thinking and talking about [individual] and state wrongdoings."[26] The Geneva Convention (1949) and other international treaties developed during this period codified states' commitments to end impunity for certain crimes.

At the same time, the Nuremberg and Tokyo trials provided the foundations for greater acceptance of the norms of accountability and individual responsibility. In particular, the belief that individuals could be held responsible for human rights abuses provided a significant departure from previous notions of accountability that dominated the human rights field.[27] Justice Jackson in his final judgment at the Nuremberg trials articulated the widespread sentiment of the time, that "just following orders" no longer justified threats to human rights.[28] Furthermore, he argued that "individuals have international duties, which transcend the national obligations of obedience imposed by the individual state."[29] Finally, the Nuremberg and Tokyo trials established prosecutions as accepted practice for confronting human rights crimes. To that end, World War II trials had a lasting impact on the practice of transitional justice.

As previously indicated, however, it was not until the "third wave of democratic transitions" that transitional justice as we understand it today began to take shape.[30] Transitions were understood as "periods of political change," most commonly from "repressive regimes to democratic societies."[31] As Ruti Teitel explains, "conception[s] of justice" during this period were "characterized by legal responses to confront the wrongdoings of repressive predecessor regimes."[32] Accountability in this context was viewed in strictly retributive (legal) terms. The priority for states, therefore, was to punish those deemed "most responsible" for the human rights abuses committed.[33] As such, trials, and to a lesser extent TRCs, were perceived by newly formed democratic states as a way to distinguish their regimes from the actions of the previous government.

During this period, states pushed to reassert responsibility over the accountability of their citizens, and thus justice implemented at the national level took priority over international and collaborative approaches. At the same time, transitional justice practices in Latin America revealed tensions between politics and accountability as justice became intertwined with nation-building. The complex political structures associated with accountability were further evident in Argentina, where the protests and violence that followed the initial trials resulted in a series of amnesties being granted to military officials. These impunity laws utilized in Chile and Argentina raised questions amongst practitioners and scholars regarding the intent of transitional justice practices.[34] Dustin Sharp observes that "the transitional justice initiatives of the period fostered pragmatic compromises" rather than justice for the victims, as states aimed to balance the politics of transitions with the moral imperative to provide recourse to those most impacted by the violence.[35] The instability associated with transitional justice across Latin America prompted states to rethink the nature and goal of justice. While accountability remained an important focus for states, this was mitigated by the need to ensure stability during and after the transition.[36]

Beginning in the mid-1990s, ideas about transitions evolved to account for the increased use of accountability mechanisms, most notably amnesties, trials, and truth commissions "following . . . period[s] of conflict, civil strife or repression."[37] Indeed, transitional justice mechanisms were utilized by states and the international community during "post-conflict peacebuilding situations . . . including those that [did] not involve a liberal transition."[38] Here transition denoted a move from violence and instability to peace and development often procured through peace agreements, orchestrated by external actors in consultation with the multiple stakeholders, both international and domestic. Scholars have increasingly observed that justice is an integral part of peacebuilding and conflict resolution as states aim to respond to the human rights abuses committed by *all* parties to violence.[39]

The post-conflict transitions of the twentieth century further solidified the contributions of trials and TRCs to the pursuit of accountability following human rights abuses.[40] Transitional justice mechanisms used during this period demonstrated the complex yet mutually reinforcing relationship between peace and accountability. Furthermore, these transitions established an expansive set of rules and norms for the practice of transitional justice. For example, the tribunals in Rwanda and the former Yugoslavia reestablished the norm of collaborative justice (between the international community, NGOs, and the state), which had been abandoned during the transitions of the 1980s.[41]

Similarly, the landmark TRC in South Africa (along with those in Chile and Argentina) established a precedent for the pursuit of justice through nonlegal measures. It is here, beyond the strict procedural rules of trials, that spaces exist for the voices and stories of the most marginalized, notably young people. While TRCs were initially viewed as counter to the norm of accountability, the transitions of the 1990s, specifically the South African case, demonstrated their capacity to produce a complementary form of justice to trials. The notions of justice, which emerged at the South African TRC, advocated for the "right to truth," which was underpinned by the belief "that only once the wrongs of the past had been aired would it be possible . . . to move forward toward true societal reconciliation."[42] Justice in the context of TRCs considers the relationship between truth, accountability, and social restoration, thus creating potential opportunities for inclusive storytelling and participation. As Jeffery observes, a right to truth "is founded on the notion that both victims of human rights crimes and their families possess the right to know the circumstances" that led to their harms and to speak their truths about these experiences.[43] Truth commissions with their more expansive and inclusive parameters are thus more capable of revealing these truths, as they are not subject to the same strict procedural rules of trials. Moreover, as Joanna Quinn explains, "Truth commissions avoid retributive outcomes," instead focusing on "[providing the] victim and perpetrator an opportunity to share their past experiences."[44] In this way, the truth commission process is underpinned by restorative justice principles where participatory storytelling and the voices of individuals are integral to the realization of meaningful justice.

Restorative Justice

Today transitional justice is conceived and cast in restorative and transformative ways. In contrast to retributive justice, which considers crime to be a violation against the state, restorative justice perceives crimes as a "violation or harm to people and relationships."[45] As such, it prioritizes the restoration of social conditions over the imposition of punishment for perpetrators. The harm experienced by individuals, groups, and the broader community are the primary focus of this approach to justice. Given this, the goal of restorative justice is to repair social relationships and to encourage reconciliation between parties. This emphasis on community and relationships necessitates the participation of a broad cross section of the actors. Thus, it is where opportunities for youth to own their conflict stories exist.

Restorative approaches to transitional justice have become increasingly popular, as they provide "open textured . . . standard[s] that allow a lot of space for cultural difference and innovation while giving us a language for denouncing uncontroversial bad practice."[46] Given this, restorative justice approaches enable an inclusive forum for traditionally marginalized groups, such as youth, to claim agency over their conflict experiences. Thus the implementation of transitional justice mechanisms capable of reflecting the diverse perspectives often associated with violence and instability aids this level of participation in transitional context. As Kerry Clamp observes, restorative justice provides communities with an opportunity to "repair harm and restore loss" in ways specific to their contexts.[47] It enables spaces for communities to come together to confront their history of violence in responsive, expansive, and unique ways.

Restorative justice, therefore, seeks to acknowledge and confront the past while remaining mindful of the need for transitional societies to develop and grow. This approach to justice is a significant departure from classical, retributive approaches as it allows for consideration of the long-term, social, and development needs of individuals post-conflict. To that end, it attempts to make the transitional society whole again by "restor[ing] the victim and the perpetrator back into the community, and restor[ing] the relationship between them."[48] Moreover, restorative justice pursues accountability at the community and individual level, thus providing a more inclusive and comprehensive approach for the pursuit of justice in transitional states. Restorative justice approaches acknowledge that human rights abuses do not exist in a vacuum; rather they are the product of the social and political conditions that perpetuate and facilitate conditions of instability. Given this, the aim of this form of justice is to encourage reconciliation within the community and to ensure that the needs of victims, their families, the perpetrator, and society are addressed.

Proponents of restorative justice highlight that its fluid and ambiguous nature addresses common critiques of the retributive approach, which suggest that transitional justice is ineffective because it relies on a one-size-fits-all response to human rights violations.[49] This ambiguity, however, also serves as the central criticism of restorative justice, as scholars suggest that this vagueness creates practical limitations and challenges its legitimacy.[50] As the cases presented in this book highlight, however, transitional justice practices that follow strict institutional rules often fail to represent and engage the most marginalized members of post-conflict communities. The flexibility of these restorative approaches provides young people with the space to participate in transitional justice and to challenge externally derived representations about their roles in the conflict that may emerge.

Similar opportunities for inclusive participation of youth exist due to the emergence of holistic and transformative approaches. Holistic transitional justice "treats all rights as universal, interdependent, and indivisible and situates violence on a continuum that spans interpersonal and structural violence, rather than simply focusing on acts of political violence."[51] As such, it acknowledge the diverse ways in which individuals experience violence and instability. This is particularly beneficial when considering the interests and needs of youth, who often experience conflict in unique and surprising ways. Furthermore, these approaches use multiple mechanisms, both judicial and nonjudicial, in the pursuit of accountability for human rights abuses.[52]

Amongst the most significant contributions of the holistic approach to the transitional justice field is the claim that development issues are central to ensuring accountability in post-conflict contexts and thus should be a primary concern throughout the transitional justice process.[53] This framing compels architects of transitional justice practices to ensure that they assess accountability and justice in ways that speak directly to local needs. In this way, holistic approaches acknowledge the expectations of conflict participants who often understand the pursuit of justice in developmental terms.[54] Transitional justice processes that conceive of justice, peace, and development as mutually inclusive are often better equipped to acknowledge the agency and diverse justice needs of youth and to represent their stories in meaningful ways. Given this, holistic and restorative approaches to transitional justice are well placed to provide a space for youth to engage and to have their voices heard.

The inability of transitional states to prosecute all individuals, coupled with institutional immaturity and scarce resources, limits the effectiveness of retributive approaches to justice. In response, holistic and restorative approaches provide an alternative for states looking to confront past human rights violations. Indeed, the capacity of these approaches to deliver a combination of accountability, reparations, truth, reconciliation, and social transformation suggests that they can provide justice in diverse contexts. Ultimately, shifts in the way we understand justice, accountability, and transition have seen holistic and restorative approaches emerge as best practice throughout the transitional justice field.

Reconciliation

The underlying ethos of acknowledgment has become increasingly prominent in the transitional justice field as our approach to justice has evolved in its nature and scope. Restorative justice allows for an open and "flexible" approach to justice, which "further[s] the restoration of both the offender and his ambient broken relationships."[55] In this sense, restorative approaches create social conditions, where achieving accountability *and* reconciliation does not require an either/or approach. As Daniel Philpott observes, while "trade-offs between reconciliation and accountability will still occur," this compromise is not "because the concepts are intrinsically incompatible."[56] Rather, it is the politics associated with justice in transitional contexts that allow some stakeholders to leverage their participation in reconciliation for impunity. Moreover, conditions of "extreme instability and lawlessness" often render retributive approaches to justice ineffective at facilitating accountability.[57] Given this, justice conceived through an expansive, pragmatic lens that prioritizes acknowledgment as a form of accountability has the capacity to promote reconciliation, and thus in the practice of transitional justice the two concepts are increasingly recognized as complementary.

Despite the increased prominence of reconciliation in the practice of transitional justice, its nature, scope, and form remain highly contested. While there are many definitions, the central theme of the literature suggests that the process of reconciliation is fundamentally "about building relationships of trust and cohesion" by "addressing conflictual and fractured relationships."[58] That is, notions of reconciliation in these contexts emphasize the importance of interpersonal relationships to the production of meaningful and lasting peace and stability. As John Lederach observes, reconciliation is an "adaptive" series of practices, the purpose of which is to "build" and "heal relationships and societies and ultimately, achieve . . . a positive peace."[59] In addition, Susan Dwyer suggests that reconciliation in practice requires "bringing apparently incompatible descriptions of events into narrative equilibrium."[60] Reconciliation processes produce representations of conflicts where competing stories often sit uncomfortably side by side. This suggests that for young people, reconciliation mechanisms, namely TRCs, have the potential to provide a platform for exploring the varied and often contentious interpretations of the roles they occupy during conflict, as well as the range of youth representations that evolve throughout the reconciliation process and the construction of the formal conflict narrative.

Daniel Philpott suggests that political reconciliation seeks to "restore an entire political community, or a relationship between political communities, to a condition of respected citizenship, the rule of law, legitimacy, and trust."[61] The aim of reconciliation, therefore, is to create and restore productive social and political relationships that can maintain peace and stability. Political reconciliation ensures that post-conflict communities "are not haunted by the conflicts and hatreds of yesterday" by providing a process for the development of an open and inclusive confrontation of the harms associated with violence and instability.[62] In addition, political reconciliation in post-conflict societies requires a widespread commitment to "social inoculation against a future return to violence."[63] A holistic transformation of these conflict societies is thus essential for the prevention of further violence and a relapse of the conflict.

While political and interpersonal reconciliation share the same broad goal of restoring relationships, the types of connections they prioritize differ. Political reconciliation derives legitimacy via institutions, which are authorized by governments, and thus it prioritizes top-down notions of restoring relationships.[64] In contrast, interpersonal reconciliation which is predominately enacted at the grassroots level, and is situated within communities preferences notions of relationship (re)building that are bottom-up and culturally responsive.[65] The scope of these approaches to reconciliation varies significantly despite both forms pursuing the restoration of trust and the elimination of negative beliefs amongst stakeholders.

Interpersonal reconciliation prioritizes individuals as it is focused on reframing the "right relationship between the perpetrator and victim [in the context of] non-political harm—for example, an act of theft or domestic harm."[66] In contrast, political reconciliation emphasizes the importance of reframing the harmful collective relationships and structures that perpetuated past instances of violence. This is achieved by exposing the "presence of pervasive and widespread negative attitudes" in order to "rebuild trust within the polity by reinforcing normative expectations, or to reconstitute [the] political community."[67] Together these two approaches to reconciliation complement each other and facilitate a holistic and inclusive outcome that creates a post-conflict environment capable of maintaining stability, as both the structures and relationships within the community have been restored.

Reconciliation is an obvious entry point for youth into transitional justice processes because it provides the community an opportunity to hear and, most importantly, take seriously the experiences of youth as distinct from children. In addition, reconciliation processes offer a space for youth to assert agency as they involve "active participation, in which the wider community deliberates" and unites in collective truths.[68] In this way, the process of reconciliation is a collective and inclusive process whereby marginalized individuals claim opportunities to influence justice outcomes as political agents.

Reconciliation does not occur in a vacuum, as the experiences of stakeholders are defined by their interactions and interpretations of the environment in which the conflict occurred. It is these contextual factors that provide a rich tapestry for understanding the interactions of different political stakeholders with the process of reconciliation. Reconciliation focuses on the collective while prioritizing the healing of the individual; although it aims to produce broad social outcomes, its success is reliant on the will of the individuals it engages. The capacity of reconciliation processes to contribute positively to peace and justice in these contexts is determined by how well stakeholders "relate to one another."[69] Indeed, as Quinn concludes, "There is a strong and causal relationship between acknowledgment and forgiveness, social trust, democracy and reconciliation."[70] A truly comprehensive and inclusive reconciliation process, therefore, will be inclusive of a wide range of individuals and take seriously the meaning they attribute to their stories.

Although today the claim that healing occurs through the process of acknowledgment is highly contested, it remains the key justification for the implementation of TRCs.[71] The belief that "revealing is healing" suggests that "psychological restoration and healing can only occur through providing space for survivors of violence to be heard."[72] That is, the notion that "revealing is healing" highlights the relationship between agency, acknowledgment, and reconciliation. In this respect, acknowledgment is "responsible for the creation of the bonds of social capital and social trust."[73] This is particularly important in instances where these elements have been noticeably absent from the pre-conflict environment. It assumes that when individuals are given the opportunity to voice their experiences in a public forum, the process of understanding associated with this recognition produces trust amongst the community. As Rejeev Bhargave observes, "Without a proper engagement with the past and the institutionalization of remembrance, societies are condemned to repeat, re-enact, and relive the horror."[74] Thus, ensuring ongoing peace and stability post conflict requires communities to confront past human rights abuses in transparent and inclusive ways that reflect a wide range of beliefs about the violence by those most impacted.

In transitional justice contexts, truth telling is the "public discovery and revelation of past injustices," which is undertaken most commonly by TRCs.[75] Truth telling facilitates the restorative goals of political reconciliation because it not only exposes past human rights violations, but it also "provides public recognition that the victim's rights as a human and a citizen were violated" and previously hidden.[76] In post-conflict environments, the nature of truth deviates from everyday factual truth due to its relationship to healing, reconciliation, and political agendas. Scholars highlight the distinction between knowledge of facts and acknowledgment of deeds, which is more diverse in scope yet also informed by the political environment in which it is situated.[77] Truth telling in transitional justice contexts "involves [perpetrators] stating their injustices publicly, admitting the suffering of the victims, confirming their membership in society, and thus restoring their dignity."[78] It necessitates acceptance by victims and the community of these stories and their situatedness within their own narratives. Reconciliation, therefore, is produced through the creation of a public narrative, which acknowledges the experiences of the combatants, the victims, and the community. Public recognition accomplishes justice through reconciliation as it allows victims to reclaim or, in the case of marginalized demographics, assert agency over their conflict experiences.[79] By engaging with public truth-telling processes, traditionally marginalized individuals can enact, demand, and invoke their citizenship and thus claim ownership of their stories.[80]

When youth are given the opportunity in reconciliation processes to speak their truths, free from the constraints of institutional barriers, they demonstrate often unexplored agency, capacity, and ownership as political actors. Scholars such as Jessica Senehi and Sean Byrne conclude that storytelling "provides for a collaborative process of meaning making and relationship building that . . . mediates between the personal and the political."[81] For youth in particular, the development of a conflict narrative derived directly from their firsthand accounts challenge the narrow representations often associated with their experiences. Moreover, the process of storytelling "engages" youth "in an interactive process that empowers their voices" and thus legitimizes their claims of agency and citizenship.[82] The creation and dissemination of their unique and diverse conflict narratives, as such, reenvisages the relationship between youth and the broader transitional justice community. In doing so, reconciliation processes such as TRCs, which enable this storytelling, act as a public forum for youth to establish meaningful relationships with other key stakeholders and to have their stories widely acknowledged.

Since the landmark South African case, mechanisms that facilitate justice through reconciliation have provided a public space for a cross section of the community to come together and acknowledge both individual and collective experiences of violence. In recent times, TRCs have become a "routine approach to the problem of how transitional states can best address human rights violations."[83] TRCs today allow post-conflict states to pursue a diverse accountability mandate, which incorporates retributive forms of justice and delivers accountability, albeit in a different form. This broad mandate facilitates the meaningful participation of actors that are typically excluded from traditional approaches to justice. As a result, TRCs have the capacity to represent a diverse range of conflict experiences.

An evolving body of research on the participation of traditionally marginalized individuals with transitional justice practices, however, demonstrates that many barriers to agency remain. Furthermore, scholars highlight that efforts to involve and make visible the voices existing on the margins of transitional societies have been mixed.[84] As Sharp contends, "The historically marginalised aspects of transitional justice remain at the field's edge," despite the normalization of the pursuit for accountability within post-conflict states.[85] Despite the prominence of restorative justice approaches today, which enable a more open and participatory environment, the inherent political nature of transitional justice remains an obstacle to the provision of meaningfully inclusive practices. A tension exists within the practice of TRCs due to attempts to balance the broader reconciliation demands of the transitional state and aspirations for an inclusive and open process, which acknowledges the wide array of actors that experience human rights abuses during instability. While the needs and interests of youth are increasingly visible in the TRC process, representations of their experiences, particularly in the institutional reporting, perpetuate marginalizing, dichotomous stereotypes that deny ownership and agency.

Truth and Reconciliation Commissions

TRCs are widely used in transitional contexts to facilitate reconciliation. They have proven to be a popular mechanism in the pursuit of justice, as they provide an alternative to trials that "balances political constraints" with calls for accountability.[86] Scholars have written extensively on the range of possible goals for TRCs in an effort to quantify their successes and failures.[87] While far from exhaustive, stated goals include "promoting victim and societal healing, establishing accountability, facilitating reconciliation, and preventing conflict recurrence."[88] These goals can be broadly characterized under the themes of acknowledgment, engagement, and reconciliation.

Alongside debates about the goals of TRCs sits an extensive discussion surrounding how to define them. TRCs are most commonly defined as nonjudicial, temporary, and officially sanctioned institutions mandated to produce a report on the nature and causes of violence in transitional contexts.[89] Classifications of TRCs differ in their views on the necessity and importance of the reporting aspect of the TRC. For example, while scholars such as Priscilla Hayner believe that the final report is a mandatory feature of TRCs, others remain silent on the reporting aspect.[90] Adding to the litany of claims surrounding the importance of final reports are those scholars who advocate for a flexible approach. Indeed, scholars contend that while the production of a report is a desirable outcome for any truth commission process, it is not indicative of a commission's overall success or failure.[91] Nevertheless, Jeffery and Mollica argue that in instances where final reports are produced "the failure of governments to undertake [the] programs of reform recommended . . . undermines the purpose and legitimacy of the TRC processes."[92] TRC reports, therefore, establish the parameters of engagement between the transitional government and the community.

Although not a necessary outcome of the reconciliation process, TRC reports are important because they provide a public and transparent record of human rights violations. This record is produced following a comprehensive investigative process that collects the stories of conflict through public and private hearings, written statements, and focus groups. The institutionalization of this narrative limits the potential for "states, societies and perpetrators to deny uncomfortable truths about their pasts" and "the range of permissible lies" told by stakeholders "whose interests are not . . . served by the truth."[93] In addition, TRCs often guide the development and rebuilding practices of transitional states by making "specific recommendations for reform," which aim to "prevent the repetition of past crimes" by "[identifying] ways to help former opponents live side by side peacefully."[94] The recommendations component of final reports is particularly important for marginalized communities, such as women, children, and youth, as their participatory capacity is often the focus of these reforms. This is evident in the cases examined in this book, as child and youth development and education programs are a principal component of the recommendations.

While transparency and acknowledgment are enabled by the development of a TRC report, the stories produced often neglect individual voices that do not fit the linear conflict narrative. Final reports thus often represent a pragmatic compromise that highlights the broad causes and events that took place during the conflict rather than a retelling of all truths. For young people, the process of testifying at the committee and providing statements to thematic hearings is more important than the production of a formal report. These inclusive and open processes allow youth to tell their stories, have their voices heard, and thus claim agency and ownership over their conflict experiences and their role in the post-conflict processes of transitional states. In contrast, the final report can produce and perpetuate marginalizing narratives that minimize or misrepresent the contributions of youth. While often marginalized groups such as women, children, and youth are visible in the TRC processes of transitional states, hearing, reflecting, and responding to their stories remains a significant challenge. The formal narratives produced in the final reports of TRCs are often informed by beliefs about youth rather than the reflections of youth. The distinction between these two sets of beliefs creates a dilemma for post-conflict states that aim to provide justice through reconciliation and acknowledgment. The pragmatic compromises required to produce a linear and politically accepted narrative of the causes of conflict often reduce the stories of youth to their most basic and logical form. When transitional justice processes are codified through processes such as formal reports, they silence, often subconsciously, the dynamic voices of youth, as well as their claims to citizenship in favor of other political agendas. Substantive participation in transitional justice practices by those traditionally denied agency in these processes reflects claims to political will by these individuals. By claiming ownership over and recounting their experiences, as well as the meanings attributed to these recountings, youth assert their citizenship and thus challenge the use of their stories as simply embodiments of peace and broader political agendas within transitional justice processes.

Conclusion

Reconciliation practices such as TRCs are important sites of engagement for young people following conflict. Yet their potential for inclusion is often constrained by traditional cultural hierarchies and endemic, technocratic power structures. Nevertheless, when young people's stories are heard through these formal practices, it can contribute substantively to a deeper and more nuanced understanding of the causes and consequences of violence and instability. In addition, young people's participation offers reciprocal value to reconciliation, as their engagement with TRCs has transformative potential. Substantive inclusion of young people, which acknowledges their leadership and capacity as decision makers, can offer new and diverse opportunities for these institutions in their pursuit of responsive and holistic justice.

However, attempts to meaningfully represent the voices of young people in formal mechanisms such as TRCs are limited by narrow framings of who these young people are. While they are visible, their stories are often used to reflect the aspirations of powerful actors. Thus, when young people are represented as the embodiment of political goals, their experiences are rendered silent by the structures and norms that guide these formal processes. To overcome these challenges and to complement the stories about youth reproduced by formal mechanisms, youth have turned increasingly to informal mechanisms as demonstrated in the introduction. Yet the pursuit of reconciliation through informal practices does not negate the importance of creating substantive inclusion in the formal justice architecture of transitional states. Amplifying young people's voices in transitional justice highlights the complex interplay between agency, voice, subjecthood, and resilience. Therefore, young people's political will, and their substantive participation in the design and implementation of reconciliation mandates, enables a more responsive and holistic approach to accountability.

Chapter 2

Locating Young People in Peace and Conflict
The Development of Scholarship for Children and Youth

> Childhood is basically an elaborate and very powerful adult myth, a series of stories and accounts that locates children as subordinate figures in society.
>
> —Michael Wyness, *Childhood and Society*

The question of how youth and their participation in conflict should be represented, harnessed, and understood post conflict is one of the contemporary challenges facing transitional justice. Since the Secretary General's 2004 report *The Rule of Law and Transitional Justice* outlined and advocated for an inclusive, agent-centered approach practitioners have increasingly sought to ensure the substantive participation of a wide range of actors, including victims' families, local communities, women, refugees, civil society, children, and most recently youth.[1] As chapter 1 demonstrates, TRCs have proven instrumental in enabling the participation of a diverse range of voices in the pursuit of accountability in transitional states. Attempts to create transitional justice approaches that value and consider local ownership and agency have inspired an empirical turn within the transitional justice scholarship as it seeks to explain and assess the capacity of the "transitional justice toolkit" to meaningfully engage with those traditionally excluded from the practice of transitional justice.

The inclusive mandate of TRCs has broad implications for this praxis. As Holly Guthrey and Karen Brounéus observe, TRCs that consider the local and "provide an inclusive and participatory space" for the voices of those most impacted by the conflict are better able to ensure the goal of reconciliation, as inclusion encourages ownership and legitimacy.[2] TRCs have increasingly acknowledged the role of youth in conflicts, as well as their importance to the reconciliation process. However, their distinct voices often remain silenced, and thus their ownership and agency over their reconciliation narratives remains limited. While TRCs today recognize that youth experience conflict in a manner distinct from children, narrow representations of youth that rely on norms and assumptions constructed by external actors hinder their capacity to reflect these differences. Youth are, at the same time, increasingly visible in TRC processes and silenced in the development of the formal conflict narratives produced by TRCs. This chapter examines the developments and challenges associated with conceiving and casting youth as "innocent victims" and as "deviants" before offering an alternative model that highlights the capability of youth in peace and conflict contexts. Representing youth and their substantive participatory capacity requires a critical exploration of the ways in which their experiences are informed by their status as youth. To overcome the limitations evident in current depictions of youth, this chapter proposes that an agent-centered, pragmatic lens be applied when describing youth engagement.

The youth agency lens has the capacity to provide transitional states with a framework to guide the development of programs that would actively respond to the interests and needs of youth.[3] The implications of this framework across a range of contexts, however, have yet to be extensively examined. Developments in the peacebuilding field suggest that centering youth voices offers opportunities for a more nuanced and holistic representation of their experiences. At the center of this model is the belief that youth possess agency and that understandings of who youth are and the roles they play post conflict must start by acknowledging their agency and its relationship to their capacity for autonomous decision-making. The youth agency lens "recognizes that young people live, work and act independently of organizations and programs" and that their interactions impact society in diverse and complex ways.[4] It suggests that the meaningful inclusion of youth requires agents to conceive and cast them "as an organic social force, all the time enmeshed in cultural and conflict reproduction," rather than as subjects and actors in other individual's agendas.[5] As such, when recounting their stories of conflict and reconciliation what matters is the meaning they ascribe to experiences, not that which is attributed to them by other stakeholders.

Before turning to an examination of the agent-centered approach, it is important to consider the different frameworks that are prominent in both the policy and scholarship on young people's participation in peace and conflict. First, this chapter considers the evolution of the normative frameworks that underpin beliefs about children and youth and their relationship to agency. Next, it examines developments in the classifications of young people, including the definitional boundaries, international instruments, social constructions, and theoretical models that inform ideas about children and youth in conflict and post-conflict processes. These models are significant for our understanding of youth in transitional justice, as they produce traditions about young people that have implications for representations of youth in TRCs. Following this, the chapter evaluates scholarship that perpetuates and critiques the dominant dichotomies used to classify young people in peace and conflict, youth as innocent victims and youth as deviants. In the concluding section, this chapter considers the contributions of the peacebuilding field to our understanding of young people in transitional justice. Specifically, it highlights the value of framing young people as empowered political agents. Taken together, the victim/perpetrator binary and the youth agency model form the theoretical framework used throughout the rest of this book to examine representations of young people during formal reconciliation.

Normative Frameworks and Their Relationship to Agency

Agency is understood as "the role of creative individual activity in the constitution of human society."[6] It suggests, therefore, that individuals actively construct their social and political world. Acknowledgment of youth agency recognizes the capacity of youth to "shape . . . their own and other social conditions" as well as "their intentional roles . . . as knowledge producers."[7] Consideration of youth agency in transitional justice contexts requires an understanding of the dynamic nature of their participation in conflict and the structural conditions that perpetuate interactions and environments that continually deny their voices. For youth to have agency, therefore, means to challenge, negotiate, and question the systems in which they act, speak, or are silenced. It suggests that the behaviors of youth in peace and conflict are fluid and constantly shifting. They are not simply victims and/or deviants, they are also "agents of change" capable of contributing both positively and negatively to transitional justice.[8] Theories of youth that recognize their substantive and meaningful contributions have emerged in recent years in the peacebuilding field. These models of youth agency highlight the importance of a "holistic understanding of youth behavior" particularly in the development of youth-led practices.[9] As the cases in this book demonstrate, while TRCs often fail to utilize this holistic notion of youth, particularly in the formal narrative, the processes associated with conducting TRCs provide a forum for them to highlight their diverse experiences of conflict. Dominant representations of youth rely on dichotomous normative assumptions, rather than reflections of their on-the-ground experiences, and thus they are linked specifically to normative classifications that merge women and children.

Cynthia Enloe was one of the first feminist theorists to construct a framework for the representation of children in international relations that drew attention to the institutional silence they experience. Central to her framework was a constructed politicized relationship that conceived of "womenandchildren" together. By representing these distinct demographics as one, Enloe questions the marginalizing instincts of international systems, which assume a symbiotic relationship between "women and children as the non-political . . . innocent, voiceless and passive" subjects of human rights violation.[10] While scholars such as Erica Burman have challenged the validity of this representation, due to its narrow understanding of women and children as "objects" without agency, it remains dominant in the practice of transitional justice and is often still utilized to inform interactions with these groups.[11] Similarly, the link between children and youth has become increasingly prominent in transitional justice discourse as their experiences are often represented together, particularly in reports produced by NGOs. For example, the International Centre of Transitional Justice have developed a series of policy reports on "children and youth." In these reports, youth are often relegated to a secondary position in the common vernacular.[12] This representation is incomplete as it fails to acknowledge that youth engage with conflict and transitional periods in varied, often devastating, ways that are distinct from children's experiences. Moreover, their unique needs and interests are often obscured or conceived in a way that takes the experiences of children as universal and linear. As Katrina Lee-Koo observes, "At no other stage in a person's life does ten years make such a stark difference."[13] The use of terms such as "baby, toddler, child, teenager, adolescent, youth and young adult denote . . . stages of development and different capabilities and attributes."[14] Rarely therefore does literature, which speaks of children and youth combined, see and reflect their unique interests and needs. These two linked representations produce a normative framework that fails to reflect displays of agency by youth or the experiences that are unique to their status as youth.

In addition, predicting and classifying their interests through a singular, linear framework presents inaccurate normative assumptions, as youth, like most individuals, are inherently unpredictable and thus respond to external pressures in diverse ways. When speaking of or about youth therefore, it is crucial to utilize an expansive lens and to establish a clear point of departure from children and adults. Understanding the differences between these three social demographics is critical for peace and conflict scholars and practitioners, as classifications inform and influence transitional justice practice. In the case of youth, Siobhán McEvoy-Levy observes that "ideas about young people shape policies and programs which, in turn, shape local and global ideas about youth."[15] Once institutionalized, representations of youth have a lasting impact on their interactions and relationships. Where reconciliation narratives are concerned this is an important consideration, as these accounts seek not only to restore relationships but also to establish a long-term development agenda (through the recommendations outlined in the final report) for the transitional state. It is therefore crucial that representations of youth codified in these final reports reflect the diversity and complexity of youth's conflict experiences, as well as the nature and extent of their capacity to meaningfully contribute to the reconciliation processes of these states.

Prominent understandings of youth, in scholarship and practice, reveal significant obstacles to their substantive participation and meaningful representation. Most notably, the political nature of the discourse has produced ideas about youth that are problematically tied to explorations of children and childhood. As a result, youth are often characterized as innocent victims without political agency. Bina D'Costa observes that "a disproportionate percentage of the international community's attention focuses on child soldiers" and their vulnerability, even though young people occupy a multitude of roles as civilians, witnesses, combatants, and targets.[16] When youth are considered in literature as a distinct social group, they are commonly cast as deviants or perpetrators of violence. These models for understanding youth focus on the structural impact of their engagement with the post-conflict environment. In doing so, they prioritize collective notions of youth and their participation rather than acknowledging the individual and diverse voices of youth. The most dominant model is the "youth bulge" theory, which persists in many policy circles. This theorizing is problematic for representations of youth at TRCs because it overstates the threat posed by a large youth population and thus obscures display of agency and substantive participation.[17] Despite several sound empirical critiques of the legitimacy of this theory, policy actors continue to use its underlying normative principles to create narrow policies and justify protectionist strategies when interacting with youth in political spaces.[18]

Young people in conflict and post-conflict states, therefore, are perceived to have had their childhoods "lost" or "stolen."[19] As a result, they are often viewed and represented in one of two ways: as "out-of-place and dangerous because they have transgressed what is seen as appropriate behavior" for young people or as passive objects and victims of violent governments or rebel forces.[20] These depictions of youth have implications for the representation of their experiences in the final reports of TRCs, as adult understandings of young people and institutional representations are informed by these binary classifications. The victim/perpetrator binary remains the dominant lens in the transitional justice field, appearing frequently in reconciliation narratives produced by TRCs. Considered together, these two representations of young people suggest that the experiences of youth are fixed and universal. Representations of youth informed by this dichotomous framework are insufficient to construct an inclusive, holistic conflict narrative because they conceal the fluid and complex nature of youth and their relationship with peace, conflict, and reconciliation. As demonstrated later in this chapter, however, youth often occupy crosscutting roles and the realities of their interests are often not easily characterized. As Paul Gready has observed in the case of South Africa, youth were "both victims *and* perpetrator, or political activists *and* criminals" (emphasis in the original).[21] Recognition of agency therefore necessitates that interactions with youth take seriously their heterogeneous (re)claiming of identities.

Until recently, the firsthand voices of youth had been consciously absent from the discussion, despite increased practical recognition of their status as political agents, who like children "inherit . . . the results of transition."[22] The prominent classifications that have evolved in the scholarship on youth present a homogenous and narrow lens for describing their experiences and interests. Yet as the collection of works by Albrecht Schnabel and Anara Tabyshalieva demonstrate, youth are complex characters who actively demonstrate agency and ownership over their conflict experiences through meaningful participation in post-conflict peacebuilding practices.[23] As the cases presented in this book demonstrate, the multifaceted and dynamic nature of youth engagement is consistent across all post-conflict contexts, yet our capacity to represent this diversity at the institutional level is hindered by an overreliance on the victim/perpetrator binary by external stakeholders, specifically governments and civil society. Given this, standardized representations of youth are unable to accurately reflect the nature and extent of their engagement. This chapter offers an alternative conceptualization of youth that is grounded in discursive recognition of their capacity, their voices as active political storytellers, and the complexity of their experiences.

Children and Youth in Conflict and Post-Conflict Processes

Research on youth in peace and conflict is a rapidly evolving, yet still intermittent, sub-field of inquiry. Despite a few notable exceptions, scholars of transitional justice and peacebuilding rarely focus solely on the experiences of youth distinct from children.[24] Common characterizations of children *and* youth within these contexts homogenize their experiences, rendering invisible diverse displays of political will and agency. When children and youth are cast as possessing a singular identity it positions them within the political space as objects for the protective practices of others (namely adults) who are accepted as the real political subjects. This failure to recognize and speak to the demographically distinct nature of children and youth, and within that the diverse character of their experiences, reveals the ephemeral, shallow role assigned to young people across a large cross section of the international relations literature.[25] Similar trends exist within policymaking for peace and reconciliation, as perceptions that *all* children and youth exist in nonpolitical spaces and in apolitical ways results in a predisposition toward treating them as cases rather than political persons.[26] Katrina Lee-Koo's work echoes these claims, revealing an overemphasis on the role of young people as nonpolitical agents throughout the preexisting literature on peace and conflict.[27] This literature is informed by early sociological and psychological notions of children and childhood, which assume that being young is a universal experience and thus all young people "have the same basic needs," capacities, and experiences.[28] It prioritizes a protectionist lens, which casts young people as passive bystanders to the events that shape their lived experiences. Thus, it denies opportunities to see and empower their capacity for autonomous decision-making.

Combining the experiences children *and* youth in a linear, singular narrative also reinforces dominate discourses in these contexts, which situate them as submissive, political resources. Within institutions, notions of childhood are constructed to be static and generalizable across time and space, creating a framework for understanding young people's capacity to participate that is predictable yet unresponsive to the reality of children, adolescents, and youth.[29] The liminality of *childhood* and *youthhood* creates challenges for the traditional social hierarchies of post-conflict institutions. To overcome these ambiguities, the architects of institutions often construct and perpetuate discourses about children and youth as a singular identity that maintain the social and political status quo. Decisions about how transitional justice institutions interact with children *and* youth's stories, therefore, are made to bolster the institution's legitimacy or to further the political agenda of those in power. As such, their stories are deployed to embody the prospect for peace, which can be facilitated by the institution, rather than to rebuild relationships between children and youth and the transitional community. In reconciliation contexts, these linear stories produce a complex and intentional paradox that objectifies children and youth and denies them political agency, as belonging is bestowed by adults rather than inherent to their positioning as citizens.

For centuries, scholars and practitioners have asked, "Just what, after all, are we to make of children?" Increasingly, the same question applies to youth, as notions of childhood and youthhood remain "perpetually diffuse and ambiguous," and thus reflects the realities of their experiences rather than a classificatory restraint.[30] However, conceptual uncertainty, or as I suggest fluidity and diversity, presents significant challenges for discourses and institutional practices that seek to maintain the status quo of traditional hierarchies and distributions of power when engaging with children and youth. As such, combining children's and youth's stories within the institutional narratives of post-conflict practices such as TRCs has become a problematic practice that requires reconsideration to ensure that the substantive participation of both children and youth reflects their lived realities and capacity for leadership. As highlighted by the cases in this book, consolidating children's and youth's experiences excludes important stories from the reconciliation discourse of a community. In doing so, it silences all young people and creates blind spots that are a threat to the realization of the reconciliation mandate. While the following chapters illustrate that significant strides have been made toward the substantive and distinct participation of both children and youth, due in part to the advocacy of youth-led organizations, homogenized identities persist within the formal institutionalized narratives. To understand the preservation and embeddedness of these marginalizing narratives it is necessary to examine their theoretical origins.

Early notions of the child conceive of them as incomplete and developing individuals requiring protection and care.[31] These understandings of "the child," Chris Jenks suggests, have informed "the powerful commitment to children in Western society" and thus the moral obligation to look after young people.[32] States and the international community, as such, assume responsibility for the protection of children, as well as the task of instituting systems and structures that will facilitate their transition into adulthood.

As David Archard observes, the notion of childhood "require[s] children to be distinguishable from adults in respect of some unspecified set of attributes."[33] Amongst the most widely used depictions include the innocent child, the unruly and deviant child, and increasingly children as autonomous agents. This list, however, is far from exhaustive; as David Nelken observes, "the child" is fraught with "contradictions, tensions, projections and conflicting ideals," yet those with the power to challenge these framings are often those whose interests it serves to maintain them.[34] This view conceives all young people as incapable of determining their own parameters for representation. In doing so, it produces a framework for understanding young people that focuses on children and neglects youth.

Understandings of childhood as a social construct began to take shape in the twentieth century. Since then, the identities of young people have been shaped and understood through their interactions and relationships within the social and political structures where they exist. Michael Freeman contends that images of children and discussion of their rights represent "aspirations for the accomplishment of particular social or moral goals,"[35] as opposed to pragmatic reflections of their experiences. When assigned public meaning and problematized as objects that reflect external aspirations, stories of children and youth perpetuate unrealistic assumptions about their role and capacity. This creates a disconnect between young people and the institutions promoting these representations, which threatens their overall legitimacy and aims in the eyes of young people. While helpful in the production of linear and easily digestible reconciliation narratives that further particular political truths, the continued promotion of universal classifications alienates young people and discourages buy-in for the outcomes. When the underlying normative characteristics of this view are used to describe the experiences of young people in reconciliation as such, they contribute to the silencing of youth, a denial of their agency and a refusal of ownership over the meaning attributed to their stories.

Children, Youth, and Human Rights

Following developments in the international dialogue on young people and the almost unanimous ratification of the Convention on the Rights of the Child (CRC), children have become increasingly visible in conflict and post-conflict contexts. Representations of young people in transitional justice, and specifically in the formal conflict narratives produced by TRCs, are informed by notions of human rights embedded in the CRC. In response to this evolution in the nature and extent of young people's political participation, theoretical and empirical scholarship has focused on understanding the relationship between children, human rights, and political participation in a range of contexts. The visibility of young people in peace and conflict contexts is often directly associated with the CRC, as notions of childhood are directly tied to human rights and their protections. Indeed, the CRC establishes a universal set of rights for children, underpinned by the normative belief that while children can "claim" rights, it is the responsibility of the state and thus adults to determine the nature of these protections. While widely accepted, the CRC is not without its critics, who argue that the "child's rights regime," which underpins and is furthered by the convention, produces an unrealistic depiction of childhood as universal.[36] Furthermore, this mediated approach to rights, which emphasizes entitlements over claims, sets a problematic precedent with respect to recognizing the political agency of young people.

In addition, Boyden contends that the "world's children" framework underscored by the CRC is susceptible to manipulation and overuse by NGOs in policy development, as it presupposes a singular and linear view of childhood, which is highly emotive but also blind to context and experience.[37] Relying on homogenous and institutionalized concepts of childhood does not allow for outliers to the narrative. Opponents of universality have highlighted its inability to respond to the diverse nature of children's experiences, concluding that the "well established but narrowly conceived framework through which we view children" obscures other potential, more responsive and reflective classifications that acknowledge their place in the creation of knowledge.[38] For example, amongst the most widely studied group of young people are child soldiers.[39] While the needs and interests of this group of children warrant considerable attention, the dominance of their narratives within the literature and in the practice of transitional justice obscures the other diverse roles children and youth occupy in conflict. The emphasis placed on giving child soldiers a voice has as such inadvertently silenced other stories not represented by this narrative.

While research on children in conflict has evolved, much of the work on child soldiers continues to be informed by the idea that children are irrational and incomplete beings. As a result, young people are characterized as being "universally and negatively" affected by conflict.[40] External classifications of child soldiers focus on protecting their innocence, as they are perceived as not yet fully formed individuals and thus vulnerable to manipulation. At the core of these discussions is a thematic emphasis on the evolution of children's rights within the broader discourse on international criminal justice. The moral ambiguity associated with the participation of young people in conflict produces theoretical discussions that emphasize their innocence and passivity. This discussion is framed using a rights-based approach that emphasizes protectionism and the need to generate "safe avenues for children to participate" in the social and political world.[41] Yet heavily mediated participatory parameters present significant challenges to children's agency, as they deny them the right to decide how their conflict stories are told. These barriers are further exacerbated by the temporalities of justice, which asks youth to reflect on their experiences as child soldiers.

In contrast, where youth are concerned their exclusion from institutional legal frameworks creates uncertainty around their role in the conflict. To that end, the notion that youth are more capable of thinking and acting for themselves has produced representations in the literature that emphasize their "destabilizing potential."[42] As outlined in the introduction, the rigid classificatory framework of the CRC, which labels any individual under the age of eighteen a child, produces an exclusionary legal framework that neglects youth and is blind to social and cultural representations of young people. Although this notion of the child is widely accepted, there is no clear explanation in the scholarship or in policy of what distinguishes a seventeen-year-old child soldier from a nineteen-year-old combatant. Scholarship has failed to determine why the seventeen-year-old is innocent and vulnerable, yet the nineteen-year-old is a troublemaker.[43] What the literature in the peacebuilding field has determined, however, is that "the blurred distinction between child and youth creates ambiguity and tension around how to deal politically and socially" with youth in peace and conflict.[44] As the cases in this book demonstrate, this tension is evident in the institutional representations of youth at TRCs.

Although perceptions of victimhood persist, there is increased recognition within the scholarship that all young people possess political agency. Yet this literature is intermittent and often fails to inform the relationship between children and the international community, particularly in policy. It is important, however, to briefly visit the underlying claims of this literature as it informs current understandings in the peacebuilding field, which consider the contributions of young people essential to the development of sustainable peace. Literature on children as political agents contends that while they are still evolving and developing cognitive skills, their views and experiences are valid and thus warrant consideration within the social and political structures that emerge following conflict.[45] Children and childhood, as such, are both socially constituted and impactful. As James and Prout observe, children are not merely passive and vulnerable; they also actively engage with and inform the world around them.[46] By acknowledging the potential of children as agents and contributors, these scholars recognize the importance of allowing children the space to utilize their voices as well as the significance of providing them with a seat at decision-making tables.[47] In doing so, this body of work opens up the experiences of children as "sites of knowledge" in peace and conflict.[48] The literature on children in transitional justice attempts to justify and establish the importance of examining the active and meaningful participation of children. As Alison Smith contends, children "far outnumber adults in many countries requiring transitional justice," and thus "excluding them may exclude the majority of the affected population."[49]

Understanding young people's political agency and capacity requires an interrogation of the nature of their participation to ensure it is meaningful and responsive to their interests. When measuring young people's engagement with post-conflict practices, quality and clarity matters. The recognition that young people's participation in conflict makes them sites of knowledge production is an important yet unexamined lens through which to consider the value of their voices. At the center of this research on the participation of children as stakeholders in the practices of transitional justice is the recognition that "children can claim certain individual rights even in adverse situations, transcending borders and conflict lines."[50] These claims are informed by legal provisions in the CRC, in particular Article 12, which outlines children's rights to participation. Yet, as previously indicated, the guiding principles of the CRC say nothing about the capacity of youth to participate or the impact of their unique status as youth on their experiences and their relationship to transitional justice. While the participation of youth may be implied and interpreted in the evolving nature of Article 12, the strict numerical parameters of the CRC suggest that this framework does not inform how the international community interacts with all youth.

Defining Young People

Recent scholarship has sought to distinguish between the youth, child, and adolescence classifications. The transitional and fluid nature of youth produces a complex lens through which to understand the diversity and magnitude of their conflict experiences. The rapid period of change associated with youth ensures that their interests, needs, and motivations are constantly shifting. Yet the prominence of the CRC throughout the dialogue on all young people in peace and conflict has produced a discursive framework, which relegates the interests of youth to the margins. Attempts by youth scholars to challenge these normative barriers have contributed to an evolution of the discourse, yet the operationalization of this expansive notion remains elusive.

This increased focus on youth stems from the on-the-ground reality that the demographic is often a transitional society's largest, and thus youth have the potential to be highly influential as agents of change or spoilers to peace processes. As the cases in this book highlight, youth are uniquely positioned to contribute to post-conflict practices, particularly as communities look to rebuild and restore relationships. In recent years, the interests of youth have also received greater recognition within public and political discourses, as they lend their voices to a wide range of issues across a variety of contexts. For example, youth parliaments and state-based youth policies are becoming increasingly prevalent, particularly in post-conflict settings as governments acknowledge the importance of the demographic to the stability of the country. Youth representation in these programs and policies, however, remains a significant challenge because of the different and often competing notions of who youth are, which continue to resonate throughout policy, practice, and scholarship. Indeed, the difficulty associated with characterizing youth produces potential obstacles to meaningful engagement.

Defining "youth" is a challenging yet necessary endeavor as this classification provides a foundation for their engagement in the reconciliation processes of transitional states. Specifically, they establish practical parameters that can be used to determine the nature, scope, and feasibility of the TRCs investigation. In addition, definitional boundaries can be both inclusive and restrictive. On the one hand, these classifications provide individuals with a collective sense of belonging, which in the context of reconciliation can be restorative. On the other hand, they can act as a barrier to participation, particularly where individuals fall outside the classifications.

Numerical classifications, particularly those established by international organizations, have been the most utilized yet highly contested definitions of youth. The United Nations defines youth "for statistical purposes, [as] . . . those persons between the ages of 15–24 . . . without prejudice to other definitions by Member States."[51] Similarly, the World Health Organization (WHO) has "outlined three categories of youth-adolescence (10–19 years old), youth (15–24) and young people (10–24 years old)."[52] While numerical boundaries establish practical and transparent participatory parameters for the development of policies and programs, they are exclusionary by design and thus fail to capture individuals within a post-conflict community who identify as youth regardless of their biological age. To ensure responsiveness, youth as an identity marker should be primarily understood as a fluid category that is individually (re)claimed, as well as culturally and socially determined.

Classifications of young people that are mindful of how social and political forces shape their experience are far more useful for the study of representation and engagement. Alice Schlegel contends that youth is "a period between childhood and adulthood during which its participants behave and are treated differently than either their seniors or their juniors."[53] Youth is a period of transition and discovery. To that end, representations of youth engagement in the reconciliation narratives of transitional states need to reflect the full spectrum of ideas about youth and their roles in conflict.

YOUNG PEOPLE AS REPRESENTATIONS OF THE SOCIAL LANDSCAPE

Contemporary portraits of young people in peace and conflict reflect long-standing tensions between different constructions of children and youth in political spaces. Whether young people are represented as victims or threats, as agents of change or potential spoilers to peace, or as a collective group or a range of diverse individuals is determined by the political climate in which they interact. In post-conflict contexts in particular, children and to a lesser extent youth are depicted as symbols of suffering and aggression and/or the future potential of society. There is a large body of literature that casts young people as political symbols for a range of political ends. For example, Helen Brocklehurst's work demonstrates that images of children are "central to the practices of militarization and nationalization."[54] Highlighting the case studies of Nazi Germany, South Africa, and Northern Ireland, she argues that "children's bodies have a political function . . . they are used as an emotional sphere against which to normalize and legitimize violence."[55] In this way, children and childhood are seen as a tool to further the ideological and practical aims of society. This has implications for our capacity to understand their interests, as children who do not fit into these social narratives are excluded from representation. The evolving independence of youth and the perception that they are "mischievous instigators" of violence fails to fit the emotive narrative, and thus rather than consider the implications of their unique voices they are either excluded from the discussion or amalgamated with children.

Charli Carpenter's research on children born as a result of wartime sexual violence highlights similar problematic assumptions, which are established when children are used as solely representations of atrocity. Throughout this research, she shows that these children are used by international organizations to set the parameters of policy intervention, as they embody a dialogue on innocence and vulnerability that creates as a moral necessity the need to protect young people at all costs.[56] As such, in the global public discourses surrounding peace and conflict, rarely are young people conceived and cast as unique individuals with their own diverse set of interests.

When youth are considered, a similar phenomenon exists as external actors assign meaning to youth behavior without consideration of their actual intent. Rather than emphasizing the vulnerability of these individuals, however, these representations draw on the perceptions that youth are instigators and troublemakers. Narratives created by media, advocacy networks, the institutional structures of local governments, and the international community dominate popular and scholarly discussions of young people and their roles in post-conflict environments. As Siobhán McEvoy-Levy highlights, "The Western media reports riots and demonstrations by Palestinian 'youth,' but the plight of 'children' displaced by war in Kosovo."[57] Likewise, think tanks and NGOs prioritize the suffering of children rather than the capacity of youth. Indeed, these actors produce narratives of young people that are politically motivated and highly contested. Given this, there is a growing body of work that examines the symbolic nature of children in political contexts, which Karen Wells has termed the "politics of pity."[58] Young people provide a powerful image, which rallies support for the mandates of a burgeoning global advocacy network. For example, as Lee-Koo demonstrates, "the African boy" reflects and reinforces preexisting stereotypes of post-conflict communities as "morally defunct zones of tragedy" that require the guidance and support of the international community.[59] External actors are, as such, often selective in their representation of the actions of youth, as they spotlight and assign meaning to their behaviors that perpetuate the narrative that fits their agenda. In this way, representations of young people are uniquely tied to the social and political environment. Prominent notions of young people in scholarship and in transitional justice practices prioritize external, often top-down representations rather than context-specific self-reflections.

These depictions, scholars have observed, "are mostly emotive and/ or reductionist" in nature and thus are often used to further political and social agendas.[60] Representations of young people are value-laden and externally derived, and thus they often reveal the broader political tone of their communities. As such, representations of the child or youth are a product of the world around them rather than a reflection of actual participation in society. The choice of classification highlights cultural norms, political will, and the emotional and moral struggles of powerful external actors. For example, as David Rosen observes, "The child-soldier crisis is part of the contested domain of international politics in which childhood serves as a proxy for other political interests."[61] Similarly, Jenny Kuper concludes that the protectionist mandate, which underpins the CRC, is derived from a global perception that children are both "particularly vulnerable" and "the new generation . . . to be cherished in that they represent the future."[62]

The use of children and youth to frame social causes and further political mandates challenges emerging claims within the literature that advocate for and demonstrate the political agency of children.[63] That is, these notions of childhood seek to reflect the roles and experiences of children through a normative lens that sees the value of children as children. Moreover, they represent an understanding of the child that acknowledges their unique contributions to politics because of their status as children. While this perspective of children is slowly emerging in the literature on peace and conflict, its influence and impact is crowded out of broader policy discussions, as these representations do not help to further the causes of adults as protectors and fully evolved beings. Furthermore, the impact of this new way of thinking about children in the public space has yet to be extensively empirically tested. Indeed, the theoretical origins of childhood still maintain prominence in the scholarship that evaluates and frames the roles of children in peace and conflict. It is therefore important to briefly revisit this literature, as it forms the foundation for the children and youth as victims classification.

The Theoretical Origins of Childhood

External depictions of young people remain deeply rooted in the academic discourses of childhood, despite extensive critiques regarding their capacity to reflect the heterogeneity of young people's experiences. As Jean-Jacques Rousseau contends, "We know nothing of childhood, and with our mistaken notions the further we advance the further we go astray." By "always looking for the man in the child" our interactions discount and render invisible "what he is before he becomes a man" and the political contributions stemming from this positionality.[64] Ideas about childhood, therefore are conceived from above to reflect the ways in which adults interpret children's interactions, rather than considering how they themselves ascribe meaning to their experience. It is "adult cognition, morality and emotions," that frame the most utilized public discourse on young people.[65] As a result, rarely do representations of young people reflect the complex nature of their relationship to the broader community. This is evident in contexts where conflict has forced young people to transition between commonly understood Western understandings of development in a shortened period.

In addition, "childhood" and the representations associated with it create distinguishable boundaries between adults, children, youth, and adolescents that denote social and public responsibilities. As Archard observes, the notion of childhood "requires children to be distinguishable from adults with respect to a series of unspecified . . . attributes."[66] As such, if adults are conceived and cast as political, mature, and engaged, then children exist in a normative space that casts them as pre-political, immature, and disengaged. Lee-Koo suggests in her critique of the theoretical origins of children that the collective childhood construct describes young people as individuals "yet to develop . . . a political consciousness and the capacity to bear the burdens" associated with political responsibilities.[67] Unlike adults, children do not carry the responsibilities associated with an individualized public persona. Their identity, to the extent that one exists in the public sphere, denotes innocence, vulnerability, and the collective potential for a peaceful, prosperous future.

As previously mentioned, early writings on childhood reveal the origins of several dominant narratives that persist throughout the scholarly literature to describe the identities of young people in post-conflict contexts, namely the innocent child and the unruly child. These narratives of childhood envisage a young person who is passive, is incomplete, and requires socialization. Their development and transition into adulthood is viewed as a condition of their surroundings and their interactions and relationships within this environment. The innocent child, therefore, represents purity and a manifestation of love.[68] In the eighteenth century, Rousseau envisaged a child that was "naturally" good, the embodiment of grace in need of protection from corruption.[69] In contrast, the unruly child is a direct product of a disorderly environment and the embodiment of society's failure to protect them from corruption in society.[70] These early notions of childhood persist today in the protectionist framework, which forms the foundation of the child soldier narrative.

Collective Representations

Rarely are children conceptualized as individual agents. Increasingly, scholars have acknowledged the problematic nature of conceiving the identities of young people as a collective. Brocklehurst concludes that in many societies the ideas about children are conceived and cast at the community level, rather than considering the unique and diverse interests of children as individuals.[71] Collective representations prioritize belonging and see value in identifying as part of a social group. In this way, collective social representations do not necessarily consider "whether that membership was chosen by them or ascribed to them by others."[72] That is, when viewing an individual as part of a collective group, it is often unclear whether the individual themselves directly identifies with the defining characteristics of the group.

Both proponents and opponents of these collective frameworks highlight their capacity to reveal the specific relationships and positions that a group maintains in the social and political world. Scholarship on collective representation suggests that they denote broad social expectations and impose characteristics on individuals based on "historical practices, cultural norms, social attitudes, religious values, legal dictates or the needs of the society."[73] Advocates of collective representation highlight the value of this for creating structure and order in society. In contrast, opponents conclude that these representations are problematic because they leave little room for self-identification. Furthermore, they point directly to the externally constructed nature of these representations to highlight that a group's position in society rarely reflects the actual role of these individuals, as behavior exists on a constantly shifting spectrum while collective representations often remain fixed and unresponsive. Although an individual may fit the mold ascribed by this collective representation one day, their actions the next day may diverge significantly, thus challenging their place within this collective space.

This is particularly problematic for young people, as prominent social depictions often rely on "identities of exclusion," which ignore actions that suggest any deviation, including displays of agency.[74] In addition, as Cecilia Jacob observes, the identities of young people are often symbolically constructed to "influence domestic and international politics."[75] These social classifications rarely acknowledge the often ambiguous reality of the engagement of young people in peace and conflict. Thus the distinction between children and youth had until recently gone unacknowledged, particularly in the transitional justice field. As Boyden explains, research on adolescence and youth has been sporadic, piecemeal, and "largely confined to the Global North."[76] This research has produced inaccurate normative assumptions about their capacity, and by depicting them solely as children, it has cast their conflict identities through the lens of innocence and passivity.

Furthermore, when youth are considered, there is a propensity throughout the peace and conflict literature to construct their behavior in exclusively "pejorative terms, as deficient . . . delinquent . . . or dysfunctional."[77] This narrative of youth as children is perpetuated by NGOs that until recently had dominated the field of inquiry with respect to understanding young people's role in post-conflict contexts. The actions of these institutions are derived from specific mandates and political agendas that guide their analysis. Despite the significant contributions that these institutions have made in advocating for the increased visibility of children, the underlying protectionist framework used in this work curtails the visibility of youth as a demographic distinct from children. Indeed, youth are often reduced to the status of children in these reports because these institutions need to work within pragmatic and popular boundaries to ensure the sustainability of their agendas.[78] As Cecilia Jacob demonstrates in her work on child security in Asia, NGOs "lean . . . heavily towards Western liberal associations of individual child rights" and rely on "emotive" imagery to invoke sympathy amongst donors and the general public.[79] In doing so, they create and perpetuate narratives about youth that fail to reflect the diversity of their lived experiences.

THE CHALLENGES OF SOCIALLY CONSTRUCTING CHILDHOOD AND YOUTH

It was not until the early twentieth century that notions of children as autonomous agents found form in scholarly research. This research acknowledged that all young people were political stakeholders and that their rapid development and inexperience did not render them passive actors.[80] Despite this, representations of young people's political agency have yet to consistently appear in practice, particularly those that are institutionalized. This creates cycles of exclusion where substantive social constructions of their agency and capacity fail to trickle down in ways that inform the practices of post-conflict states. As Helen Berents argues, "taking young people seriously" as knowledge producers and productive political actors requires a "centering of the margins" where their performative capacities are revealed.[81]

In the case of youth, scholars have increasingly sought to examine the diverse ways youth are represented and their interactions with different social and political contexts. Scholars concerned with the positive contributions of youth to peacebuilding argue that their agency and capacity is essential for sustainable, meaningful peace.[82] This work draws extensively on empirical cases from all regions of the world and provides significant insights into the challenges and opportunities for youth's engagement and leadership. In addition, in the psychology field, empirical research has engaged extensively with how adolescents manage the trauma associated with conflict.[83] This research aims to provide a framework for understanding the unique ways youth experience traumatic events. Furthermore, it seeks to highlight the unique and long-term consequences of war-related trauma on youth.

Finally, anthropologists have explored the impact of displacement on adolescents.[84] This body of literature contributes substantively to ideas about who youth are in peace and conflict contexts. The empirically driven nature of this research has provided significant insights into conducting ethical research with youth.[85] The study of youth, therefore, is a rapidly emerging sub-field across a range of disciplines. The existing literature, however, is merely a starting point. Despite a few notable exceptions, the research currently available struggles to reflect the nuance and complexity of youth's experiences in post-conflict environments because it prioritizes the telling of stories about youth rather than by youth. Furthermore, this body of research fails to acknowledge the multiple ways in which key stakeholders understand and represent youth. Indeed, research to date has focused on examining the ways in which policymakers and elites understand youth and their experiences. As a result, within research on youth and conflict, notions of victimhood and deviance dominate attempts to define young people and the roles they occupy in conflict and post-conflict processes. As we will see in the following sections, the dominant account of youth as victims stems from the extensive literature on child soldiers, and the notion that youth are deviants is underpinned by the youth bulge theory.[86]

Youth as Innocent Victims

Children and youth are increasingly being recognized as distinct demographics, with a diverse range of interests unique to their status and developmental progress. Yet when discussed throughout the literature their experiences are often classified together. Moreover, when the narratives of children and youth are institutionalized, their experiences are often amalgamated to fit a streamlined and linear representative framework. As already highlighted in this chapter, the interests and needs of child soldiers dominate discussion throughout transitional justice literature. This body of research expanded rapidly in response to the 1996 *Graça Machel Report* commissioned by the UN General Assembly to examine the "problem of children in conflict."[87] This report was a landmark study in the peace and conflict field as it was the first to highlight generalizable trends regarding the experiences of children in conflict on a "global scale."[88] Amongst the most startling findings of the report was the recognition that young people are a target for recruitment, as they are perceived as vulnerable and easy to manipulate.[89] The underlying theoretical claim that resonates here is the perception that children are not fully formed. This belief about the nature of children is embedded in the youth as innocent victims framework, which assumes that all young people are pre-political and highly susceptible to the negative effects of conflict. Moreover, this classification reflects the dominant claim, in both the scholarship and practice of transitional justice, that children are innocent as they are "yet to develop an individual political consciousness and the capacity to bear the burdens" of participation and agency.[90]

The victim classification has significant implications, both positive and negative, for our interactions with young people in peace and conflict. In the human rights field, the victim model is used to enshrine protections. In contrast, rebel forces have interpreted and manipulated the beliefs inherent in this framework to further their violent causes. This is evident in the child soldier narrative, which relies on representations of a childhood lost or stolen.[91] When the child soldier narrative and the victim lens more broadly are applied in transitional justice practices, our interactions with young people are limited. Similarly, when the victim lens is uncritically applied to explain children's behavior, it perpetuates notions of the dichotomous child combatant, which represents them as either the passive victims or the unwilling pawns.[92]

Although a small section of the literature on child soldiers explores their motivations for participating in the violence, these discussions are based on the perspectives of the recruiters rather than the children and youth. For example, Brett and McCallin demonstrate that rebel armies recruit children due to their perceived obedience.[93] This sentiment is reflected across the social sciences as young people are portrayed as easy targets for rebel groups in conflict environments.[94] In addition, Singer and Brett and Specht highlight technical innovations in weaponry as key factors that motivate young people to engage in conflict, but they also highlight that these innovations often require the use of "small fingers," which makes young people a target for recruitment.[95] The underlying premise of this classification is that "children need special protection because they are innocent and dependent actors in an adult world."[96] This description of young people assumes that they are merely subjects and recipients of peace without the capacity for meaningful decision-making. Similarly, under this construction of identity, youth are viewed as "apolitical, sheltered and separate from the political realm," thus they are constructed to be solely individuals without an autonomous voice.[97] Kemper, for example, highlights that armies view "younger generations as cheap, effective, and obedient fighters" without substantive reference to the reciprocity received by youth who fight.[98] Scholarship, through its emphasis on revealing the perceptions of powerful stakeholders (specifically militants and rebel groups), has constructed an image of young people as submissive targets for recruitment. While this is an important part of the story, its discursive dominance in the transitional justice field silences youth's distinct voices, rending invisible their self-representations.

Youth as Deviant Adolescents

In contrast to the scholars who emphasize the youth as innocent victims framing are those who prioritize their deviance. These negative representations portray youth as a "demographic ticking time bomb" capable of instigating violence and conflict.[99] Specifically, the reporting on youth combatants to date stigmatizes youth "as evil (as 'bandits' and 'vermin')" without recognition of the nuance and complexity inherent in these framings.[100] For example, Peters and Richards observe that rural youth in particular are described as barbarians lacking control and capacity.[101] This classification of youth reflects the othering critique, which is often leveled at social and collective representations of youth generally.

The central premise driving this research is the youth bulge theory developed by Henry Urdal. Urdal contests that a high-density youth population (predominately male) increases the likelihood of social instability. He contends that "when youth make up 35% of the adult population, which they do in many developing countries, the risk of armed conflict is 150% higher than it is in countries with an age structure similar to most developed countries."[102] The youth bulge theory assumes a causal connection between violence and a large male youth population and casts youth through a narrow lens as solely the instigators of violence and spoilers to peace. Similar to the youth as victims classification, youth remain a social and political challenge, yet rather than protecting them, the deviance lens calls for youth to be managed.

Furthermore, the youth bulge theory postulates a causal relationship between social instability and a lack of opportunities for young people. Urdal suggests that the potential for volatility is heightened when the social environment fails to accommodate the needs of the youth population.[103] Notably, several other scholars examining the causes of conflict have identified youth dissatisfaction (and deviance) as a primary factor in the instigation of violence. For example, Kaplan's new barbarism theory and Huntington's research suggest that structural factors including elevated levels of poverty and unemployment coupled with a high proportion of youth create environmental instability that inevitably leads to violence.[104] Yet, as demonstrated in the following chapters, emphasizing deviance obscures the complexity of youth's stories and results mainly in their alienation from community and political spaces.

At the core of these arguments are normative claims concerning youth's motivations for violence. Indeed, Urdal's work attributes youth's dissatisfaction with the social and political structures of their environment as a primary cause of violence in transitional states.[105] The notion that youth are troublemakers who initiate widespread social instability creates a narrow and harmful simplification of their identity. Additionally, this representation of their interactions with social and political structures lacks nuance and thus fails to reflect the idea that the youth demographic is expansive and diverse. Regardless, these normative assumptions about the association between social prospect, youth deviance, and violence prevail and continue to inform institutional engagement with youth in post-conflict states.

While the youth bulge theory remains the dominant explanation for youth deviance, several other scholars have attempted to explain youth's propensity for violence in various settings. For example, Kelly Greenhill and Solomon Major adapt the spoiler theory to explain the motivations for youth violence in post-conflict settings.[106] While traditionally the spoiler theory is used to describe the behavior of elites, Greenhill and Major suggest that all individuals and groups have the potential to act as spoilers given the right set of circumstances. They introduce the term *latent spoilers*, which they define as "determined but weak actors who would oppose the implementation of a peace accord, if only they had the material wherewithal to do so."[107] This term has been used to characterize youth post conflict, as there is the common perception that "despite the high expectations for what a resolution of the conflict might bring, in a peacetime environment youth are likely to lose much of the power they once held."[108] The latent spoiler classification, however, is insufficient when it is the only representation used to describe youth experiences. By examining only the potentially negative impact of youth on post-conflict practices, the spoiler theory obscures claims of agency and power derived from the meaningful and substantive participation of youth in post-conflict reconstruction.

Similarly, Collier and Hoeffler propose an economic opportunity-cost model to predict the potential for youth's engagement in conflict.[109] Their research suggests that environmental factors, lack of opportunity, and the perception of few political obligations makes joining rebel forces a viable, realistic opportunity. Their research contends, therefore, that youth cohorts are susceptible to deviant behavior due to a lack of social engagement and minimal family obligations. Indeed, they conclude that guarantees of "food, education, camaraderie and power" from rebel armies "provide enticing opportunities for youth."[110] The greed-grievance model examines the opportunity costs associated with participating in violence in an attempt to predict conflict.[111]

This model assumes that young men are prime targets for recruitment due to their lack of obligation and their susceptibility to material objects. It thus fails to consider instances where youth are fighting for something and thus their participation in the conflict is derived from intrinsic motivations rather than the capacity of rebel forces to manipulate and lure them into the conflict. As Stephanie Schwartz explains, the youth bulge and greed-grievance models highlight the capacity of youth to cause conflict, but they say nothing about the youth role either during the conflict or in the transitional justice phase.[112] Likewise, Lesley J. Pruitt suggests that these approaches when emphasized in scholarship or drawn on in policy development perpetuate stereotypical assumptions about gender without substantively engaging with "gender theory or the influence of gender norms in young people's lives."[113] As revealed by the cases in this book, public representations of young people matter because they inform the character and extent of their access, particularly to the formal peace and transitional justice architecture. As such, critical consideration of these visible representations is necessary to ensure that institutions do not perpetuate insecurity and marginalization for young people.

These models offer little to our understanding of substantive participation because they produce inaccurate representations of young people that deny their agency and capacity. Their emphasis on behaviors and motivations during times of instability obscures broader interactions and discourses with and between young people. As such, the youth bulge and greed-grievance models "overgeneralize and fail to engage with the complexity of young people's lives and the diverse ways that young people assign meaning to their experiences."[114] Thus, significant elements of young people's stories are missing from policy and analysis that use these approaches. To better understand young people's positioning and contributions to sustainable peace and reconciliation, discourses must also incorporate public representations of young people that are illustrative of their capacity to contribute meaningfully to society during transitions or peacetime (examples are included in introduction).

Models that solely emphasize deviance offer a problematic yet highly influential representation of young people that continues to permeate political discourse, creating cycles of exclusion within formal institutions. Several scholars suggest that perceptions of youth deviance persist due to the stereotype that youth are the cause of social upheaval. As Griffin explains, in modern Western societies, the inevitability of trouble is expected and normalized as part of a natural process to test the boundaries of independence.[115] These normalized constructions of youth as negative social actors are particularly problematic as research demonstrates they have permeated youth's perceptions of their political positionality. As Clay explains, youth see themselves as a "low priority in society" who are relegated to the political sidelines by external actors.¹¹⁶ These representations present a challenge for youth agency when they persist to create silences about and for their active participation. Yet as empirical work in peacebuilding contexts demonstrates, these margins are also sites of opportunity when claimed by youth as avenues of political participation.¹¹⁷

The victim/deviance binary presents a challenge for the construction of a reconciliation narrative that is inclusive of the diverse experiences of youth and that reflects the scope and extent of their participation in conflict and post-conflict practices. The underlying theoretical lenses central to both these classifications produce narrow and linear representations of youth that are hard to overcome. For example, the protectionist lens embedded in notions of victimhood is problematic because it relies on the belief that children lack capacity. It promotes an image of young people as passive subjects, lacking the potential for agency often demonstrated by the youth demographic in post-conflict environments. Similarly, the deviance lens is troubling because it fails to capture the nuances of youth's roles in conflict and post-conflict contexts. Both representations obscure the multitude of other, often overlapping roles that youth take on in conflict and post-conflict environments as peacemakers, mediators, survivors, activists, and storytellers. To address this, I propose using a youth-centered lens that situates young people's voices as central in the production of knowledge about violence and instability.

Youth as Empowered Political Agents

McEvoy-Levy identifies four popular lenses used to classify the interactions of young people within the post-conflict environment:

1. Children have rights and should be protected

2. Youth are a development asset

3. Youth are a threat to security

4. Youth are agents of change¹¹⁸

These discourses provide a sound starting point for the meaningful representation of youth participation in transitional justice contexts.

Collectively they allow for a broad and fluid representation of youth as a demographic with constantly shifting needs and interests. Aside from a few notable exceptions, however, stakeholder biases and institutional limitations produce an overreliance on child protection and security threat classifications. As indicated throughout this chapter, frameworks one and three currently dominate interactions with young people in post-conflict contexts. Yet on their own they fail to recognize the agency and capacity of young people to claim rights and participate positively in society. These frameworks are the underlying claims of the victim/perpetrator binary, and thus they obscure the dynamic nature of youth participation. Framework two, while acknowledging the capacity of youth to participate, views youth as a product and agent of a broader political agenda. Therefore, while it recognizes that young people have a distinct voice, it emphasizes using that voice to the agenda and mandate of other agents. In these instances, while their participation is substantive, it is not necessarily meaningful as it is not owned or claimed by youth. Framework four provides the central conceptual ideas drawn on throughout this book to demonstrate the capacity of youth to engage meaningfully with TRCs. Further it provides a basis for revealing the implications of youth's substantive participation in creating a more holistic reconciliation narrative. Yet the stories herein also reveal that youth representations that are true to their experiences must reflect the dynamic nature of young people. Thus, it utilizes the conceptual underpinnings of the other three frameworks to inform discussions of the complexity of youth's interactions with TRCs.

Representations of youth in peace and conflict contexts today have become more expansive and inclusive. Peacebuilding discourses have paved the way for an examination of young people's substantive participation and agency in post-conflict contexts. As a result, recognition that youth are catalysts or agents of change have emerged as prominent classifications to guide our understanding of inclusive practices. The youth agency lens starts with youth themselves rather than with rights, development, or violence.[119] It examines the distinct experiences and roles of young people by studying the behaviors and voices of youth, free of external influence or social presuppositions. At its core, a youth-centered approach acknowledges the ability of youth to "effect change independent of outside actors" and thus possess leadership in these spaces.[120] To that end, youth have and exert agency, as opposed to being given it, due to their participation in conflict and post-conflict practices. When navigating the social and political landscape, young people demonstrate capacity to challenge the status quo and to claim ownership over their conflict stories. This is not to suggest, however, that representations of youth are free from external influence. As Schwartz's demonstrates, outside agents have a key stake in defining and classifying the role of youth.[121] However, a more nuanced understanding of young people's interactions with the political world indicates that powerful actors are not the only arbiters of these classifications; young people are also knowledge producers and experts in assigning meaning to their experiences. This view prompts consideration of the wide range of roles that youth occupy in post-conflict contexts. It contends that while youth are victims and perpetrators, they are also witnesses, bystanders, peacebuilders, development agents, and politicians.

Agent-centered approaches have come to dominate the discourse on youth inclusion. Despite this, operationalizing this framework has proven problematic within the formal peace and justice architecture of post-conflict states. Yet a growing body of empirical research provides significant insights into the impact of this approach on how we understand young people and their conflict experiences. Pruitt, for example, in her empirical study on the relationship between youth, music, and peacebuilding, argues that "across the globe young people are challenging their elders to address the root causes of conflict and engage in the peaceful resolution of differences in pursuing peace."[122] Pruitt's work is not unique in this finding, as other scholars have also demonstrated youth leadership in the design and implementation of peace and justice practices that operate parallel to the formal institutional structures.[123] Echoed across this emerging and influential body of work is the recognition that young people have unique abilities and the political will to engage and contribute to peace. Moreover, this scholarship suggests that when empowered and enabled, young people can navigate the political landscape in ways that contribute substantively to the pursuit of meaningful justice.

In addition to this empirical work on youth peacebuilding, several scholars have highlighted the importance of youth voices in creating transitional environments capable of sustaining peace. John Paul Lederach observes that in the pursuit of peace it is crucial to garner the opinions of a wide cross section of the community. He notes that talking only to "politicians and military leaders" provides an incomplete picture of conflict and thus an unsatisfactory framework for the development of post-conflict practices. Lederach's work acknowledges the value of "talking to taxi drivers . . . to construction workers and housewives . . . to elders, shamans, and for goodness' sake, talk to children."[124] In doing so, it looks within, across, and to the margins, where, as Berents reveals, the capacities of young people are most visible.[125] Agency and voice are inextricably connected in this framework. Indeed, the youth as empowered political agents framework distinguishes between the visibility of youth and the substantive and meaningful consideration of their voices in post-conflict practices. This has implications for the representation of youth in transitional justice, as the youth as empowered political agents framework suggests that hearing and responding to the voices of youth distinct from children allows for the development of more inclusive polices and responsive institutional structures.

Conclusion

This chapter has examined developments in the scholarship on children and youth in international relations, peacebuilding, and transitional justice. It revealed the challenges associated with representing the experiences of youth in transitional justice through the victim/perpetrator binary, arguing that this narrow dichotomy does not provide an adequate framework for understanding young people's political agency and capacity to act as knowledge producers because it constructs a linear and externally derived reflection that silences unique and diverse voices. To overcome the assessed limitations of the youth as victims and youth as deviants frameworks, this chapter offers an alternative youth-centered approach. This approach considers the contributions of youth to the development of social structures and political institutions. In doing so, it acknowledges and prioritizes the belief that youth are political actors with agency and that they possess the capacity to claim ownership over their conflict experiences.

As such, this chapter suggests that when youth are empowered as political agents, institutions have greater capacity to see and hear their experiences. The participation of young people in TRC processes, therefore, needs to be considered through this approach, which starts from the position of youth themselves. It considers the role of youth in conflict and reconciliation by examining how their unique status as youth informs and is constituted by their interactions with social structures and institutions. This approach provides a more nuanced and complete understanding of young people and their experiences, as it applies a pragmatic lens to the relationship between young people and reconciliation and helps to expose institutional slippages between classifications of children and youth. Moreover, this youth agency approach allows institutional structures to see, acknowledge, and respond to the meaning young people assign to their own stories, as well as the multitude of roles they occupy in conflict and post-conflict environments.

Chapter 3

Establishing Visibility

A Human Rights Approach to the Involvement of Young People at the TRC in South Africa

Hope for Tomorrow, Yesterday's Heroes
  —Desmond Tutu, foreword to *Between Anger and Hope*

Children are the living message we send to a time we will not see.
  —Neil Postman, *The Disappearance of Childhood*

It takes a village to raise a child
  —African proverb, cited in *Between Anger and Hope*

The relationship between young people and transitional justice processes reflects a complex interplay of competing ideas regarding their capacity to behave as political actors. While they are increasingly visible in the public spaces where formal transitional justice occurs, other political actors often claim their presence as the embodiment of a commitment to reconciliation and a more peaceful future. Young people, as the quotes above reveal, are cast as symbols and aspirations often without acknowledgment of their own agency.

Over time, young people have become increasingly visible in formal reconciliation practices. Yet the mode and function of this visibility is often passive, demonstrating a tension between the narrow, institutionalized notions about young people's ability to participate and the complex reality of the relationship between youth, children, reconciliation, and engagement. While the scholarly discourse on young people started to evolve during the 1990s to reflect agency, voice, and diversity, institutional narratives within the formal transitional justice architecture remain largely static, narrow, and one-dimensional. Perceptions of young people as "social shifters" or as "an entry point for unravelling the ways in which processes of change invoke people's agency" were atypical and mostly conceptual.[1] These representations produce collective classifications of identity that connect young people's place within the community to moral claims about the peacefulness of transitional states. Where discourses around engagement are concerned, this tension is heightened by classificatory slippages between the stories of children and youth.

The South African Truth and Reconciliation Commission (TRC) set new international justice precedents as the first to encourage the substantive participation of young people, to pay attention to their conflict stories and to hold public hearings on their needs and experiences. Visibility of these stories proved integral to gaining an understanding of the human rights violations committed during apartheid (1948–1994). Thus, the TRC's engagement with these experiences provides important insights regarding the relationship between young people and formal reconciliation practices. During apartheid, children and youth played key roles in the resistance (occupying catalytic places in anti-apartheid structures) and more passive roles as indirect and direct targets of violence.[2] They were central activists in the 1976 school protests, leaders in the resistance movements of the 1980s, and participants in the alternative community governance and security structures that found form in the 1990s, including the self-defense units.[3] Between 1984 and 1986 alone, between 26 and 46 percent of detainees were young people held, often without a trial. Apartheid and the state's efforts to maintain marginalizing structures also affected young people's education, prospects for employment, relationships, and safety.

South Africa's TRC established the initial approach for reporting the stories of young people, and these parameters continue as the starting point for their participation. Practices that were viewed as innovative at the time, including the consideration of children in TRC recommendations and the provision of a separate reporting chapter on the experiences of young people, are now expected practices within the mandates of formal reconciliation processes. The South African TRC is broadly considered to be a landmark case within the transitional justice field as the first of its kind to hold public and televised hearings and to offer amnesties for the testimony of combatants. In doing so, the South African TRC established a new model for understanding justice as the acknowledgment of harms. By preferencing narrative justice, it created space for the participation and visibility of a range of actors, amongst them women and young people. The South African TRC, particularly its structure and events, contributed substantively to debates about truth versus justice, as it legitimized truth commissions as instruments of justice. It is therefore a logical starting point for our understanding of how young people's participation in formal reconciliation has evolved.

Before examining representations of young people at the South African TRC, this chapter outlines the shift in the discourse on childhood from the private sphere to the public. Following this, it provides an examination of the normative foundations of the victim/perpetrator dichotomy to conceptually ground the analysis of the TRC process. I suggest that discourses on human rights for children and the dominance of the protectionist framework created narrow institutional frameworks that obscure and mischaracterize displays of agency by youth. To demonstrate this the chapter then turns to the stories of children and youth at the South African TRC, revealing the implications of this linear international discourse on the character of children and youth's participation.

The South African TRC was a turning point in the visibility of young people in institutionalized reconciliation. Yet, the type of participation enabled by this TRC homogenized their stories and created barriers that prevented opportunities for substantive participation and the realization of their diverse voices. As evident in the final report, the character of children's and youth's participation had implications for how their stories were represented. Throughout the South African TRC process, a blurring of the boundaries between representations of children and youth occurred, which failed to reflect the ambiguity of their experiences and their heterogenous voices. Moreover, the interactions between children, youth, and the TRC in South Africa laid the foundations for a narrow reconciliation discourse about their capacity to participate and the contributions of their stories, which informed how the architects of future TRCs defined the parameters of participation for all young people.

Consideration of the stories told about children and youth in the South African TRC report, coupled with an examination of their engagement with the actual TRC process, helps us to understand how representations of young people have changed and evolved. This chapter therefore argues that the South African TRC reflects a broader shift in the interactions of children and youth with transitional justice practices, as their reconciliation and conflict stories move from the private to the public sphere. Children and youth were visible throughout the TRC process, yet the decision by the Commission to hold hearings about the experiences of children, rather than for children, resulted in the production of an institutional conflict narrative, where the voices of youth acted as a proxy for all young people. As a result, their distinct voices were silenced.

The participatory parameters established in South Africa are significant as they inform future discourses of agency and ownership for young people in reconciliation. This is evident, in the subsequent chapters, but also in the examples from the Peruvian TRC presented later in this chapter. Here, the interactions of young people echo the storytelling, participatory approach established in South Africa. This chapter as such provides the starting point for a discussion of the social and political structures, beliefs, and norms that foster and promote the engagement of youth with the reconciliation practices of post-conflict states.

Reflecting on Classifications of Young People

Within the report of the South African TRC, young people are recognized as the "hope" and the "heroes" of South Africa. Representations tied explicitly to social perceptions of their future-making capacities and evolving leadership potential. This dual classification echoed an emerging global trend on the evolving significance of young people to post-conflict discourses associated with the pursuit of accountability for sustainable peace. Using young people's experiences to motivate activism was commonplace during apartheid and is central to how their stories were told within the TRC report. At the special hearing on conscription, for example, Dr. Laurie Nathan, a founding member of the End Conscription

Campaign (ECC) in 1983, shared the declaration of the ECC, which uses the narrative of harms experienced by young men as a rallying call for participation. As Nathan exclaims, "Young men are conscripted to the illegal occupation . . . and to wage unjust war against foreign countries. Young men are conscripted to assist in the implementation and defense of apartheid policies. Young men who refuse to serve are faced with the choices of a life of exile or a possible six years in prison."[4] The repetition of "young men" in this declaration is significant because it creates a strong image for the commissioners and participants of the impossible choice for those most impacted by conscription. This imagery of young men evokes common masculinity framings, which cast young men as inherently violent yet without agency over that violence, to inform the activism of the organization.

While these classifications can offer opportunities for activism and engagement amongst young people, they also present a static perception that does not acknowledge their transitional identity. Furthermore, missing from these stories are the varied and constantly shifting roles they occupy during conflict or in its aftermath. This is particularly evident when the classifications are used by external stakeholders whose beliefs about the roles young people occupy are underpinned by normative traditions of universal children's rights. International discourses on children's rights are problematic when not embedded and informed by local contexts. This framework presents challenges for recognizing young people's agency as rights claimants within reconciliation because it assumes a universal yet conditional notion of rights where the parameters for ownership and agency are established by gatekeepers rather than by young people. In the South African context this is evident in discussions by the TRC about witness selection, which note that "women and men should be heard; and the experiences of youth should be considered."[5] Attempts to engage with young people at the South African TRC, while an important turning point in our understanding of their role in formal reconciliation, also established a narrow framework for the *ideal* young participant as a technocratic performance defined by their silent visibility. This performative engagement continues within formal reconciliation and peacebuilding practices today, as the character of young people's participation often remains limited by a culture of power that values high-level stakeholders and government actors.[6]

This chapter as such is concerned with the external norms about young people that inform how they engage with formal reconciliation practices. Overreliance on these beliefs and traditions were prominent in South Africa and limited the TRC's capacity to represent the unique and diverse experiences of young people. The process and institutional narrative prioritized a conceptual idea of their potential, and their embodiment of the future, rather than their participation as active political and social actors. In part, the production of this politicized narrative derives from the normative slippage of classifications of children and youth that persisted across the investigation and reporting stages of the reconciliation process. The distinction between beliefs about youth and the beliefs of youth therefore, presents a significant challenge for TRCs and the traditions within international relations that guide our interactions with children and youth in transitional justice.

The engagement of youth with TRCs continues to evolve, yet to understand the current state of youth representation and engagement it is necessary to examine its origins. The purpose of this chapter, therefore, is to explore the contributions of the South African TRC process to our understanding of youth representation in the reconciliation narratives of transitional states more broadly. As the first TRC to hold special hearings on children and youth, the South African TRC provides valuable insights. This chapter demonstrates the complexity associated with accurately representing the conflict and reconciliation stories of demographics as diverse, unique, and fluid as children and youth. Moreover, this chapter explores the normative foundations of what remains a problematic tension within the reconciliation discourse today. It highlights some of the earliest challenges associated with constructing a narrative of the conflict experiences of young people, which balances the representations *of* youth with the stories *by* youth. In doing so, it suggests that when representations of young people fail to reflect the stories of youth, distinct from children, their voices are marginalized and relegated to the fringes and the institutional narratives cast the experiences of children and youth as universal. This has implications for the reconciliation goals of transitional states, as the failure to include the distinct voices of youth challenges the inclusiveness that TRCs aim to facilitate. Critical exploration of the participation of young people in reconciliation offers substantial insights into how youth push back against the dominant representations that perceive and cast all young people as victims and/or perpetrators.

Examining the nature and extent of youth engagement reveals the ways in which agent-centered approaches to transitional justice can produce more inclusive reconciliation narratives. As demonstrated in chapter 2, youth are motivated and engaged agents, yet they are rarely represented this way in the formal, institutional structures of transitional justice. When youth are considered, it is often through the lens of the victim/perpetrator binary. Understanding the origins and persistence of these classifications provides significant insight into the ways youth challenge these marginalizing perceptions. The experiences of youth represent a site of tension for transitional justice, as they challenge the political and structural hierarchies inherent to the victim/perpetrator classification.

Childhood: Moving the Dialogue from the Private to the Public

Notions of childhood and youth have become increasingly politicized and thus subject to significant debate and commentary. Shifts in the recognition of children from the solely private to the public sphere have globalized ideas about childhood, which are today normalized and embedded in international institutions. As a result, universal representations of childhood are prioritized and promoted by these structures. The institutionalization of childhood, embedded in a system of rights, solidified in the twentieth century through a series of formal dialogues held between states.[7] The notion that a catalog of rights was needed, one that specifically addressed the needs of children, first emerged in 1979 during the International Year of the Child.[8]

In the resolution codifying Member States' commitment to the Year of the Child, the United Nations General Assembly acknowledged, "the vital link between programs benefiting children and the observance of their rights."[9] The focus on programming *for* children indicates a shift in their visibility, yet the focus on the role of adults in this resolution, rather than the voices of children, also highlights beliefs about the need for limits on the agency of young people. Indeed, the resolution outlines the responsibility of governments, to implement measures capable of producing "lasting increased benefits for children" via "specific national targets and goals" targeted at addressing children's needs.[10] By framing responsibilities for children rather than with them, the resolution perpetuates beliefs about the "infantilized" and "vulnerable" nature of young people.[11] Although young people are visible in the public space, their agency and ownership is mitigated by a singular representation of their relationship with the international community as protector. During this period, ideas about the importance of protecting children from harm and manipulation were prominent within the discourse on children's rights. As such they were a central theme of the institutional structures created to articulate states' responsibilities for children and instrumental in guiding their interactions with children.

Recognition that children have rights indicated a notable shift in ideas regarding the representations of young people from purely subjects to actors with evolving agency who require protection to continue their development. While this shift indicated a positive development in the discourse on children in international relations, tension between the rights *of* children and human rights *for* children emerged and continues to inform our interactions with young people today.[12] Most notably, it continues to challenge claims of agency in the practice of transitional justice. In addition, silenced by and absent from the discourse informing this resolution is recognition of the youth demographic as distinct from children.

The Year of the Child fell strategically on the twentieth anniversary of the Declaration of the Rights of the Child. Thus it provided the international community with an opportunity to evaluate the progress made toward recognizing the needs of young people outside of the private sphere.[13] In this respect, the notion of a designated and universal set of children's rights "was seen as an appropriate political signal" to highlight the normative shift taking place globally toward the "greater visibility and protection of children in national and international politics."[14] During this period, a culture of childhood evolved that understood this period in an individual's life to be "one free of responsibilities."[15] Representations of children thus reflected the belief that while they were actors with needs and rights, they were not political agents with the capacity to contribute to the structures, norms, and institutions of society.

In addition, in the 1980s, a related yet distinct development in the norms related to the visibility of young people occurred that reframed ideas about their agency. During this period beliefs about children evolved from an exclusively protectionist framework to one that recognized their limited independence and potential to act as empowered individuals.[16] This shift situated children at the center of international efforts to fulfill a humanitarian ethic of responsibility. That is, they were perceived as agents who were entitled to claim certain universal and inalienable rights and protections that were once perceived as irrelevant due to their absence from the public space.

This development had implications for the types of rights children could pursue. Most notably, it prioritized "welfare rights," specifically the guarantee of food and water, over "agency rights," the right to participation and influence over their experiences.[17] In this way, children were perceived as actors with needs, as opposed to previous beliefs that cast them as purely "objects of charity and benevolence."[18] Yet the agency associated with these entitlements was limited, conditional, and bestowed upon them in accordance with perceptions of their evolving capacities. Notions of children that prioritized innocence and purity remained central to their collective representation, particularly within institutions. These different social constructions revealed a tension between children's emerging political identities and traditional constructions of children as nonlegal, innocent, developing subjects. While nods to their evolving capacity signaled early acknowledgment of the diversity between children and youth, it had yet to be fully realized in ways that would inform their interactions with reconciliation processes.

Where transitional justice practices are concerned, the participation of children has become normalized and expected, particularly in practices that promote restorative justice, namely TRCs. As the South African case demonstrates, children and youth were a thematic category for exploration in special hearings. The purpose of these hearings was to "identify patterns of abuse experienced by individuals and groups" by capturing the stories of vulnerable demographics.[19] Thus, the stories of children and youth were an essential component of the TRC because they highlighted a systematic pattern of abuse by external agents and institutions. Given this, the experiences of young people at the South African TRC provided a powerful symbol of apartheid. Recognition of their role as political agents, however, failed to generate significant attention within the institutionalized narrative.

The manifestation of this normative shift toward the visibility of children, though absent agency, has received minimal attention in the literature. In particular, the scholarship has largely failed to consider the implications of these evolving norms on our capacity to understand the distinct experiences of youth. While there is awareness amongst the international community and transitional states that "young people have the right to participate" in reconciliation, "their voices have been historically absent" or, in the South African, case misrepresented.[20] As the examination below demonstrates, the voices of youth are predominately employed to represent the experiences of children, as the dominant norms that informed their participation, namely the imperative to protect their human rights, resulted in a silencing of the distinct experiences and interests of youth. There remains a need in both scholarship and practice for a more critical exploration of the ways in which children and youth are represented in the public space, most notably reconciliation, to ensure that these representations reflect their stories and hear and respond to their voices. The representations of children and youth at the South African TRC highlight tensions between the international norms of children, the beliefs of external stakeholders, and the lived experiences of young people in conflict and post-conflict practices.

As the reconciliation narratives of young people in South Africa demonstrate, representations of youth were inextricably tied to children, which silenced the unique and diverse needs and interest of youth following apartheid. Broadly speaking, conceiving and casting the experiences of children and youth together has implications for how we understand the interactions of young people with conflict, justice, and reconciliation. The direct participation of young people, however, has the potential to serve two main functions. First, on a practical level, their participation makes young people visible within the institutions and processes responsible for producing a formalized public conflict narrative. Second, it allows for the development of recommendations that directly target their needs and interests. These outcomes are evident in the South African and Peruvian TRCs, which, as the discussion below reveals, share many parallels regarding young people's participation. Taken together, these TRCs reflect the normative traditions and beliefs of the period that were emerging in the international discourse of children and rights. These beliefs highlighted the importance of seeing young people, yet they did not provide any consideration for the diverse experiences that arise as children transition through youth and adolescence. In this way, the TRCs of South Africa and Peru provide insights regarding the origins of the victim/perpetrator dichotomies in reconciliation narratives. Yet to understand how representations of children and youth in the formal narratives of TRCs have evolved, we must first consider the developments that led to the increased visibility of children in international relations. These developments are significant because they provide the context in which the stories of and engagement with young people during TRCs are situated.

Evolving Notions of Children to Youth

Complicating representations of young people are the biological and developmental aspects that determine how external actors see their agency. This is particularly challenging, in the case of children and youth, as these individuals move rapidly through stages from infancy to childhood, adolescence, and youth. At each stage, they acquire skills that both inform and are informed by their experiences. In recent years, institutions have sought to understand and reflect this evolving capacity. Indeed, this notion has been readily acknowledged by the international community and codified in the CRC in multiple articles, which require state parties to ensure not only that young people are given the opportunity to express their own views but that these views are given "due weight in accordance with the age and maturity of the child."[21] That is, there is an expectation that young people will be afforded the opportunity to exercise agency in accordance with their expanding capabilities.

Where transitional justice and reconciliation practices are concerned, upholding this widely agreed upon principle has proven challenging. Creating a responsive space for young people to interact with and speak in public spaces remains constrained by the stories told about them to fulfill political mandates beyond and around their experiences. Much has been written about the diverse ways in which institutions can ensure the visibility of children. Yet there is an absence of research that considers the implications of this rapidly evolving understanding of young people on their capacity to participate meaningfully in reconciliation. Complicating matters further are the different beliefs about the participation and role of children and youth in conflict that have been used to construct representations of children in transitional justice contexts. Understanding these differences is crucial for our capacity to produce inclusive reconciliation narratives because these representations have direct implications for how we understand the ways they participate in reconciliation processes.

The CRC established a sliding scale for the participation of the young people in politics based on age and other factors. As Katrina Lee-Koo observes, the CRC, in theory, acknowledges that childhood is not one state of being but many: "It is a dynamic and fluid period of human development that is constantly changing."[22] Ensuring that this translates into practice, however, remains a source of tension within the transitional justice field and in post-conflict environments where children take on roles traditionally perceived as belonging to adults.[23] Nevertheless, ensuring that transitional justice mechanisms apply the Article 12 provisions in the development of programs and practices is integral for the visibility of young people. Article 12 allows for the level of young people's participation to reflect their capacity and learned experiences, thus reflecting more accurately their agency and ability for autonomous decision-making.[24] Despite this discursive recognition, children's increased visibility has resulted in the emergence of universal and static beliefs about children and childhood rather than a recognition of their distinct voices and capacity to own their stories.

The two most common archetypes used to describe human rights for children act as significant barrier to inclusive and meaningful political participation. A tension exists in reconciliation between prioritizing the *special needs* of children and their capacity to *actively claim* their rights. Transitional states and the international community have struggled to find a balance between ensuring the self-determination of children and the long-standing moral responsibility to protect their welfare.[25] This debate reveals "the distinction between two approaches to children's rights . . . the 'nurturance' and the 'self-determination' approach," which emerged as children became more visible in political spaces.[26] At the center of this debate are "highly ideological and value laden" constructions of childhood appropriated by adults to meet specific moral, social, and political ends.[27]

While both approaches have impacted our understanding of the experiences of young people in a range of contexts, the nurturance model remains the principal framework for informing international and domestic policy with respect to children and for guiding scholarly debate. As Michael Freeman observes, "Childhood is . . . a man-made phenomenon: those in authority determine who is a child" and define the parameters of this classification.[28] The dominance of this model is problematic, particularly in transitional justice contexts, as it is central to the ways in which key stakeholders construct representations of children and youth within the formal reconciliation narratives. These classifications are then used to justify and institutionalize narrow participatory parameters for young people in the politics following reconciliation. External agents rely on these representations to explain the patterns of behavior for young people in ways that further their agendas for peace and prosperity. By emphasizing stories of their capacity to nurture children, the post-conflict state represents itself as a responsible, future-focused actor, thus distinguishing itself from the human rights perpetrators of the past. This nurturing narrative, however, mediates the participation of young people through an adult lens. While this may be an important political narrative, using children solely as symbols discounts instances of autonomous decision-making by all young people during conflict and in reconciliation.

CHILDREN'S RIGHTS AS A MOVEMENT

The earliest iterations of the children's rights movement are evident in the 1852 article "The Rights of the Child" and the 1879 novel by Jean Vallès *L'Enfant*, which portrays children as objects in the protectionist narrative of the state.[29] The focus of discussion during this period was on promoting the community's moral responsibility to save children from harm and delinquency.[30] This perceived obligation was derived from the underlying claims of protectionism and collectivism that were central to the human rights discourse at the time. As a result, governments during this period prioritized practices that enabled childhood and thus maintained innocence.[31] These understandings of children's rights, however, failed to recognize that young people are individuals capable of claiming their rights. Instead, policies and practices were derived from a belief that children have a collective identity, and thus their needs and interests can be universally represented. The first phase of the children's rights movement afforded limited consideration of factors such as agency, ownership, and freedom when discussing the spaces children occupy in the political world. While perceptions of children's rights have evolved, remnants of these normative beliefs remain in the ways in which young people are represented in formal conflict narratives produced by TRCs.

Initial attempts to institutionalize children's rights are evident in the Geneva Declaration, adopted on September 26, 1924.[32] While nonbinding, the declaration provided states with a limited set of guidelines regarding the welfare of children. This framework for action promoted the state's "duty" toward children, concluding that "mankind owes to the child the best it has to give" with respect to a range of issues including justice, development, freedom from exploitation, and relief in times of emergency.[33] As Freeman observes, it viewed "children . . . as an investment for the future" rather than political leaders now.[34] That is, children during this period were cast, at an institutional level, as representations of the state's potential, as the declaration promoted a collective understanding of their place in the community rather than their capacity as individuals. In this way, the declaration furthered a needs-based representation of young people, reliant on the responsibility of external actors as opposed to the agency, ownership, and abilities of young people. While children were visible in this model, the scope of engagement was limited, as adults were required to exercise human rights on behalf of children.

Following the Geneva Declaration, the dialogue on the rights of children remained largely static until the 1950s, when it gained momentum against the backdrop of a global shift toward universal human rights. During this period, discussions centered around whether the declaration accurately reflected beliefs and ideas about child welfare.[35] In response to these evolving beliefs, on July 11, 1950, the Social Commission of the Economic and Social Council (ECOSOC) proposed the Concept-Declaration of the Rights of the Child. This proposal, however, was stymied by a lack of political will regarding the codification of these issues. Many states viewed the recently created Universal Declaration of Human Rights to be a sufficient avenue for the protection and discussion of children's rights.[36] The specific challenges associated with the rights of children, therefore, were not given priority outside the broader discourse on human rights.

It was not until the twentieth century that the unique position children now occupy in the public space began to take shape. Specifically, the notion of "the global child" emerged as NGOs and states sought to institutionalize and make visible the needs of children.[37] Indeed, during this period, a significant shift occurred in the social attitudes toward young people from ambivalence to protectionism. This shift was set in motion in 1976, when the UN General Assembly declared 1979 the International Year of the Child. This resolution introduced a "framework for advocacy on behalf of children and for enhancing the awareness of the special needs of children on the part of decision-makers and the public." Central to these guidelines was a recognition of the value of "programmes benefiting . . . not only . . . the wellbeing of the children but also . . . broader efforts to accelerate economic and social progress."[38]

Despite this noteworthy progress, it was not until a decade later, in 1989, that the CRC institutionalized the normative developments that had been taking place with respect to the rights of children.[39] As previously indicated, the CRC instrument created a codified language for talking about the nature and extent of children's rights. Moreover, the almost unanimous ratification of the convention suggested that there was "a strong consensus among states as to the substance and universal applicability of the rights of the child."[40] The institutionalization of these norms, however, was not without its challenges. Scholars such as Bina D'Costa and Katrina Lee-Koo have observed that the norms prioritized within the CRC reflect a Western understanding of children.[41] This created a global standard for discussing children's rights that excluded a substantial proportion of developing nations, specifically those in conflict zones, where children are exposed to human rights violations that often have lasting physical, social, and psychological effects.

These international instruments used a "caretaker model," which denotes a hierarchical interaction between children and the state in reconciliation practices, where young people are passive actors reliant on others for the pursuit of their rights.[42] The CRC emphasizes the importance of protecting children collectively and prioritizes their safety and welfare as a group in order to outline the paramount responsibilities of states' to them.[43] Children are thus afforded limited individual agency and ownership over their unique experiences that diverge from these collective stories due, in part, to their innocence status. As Harry Hendrick observes, the caretaker model is based on the biological notions that children are physically and psychologically weaker, "independent of time, geography and social class."[44] Thus, children garner significant attention *because* they are universally perceived as being a vulnerable collective.[45]

Therefore, the visibility of young people in reconciliation practices, and international relations more broadly, is reliant on the beliefs of external agents about their innocence. It is further reinforced by perceptions that states possess a moral responsibility to maintain and guard that innocence. As scholars have observed, individuals under the age of eighteen "are believed to have specific needs due to their immaturity and particular susceptibility and are accorded special rights in relation to societal protection and provision."[46] Complicating matters is the presence of youth within this classificatory range who, due to their coupling with children, often have their ownership and participatory capacity silenced by the good intentions of protectionist models. This normative lens has guided the representations of all young people (children and youth) in reconciliation practices, regardless of how they self-identify, and as demonstrated below, has produced incomplete narratives of their experiences in formal reconciliation.

Visibility Parameters

In 1995, the parliament of the Republic of South Africa passed the Promotion of National Unity and Reconciliation Act (the Act), which established a set of parameters for the creation and implementation of a truth commission. In accordance with the Act, the South African TRC was mandated to investigate and report on the "causes, nature and extent of the gross violations of human rights" committed between March 1960 and May 1994.[47] Due to the scale of the investigation and the broad nature of the reporting mandate, three committees were established to ensure successful completion: the Committee on Human Rights Violations (HRV), the Committee on Amnesty, and the Committee on Reparations and Rehabilitation.

Following the initial public hearings, the HRV committee conducted a series of institutional investigations into the experiences of groups whose stories and thus beliefs sat outside the initial scope of the examination. This targeted investigation reflected the TRC committee's belief that these were important voices whose experiences of apartheid warranted consideration, despite their exclusion from the initial mandate. Amongst these groups were children and youth, who the investigative process demonstrated were key stakeholders in the resistance movement. These hearings were established to "offer voice to groups that were otherwise underrepresented in the public hearings" due to their exclusion from the original reconciliation mandate.[48]

The inclusion of children in particular, required the commissioners to adopt a broad interpretation of the participatory guidelines established by the Act. The participation of children and youth in the South African TRC process was enabled by the broader goal of the TRC: restorative reconciliation, known as *ubuntu* ("humaneness").[49] In particular, the mandate of the TRC committed to the restoration of "human dignity and *ubuntu*," as well as the "restorative dimensions of a number of religious and cultural traditions in South Africa."[50] As Paul Gready concludes, "Tutu repeatedly articulated the view that all South Africans were victims of apartheid, marshalling *ubuntu* as his creed and arguing that dehumanizing relationships affect all partners to the relationship."[51] As such, the mandate conceived of the violence as a community experience that necessitated a widespread, inclusive reconciliation process. In doing so, it obligated the commission to ensure that its investigative scope remained expansive and community-focused, as the *ubuntu* ethos allowed for a broad participatory scope and emphasized the healing of victims and community relationships as paramount.

Healing and community, embedded in the notion of *ubuntu*, are two of the central tenants of a restorative approach to transitional justice.[52] This shift in the notion of what constituted justice, coupled with the normative developments surrounding children's rights internationally, enabled "a window of opportunity for . . . reformism" and the engagement of young people in the process of justice and reconciliation.[53] Accordingly, six hearings were conducted to assess the impact of apartheid on children and youth during May and June of 1997, in Bloemfontein, Cape Town, Durban, East London, Johannesburg, and Pietersburg. The primary mandate of the hearings was to examine the physical and psychological trauma experienced by young people during apartheid.

The submissions by youth inadvertently demonstrated a public, institutional acknowledgment of the active role that youth played in the resistance movement. In particular, the TRC recognized the long history of resistance amongst the youth demographic that dated "back to the formation of the militant African National Congress (ANC) Youth League in 1943."[54] Similarly, as Mr. Ndlozi described during his statement, "They [young people] said you cannot stop me from doing, from protecting the community and it was very difficult to argue that issue. You cannot stop someone else from protecting the community."[55] The political engagement and determination displayed here are representative of the attitude displayed by youth throughout the TRC process in the struggle against apartheid. Inherent in these submissions are discussions of beliefs and a sense that youth were fighting for something, both of which denote agency. Evidence of this agency was also observed by Desmond Tutu: "Many not only believed the slogan 'liberation before education' but willingly sacrificed their future careers in fighting against apartheid."[56] Furthermore, scholars have observed that the protests led by university students during the 1960s led to a culture of repression, perpetrated by the state, that saw them "routinely detained without trial, arrested and held on politically related charges, and tortured."[57] Thus, the patterns of behavior by youth through their participation at the TRC and in the conflict highlight their significant contributions to the public sphere as political agents. To exclude their voices from the reconciliation process, therefore, would have resulted in a significant oversight in the narrative regarding human rights violations.

There are no specific provisions in the Act, which outlined the nature and scope of the TRC, for the engagement of children or youth.[58] Children, however, were not invisible during this process. Notably the interim constitution under which the Act was passed also placed the rights of children on the national agenda. The constitution emphasized the importance of considering the "best interest" of South African children under the age of eighteen years.[59] This constitutional commitment, coupled with the emphasis on applying a human rights framework to the investigation of the conflict that occurred between 1960 and 1994, provided a narrow set of parameters for understanding the ways in which young people experienced apartheid.[60] That is, it created an institutionalized narrative that increased their visibility yet also blurred the distinction between representations of children and youth. Indeed, the institutional structures on which the TRC was created provided no space for nuance when considering the experiences of children and youth. While the constitution ensured that the experiences of young people were discussed at the TRC, the process highlights a tension between institutionally constructed representations about young people and the self-representations by young people.

The exclusion of young people from the mandate of the TRC reflected the dominance of the human rights agenda with respect to children in the international community during the 1990s. Specifically, the CRC was instrumental in framing the narrative experiences of children during this time. This approach, which prioritized the moral responsibility of states to protect children from harm, depicted young people as passive subjects in the conflict environment.[61] As Kemper explains, "The moral obligations . . . derive[d] from a ubiquitous belief that children suffer the most; that they are innocent; and that their welfare lies in the interests of all."[62] It established a global standard for realizing the rights of children based on the belief that they are passive subjects vulnerable to manipulation by adults.

In addition, the almost unanimous ratification of the CRC increased the visibility of the rights of children for those under the age of eighteen. In doing so, a limited framework was established for constructing representations of young people during post-conflict reconciliation that inextricably equated the experiences of youth with those of children. Indeed, as van Bueren has observed in her investigation of child soldiers, the "blinkered vision of the drafters of the Convention may have contributed to the weakening of standards in respect of child civilians" and those whose experiences are not represented by the victim framework.[63]

Establishing Visibility

The inclusion of young people in the South African TRC established an international standard for recognizing their unique experiences during reconciliation. As Graça Machel's submission at the youth hearings in Johannesburg observes:

> South Africa is probably . . . among the first countries to . . . give a face to children. Give visibility to children and to give priority to children. . . . This is one of the few experiences where children will be given a platform so that the nation, and even the international community will have to sit and listen. In other words, we have moved from [positions where we] do not acknowledge their rights to participate in the debate [or] in the shaping of their lives.[64]

Similarly, Dr. Magwaza at the Durban hearing concluded that "we, as adults, sometimes keep a conspiracy of silence around the suffering of the child because it is too painful for us to deal with it, or simply because we do not have skills." He continues: "They represent South Africa's most critical national asset, therefore today we want to share their invaluable experiences, and we would like to hear their voices."[65] The South African TRC established a range of procedures to communicate the stories of those prevented from directly testifying. As transcripts from the Durban and Bloemfontein hearings reveal, children were given the opportunity to speak privately about their experiences.[66]

Furthermore, they were asked to draw pictures to convey their conflict narratives, which helped the TRC establish and publicly acknowledge their needs, interests, and experiences. At the Durban hearing, for example, the comission presented a drawing "by an eight-year-old child. In it there's a man who's pouring petrol on the house and setting the house alight."⁶⁷ At the Bloemfontein hearing "one child made a drawing of a little boy who was killed, and that was her brother . . . she ha[d] drawn the killer with a gun, and had painted this killer black because that's the vision the child ha[d]."⁶⁸ Notably, this level of engagement with children "set new international precedents in efforts by truth commissions to address issues surrounding children."⁶⁹ For the first time, children (not their representatives) were visible in the reconciliation practices of a transitional state. By employing innovative techniques to allow children to tell their stories, the TRC process legitimized their status as individual rights holders with a claim to protection from the state. Yet these creative parameters also produced restrictive barriers for the participation of children in TRCs that minimized their capacity to claim and exert agency and citizenship through direct testimony. The voices of children, while heard by those who directly interacted with them, were controlled by external actors due to the international norms and beliefs that informed their level of participation.

For youth over the age of eighteen, the TRC hearings provided a safe space to claim ownership over conflict and reconciliation narratives. For example, as Mr. Mashalaba explained at the hearings in Eastern Cape, "We were not passive bystanders but rather acted with the naïveté of youth."⁷⁰ The consensus amongst the submissions *by* youth was that they were "heroes" and "soldiers," fighting for an important cause.⁷¹ The submission of Ms. Sandra Adonis best articulates this common belief. Reflecting on her participation in the resistance movements, she concludes: "Although we have done things that we are not very proud of, but the reasons why we have done it we are proud of them, because today we can stand with our heads up high and say that, together with the nation, we have done it."⁷² Explicit links to motivation reflected here reveal the importance of providing space for youth to self-ascribe meaning to their actions. When youth are given opportunities to own their stories, the nuances and complexities that fuel their behaviors are made visible. This enables communities to better understand the character of substantive participation by youth.

By providing youth the opportunity to testify at these hearings, the TRC made visible the broad range of beliefs about justice, conflict, and reconciliation held by youth. These reflections, however, when institutionalized in the final report, were also used to represent the experiences of children, as the direct testimony of individuals under the age of eighteen was prohibited by the commission and codified in its mandate. Thus, while youth were visible, representations of their stories reflected ideas *about* all young people, rather than the unique beliefs of youth themselves about their capacity. This is significant because narratives are experience-centered, yet when institutionalized and told in a way that fails to create space for diverse and unique experiences, they can have a marginalizing effect. While the institutional reports of the South African TRC are reductionist in their ability to represent youth, the TRC process revealed youth to be responsive political agents. The contrast between the final report and the TRC process suggests a stark contrast between representations of youth constructed *by* youth and the ways in which youth are represented in the transitional justice community.

This engagement of youth at the South African TRC operationalized Article 12 of the CRC, namely that the views of children should be "given due weight in accordance with the age and maturity of the child."[73] Moreover, Michael Wyness, Lisa Harrison, and Ian Buchanan conclude that this pattern of engagement demonstrates an "apprenticeship" framework of rights where agency is gradually afforded to young people as they evolve.[74] That is, as young people develop, their engagement with political processes becomes more nuanced, interactive, and refined.

In addition, the responsive tone of the hearings was established early on by the chairperson when he concluded: "We want to salute young people for the incredible courage that they showed for we are where we are today, very largely due to the contributions of young people and so I welcome you all . . . we are going to listen to youth. We welcome you all at this special public hearing . . . where the youth are going to give submissions about what they think happened and what their future is all about."[75] Inherent in this statement are notions of agency and a willingness to include youth in the process. The reconciliation process in South Africa, therefore, revealed the broad range of crosscutting identities that youth occupied during conflict. As Gready has since observed, South African youth were "both victims *and* perpetrator, or political activists *and* criminal" (emphasis in the original).[76] Furthermore, the inclusion of a dedicated chapter on children in the official final report established a starting point for a dialogue within the transitional justice community regarding the increased visibility of young people in reconciliation processes. However, while young people were visible at the South African TRC, the lack of nuance in distinguishing between children and youth in the final report created a narrow understanding of the conflict experiences of all young people during apartheid, which denied youth agency and silenced their voices at the institutional level.

The increased visibility of young people and their distinct post-conflict needs continued at the Peruvian TRC. Throughout the final report young people are explicitly recognized as key stakeholders and the beneficiaries of state programs designed to address the root causes of the conflict. In particular, the TRC mandated that "reconciliation finds a reflection in education."[77] The emphasis on education in the mandate of the final report of the Comisión de La Verdad y Reconciliación (CVR) reflected the vital role educational institutions played in the conflict. As Julie Paulson has observed, "Education took on a powerful symbolic role in Peru's conflict" as public-school teachers were "viewed as the face of violence and state dissent."[78] Indeed, the interaction of young people with this education system formed the foundation of their conflict experiences, which was represented in the final report. The CVR observed that the primary motivation for their engagement in the violence was the "incapacity of the State and the country's elites to respond to the educational demands of youth." In particular the commission noted that this failure "frustrated youth efforts towards social mobility and aspiration for advancement."[79] Thus, revelations about the structural limitations that deny youth agency and opportunities to reach their participatory capacity are an important nuance for the conflict narrative. Yet without youth's firsthand voices these complex considerations may have been rendered invisible; replaced instead with truths that better advanced other political agendas. Substantive participation for marginalized individuals, such as youth, is thus crucial for ensuring that the solutions borne out of these reconciliation processes meaningfully represent their interests.

The focus on educational institutions as the symbolic center of the violence ensured that the final report thematically engaged with the conflict narratives of young people. Indeed, one of the principal findings with respect to children by the CVR was that "a generation of children and young people also had their educational possibilities truncated and future employment possibilities diminished as a result of the armed conflict."[80] As a result, widespread institutional reform was a central focus of the recommendations. The goal of the CVR was to promote a dialogue through educational reform that would "promote democratic values."[81] This focus on educational reform at the TRC in Peru denoted a significant turning point in the reconciliation agenda of transitional states. Indeed, the CVR was the first TRC to appoint a designated staff member to coordinate a working relationship between the CVR and the Ministry of Education.[82] Furthermore, it was first TRC to examine the structural causes of violence against children and to recognize the long-term impact of these structural causes on the future of young people. Yet like in the South African case, when the final report was produced the voices of children and youth were represented together, which created a narrow and one-dimensional account of their post-conflict needs and interests.

Blurring the Boundaries: Collective Representations of Children and Youth

In South Africa, the decision not to allow individuals under the age of eighteen to testify directly to the TRC produced narrow representations of young people in the formal institutionalized narrative of apartheid. The chapter on children and youth does not adequately account for the diversity displayed in the submissions highlighted earlier in this chapter. Moreover, a letter submitted to the commission, not represented in the final report, told the story of a thirteen-year-old boy who fought because "he knew what was right and what was wrong and he fought for what was right and people listened to what he had to say."[83] Despite not being able to testify directly to the commission, due to the belief that at thirteen he needed to be protected, his story represents a desire to interact with the community and to fight for his beliefs, both of which denote a capacity to act as an empowered political agent. Due to his age, however, the institutional report of the TRC silenced his voice and obscured this demonstration of agency because his story did not fit the dominant narrative of children in the final report. Similarly, the author of the letter about the boy's story was an eleven-year-old girl who wrote to the commission to protest their decision to restrict the age of testimony. In her letter, political will, agency, and empowerment are common themes, as she demonstrated for the commission the value of allowing children the option to have their voices heard directly. She observed that the boy:

> Made a difference in our country and by listening to children with similar experiences could help us to do the same. . . . The main point is, children should be able to talk about things

that hurt us like sexual abuse and violence. It will also be interesting, because it is about our country's history, and we are not learning about this in schools. What I am trying to bring out is that it is necessary for children to speak, because children have opinions and feelings too.[84]

The institutionally constructed representations of young people in the final report of the South African TRC were constrained by the commission's broader mandate, which was derived from dominant institutional norms that prioritized protectionism and the vulnerability of young people. Due to these beliefs, traditions, and norms the mandate restricted the investigation of the ways in which children experienced the conflict to an examination of the gross violations of human rights committed against children. Indeed, the children's hearings were motivated by the knowledge that individuals aged thirteen to twenty-four are becoming "the largest category of victims reported to the Commission," rather than a desire to understand the nature and magnitude of their conflict experiences.[85]

While young people were visible during the reconciliation process, their individual voices were muffled by a narrow institutional agenda. Indeed, the ad hoc nature of the South African hearings nurtured collective representations of conflict, which inextricably connected the experiences of children with those of youth. As explained in the final report, the commission "felt that the formal structure of the hearings might intimidate children and subject them to additional trauma."[86] Furthermore, the "focus on gross human rights violations" in the commission's broader mandate produced a final report that emphasized the vulnerability and innocence of young people.[87]

While the report is transparent regarding its inability to represent all children and youth, its justification challenges the fundamental goal of TRCs to provide a narrative of the violence and instability that is representative and inclusive. As observed in the final report, "Many saw themselves not as victims, but as soldiers or freedom fighters and, for this reason chose not to appear before the Commission at all."[88] Given this, the institutional narrative presented demonstrates a notable gap in the stories of young people, and thus the reconciliation narrative can be conceived as incomplete. In addition, the limited reporting mandate that focused on human rights misrepresented and overlooked the stories of many young people, particularly those who perceived agency and choice as central to their reconciliation stories. For example, while the report recognizes "the largely positive role that children and youth played in the liberation of South Africa, many of the testimonies and statements refer only to the generally negative consequences of repression in the period under review."[89] This suggests that the formal reconciliation narratives produced by the TRC failed to reflect the breadth of lived experiences of youth, as they were constrained by the limited normative frameworks produced and promoted within the international discourse of children's rights. Indeed, the chapter on children and youth conceded that "this focus on victims is not, however, intended to diminish the active role of children and youth. Children were agents of social change and harnessed vast amounts of energy, courage, and resilience during the apartheid era. For many young people, active engagement in political activity resulted in the acquisition of skills such as analysis, mobilization, and strategizing, as well as the ability to draw strength from friends and comrades in times of hardship."[90] Despite the commission's stated intention not to "diminish" their stories, the limited scope of the reporting mandate silenced the diverse voices of young people and represented their stories as one-dimensional. By acknowledging this role yet prioritizing and telling the negative stories, or stories of vulnerability, the final report inadvertently produced a representation hierarchy with respect to young people. Specifically, the final report placed universal notions of children and childhood at the center of the reconciliation narrative, which relegated notions of agency to the margins. While the narrative being told fits the reporting mandate of the TRC, it does not represent the nature and scope of young people's participation in the violence and instability associated with apartheid, which is acknowledged in the quote above. The South African TRC, therefore, provided early indications of a tension between the institutionalized reconciliation narratives of young people and the on-the-ground realities of their engagement. The TRC process provided a forum for those excluded from the final report and the mandate to tell their stories at hearings and through counselors. However, this inclusive process, as demonstrated by the South African case, does not guarantee that the stories of youth will be represented in the institutionalized conflict narratives.

Nevertheless, in South Africa the firsthand stories of youth, which demonstrated their agency, managed to break through these institutional barriers, as political will and agency are prominent themes throughout the transcripts of the hearings. As one participant's submission described,

"Children and youth faced the full force of state oppression as they took on their role as the 'foot soldiers of the struggle'—as what were called the 'young lions.'"[91] This submission, which demonstrates agency and courage through the representation of young people as lions, is echoed consistently throughout the TRC process. This was in stark contrast to many of the transcripts of youth, highlighted previously, that appeared in the final report. Indeed, the submissions of youth suggested significant dissatisfaction with the mandate, specifically its focus on the past. As Mr. Van Eedan explained, "Your mandate is to establish reconciliation, but the ideal for that reconciliation does not only depend on the fact that we can put the history in perspective, but also how the Afrikaner youth experience things at present."[92] The mandate's narrow focus on the past produced dominant representations of young people through the lens of victimhood. This was evident in the TRC's focus on themes of detention and imprisonment, "torture, and children and youth in exile" in the final report.[93] While these are devastating and important representations of the ways in which children experienced conflict, they are merely part of their broader reconciliation narrative. This is evident across many of the submissions that emphasized the importance of the future. For example, Mr. Van Eeden urged the commission to recognize that youth do not "want to stand here with our hands open asking for charity. We want to make a contribution to the future."[94]

In addition, the dominant narrative of the TRC report was challenged by displays of leadership and bravery, as well as a focus on the future, in the submissions provided to the TRC hearings on children. For example Dr. Coleman described youth "as the glue of township resistance" and the "foot soldiers of the struggle."[95] Yet the decision to focus the final report on the past and on stories of victims denoted a strict adherence to the humanitarian principles that dominated the discourse on children in international relations during the 1990s.[96] Interestingly, the report acknowledged this limitation, concluding that because "many saw themselves not as victims, but as soldiers or freedom fighters" they "chose not to appear before the Commission at all."[97] That is, young people overtly resisted the ascribed representations and assumptions prescribed by the mandate of the commission. The commission's acknowledgment that youth actively decided not to participate in the hearings of the TRC is a significant development, as it broadens our understanding of the role of youth post conflict. By formally recognizing youth's refusal to engage with the process, the TRC afforded them ownership over their reconciliation experience. In this instance, youth's agency is prominent, as the submissions demonstrated their capacity to impact the structures and processes of the commission by denying them the use of their stories and voices.

In addition, the engagement of young people with the TRC in South Africa echoed a broader global trend that prioritized and adhered to a narrow set of beliefs about their place in society. These perceptions persist today in ways that mediate interactions with youth through an unproductive protectionist visibility lens. As McEvoy-Levy observes, "Once negotiations began . . . the young were instructed to stand-down and return, if possible, to more normal pursuits for their age group."[98] This denotes a belief amongst the community that "youth have special needs"; however, as scholars have suggested, "Youth themselves felt cheated of decision-making power."[99] Designations that youth should exist in certain spaces or speak only on specific issues result in mediated political interactions that deny ownership. To accept that youth have agency and the capacity for autonomous decision-making necessitates a shift in perceptions about how, where, and on what youth participate. All issues are youth issues, just as youth are leaders now as well as in the future. This evolution should be led by youth and taken up unreservedly by political communities. In the context of the South African TRC, while every effort was made to protect children from harm, the voices of youth and their participation in the hearings solidified a representative amalgamation of two distinct demographics. In doing so, the TRC established the foundations for conceptualizing institutional representations of children and youth in narrow and marginalizing ways. This has had lasting implications for youth participation in reconciliation and their capacity to own their stories.

Notions of victimhood also dominated the representations of young people in the final report of the Peruvian TRC. This is due to the exclusion of young people from the decision-making about the TRC, and an overreliance on the CRC as the framework for establishing the parameters for their participatory capacity. The children's section, for example, explains that "the CVR shares with the doctrine of comprehensive protection of children, recognition of children as subjects of rights. In this regard, it states that children the factors affecting their integrity and proper training must be protected. The violence experienced by Peru during the internal armed conflict, ignored all these considerations and children became victims of violence that affected them with particular intensity."¹⁰⁰ The Peruvian case thus shares many parallels with South Africa with respect to its mediation of young people's voices. Most notably, interactions with and reporting on children emphasized the caretaker role of the state, without considering its homogenizing effect. Thus, in both TRCs the agency of many young people was rendered invisible by the attribution of meaning to their stories on their behalf.¹⁰¹

The South African model perpetuated the belief that while the human rights of children are important, the responsibility for claiming those rights lies with the adult community. This is evident in statements in the final report, which recognized that "our country is soaked in the blood of her children of all races and all political persuasions."¹⁰² In addition, the TRC report also acknowledged that the "commission took statements from deponents of all age groups, except children . . . those below the legal age of majority."¹⁰³ That is, while children and their needs were visible, their voices were largely excluded due to the beliefs of external stakeholders, which derived from the dominant international belief that children required protection. This normative protection framework embedded in the CRC casts "children as ideally apolitical" and "victims of adult political action," thus requiring adults to shelter them.¹⁰⁴

As a result, many of the special hearings on "children and youth" throughout the country solicited testimony *about* children rather than directly *from* children. For example, at the children's hearings conducted on June 12–13, 1997, few children testified, and therefore the beliefs regarding how children experienced apartheid "consisted mainly of submissions from organizations that had dealt with children and children's issues for many years."¹⁰⁵ These submissions reflected the beliefs of external agents rather than young people themselves. The stories of youth "were presented at the hearings by caregivers and [through] recordings."¹⁰⁶ So while their experiences were visible, they were not afforded the opportunity to directly engage with the commission, and their stories were controlled and interpreted by external agents rather than claimed by children themselves. Consequently, children in the final report of the South African TRC were assigned representations that emphasized dependency, innocence, and vulnerability. Furthermore, the report's framework for examining the experiences of children, which prioritized the moral imperative of the state, cast children as subjects in the conflict narrative rather than agents in their own conflict and reconciliation narratives. Indeed, representations of children were constructed through the victim lens. In doing so, the most visible characteristics of children and youth were vulnerability and innocence, representations that deny active agency.

Reliance on these classifications in the final report of the Peruvian TRC also silenced and obstructed the experiences of youth that did not fit the victim framework. As one participant described, "We were attacked by the Shining Path. We were scared and we climbed up to the hills and we saw how they burned down our homes, how they stole our clothes, our chickens. . . . We were afraid to stay in the house or to go to the fields to work."[107] This emphasis on the vulnerability of children in conflict coincided with global discourse at the time, which sought to address the growing prevalence of child soldiers. Indeed, following the release of Graça Machel's landmark report, *The Impact of Armed Conflict on Children*, the need to recognize and protect children in conflict zones became a critical imperative amongst the international community.[108] The child soldier description dominated the section on children in the final report. For example, it notes,

> The PCP-SL had a persistent, repetitive, and continuous policy of forced recruitment of children, especially in areas of Ayacucho, Huancavelica, Huánuco, and Junín. Considering children as part Guerrilla Army, for it formed the organization of the "pioneer's children" or "red pioneer" who from an early age performed surveillance work, espionage, provision of food, among others. From age 12, the Main Force pioneers taught the children the use and handling of weapons, spears, knives, and slingshots. The aim was to train them to take part in armed actions and clashes.[109]

In addition, the experiences of child soldiers represented in the final report aligned with the global trends highlighted in the *Graça Machel Report*. For example, the report observes that while children traditionally served in supporting roles "as cooks, porters, messengers, and spies. Increasingly . . . [rebel forces and armies were] deliberately conscripting children as soldiers."[110] This was also evident in the Peruvian case where the CVR notes that "forced recruitment and abduction have themselves been targeted practices against children by the PCP-SL because they were arrested and forced to participate in military events and indirect jobs that would allow development of clashes."[111]

The decisions by the CVR, therefore, to make visible the violence committed against children during the conflict reflected the focus of the international community with respect to children. The dominance of these representations, in both the South African final report and at the CVR, presented the experiences of young people in conflict as static. In doing so, the institutional reporting of TRCs during this period failed to account for the possibility that as young people grow and develop, they have a greater capacity to contribute meaningfully and actively to conflict and reconciliation. Moreover, these narrow and static institutional narratives discounted instances where the experiences and representations of youth were informed by their interactions and relationships.

A reliance on the victim classification and the dominance of the stories of child soldiers in these reports does not account for the potential agency and empowerment that young people exhibit during TRC processes, and post-conflict practices more broadly, as consequences of their conflict experiences. Accordingly, the dominant representations applied to the experiences of children at the Peruvian TRC and at the South African TRC failed to reflect the resilience and determination displayed by children following the conflict. Submissions to the CVR demonstrated that although young people were victims in the conflict, their conflict story was more diverse than the report and its recommendations revealed. For example, as one young girl described:

> There is no comfort for the death of our parents because we were left abandoned. I had to take on a role of mother and father to my younger sister when I was only 13 years old. . . . People are abusive, and worse when you are a woman they mistreat you, they exploit you. . . . Even though I have suffered through some difficult times, this has not made me dwell on it. I want to improve my lot. I am now studying Engineering. My sister is studying to be a teacher. Sometimes I think that I have been dreaming and that one day I will wake up and see my parents.[112]

This submission suggests that regardless of age, some children have an extraordinary capacity to take on roles that challenge the validity of the victim lens. Despite experiencing tragedy, children "are agents in their own right who have their own identity and values."[113] In fact children often occupy multiple shifting identities that the static representations presented in the final report failed to reflect. Not only is this child a victim, her submission revealed that she is also empowered, future-orientated, and responsible—all themes that denote agency. The limited scope of the investigation in Peru, however, coupled with the reliance on the CRC to guide the parameters of investigation, resulted in a highly visible yet narrow representation of young people in the formal conflict narrative.

Unlike the South African case, where the representations of children and youth were combined and reflected through the stories of youth, the Peruvian TRC limited its discussion to those classified under the CRC as children.[114] While there are mentions of youth in the report, they are sporadic and brief. For example, the introductory section of the report exposes the role of youth as leaders of the resistance. It describes a resistance protest in June 1995 that was largely "led by university students who assumed a vanguard role in the struggle for [the] restoration of democracy."[115] This depiction of youth as leaders lends credence to claims that youth have the capacity to act as "empowered political agents" and "agents of change" in conflict and transitional justice contexts.

In contrast, the final report also describes youth as "resentful, live renegades, bored with life because they have passed things."[116] Clearly, the deviance classification was also prominent in the institutionalized narrative of the TRC, which was tasked with making visible the roles youth occupied in the Peruvian conflict. The ideas that youth were resentful and bored prioritizes stereotypes and normative frameworks *about* youth, which are underpinned by the beliefs that they are troublemakers or spoilers. Moreover, this rhetoric emphasizes the generalized assumption that youth have a propensity for deviance, which as demonstrated in chapter 2 has come to dominate representations of youth in these contexts. Given this, the sporadic representations of youth in the Peruvian TRC report demonstrate that the deviance lens produces the same institutional silencing as the victim lens, as it denies agency by casting the experience of young people as negative and emphasizing only their propensity for violence.

Taken together, the victim (child soldier) classification and the deviance description create narrow boundaries for the representation of young people in the final reports of TRCs, as not only do they mischaracterize and overlook the diverse experiences of young people but they also fail to reflect the stories of young people that do not fit within these binaries. For example, although representations of the role of youth were absent in the final report of CVR, youth nevertheless played a pivotal role in the reconciliation process. Peruvian youth participated in Promotores de la Verdad (PROVER), a program designed to promote and distribute information on the CVR. Youth volunteers actively engaged with the work of the TRC through taking statements, organizing, and developing a community forum to encourage other young people to participate.[117] Their role in this program demonstrates the capacity of youth to act as agents of change, particularly in circumstances where they are excluded from formal processes and required to operate on the fringes of society.[118] Since the Peruvian TRC, many scholars have noted the capacity of youth to exercise agency and ownership over their post-conflict experiences in this way.[119] Moreover, as highlighted in chapter 2, empirical research on youth in peacebuilding demonstrates that the voices of youth are often the loudest when they are forced to be occupy the spaces outside the formal reconciliation and transitional justice structures.

Social Representations of South African Children and Youth: A Tale of Binaries.

Dominant throughout the South African final report's chapter on children are stories that perpetuate the notion of young people as the subjects of an adult agenda. Indeed, an emphasis on the capacity of young people to be manipulated and the reproduction and use of binary representations are prominent features of the stories told *about* young people in the final report. This is problematic because not only does it reduce the stories of young people in South Africa to a singular experience, but it also fails to capture their underlying motivations and self-reflections. These representations echoed the international discourse that was evolving at the time around notions of the "deviant other," or more specifically the notion that young "bad boys need to be saved."[120] Indeed, the increased visibility of young people in the peace and conflict environment produced a range of assumptions about their role in the violence and instability. The dominant representations of youth in the final report, therefore, start from a position of limited responsibility and control. For example, the report suggests that during the conflict the security establishment "engaged in the informal repression of children by hunting down 'troublesome' youth and developing an informer network."[121] Young people are thus represented here as puppets of powerful individuals, namely rebel groups and political elites.

Moreover, these representations furthered the stereotype of a demographic susceptible to manipulation by those who employed negative socially constructed beliefs about youth for their own gain. The submission by Mr. Maxlesi, a representative of the Eastern Cape provincial youth commission, echoed this sentiment. Specifically, he observed that "youth are products of the highly militarized confrontational past of South Africa."[122] Central to this classification is the notion that they are *troublesome* and easily manipulated, a theme that is repeated on multiple occasions throughout the chapter on children and youth.

By prioritizing this classification in the institutionalized reconciliation narrative of South Africa, the report promoted the same normative trend that was emerging throughout other subsections of the peace and conflict discourse, namely the notion of the deviant adolescent. The formal and public reconciliation narrative of the South African TRC produced and disseminated a narrow, reactive, and homogenous understanding of the conflict experiences of youth. Representing youth as products of the establishment ignored the capacity of young people to "actively and independently cause tremendous suffering and destabilization," as well as their capacity to resist manipulation.[123] Taken together, these narratives denote an externally determined portrait of youth, where their stories are cast as a consequence of other people's actions rather than the result of their own agency. In doing so, these representations, which are prioritized in the final report, minimized the responsibility and agency young people had over their own conflict behavior. Moreover, rather than telling the story of how youth were affected by the conflict, the focus on the militarization of youth represented them as merely subjects in a political game. Without submissions by youth, which have the capacity to challenge assumptions and expose their reasoning for becoming combatants, the reconciliation narratives of youth remain incomplete and narrow.

The South African TRCs final report also used the youth as victims classification to tell the stories of youth. Indeed, the stories of trauma and anger told throughout the report utilized the image of the child to represent the frustrations of the adult community toward the government. For example, as one participant described, "One morning a 'bum' will be found dead—a child of God whose only mistake was to fight for his country. . . . When you see the mothers sobbing for their children on TV you can understand how I feel. I hate the government for turning my son into a zombie."[124] The zombie imagery, coupled with evoking innocence through calling the young person a "child of God," uses the child to represent a social and political discourse about the devasting impact of conflict. In addition, the image of the mother sobbing is used to represent the expansive social and emotional implications associated with the engagement of young people in apartheid. Throughout the final report of the South African TRC, young people and their images are employed to symbolize the devastation and trauma of others. Similarly, a psychologist, when testifying on the nature of the posttraumatic stress disorder experienced by adults as a result of apartheid, invoked the image of the child. He explained that "the pain of all those who died becoming sensed around this experience of a solitary child's death. There is nothing more vulnerable and in need of protection than a child, and there is little else that shows up the barbaric nature and violence of war than when a child is killed."[125] While the deaths of children in war are traumatic events, using their images and experiences to highlight the trauma of others perpetuates the belief that they are subjects in a political system as opposed to agents with their own individual traumas. Here the assumption that childhood denotes vulnerability and innocence is used to represent the experiences of adults rather than to tell the conflict stories of young people. In doing so, the final report of the South African TRC legitimizes narrow binary representations that were solidifying during the 1990s in response to the evolving norms about the rights of children and their capacity to claim these rights. Moreover, as the first TRC process to engage young people in a formal and institutionalized manner, it established problematic foundations for future TRCs regarding how to represent the experiences of young people.

Conclusion

The South African TRC laid the foundations for our interactions with young people in TRC processes. It established parameters for the engagement of children and youth and for the reporting of their stories in the final reports of TRCs. It is during this TRC process that an important discursive distinction first emerges between reporting of and reporting by individuals during reconciliation. As the South African case demonstrates, throughout the twentieth century the visibility of children in reconciliation practices was informed by the broader human rights narrative that was beginning to find form. This narrative was produced by adults and institutionalized through the United Nations' architecture. The inclusion of youth within this story was in large part a consequence of the limitations created by institutionalizing this human rights narrative for children. Specifically, in the final report of the South African TRC, youth and their stories are used as substitutes for children, whose participation was limited due to the belief that they are vulnerable and innocent. The visibility of children at the South African TRC foreshadows the inclusion of youth in reconciliation processes; however the TRC's depictions of young people were not necessarily accurate or helpful for understanding the diverse ways youth and children experience conflict. The Peruvian TRC process would later perpetuate these binary representations of young people, suggesting that while the engagement of young people in TRCs evolved significantly during the 1990s, instances of backsliding were prominent.

The South African TRC also reveals a tension between the ways in which different agents represent children and youth in reconciliation processes. On the one hand, the behavior of the state highlights the moral responsibility to protect norms derived from international human rights instruments such as the CRC. This convention facilitated the creation of a universal understanding of the child that prioritized "welfare over their autonomy."[126] In contrast, the patterns of behavior exhibited by young people, and those who interacted closely with them during the TRC process, revealed a shift in their visibility and recognition of their agency and capacity during the reconciliation process. Indeed, the direct engagement of young people with the truth and reconciliation process in South Africa exposed claims of agency, which challenged the commission's focus on their vulnerability and primary status as victims. Given this, the South African TRC highlighted the complexity associated with institutionalizing the conflict and reconciliation stories of young people. Moreover, this chapter has demonstrated that external agents often grapple with displays of agency and reconciliation stories of young people that do not fit the institutionalized notions of children embedded in the CRC.

Furthermore, a variety of push-pull factors are evident in the submissions of and reporting on children. Among the key challenges is how to reconcile the stated international obligation to protect young people, with an emerging responsibility to ensure that their voices and thus agency are not stifled by the manifestations of a protectionist approach. Reconciliation practices, such as TRCs, aim to produce a transparent truth, yet questions of whose truth often remains ambiguous. Incongruous narratives emerge that are either perpetuated or stifled by at times well-meaning political agendas. In the context of young people's truths, this complexity, which was made visible in South Africa, continues to evolve in the cases of Sierra Leone and Timor-Leste (chapter 4).

The South African case highlights the visibility of children, prefiguring the formal and institutionalized inclusion of youth, as a separate demographic in the conflict narratives of transitional states. While youth were key stakeholders in the process, when institutionalized their stories were combined with the experiences of children. As a result, youth were visible, yet their reconciliation narratives and thus their voices remained silenced. The representations of children and youth in the South African context are significant because these informed the participatory conditions for young people in future TRCs.

Chapter 4

Claiming Ownership?

Contrasting Narratives of Agency and Participation at the Sierra Leone and Timor-Leste TRCs

> In Sierra Leone, the youth is the lifeblood of the nation . . . [they] constitute forty-five percent of the country's estimated 4.5 million population.
>
> —*Witness to Truth*, 3B:343

Representing young people's participation in conflict presents a complex challenge for transitional justice institutions seeking to reconcile political agendas and diverse "truths." When young people claim ownership over their stories of violence during processes such as TRC, those engaging with these stories are offered important insights into their contributions to peace and justice by an often undervalued citizen demographic. Where youth have participated substantively in the violence, as was the case in Sierra Leone, either through recruitment or by choice, representing their role in the conflict is often complex. Contradictory beliefs about the nature of their participation can hinder the production of a cohesive story that reflects the rich tapestry of their experiences. Steadfast adherence to normative frameworks that emerged in previous TRCs, and that exist in the discourse on youth in peace and conflict more broadly, can obscure demonstrations of agency and ownership. Institutional slippage between classifications of children and youth within the public representations of TRCs reflect political agendas and the belief that reconciliation requires a linear conflict narrative that presents a shared and unified truth. At the Sierra Leone TRC, young people's prominence as political actors in the conflict magnified their voices throughout the reconciliation processes, creating more opportunities for them to exert meaning over their stories. Yet the agendas of powerful actors, which imbue young people's stories with political meaning and aspirations, also persisted, creating notable tension between the stories of youth and stories by youth.

In Sierra Leone, youth were cast as "key sites of cultural reproduction," transformation, and knowledge, whose stories provided critical insights regarding the nature of the conflict.[1] Public representations also centered their voices to demonstrate the need for relational dynamics and community building conditions in the pursuit of holistic reconciliation. These reflections of young people at the Sierra Leone TRC acknowledged their role as a bridge between the future and the past by telling stories that seek to ensure that conditions where human rights violations thrive are not repeated. Yet an emphasis on the traditional deviance roles complicates the narrative around young people's substantive inclusion and leadership in the construction and dissemination of the Sierra Leone reconciliation narrative. By emphasizing deviance, young people are cast as the problem to be controlled, which promotes reconciliation conditions that mediate their participation and denies them opportunities to contribute to trust building, which is central to the mandate of reconciliation practices.

During the Sierra Leone TRC process, the stories of young people's conflict experiences therefore reflected the challenges associated with balancing the competing beliefs of stakeholders regarding their ownership and agency. This balance reflects the broader challenge of formal transitional justice practices, which today remain limited in their capacity to genuinely consider young people's leadership, due in part to long-worn power structures. Complicating this narrative further is the problematizing of young people within the reconciliation discourse that ties their experiences to the future aspirations of the transitional community. As the above quote demonstrates, the stories and meaning ascribed to young people acknowledge their importance to the future political success of the state without necessarily considering how this meaning reflects the uniqueness of individual stories. While the institutional narrative intermittently acknowledged the ownership that young people possess over their conflict experiences, it also prioritized the deviance discourse in its discussion of their experiences to promote a conflict narrative where reconciliation is pursued by managing youth. The experiences of youth, as such, were used to symbolize the violence and instability of the conflict. Interestingly public representations of deviance were not solely externally ascribed during the Sierra Leone TRC process. Notably this chapter also reveals attempts by youth to pursue ownership over the deviance discourse.

Scholars have considered the problematizing and passive ascribing of meaning to the experiences of children; however, little research exists that highlights the impact of these dual and often competing stories on youth and their capacity to substantively participate in reconciliation discourses.[2] To that end, this chapter seeks to highlight the ways in which different stakeholders construct representations of youth and to assess how these representations influence our understanding of their conflict stories. In doing so, it reveals the dominance, origins, and persistence of the deviance lens, as well as the claims of ownership, empowerment, and agency within the stories of youth. This chapter argues that while the deviance classification remained a significant component of the youth reconciliation narrative in Sierra Leone, youth attempted to claim ownership and agency over this discourse and to challenge the meaning of this public representation to demonstrate political agency. The voices of youth are a prominent feature of the TRC report alongside those of external agents. In this way, this chapter identifies a turning point in the evolution of young people's engagement with formal reconciliation practices. Not only were youth afforded a separate chapter in the final report, but the stories told reflected their diverse and unique experiences during the conflict as well as their potential to substantively contribute to formal reconciliation structures. The Sierra Leone TRC represents a shift in the discourse as the process enabled youth to act as knowledge producers.

While chapter 3 explored the challenges associated with the increased visibility of young people in reconciliation processes, this chapter examines a normative transition in beliefs about the nature of youth participation. Yet it also considers how embedded institutional discourses of deviance resist challenges from young people and attempts to claim this identity for themselves. It highlights an evolution in the reconciliation dialogue that resulted in a separation of the collective narrative often used to talk about children and youth and considers how the TRC process in Sierra Leone shifted the conversation to include the unique experiences of youth separate from children. It argues that the case of Sierra Leone, which is broadly considered a model for encouraging the participation of children in truth-telling practices, also reveals a partial solution for the creation of a more representative institutional narrative of youth.[3] The TRC process in Sierra Leone as such denotes a significant departure in how youth are *talked about* and *talked to* in reconciliation processes. Yet this chapter also argues that this evolution in the nature and scope of youth representation in reconciliation processes has not become embedded in the practice of transitional justice. Drawing on examples of youth representation embedded in the TRC report of Timor-Leste, it demonstrates that the victim/perpetrator binary continues to inform the beliefs and traditions of reconciliation practices with respect to the substantive participation of young people. The disjuncture between these two narratives of youth indicates the presence of a dilemma within the relationship between youth and transitional justice during the twenty-first century.

Before turning to a discussion of youth representation in the TRC of Sierra Leone, this chapters considers the prominence of beliefs regarding substantive participation and collective representative during the TRCs of this period. Next it explores developments in the international discourse on young people to situate the relationship between youth and the Sierra Leone TRC in broader historical and social context. This chapter assesses the value of the evolving international empowerment dialogue to the development of more substantive inclusive TRC processes. Following this, the chapter turns to its discussion of young people at the Sierra Leone TRC. It reveals that the meaningful engagement of youth with this TRC process facilitated the creation of an institutionalized conflict narrative, which balanced stories of agency with notions of deviance and thus created a discourse where young people were valued as knowledge producers. The chapter then examines the contributions of the Sierra Leone National Vision Project to the development of a more substantively inclusive TRC narrative that recognized the ownership and agency of youth. Finally, this chapter examines whether the level of engagement established during the TRC process in Sierra Leone was part of a broader trend in the transitional justice field. To do so, it considers briefly how the final report of the Timor-Leste TRC represented the voices of young people.

The Persistence of Socially Constructed Representations

The increased visibility of the young people in the public sphere challenges traditional constructions of the relationship between the community and those it conceives as experiencing *youthhood*. Within the TRC report for Sierra Leone, youth's political agency following the increased tyranny of the one-party system of the 1970s and 1980s is visible through the acknowledgment that they "formed the only opposition to the ruling All People's Congress (APC)" when "the other local parties had been co-opted into the government."[4] The narrative of their political participation within the report begins as one of courage, presence, and influence, acknowledging that "when institutions and their leaders in so many sectors . . . failed to speak out against the injustices of the APC regime, invariably it was the voice of youth that called for accountability."[5] Youth, in this instance, were key advocates for ending political impunity, thus furthering a long-held aim of the transitional justice project. Representations of youth as a positive political presence within the report are sporadic, as images of youth as "instruments of oppression," as "vicious thugs," and as outcasts "struggl[ing] to find" their "rightful place in society"[6] create a form of visibility that aligns with the political and social narrative of reconciliation supported in post-conflict Sierra Leone.

Prominent in the political narrative of the TRC was the perception that addressing "the youth question" was essential for producing peace. By framing their stories and experiences as a question requiring a solution, TRC reporting created limited discursive opportunities for youth's visibility to be meaningfully transformative or to serve an interpersonal reconciliatory function. Subsequent institutional efforts to resolve this question, including the creation of the Ministry for Youth and Sports in 2002 and the publishing of the National Youth Policy in 2003, had similar marginal impacts, as the emphasis was on resolving a question that had been generated from the politicized, top-down narratives prioritized during the aftermath of the conflict. Without targeted attention on diverse, local points of view, the capacity for meaningful reconciliation remains fragile. Attempts by the Sierra Leone government to answer the youth question through development programs are illustrative of this disconnect. As the TRC reporting notes, the youth ministry "faces the challenge of convincing people" that the youth question is "a national priority that demands national mobilization."⁷ Social constructions of youth within Sierra Leone, which denied them agency in comparison to elders, informed this reluctance. While visible, the power dynamics within the community ensure that the stories of youth hold less authority. This is further exacerbated by the way narratives of youth's experiences are institutionalized through politicized reconciliation.

Visibility is central to reimagining young people's place in the community following conflict. Yet how this visibility is cast within institutions (such as truth commissions) to represent participation is not siloed. It is embedded within wider political narratives about how violence and instability inform a nation's past and its potential for the future. Young people's place within reconciliation is steeped in political meaning. Their identities are imbued with a sense of promise and opportunity for a nation emerging from the trauma and violence of conflict. However, when the political agency evident in their visibility expresses a counternarrative, particularly to the one that officials perceive will facilitate reconciliation, it is often represented by institutions as deviance or manipulation. Despite evidence of their political agency, interactions between institutions and youth are informed by classificatory frames that emphasize their passivity, their dependence, and the imperative of managing their participation. Following the Sierra Leonean conflict, the TRC outlined that in examining the participation of youth the aim was to develop recommendations that "respond to the challenges created by misguided youth in the past and . . . to restore youths as productive members of their community." The commission also noted that "Sierra Leone . . . witnessed what the lethal cocktail of youth marginalization and political manipulation can produce."

While youth occupied diverse and at times violent roles in the conflict, the socially constructed representation of their aims as "misguided" and "manipulated" denies the political agency underpinning this violence and fails to recognize the diverse participatory motivations of youth. Indeed, scholarly work on young people continues to grapple with the significance of the "emotive and reductionist" social images commonly used to describe their place and role in society.[8] The resilience of these images is the result of a belief among policy and decision makers that children and youth are a valuable commodity. As recent empirical work on children and youth in international relations demonstrates, throughout history children and childhood have been used to further political agendas.[9] Moreover, this scholarship contends that even when children are visible, their identities are heavily regulated and managed through institutions, legislation, and an overreliance on protectionist discourse.[10] Brocklehurst argues that there is a discursive separation of the child and the public sphere, a "containment" and perpetuation of the view that to be a child is to be apolitical.[11] Representations of young people, therefore, are often reflections of the current political environment rather than manifestations of their nature or their capacity to influence social structures and institutions.

The child soldier remains one of the most prominent and morally ambiguous representations assigned to young people. Rosen concludes that "the child soldier crisis is part of the contested domain of international politics in which childhood serves as a proxy for other political interests."[12] This image of the conflict experiences of young people remains prominent as it reflects not merely the role of children in war but also a broader conversation about rights, development, and the morality of intervention. Indeed, the moral implications of children's participation in conflict motivate critical debates regarding the needs of children.[13] This discussion is framed using a rights-based approach that emphasizes the need to protect children and to generate "safe avenues for children to participate in the justice and reconciliation process."[14] As Shepler observes, the child solider representation "carries a range of meanings and implications and serves as a site, both discursively and in the bodies of children themselves for reform."[15] That is, children are increasingly acknowledged to be important stakeholders in the dialogue regarding a country's future. Yet throughout this body of work children are predominately described as subjects of the state. They are conceptualized as a collective group without individual agency and represented in ways that often fail to acknowledge points of difference between the experiences of young people.

Externally constructed social representations deny youth the opportunity to claim ownership over their experiences. They are therefore denied recognition as fully rationalized political actors with the capacity for political agency and contribution.[16] While young people are visible in the public space, they exercise minimal control over their position and are further marginalized and silenced by these constructs. There are thus significant power relations evident in socially constructed representations of young people, as they have little ability to contest the ways institutions and other stakeholders describe their experiences.[17] The same conditions also perpetuate the silencing of youth as they are subject to the same disempowerment through the imposition of representations that inherently diminish their ability to claim their actions and their citizenship.

Capacity and agency are associated exclusively with adulthood. This association implies that participation in social and political mechanisms is limited to the behavior of adults. As Berents explains, the common assumption throughout the literature and in the peace and conflict field is that "the adults who surround young people in everyday life . . . know best and can speak on their behalf, in their best interest, *for* them."[18] Children and youth, however, are not inactive or incapable of participation in these contexts. Instead, transitional justice practices and institutions often fail to recognize their actions outside these socially constructed representations. Cordero concludes that children are considered incompetent, dependent, and vulnerable, not because they are but because the public discourse conceives them in this way.[19] Indeed, the identities of children and youth are used to provide a point of difference between various life phases, most notably the transition into adulthood. If children and youth are passive, vulnerable, and easily manipulated, then adulthood denotes a shift to rationality and productivity.[20] Within this framing, children are associated with these identities as a "way to give the desired shape and order to future adults" and their role in political activities.[21]

Benefits and Challenges of Collective Representations

TRCs offer opportunities for inclusive participation compared to retributive practices, such as trials. They provide an expansive forum where marginalized individuals are empowered to tell their stories. However, their focus on creating broad conflict narratives also prioritizes collective social representations. As Erin Baines observes, mechanisms that examine conflicts "beyond individuals can explore interconnecting levels of responsibility" and thus "produce social understandings of victimhood."[22] This is particularly relevant in the case of child soldiers, where the emphasis is on attributing blame for the conflict experiences of young people rather than examining the behaviors of the individual that denote agency and ownership outside their classification as a child soldier. The focus on generating a complete conflict narrative through the TRC process, however, prioritizes an exploration of the societal factors that perpetuated human rights abuses. In doing so, TRCs, particularly during the reporting phase, highlight the macro consequences of violence. This emphasis on the social factors and macro consequences silences the individual motivations of young people and discounts their efforts to reclaim ownership over their experiences, particularly when their stories do not fit within the broader explanations of the conflict.

The tension apparent between collective stories about young people and by young people is heightened in cases where the reconciliation interests of the broader transitional community do not align with the aspirations of youth to be meaningfully included in the process. Indeed, TRC final reports are "highly strategic social productions" that often fail to hear youth, particularly when their stories challenge the political and social representations created and furthered by powerful stakeholders.[23] As the discussion in this chapter demonstrates, the Sierra Leone TRC represented an evolution in the relationship between youth and TRCs, as, for the most part, the institutional narrative was responsive to the truths told by youth and beliefs about their capacity to contribute to meaningful change. Yet the highly embedded nature of the victim/perpetrator binary ensured that challenges to representations of youth agency were still reflected in the report, alongside reflections of ownership and empowerment. For example, in Sierra Leone, even though youth are afforded separate consideration, the predominant classifications used to tell their stories represented the demographic as "misguided" and "lost."[24] Furthermore, these descriptors indicate the presence of a belief amongst external stakeholders that youth are meant for the community to manage, rather than active and engaged political agents.[25] While these classifications are reflective of the experiences of many youth, or more importantly of youth during different periods, they are also incomplete and static depictions. Further interrogation of the reconciliation processes that produced these narratives indicates a more complex story where young people create and take ownership over their experiences. As such, the overreliance on these marginalizing narratives within formal institutions perpetuates conditions that deny young people's agency by delegitimizing the uniqueness of their experiences and their capacity to determine their meaning.

The Evolving Dialogue on Empowerment and Substantive Participation

Acknowledgment of the importance of representing youth voices in peace and conflict practices has steadily evolved since the United Nations declared 1985 as International Youth Year: Participation, Development, and Peace. Among the stated aims of the international community during this time was a recognition of "the profound importance of the direct participation of youth in shaping the future . . . and the valuable contributions that youth can make in all sectors of society."[26] Indeed, the prominent discourse during this period sought to harness the "energies, enthusiasm, and creative abilities" of youth in a wide variety of social and political processes including nation building.[27] Genuine progress toward these aims, however, remained largely stagnant until the establishment of the United Nations World Youth Forums in the twenty-first century.

These forums provided a space for youth to exercise their capacity, exert agency, and reimagine their place in the international system. They were an opportunity for youth to enter the public sphere and change the narrative with respect to their capacity and status as political agents. Following the 2001 forum in Dakar, the participants (youth delegates from around the world) presented the international community with the Youth Empowerment Strategy that responded directly to the above aims. Among the declarations in this strategy was a direct call to acknowledge the distinction between children and youth. Specifically, while they highlighted the importance of the United Nations General Assembly Special Session on Children, and its capacity to provide "young people" with a voice, they also urged the international community to commit to their proposed recommendations at the designated General Assembly bi-annual session on youth.[28] In urging the international community to acknowledge their recommendations in the proper designated forum, these members of the youth demographic claimed ownership over their separate identity in the public sphere.

In addition, the Youth Empowerment Strategy provided youth with an opportunity to reflect and report on the social and political barriers to their empowerment firsthand. In doing so, they demonstrated a heightened level of awareness of the political sphere not typically attributed to youth, as well as their potential role in addressing these challenges. This was evident in the strategies they presented to the UN for targeted action, which sought to harness preexisting "networks of young people that are involved with United Nations agencies."[29] Specifically, youth recommended that "a youth network . . . could generate mechanisms to ensure the participation of young representatives in reconciliation process[es], negotiation and peacebuilding."[30] Here, the youth participants proposed that meaningful participation requires the international community to acknowledge and utilize youth who are already engaged within the international system. Inherent in this claim is the belief that addressing the needs of youth requires that they be given the capacity to "shap[e] their own . . . social conditions."[31] That is, the best actors to respond to the interests of youth are youth, and thus they should be given the opportunity to meaningfully engage in the development phase of peace and reconciliation.

The youth participants at Dakar identified the "culture of peace" as a potential normative space for a shift in external beliefs regarding the empowerment and engagement of youth. They observed, however, that the challenge for youth was to "increase [their] influence" and to be more outspoken in national dialogues that seek to "build a culture of peace."[32] The engagement of youth during this world youth forum exposed themes of participation that suggested a shift in the discourse to reflect beliefs amongst youth themselves that they were empowered political agents. For example, alongside their commitment to engage more directly in building a culture of peace, youth also demanded in their empowerment strategy that the international community institutionalize both the Braga Youth Action Plan (1998) and the Dakar Youth Empowerment Strategy at the General Assembly.[33] These ideas reflected an ardent desire to have their political will and their capacity to act as agents of change acknowledged and legitimized by the international community. Indeed, the language and recommendations in this document suggests that youth were no longer satisfied with being visible—they also believed they should be heard.

The participants also observed that the lack of access to institutional structures and resources continued to produce and perpetuate barriers to empowerment and the meaningful exercise of agency. In response, youth, through their recommendations in the empowerment strategy, aimed to amend the traditions and structures they believed to be responsible for this disempowerment. In particular, they called for "access . . . to policy-making bodies" and concluded that the United Nations needed to "improve its way of communicating with youth organizations."[34] They also advocated for "legislation . . . protecting [youth] rights to participation in decision making" as well as "access to quality education fostering responsible citizenship."[35] These recommendations are underpinned by themes of development, political capital, and positive potential and reflect attempts by youth to be seen by the international community as empowered political agents. In practice, these recommendations aimed to facilitate this shift by influencing the structures and traditions that inform external ideas about youth within the international community and in transitional states. This is particularly important because the institutions that facilitate these dialogues, including at times TRCs, silence these individuals through an overreliance on traditional understandings of the capacity of youth. To overcome these silences, therefore, youth must be assertive when addressing these forums to ensure they challenge the common assumptions that youth are disengaged and passive.

As the case of youth at the Sierra Leone TRC demonstrates, a thematic focus on youth in the mandates of TRCs provides a potential solution to the challenges identified at the international level. Indeed, their inclusion in these mandates compels transitional communities to meaningfully interact with the stories of youth and to consider their contributions to the conflict through an agency lens. The thematic focus provides institutional acknowledgment that youth and their actions had a significant impact on the transitional state during the conflict and that their voices are integral to the creation of a national dialogue on peace and reconciliation. For example, the TRC report for Sierra Leone placed youth at the center of the conflict narrative, concluding that "the last twenty years of Sierra Leone's history, is in large part, the story of Sierra Leone's youth . . . as students, journalists, workers, and activists they exposed injustices and the bankruptcy of the ruling elite's ideologies." This acknowledgment in the institutional mechanism of the reconciliation process in Sierra Leone denotes a shift in the representation of youth. Indeed, not only are youth visible in the mandate, but their contributions as influencers of the broader social and political systems form part of the beliefs about youth outlined in the final report. This is significant because it affords legitimacy to their stories and claims of agency, which had begun to emerge in the international discourse on youth empowerment. The consideration given to the voices of youth at the Sierra Leone TRC lends credence to scholarly claims that storytelling is an effective mechanism for youth empowerment, as it acts as a vessel through which youth can demand agency and claim ownership over their experiences.[36] As the remainder of this chapter demonstrates, participation in the TRC process afforded youth the space to claim ownership over their transitional justice experience, even in instances where their conflict stories reflected notions of deviance. Submissions by youth to TRCs, either in writing or at open or closed hearings, allow them the opportunity to speak for themselves, rather than having others speak for them. As such, deviant behaviors and displays of vulnerability take on new meaning, as they reflect the beliefs of youth rather than the beliefs of external agents that are then imposed on youth.

Significantly, a shift in the international discourse on youth was evident during this period, as the international community responded to the Youth Empowerment Strategy by institutionalizing their recommendations. Following the 2001 Youth Forum, the General Assembly in 2002 adopted a resolution on the "policies and programmes involving youth."[37] Through the language displayed in this resolution it is evident that the beliefs of international actors regarding the scope and nature of youth engagement shifted. This resolution denotes a shift in beliefs about the capacity of youth, from an acknowledgment that children have human rights that require protections through the CRC to a recognition that youth are diverse individual actors with the capacity to influence society if provided with the resources and space to do so. Indeed, the resolution made a commitment to "take into consideration the empowerment and full and effective participation of young people, and their role as a resource and as independent decision makers in all sectors of society."[38] This commitment by the international community was a significant departure from the language of protectionism, which had previously dominated the international discourse. Significantly, emerging beliefs about youth that classified them as decision makers and resources aligned with broader discursive understandings about the capacities of young people, which suggested that their abilities evolved as they transition through various life stages.[39] Also significant to these evolving capacities was the influence of the political and social environment in which youth existed and interacted with other stakeholders. Indeed, the resilience and adaptability of young people displayed during this time both internationally and in transitional states highlights their significant contributions to reconciliation processes, particularly those that associated sustainable peace and justice with development.

Youth and Substantive Participation at the Sierra Leone TRC

Representations of youth at the TRC of Sierra Leone highlight their capacity to engage and to participate substantively in reconciliation and the construction of a formal record of the conflict. This focus on youth engagement was due in part to the emphasis on progress and development in the broader reconciliation narrative. In Sierra Leone, the dominant institutional belief that informed interactions with youth was that they are "the lifeblood of the nation."[40] The emergence of this belief and framework for understanding youth's role in the conflict stemmed from their overwhelming presence as the society's largest demographic. Youth were also institutionally represented as "the driving force behind the resistance," a classification that denotes both substantive participation and the desire to facilitate change.[41] In this way, the representations of youth in Sierra Leone's final report suggest a broad community belief that youth provide a symbolic link to the country's future. To that end, this demonstrates that youth engagement, as well as acknowledgment of their reconciliation interests, are often inextricably tied to the future and progress of transitional states.

Representations of youth that portray them as a driving force and lifeblood suggest an underlying institutional recognition of the importance of youth to the broader restorative justice goal of sustainable peace through the restoration of relationships. This recognition, however, is complicated by the blurring of classificatory boundaries, which resulted from the transitional nature of childhood and youthhood. In the opening sections of the chapter on youth, the commission highlights the potential for definitional slippage, noting that "testimonies received . . . indicate that the majority of participants in the war were youths" but that "many of them were children at the time of their recruitment."[42] This fluidity creates complexity for how the experiences of young people are represented and addressed within institutionalized reconciliation processes, as it assumes some degree of evolutionary stasis and disconnectedness from the narratives. Youth are heterogenous agents within reconciliation whose agency is informed by and endowed with a particular political meaning *because* they were children of war. Yet the politics of reconciliation often includes a classificatory slippage in ways that promote narratives of young people as homogenous objects requiring international and domestic problematizing and project management.

The production of the reconciliation narrative in Sierra Leone reflected an attempt to produce an inclusive and holistic narrative. In this respect, the Sierra Leone TRC exposed a turning point in our understanding of the unique and distinct stories of youth in post-conflict contexts. The inclusive and representative process of the TRC demonstrated a shift toward greater recognition of the independence and capacity of youth to substantively participate in the reconciliation process of transitional states. Furthermore, the emphasis on empowerment, ownership, and agency in the reconciliation narrative also reflected a broader shift in the international language on youth. While the victim/perpetrator binary is still prominent in the institutionalized narrative, it is less pronounced, and thus space exists for the recognition and inclusion of a diverse range of stories.

Between the International and the Local: Navigating Reconciliation Narratives in Sierra Leone

During the twentieth century, the international dialogue on youth participation shifted to reflect a more nuanced understanding of who youth are, as well as the roles they occupy as political agents. Furthermore, in response to the heightened visibility of youth in the political space, most notably in peace and conflict, the international community sought to institutionalize a framework for their engagement. As previously mentioned, the increased practical engagement of youth in peace and conflict coincided with the broader focus on youth by the international community. This shift in the traditions of the international community was institutionalized in the adoption of the United Nations Resolution on the World Programme of Action for Youth to the Year 2000 and Beyond.[43] Among the ten priority areas identified in the resolution was a commitment to "the full and effective participation of youth in the life of society and in decision-making."[44] The resolution acknowledged the participation of youth in the design and development of policy as a crosscutting issue central to all priority areas. In addition, it identified the importance of youth to the future prosperity of society. It notes that "the capacity for progress [in] our societies is based, among other elements, on their capacity to incorporate the contribution and responsibility of youth in the building and designing of the future. In addition to their intellectual contribution and their ability to mobilize support, they bring unique perspectives that need to be taken into account."[45]

The importance of youth empowerment through engagement was also codified in a series of subsequent resolutions at the General Assembly during the mid 2000s. Specifically, these resolutions recognized the importance of facilitating "the empowerment of youth through building the capacity of young people to achieve greater independence, overcoming constraints to their participation, and providing them with opportunities to make decisions that affect their life and well-being."[46]

The emphasis on accountability and the voices and opinions of youth institutionalized in these resolutions is echoed in the beliefs and behaviors of actors, highlighted in the Sierra Leone TRC process. These resolutions reflected attempts by youth to control their stories and experiences, as they institutionalized the recommendations established at the Dakar youth forum. The belief that youth can and should control their own experiences was also evident in the Sierra Leone TRC report, which notes that "youth themselves must be integral to the planning and implementation of youth-orientated policies and programmes."[47] That is, the report acknowledges that the stories and ideas of youth are essential for their meaningful participation and for the creation of practices that directly represent their experiences.

In addition, the report also notes that "the construction of sustainable youth programmes can only be done through an authentic dialogue between youth and their elders."[48] One of the central conclusions of the report was that *listening* and *responding* to youth must be a key priority for the state as it finalized the reconciliation process. That is, the final report acknowledged that the substantive participation of youth and the direct inclusion of their stories in the institutionalized narrative provided an opportunity for youth to exert agency and ownership. This emphasis on "authentic dialogue" suggests that while hearing the stories of youth and their needs is essential, it is also necessary that transitional communities respond to these narratives through reactive and inclusive policy.

The Sierra Leone TRC process sought to legitimize the roles youth occupied during the conflict through dialogue and direct engagement. Following the conflict, the stories and experiences of youth were prioritized through creating "a separate youth ministry" and publishing the Sierra Leone National Youth Policy.[49] As the chapter on youth participation at the Sierra Leone TRC demonstrates, the priority of these practices was to "empower youths not only to make them responsible citizens but also as an investment in Sierra Leone's future."[50] Youth as such were cast in these narratives of policy development as political agents but also as development assets. For example, acknowledgment of their role as combatants resulted in their inclusion in the disarmament program being undertaken. This program focused on the future as it sought to ensure that the "more than 7,000 ex-combatants were placed in the formal education system at secondary, tertiary, and technical vocational levels. Some of these youths are already using their acquired skills to help rebuild their communities, thereby promoting the reconciliation and reintegration aspect of the programme."[51]

This dual representation as assets and as political agents, while important, is also potentially problematic because it casts youth agency as a product and symbol of a broader political agenda and thus denies youth ownership as independent actors. Moreover, the nature of these representations obscures current displays of agency and the unique contributions of youth that are informed by their status as youth. Empirical scholarship in the peacebuilding field has increasingly acknowledged the "youth as a resource" framework as central to our understanding of the roles of youth and their experiences in post-conflict practices.[52] This scholarship emphasizes the *potential* of youth as well as their future contributions to society. Focusing on their contributions to the future, however, creates a narrow and linear representation of youth. This focus on the future is further evident in the submissions to the public hearings. Indeed, as one participant noted, "I will say that youths are the leaders of tomorrow. Unnecessary provocation toward youth should be curtailed. Therefore, youth unemployment should be addressed. There should be a corridor or community area for youths to be gainfully employed."[53] This submission reflects a general trend that portrays the contributions of youth as future orientated and their present as a situation to be addressed by external agents, without consideration of the distinct voices of youth.

In addition, youth are portrayed in the final report as the central symbol of deviance and violence. Specifically, the report concludes that "the *potes* became rallying points for alienated unemployed youths and an arena for political discussion centered on the corrupt practices of the dominant political class and the stifling political atmosphere under one-party dictatorship."[54] Youth in this respect were a symbol of the political corruption occurring in Sierra Leone. Their position as "alienated unemployed youths" was used by the community to represent the degradation of society and the potential damage that sustained deviance and corruption could have on the future of society. This is significant because it denies their agency and ownership by casting their contributions as symbols rather than overt displays of independent capacity.

Submissions within the final report that used the victim/perpetrator binary classifications failed to represent or *see* the stories of their substantive and positive contributions as youth. This is evident in the final report, as the narratives that promote agency and empowerment are primarily concerned with their *potential* to actively contribute rather than their capacity and agency in the conflict and throughout the reconciliation process. The chapter on youth in the final report focuses predominately on the participation of youth in the present and on the restoration of "some of the benefits of youth" believed to have been lost due to their participation in the violence and instability.[55] Moreover, the report notes that the conflict had "entirely negative consequences on [youth] development" as it left "many youths . . . disillusioned and frustrated."[56] While the destructive nature of the conflict is undeniable, casting their experiences in only this way creates a one-dimensional and unconstructive portrait of their conflict stories. Moreover, these representations deny youth ownership over their participation in the conflict because they silence displays of agency and fail to consider the stories of youth who learned important lessons due to their participation in the conflict. Indeed, what these representations of the experiences of youth demonstrate is one side of the conflict story, rather than the complete, fluid, and often messy reality of the ways in which youth experience conflict.

Complicating notions of youth within the Sierra Leone TRC report are attempts to navigate culturally derived social status with clear demonstrations of political agency. Acknowledgment of this tension is clear in the final report, which explains that "in times of transition Sierra Leone's youth ha[ve] always struggl[ed] to find its rightful place in society."[57] TRC reporting notes that amongst the key barriers to young people's substantive participation was the practice of punishing those that spoke out against elders and chiefs. As one young activist explained, "Offenders were not allowed to speak in their own defense and became embittered at the exceedingly onerous punishments often imposed on them . . . for defying this custom."[58] Intergenerational tensions, such as those reflected in this quote, are a significant concern because if emboldened by the institutional process, they have the capacity to create a culture of silence and exclusion.

Reflections of these marginalizing conditions in Sierra Leone's TRC process paved the way for more meaningful inclusion, with the TRC's explicit focus on children and youth and its attempts to emphasize ownership and inclusive participation. Displays of advocacy by youth are prominent throughout the report and reflect attempts by young people to navigate and reconstruct the social and political landscape. Storytelling during the TRC process that revealed "the voices of youth that called for accountability," as well as stories that emphasized their voluntary participation "against the social and political ills of the day, or in the name of defending their communities," challenged the cultural stereotypes that had previously informed interactions with chiefs and elders. By sharing their stories and explaining their motivations to the commission, youth demonstrated their capacity as knowledge producers, lending further credence to calls for their substantive inclusion in political processes. In addition, recommendations supporting the development of a youth ministry and the National Youth Policy reflect a noticeable shift in the discourse in Sierra Leone of the political agency and capacity of youth. Discursive efforts to center youth's stories and reveal their advocacy reflect attempts by the Sierra Leone TRC to pursue the central tenants of restorative justice and reconciliation, namely the prioritizing of inclusive practices for meaningful accountability. The prominence of themes such as capacity, empowerment, and harnessing youth's potential throughout the final report lends credence to claims within the restorative justice literature, which contend that for reconciliation to occur the process must respond to the views and stories of those most impacted by the conflict.[59] Understanding the experiences of youth in times of transition, and how their stories are revealed within the mechanisms responsible for this process, is necessary to facilitate a socially embedded peace where stakeholders are connected to their community.

Although youth agency is a central narrative of the TRC, the report also highlights the institutional constraints associated with translating the stories of youth into meaningful participation. In particular, the report demonstrates that "convincing people that the youth question is now, more than ever, a national priority that demands national mobilization" remained a significant challenge for the broader reconciliation agenda.[60] The different beliefs of stakeholders about the role of youth and their status as political actors provided a barrier to the meaningful engagement and representation of youth in these contexts. Moreover, the chapter on youth highlights tension between the normative recognition that youth are political actors and the capacity of the state to meaningfully engage with this demographic in practice. It also demonstrates the challenges of integrating the needs and interests of youth into the formal institutional structures and practices of the post-conflict state. For example, the report concludes, "Although the youth question has been declared a priority in the [national youth] policy and the public speeches of government officials, it has been very difficult to translate such declarative emphasis into practical impact. This deficiency is symptomatic of the continued marginalization of youth."[61] While youth agency is acknowledged here and throughout the report, the dominant narrative of youth engagement in the chapter on youth is one characterized by missed opportunities. While their voices are prominent, the focus on deviance when representing their experiences produced narrow representative boundaries that restricted opportunities for meaningful reflection on the stories of youth that denote empowerment and ownership. As the report states, "Youth . . . wanted the [national youth] policy enacted into law" to compel the government to fulfill their commitment to facilitate and encourage their substantive participation in the rebuilding process.[62] That is, the beliefs and stories of youth emphasized the importance of their meaningful inclusion and the critical imperative of institutionalizing this commitment to substantive participation to ensure government accountability and transparency. In practice, however, what transpired was the "prioritization of youth at the abstract level, with few tangible benefits for youth themselves."[63] This was due in part to the commission's focus on producing a final report that reflected a "social truth" rather than a true representation of how a wide range of stakeholders experienced the conflict.

Indeed, the truth produced in the final report of the Sierra Leone TRC is the result of a range of stakeholders, including youth, debating and exchanging beliefs on the nature of the conflict. This exchange produced an institutional narrative where two seemingly competing representations of youth were represented. On the one hand, the final report produced a reconciliation narrative that used youth as a symbol by prioritizing the deviance framework in its representations. On the other hand, it also acknowledged the unique capacity of youth and thus a commitment to the restoration of interpersonal relationships through acknowledgment.

Balancing Stories of Agency with the Narratives of Deviance

The conflict in Sierra Leone is commonly described as a "crisis of youth."[64] While this representation is significant because it acknowledges their role as key participants in the rebellion, it is also highly problematic because it perpetuates narrow representations of youth. It nurtures an understanding of youth that is largely pejorative, emphasizing "deficien[cy] . . . delinquen[cy] . . . and dysfunction."[65] Despite the attention to their deviance, however, youth are often represented without significant agency. For example, Peters observes that external constructions of youth in Sierra Leone prioritized socioeconomic marginalization, which left youth vulnerable as they were perceived to be "a large reservoir to be tapped by those who wanted to cause mayhem and overthrow the government."[66] Absent from the literature on the representations of youth in Sierra Leone is a recognition of their capacity to act as independent political actors. Most importantly, there is a distinct lack of discussion on the firsthand reconciliation stories of youth, as well as an absence of any significant and meaningful discussion of how displays of agency and empowerment during the conflict and throughout the TRC process challenged this dominant language of deviance.

Broadly speaking, TRCs have been instrumental in facilitating the heightened engagement of youth in transitional justice practices. In the case of Sierra Leone, the TRC process specifically sought testimony from young people and acknowledged their status as legitimate beneficiaries of reparations in the recommendations.[67] Moreover, youth were considered key political actors from the planning phase, as the TRC commission named them as one of the twelve targeted research themes.[68] Indeed, the process acknowledged the agency of youth by highlighting their centrality to the conflict. Furthermore, by conducting public hearings on youth, which engaged directly with their testimony, the TRC process recognized the importance of their stories and their voices in the creation of an inclusive reconciliation process. Although the stories of youth were central to the TRC process, the final report at times relied on the beliefs of external agents, most notably political elites and the NGO community working in Sierra Leone, to construct the formal and institutionalized narrative. In doing so, the commission produced a conflict narrative that sought to balance the substantive participation and agency *of* youth with the popular normative assumptions *about* youth, most noticeably the deviance classification.

The representations of youth at the Sierra Leone TRC that were derived from the beliefs of external stakeholders in many respects perpetuated the common assumption that youth "are potentially dangerous subjects" and therefore a significant "problem" for the development of policy post conflict. As Goldstone observes, youth have been prominent actors in political violence since the English revolution.[69] Moreover, scholarship has conceptualized large youth cohorts in conflict in a negative way. This research suggests that a causal link exists between a high-density youth population and a state's "susceptibility to political violence and crime."[70] Amongst the most notable scholarship on this phenomenon are the youth bulge theory and the greed-grievance frameworks. For example, in Sierra Leone youth were identified in the final report as a misguided, lost generation who presented a significant challenge for the commission and the Sierra Leonean community.[71] What is more, the motivations for youth violence discussed in the final report, conceived and cast by the elites in Sierra Leone, attributed their participation to the "rebellious Freetown youth culture of '*rarray man dem*'" (the urban marginal).[72]

Indeed, the reliance on the deviance framework in the chapter on youth to represent their conflict stories prioritized a narrow understanding of youth and their capacity. For example, the commissioners concluded that "Sierra Leone's youth ha[ve] always struggled to find [their] rightful place in society . . . they all lost their youth to a career of fighting and violence."[73] The sentiment that they have lost their youth was further echoed in submissions to the TRC that represented their post-conflict status as "drifting without direction, unable to access education and employment."[74] In this submission, youth are cast as hopeless and aimless, two themes central to the deviance model. Moreover, the chapter emphasizes the "challenges created by misguided youth in the past," as well as the need to "restore youths as productive members of their communities."[75] Evident across all these representations is the rhetoric of vulnerability and helplessness. These depictions of youth have a significant impact on the way we understand the capacity of youth in reconciliation contexts.[76] By representing youth as lost, misguided, and drifting, the final report casts youth as passive subjects unable to control their circumstance or their stories. This is further reinforced by the idea that their place and position in the community needs to be restored, the implication being that this task falls to adults to facilitate.

Represented in these submissions are the beliefs of external agents. They reflect the dominant and emerging trends associated with representing the experiences of youth that emerged during the TRCs in South Africa, and to a lesser extent Peru. Indeed, many of these stories indicate the presence of a *life as told*, rather than a "life as lived."[77] In doing so, these stories perpetuate one-dimensional, linear representations of the "truth" *about* youth, rather than a holistic and fluid representation of the multiple truths that emerge when the firsthand accounts of youth are heard. While children are explicitly represented in TRC reports, conceived and cast as victims and contributors to the violence, youth are inexplicably absent from the institutionalized reconciliation narratives. Locating the stories of youth requires a close examination of the TRC process, the transcripts of the hearings and focus groups conducted by the commission, and the recommendations of the commissions. We need to look in the gaps between the external narratives *about* youth to find their complex and diverse stories. The chapter on youth in the final report of the Sierra Leone TRC demonstrates these tensions firsthand as it aimed to reflect what were at times competing and contradictory representations.

In submissions to the TRC, individuals identified "the existence of disenchanted youth" as a central cause of the conflict.[78] These representations straddle the normative line between the previous dominance of the deviance discourse and the emerging language of empowerment. For example, the report concludes that "in the common parlance of Sierra Leone at the time, 'thugs' came to mean youth who were utilized for political violence. The word 'youth' itself became a synonym for the unemployed young person who was vulnerable to manipulation."[79] An interesting dynamic is evident in this representation of youth. Namely, the passivity often associated with the victimology framework has been inextricably tied to the notion of deviance; the implication being that while young people can be perpetrators, this representation is ascribed to them by external structures, thus their participation in the public space represents an absence of agency. In this respect, the passivity and vulnerability usually associated with their role within the private sphere was also evident in their interactions in the public realm. Youth, while visible, were still unable to claim ownership of their own narrative. Similarly, the overarching question that the youth chapter addresses is how should "Sierra Leone face [the] daunting task of reclaiming a 'lost generation' of youth. The youth question is . . . central to lasting peace and development in the country."[80] This is further reinforced through the chapter's extensive discussion of the stories of those classified by the elites as thugs. As the report notes, "Thugs came to mean youths who were utilized for political violence. The word 'youth' itself became a synonym for the unemployed young person who was vulnerable to manipulation . . . they did the dirty work for politicians . . . the violence offered youths an outlet for acting out their machismo, which although loathed by society was encouraged by the political elites."[81] This submission used the deviance framework to represent the perceived immorality of elites and the interactions of youth with these individuals. Furthermore, the report notes that "most thugs were unceremoniously dumped after the completion of their violent assignments,"[82] which suggests an absence of agency on the part of youth regarding their participation in the conflict, as their engagement with rebel forces was subject to the will of the elites. In addition, the report states that "marginalized youth were known as *san san boys*. . . . Most of them never fulfilled their dreams of becoming wealthy. . . . Later they became easy prey as recruits for the purveyors of state and counter state violence."[83] Employing these cultural stereotypes to describe the role of youth in the conflict produced a collective narrative that emphasized their engagement as both dangerous and passive. The depictions of youth represented in these submissions reproduced normative stereotypes of youth as both victims and perpetrators. Indeed, the emphasis on the exploitive nature of youth, due to their vulnerability and deviance, reflected in the above submissions produced a narrative of the conflict that denied the agency of youth combatants. Throughout these representations the notion of deviance, created and manipulated by the institutions, remained a central theme.

In addition, while the report implies that young people's participation is a necessary condition for sustainable peace, their casting as a lost generation perpetuates the vulnerability and passivity stereotypes. The notion that youth are a problem for the Sierra Leonean community to overcome reflects the presence of a hierarchy of representation. Specifically, the implication in this statement is that those traditionally conceived as politically competent (namely adults) are required to manage the presence of youth in the public space.

In contrast to these representations of youth, the TRC also reflected the emerging trend in the international community toward the empowerment of youth. Throughout the chapter on youth, demonstrations of agency and political will are a key component of the stories told about their conflict experiences and capabilities. For example, the submission by the minister for youth and sports notes that "the student motto 'The self' implied the importance of self—esteem and dignity, the awareness of the right to liberate oneself and the right of the collective self to initiate liberation."[84] The report highlights that youth were motivated to participate in the conflict by the "simplistic rhetoric of the [RUF] movement," as well as the belief "that their involvement would help to reform 'the system' that had oppressed them for so long."[85] Agency and the distinctive recognition that youth were fighting for something are key themes of these submissions, which challenged the dominance of the deviance lens. Indeed, the general sentiment of the youth submissions was that they participated in the conflict as a way "to make Sierra Leone a better Sierra Leone."[86] To that end, youth demonstrated political will and empowerment, and this was reflected in their stated motivations for participating in the violence.

In 2002, the government created the Ministry for Youth and Sports, which was responsible for the production and publication of the Sierra Leone National Youth Policy. This policy aimed to harness the energy of youth for the future and to create "responsible citizens" of the demographic.[87] Given the visibility and agency displayed by youth at the TRC, as well as the attention given in the final report to their distinct conflict stories, it is evident that Sierra Leone represented a significant turning point in the patterns of behavior regarding youth participation in truth and reconciliation. Indeed, what is unique about the reconciliation narratives of youth in Sierra Leone is that there is a distinct separation between the external and internal representations of their experiences. The division of external and self-reflections allowed youth to exercise agency over their conflict narrative and to present their distinct voices to the broader Sierra Leone community. In doing so, youth constructed their own identities and took ownership of their conflict experiences, which as the submissions by youth to the National Vision Project demonstrated, were inextricably tied to development.

EMPOWERMENT AND OWNERSHIP THROUGH THE NATIONAL VISION PROJECT

The TRC of Sierra Leone had a mandate that was conducive to the consideration of youth and their unique interests. The mandate sought to develop a vision that would act as a road map for Sierra Leone's future. To that end, it sought the participation of a cross section of the community in the development of this vision by establishing a program for the creation of forward-looking policies and practices. The National Vision Project (NVP) provided "Sierra Leoneans of all ages and backgrounds" with the opportunity to "claim their own citizenship space in the new Sierra Leone and make their contributions to the country's cultural and national heritage."⁸⁸ While the NVP was not exclusively designed for the submissions of youth, many were able to carve out space within this program, which ensured that their voices were not only heard but also acknowledged by the government and the Sierra Leone community. Indeed, the winner of the written submission section produced a piece entitled "Youth Movement and People's Rights Contribution to the National Vision."

The focus on the future in the NVP presented an entry point for youth participation as it encouraged innovative and creative reflections of citizenship, governance, and sustainable peace. For example, amongst the submissions to the NVP was a working boat, painted in the national colors and named the "future boat." This boat was designed and built by two members of the youth community to reflect the potential and possibilities for youth. As the creators of the boat explained, "We built this boat as an inspiration to young people to develop themselves. This is to let the people of Sierra Leone know that they as carpenters can do something to develop Sierra Leone."⁸⁹ Here, the onus on development and growth is placed on youth themselves, and the imagery invoked reflects a belief in the capacity of youth to craft their future. In particular, the image of the carpenter is designed to encourage ownership amongst youth and to highlight the importance of their participation for the future of Sierra Leone. In addition, the imagery places youth at the center of development in Sierra Leone and emphasizes their participation as political agents.

These beliefs about the capacity of youth are reinforced in the chapter on the NVP in the final report, which observes that the "vision project encourage[d] individual Sierra Leoneans, especially the youth, to contribute to the dialogue entailed" in creating a mandate for the future.⁹⁰ The level of youth visibility in this project is also significant as it indicates a shift in the beliefs of external actors regarding the capacity of youth to positively contribute to the future of Sierra Leone. Moreover, the inclusion of youth submissions in the chapter on the NVP suggests that not only were youth heard, but political actors also made a commitment to respond to their stories and widely disseminate their contributions. To that end, the NVP projects represent displays of agency and meaningful engagement in the public reconciliation space that had not occurred during previous TRCs.

In addition, submissions to the NVP provide significant insight into the conflict stories of youth. One of the most striking submissions, for example, is a picture drawn by a young person in soft pastel colors that shows their interpretation of the reconciliation process. The communal nature of reconciliation is prominent in this drawing, as the two parts reinforce each other.[91] Furthermore, the belief that youth are central to the process of reconciliation is evident in this picture.

Similarly, the stamp designed by Mohamed Bockarie, a youth in his late twenties highlights the prominence of young people in celebrations of a "new Sierra Leone."[92] This self-reflection by a Sierra Leonean youth placed young people at the center of public action, further reinforcing empowerment and engagement. Thus the reframing of youth as political agents at the Sierra Leone TRC through the NVP reflects a turning point in the patterns of behavior with respect to young people and their reconciliation narratives. This is also evident in the submission below, which emphasizes the importance of a program for the targeted engagement of youth and highlights the relationship between youth, engagement, and peace. As one youth notes, participation in the "*Youth Reintegration Training and Education for Peace* [program] taught us to forgive since to fight with someone who has wronged you would lead to an endless war."[93] Yet Krijn Peters has observed that while the TRC was an important process for documenting the stories of victims, "Many ex-combatants held back in their accounts . . . [as] the culture of most rural protagonists strongly emphasized the importance of secrecy as an aspect of social cohesion."[94] That is, local reconciliation processes often preference silence over truthful, unrestrained testimony as a means of achieving peace within the community.

Harnessing the inherent ownership and agency that youth already possess is also a prominent theme of the recommendations in the final report. For example, the commission suggests to the government of Sierra Leone that a National Youth Commission be established to facilitate the "implementation of the Youth Policy, as well as the National Youth Plan," as it notes that the effectiveness of these programs would "address the specific" development and reconciliation issues facing youth.[95] Alongside this recommendation, the commission also acknowledges that the past "denial of a meaningful political voice" for youth "had devastating consequences for Sierra Leone."[96] In response, they recommend that "more avenues for the youth to express themselves and to realize their potential" be created.[97] That is, the commissioners advocate for the creation of a space that would facilitate the substantive and meaningful inclusion of youth in the social structures and institutions of Sierra Leone.

In addition, they suggest that "political space should be opened up so that the youth can become involved in governance and in the decision-making process. Youths must have a stake in governance."[98] What is significant about these recommendations is that they echo the sentiments institutionalized in both the Youth Empowerment Strategy and the World Program for Youth. Moreover, inherent in these recommendations are evolving notions of the importance of substantive participation. The TRC process and the recommendations of the Sierra Leone TRC reframe the conflict and reconciliation narratives of youth to prioritize demonstrations of agency. The inclusive and public forum empowered youth and provided an opportunity for them to demonstrate ownership and responsibility with respect to their roles in conflict. Indeed, the inclusive conditions that emerged in Sierra Leone reflect scholarly claims about the power of storytelling. This scholarship suggests that through storytelling youth can rebuild relationships and redefine their place within the community, as substantive participation in the reconciliation process not only allows youth to demonstrate agency and capacity, but it also highlights their political will and enthusiasm.[99]

Agency Exposed through Deviance and Exclusion

While the NVP represented the positive agency of youth, their stories also revealed agency in deviance. For example, the TRC report of Sierra Leone states, "As the conflict arrived, youths used brutality not to prop up the political elites, but to accumulate resources and power that had been denied to them previously, attacking the very foundations of the elites' society."[100] This sentiment was further echoed in the observation that "*Nijahungbia Ngornga* is a Mende phrase meaning unruly youth . . . they saw the rebellion as an opportunity to settle local scores and reverse the alienating rural social order in their favor."[101] As demonstrated earlier in the chapter, the deviance theme was a prominent belief displayed throughout submissions to the commission. Yet these submissions are different from those presented previously because the motivations of youth for participating in the conflict emphasize their agency and represent their engagement as an active choice. Specifically, they indicate that the youth in Sierra Leone claimed ownership over their behavior, rather than representing their experiences as solely a product of manipulation by the social and political elites.

In the submissions to the TRC, collective representation is also prominent and became a central part of the reconciliation narrative constructed by youth. For example, as one submission notes, "It must be realized that the young ones are not politically represented, it should be noted that the majority of the youth that took part in the war do not necessarily have any allegiance."[102] Despite their exclusion from post-conflict processes, including Disarmament Demobilization and Recruitment, the agency of youth is a prominent feature of the final report. The belief that it is possible to harness the energy of youth, as well as recognition of the potential negative implications of continuing to silence youth, resonate as dominant themes both throughout the submissions to the TRC and in the final report. Indeed, the report notes that "a huge number of these armed youths were not eligible to go through the disarmament process; they still remain largely untrained, unemployed, and idle. The option of youth organizations all over the country is therefore not surprising if the energies of these youths are not appropriately harnessed then we have a potentially dangerous situation."[103]

In addition, the signposting in the final report recognized that youth were collaborators in the conflict, thus assigning agency to their participation.[104] This representation of youth as collaborators was significant, as by casting youth as collaborators the institutional narrative of the conflict acknowledged their political agency and ownership over their role in the violence and instability. Moreover, as the report notes, "Youth were often the first residents to be sought out for information or local knowledge."[105] In this way, their agency and role as sites of knowledge was represented as a crucial part of their conflict story.[106] Taken together, these submissions and representations of youth as "sites of knowledge" denote agency and reflect an emerging belief that youth were politically engaged and empowered actors. Broadly speaking, structures and institutions that represent youth as sites of knowledge are central to our understanding of the visibility and agency of youth in reconciliation and transitional justice. These representations contend that socialization is mutually constitutive rather than a one-directional process. As such, young people's voices are integral—their experiences are not solely passively controlled by adults; they are also influential in informing how the process is constituted.[107] Representations of young people are responsive to the external environment as well as to their interactions with other stakeholders within the social and political structures of the transitional state. In the above submissions, youth are engaged in a fluid exchange of information about the conflict with the TRC, which provided youth with a space to claim ownership over their information. The case of youth representation in Sierra Leone, therefore, contributes to a growing body of empirical work that casts youth as knowledge disseminators and producers, rather than as simply receivers of information.

A significant development in beliefs about youth that emerged during the Sierra Leone TRC was the co-opting of traditionally marginalizing norms by youth. Throughout the final report deviant behaviors were used to reflect the agency of youth. Yet youth's reclaiming of the deviance narrative remained in constant tension with the appropriation of this narrative by the elites of Sierra Leone who utilized stories of their "mob" behavior to frame youth as potential spoilers. As one submission notes, "Youth not only formed 'mobs' to beat up and summarily execute civilians. They also identified suspected sympathizers or disclosed their hideouts."[108] Casting these stories through the deviance lens mitigated the agency and political will that Sierra Leonean youth were attempting to claim by testifying at the truth commission hearings about the crimes they committed and the roles they occupied in the conflict. Indeed, representations of deviance, when used by external agents in Sierra Leone, often obscured claims that youth engagement in the conflict was motivated by the belief that they were fighting for something.

Beliefs that youth were politically engaged and motivated are also represented throughout the chapter. The testimony in the chapter on youth demonstrates the positive potential of youth, the impact of their voices, and elements of social trust. These thematic classifications are meaningful as they inform our understanding of youth's role in the conflict. In particular, they indicate a shift in interpretations about youth within the reconciliation narratives of transitional states and denote a move toward the belief that youth are empowered political agents. Observations of agency are evidenced in Sierra Leone during this time, as youth increasingly occupied leadership roles that challenged the power and legitimacy of the current government.[109] This sentiment was further echoed through the belief that "when institutions and their leaders in so many sectors of society failed to speak out against the injustices of the APC regime, invariably it was the voice of youth that called for accountability."[110] When viewed through the youth agency lens, these submissions reveal the capacity of youth to influence the social structures and institutions within which they interact. This is significant, as it supports scholarly claims that youth engagement is meaningful when it is "transformative" and "shapes . . . social conditions."[111] That is, one of the indicators of youth agency is the recognition within institutional structures that the substantive participation of youth facilitated changes to the status quo.

As the analysis in this chapter demonstrates, shifts in the international discourse on youth empowerment brought about a pragmatic shift in the nature of externally constructed social representations of youth, which was evident at the Sierra Leone TRC. The nature of this shift, however, was not embedded into the broader discourse of transitional justice and reconciliation. Indeed, the case of Sierra Leone, while a significant turning point in the evolution of youth participation in reconciliation following conflict, was also an outlier with respect to the level of youth engagement supported and facilitated by the process. In addition, the TRC of Sierra Leone was also unique in its capacity to represent the voices of youth in a more meaningful and substantive way.

Chega! A Continuation of the Evolving Norm or the Maintenance of the Status Quo?

In contrast to the Sierra Leone TRC sits the TRC process in Timor-Leste. As demonstrated in the introduction, these two truth commissions ran almost parallel to each other and thus were informed by the same traditions, such as the evolving international discourse on youth. Despite this, representations of youth in the Timor-Leste final report are similar to those of South Africa and Peru discussed in chapter 3. For example, the chapter on children in *Chega!* ("No more, stop, enough"), the final report of Timor-Leste, as well as the scope of the investigation mandate, was informed by the CRC, which was ratified by Indonesia in 1990. To that end, the report is focused on telling the stories of children whose experiences could be classified as "violation[s] of the Rights of the Child" and on the protection of these children.[112] The TRC reporting prioritized the narratives of children who were forcibly recruited by the *Tenaga Bantuan Operasi* (TBO), "a civilian group formed by Indonesia to support its forces in Timor-Leste."[113] In doing so, the institutional narrative produced and disseminated by the commission provided a linear and one-dimensional account of the ways in which young people experienced the violence of instability associated with the conflict.

While the stories of children in Timor-Leste who experienced human rights violations are important, as the "physical, sexual, gendered and community rights violations [they experienced] . . . profoundly affected their lives," they are only one component of young people's conflict narrative.[114] That is, the focus on human rights violations presents a homogenous representation of young people as victims, which discounts the other roles occupied by young people as well as the different interpretations of how these human rights violations affected youth. The CRC framework when applied in TRCs has the potential to create narrow, exclusionary, and reactionary boundaries for the collecting and retelling of the stories of young people. This was evident in the case of Timor-Leste, as the chapter on children prioritized stories that reflected the belief that children were "physically vulnerable, more impressionable and more easily controlled than adults."[115] Inherent in this acknowledgment by the commission is the caretaker model, which casts all young people as passive subjects and recipients of peace by emphasizing welfare over autonomy and obstructing displays of agency by young people.[116] While the emphasis on paternalism in the caretaker model, which "represses children and embeds incompetence," has led to challenges to the model's legitimacy within the scholarly literature, its underlying characteristics continue to manifest in the beliefs and interactions of external stakeholders and in the institutional narratives of TRCs, including Timor-Leste.[117] Conceiving and casting young people predominantly through this lens has significant implications for their capacity to participate in post-conflict practices because it creates arbitrary parameters for their participation that are built on beliefs and assumptions rather than the actual capacity of the individual child or youth.

The persistence of the caretaker model, and representations of young people as victims, is also evident in the recommendations of the Timor-Leste TRC. Many of the recommendations for children and youth spoke of changes that needed to be implemented institutionally or by adults, and little space was given to the meaningful and substantive engagement of children and youth. For example, the TRC recommended that "the harmonising [of] Timor—Leste laws with the Convention on the Rights of the Child (CRC) is continued, [and] that adequate capacity is provided to institutions responsible for the implementation of the CRC."[118] In addition, the TRC suggested that "a public education campaign . . . be undertaken to educate parents, teachers, and the community about the effects of physical and emotional violence on children and to provide alternative forms of behavioral control and character development."[119] These recommendations cast children and youth as the subjects of reforms rather than active agents in the process, as they prioritized what the broader community needed to do *for* children over the direct and meaningful engagement of children and youth. Indeed, the themes of protectionism and responsibility, and the beliefs that young people are subjects and recipients of peace, are deeply entrenched in the recommendations of the Timor-Leste TRC. To that end, the dominant narrative throughout the Timor-Leste report is underpinned by the innocent victims model, which suggests that the evolving norm of youth empowerment emerging in the international system had yet to take hold throughout the transitional justice field. The one notable exception in the recommendations, which spoke directly to the inclusion of children and youth, was the suggestion that "adequate resources be allocated to the development of sporting infrastructure and management so that the potential of sport to contribute to community relations and the holistic development of youth, including equal access for girls and young women, is realised."[120]

This is an innovative and thoughtful approach to reconciliation and development; however, this recommendation placed the participation of youth on the fringes outside the political decision-making structures. In doing so, it created a transitional community where youth were visible, yet their voices were not heard or responded to. That is, the Timor-Leste TRC report reflected normative conceptions of young people that conceived them to be "apolitical, sheltered and separate from the political realm."[121] While their inclusion in sporting activities goes some way toward rebuilding their relationships within the community, without the meaningful inclusion of youth in the institutions that develop strategies for peace and development they are not truly afforded agency as political actors. The recommendations of the Timor-Leste TRC, therefore, perpetuated the normative model for understanding the role of young people that emerged in South Africa. This model conceived and cast the capacity of children and youth as universal, thus denying their "political consciousness" and relegating their "lived experiences" to the margins beyond institutions and their support.[122] In doing so, these representations challenged claims within the transitional justice field that TRC processes are inclusive and representative of a diverse range of voices. Indeed, the broader focus on political reconciliation in TRCs, which prioritizes community reconciliation over the restoration of interpersonal relationships, produces a framework for the development of conflict narratives that silence youth whose stories do not fit beliefs about how young people *should* experience conflict and participate in reconciliation.

In addition, the voices and beliefs of young people at the Timor-Leste TRC were marginalized by the prioritizing of external beliefs and actions of more powerful stakeholders within the TRC report. For example, the report notes that it was "the responsibility of all parties to fulfil their duty of care towards children" as they are "owed special protections under international legal principles."[123] This emphasis on the behavior and responsibility of adults in a chapter on the experiences of children denied young people ownership over their conflict stories and their post-conflict role because it framed their stories through an external lens. Moreover, when the voices of children are visible in the chapter on children, they are often recounting their stories through the actions and behaviors of adults. For example, as one participant observed, "They were always trying to persuade me. That is why I went with them. They brought me cakes, clothes, trousers. They didn't threaten me."[124] The emphasis of this story is not the young person's choice to participate in the conflict, but rather their susceptibility to persuasion and manipulations by adults. While the child's voice is visible, the story is employed by the report to emphasize their vulnerability, which leaves little room for the acknowledgment that the child may also have been displaying agency. In doing so, it prioritized the actions of the external agents over the child. This assessment is supported by D'Costa's observations of the TRC reporting process in Timor-Leste. She suggests that despite the commission's commitment to interviewing children, the report "does not clarify the extent to which these interactions . . . helped children to come to terms with their part."[125] Furthermore, she observed that the report does not address "what motivated children to come forward to share their stories in the hearings."[126] The reporting in Timor-Leste, as such, failed to consider comprehensively the *beliefs* of young people, instead emphasizing the traditions and beliefs of external actors and the international protectionist norms. The TRC report created a silencing amongst the youth demographic in Timor-Leste, which stemmed from its reliance on the rigid classificatory boundaries of the CRC when framing the narrative on children's experiences. As a result, the unique experiences of individuals over the age of eighteen were left out of the conflict narrative told through the TRC process or mischaracterized to fit the protectionist mandate associated with the CRC.

In addition, the conflict experiences of children in the report are cast through a collective lens, as the report notes forced recruitment as a significant factor in the militarization and polarization of society.[127] Children and their actions, as such, were cast as symbols of the society's social condition rather than as individuals with unique needs, interests, and experiences. This is also evident in the discussion contained in the report on the motivation for TBO's recruitment of children. For example, the report notes that "the special position of children in Timor Leste does not arise only from the universal acknowledgement of their unique status. It is also derived from the fact that children represent the future."[128] The report concludes that this belief about young people prompted "both sides . . . to cultivate loyalty to their cause among children from a young age."[129] The belief that young people represent the future denies individual agency and ownership because it cast the experiences of youth as homogenous. Moreover, employing the experiences of young people as a symbol for a country's potential ascribes a collective classification to children and youth, which imposes social expectations. Finally, these collective representations are problematic for the capacity of youth to claim agency over their experiences because they assume characteristics about individuals based on "historical practices, cultural norms, social attitudes, religious values, legal dictates or the needs of the society" rather than individual beliefs and self-reflections.[130] As was the case in South Africa, these symbolically constructed representations create notions about youth derived from external influences, including "domestic and international politics."[131] In doing so, they create conditions within transitional justice practices that allow children and youth to be seen, but that results in their fluid, lived experiences remaining unacknowledged.

Finally, as in South Africa, the experiences of youth were represented together with those of children. For example, the central question that guided the Timor-Leste TRC's investigation of young people was why children and youth were selected for participation as combatants.[132] In addition, the chapter on children also found that "the leadership of the Resistance recruited children and youth into the clandestine movement precisely because of the unique contribution they could make."[133] The consolidation of representations of children and youth also occurred in the recommendations of the commission. For example, the recommendations conclude that "special consideration is given to the situation of East Timorese children who have been disadvantaged educationally and in other ways because of their clandestine work and sacrifices as youth for the liberation of Timor-Leste."[134] The reliance on children and youth throughout the final report in Timor-Leste demonstrates the challenge associated with hearing and responding to the diverse experiences of young people at the institutional level. Moreover, the coupling of these terms denotes the embeddedness of homogenous classifications of young people within transitional justice practices. Indeed, like in South Africa and Peru, the final report employed the terms children and youth interchangeably when discussing the recruitment of young people as combatants to such an extent that it was often difficult to discern who these institutional narratives sought to represent.[135] This suggests that universal ideas about who young people are, discussed in chapter 3, remained rooted in the beliefs of the stakeholders responsible for the development of the Timor-Leste final report. As was the case in South Africa, youth were visible, yet their agency remained stymied by the institutional slippage that amalgamated the experiences of children and youth. Their distinct experiences and diverse and unique voices were universalized to present a pragmatic conflict narrative.

 Reflecting the complexity associated with representations of youth in transitional justice, the chapter on children in Timor-Leste on several occasions uses the term "youth" as the sole descriptor when recounting the narratives of young people. The use of this classification, however, was employed to discuss beliefs about deviance and social disruption, thus perpetuating the dominance of the victim/perpetrator binary. For example, according to one submission, "In the eyes of the Indo [sic] invaders, the youth appeared to be the most dangerous segment of society."[136] In addition, the report notes that "arrests followed the assault of an Indonesian soldier by East Timorese youths, the taunting of an Indonesian official at a junior high school, and the appearance of anti-Indonesian graffiti on the walls of the Externato School."[137] In the above quotes, which describe antisocial and spoiler behavior, the term "youth" is used separate from any descriptions of childhood. As such, the Timor-Leste TRC final report perpetuates the victim/perpetrator binary, which emerged as a distinct framework for understanding the engagement of young people at the South African TRC. Beliefs about youth as deviants are also inherent to the discussion of activism within the Timor-Leste chapter on children. For example, the report states that "public demonstrations, usually organised and attended by student and youth activists, began as a tactic to attract international attention. The activists used techniques such as throwing stones, asking Indonesians nearby 'When are you going home?' writing anti-integration graffiti or posting flyers and posters in public places."[138]

The emphasis on antisocial behavior in these institutional representations of activism highlights the continued resonance of the notion of deviance, particularly amongst the beliefs of external stakeholders. Yet also significant in the quote is the acknowledgment that "public demonstrations . . . [were] a tactic" used by youth activists. This recognition further highlights the complexity associated with representing youth in reconciliation during this period as it denotes a belief in the agency of youth, which is absent from the rest of the narrative presented in the Timor-Leste TRC report. Here, the actions of young people are represented as intentional and purposeful and challenge claims that young people are intrinsically dependent on others and thus cannot "speak in [their] own voice because there is no voice, which counts as [theirs]."[139] The above reflection on youth activism challenges the belief that youth voices should not be entitled to the same consideration as adults. While this recognition is significant, it is the exception rather than the norm in the institutional narrative disseminated by the Timor-Leste TRC.

Broadly speaking, the distinction between representations of young people at the TRC in Timor-Leste and in Sierra Leone exposed a dilemma within the reconciliation practices of the period. While the norms of youth empowerment and agency were evolving and solidifying within the international system, transitional justice practices struggled to balance new ideas about youth with the embedded norms of innocence and deviance.

Conclusion

Representations of youth at the Sierra Leone TRC denote a turning point in youth engagement within the reconciliation practices of transitional states. This chapter has demonstrated that a distinct evolution took place in the dialogue surrounding youth, which is most evident in the separation of youth and children in the reporting process of the

TRC. These developments in youth participation and representation are informed by an evolution in the beliefs of international and local stakeholders regarding youth empowerment and the scope of their participation. In the Sierra Leone TRC, and in the international dialogue on youth, the voices of youth are not only visible but also heard, as both the government of Sierra Leone and the international community legitimized their voices and agency by institutionalizing their interests and experiences in the final report.

While deviance is still prominent in the representations of youth presented by the Sierra Leone TRC report, agency and empowerment are also dominant themes in the narrative. Indeed, the stories of youth in the final report indicate that youth took ownership of the deviance narrative, despite attempts by elites to employ this classification to further their own political agendas and conflict narrative. This chapter has also suggested that TRCs that undertake local storytelling initiatives are better able to meaningfully engage with the distinct voices of youth and to represent their stories at the institutional level. The establishment of systems and structures that sought to harness the agency and creative energy of youth, such as the NVP, allowed for narratives of youth engagement at the TRC to emerge that challenged the normative frameworks of young people that have traditionally informed understandings of their experiences and engagement.

The case of the Sierra Leone TRC demonstrates that there is space within the formal narratives of TRCs for the firsthand beliefs of youth and representations of their agency. This finding has potential implications for future TRCs because it creates a starting point for the development of traditions around the interactions of youth with reconciliation practices. Moreover, this chapter has indicated that when a range of beliefs and traditions are accounted for in the institutionalized narratives of TRCs, they can provide an inclusive and holistic narrative that acknowledges the distinct voices of a broad cross section of the community.

Evolutions in the engagement of youth with TRCs, however, were far from becoming normalized traditions during this period, as the beliefs about youth agency appear not to have fully solidified within the normative reconciliation models. Indeed, this chapter also demonstrates that discursive frameworks, such as the victim/perpetrator binary, were deeply embedded in the institutional structures of reconciliation processes during the 1990s. This was evident in the Timor-Leste case, which perpetuated the models of representation for young people that emerged during the TRC process in South Africa.

Chapter 5

Seeing and Hearing Youth
The Solomon Islands Truth and Reconciliation Process

> It was not hard to get youth to talk but they benefited from the collective environment of focus groups when sharing their reconciliation stories.
>
> —Interview, Solomon Islands, Oct. 2015

Truth and Reconciliation Commissions (TRCs) have been instrumental in facilitating the heightened engagement of those traditionally excluded from retributive justice approaches.[1] By providing victims and the broader community with a forum for telling their stories, TRCs act as spaces where individuals claim ownership over their experiences and the way they are represented. As demonstrated in the above quote, the performative public spaces of the Solomon Islands TRC process created opportunities for peer solidarity, where shared experiences were enacted and publicly validated, lending legitimacy to the stories of Solomon Islander youth. Interviews with youth about their participation at the Solomon Islands TRC reflect a complex push and pull between ownership and appropriation with respect to how their stories were assigned meaning once institutionalized in the TRC report. Yet all echoed similar sentiments regarding how trust built and manifested through the shared experiences of contributing to TRC focus groups created more meaningful opportunities to be seen and heard, particularly amongst their peers.

Youth are unlike any other demographic, as the transitional nature of their identities makes capturing their experiences complex, particularly for the rigid, institutional structures of the TRC's reporting mandate. However, understanding how youth enact political will and agency in these contexts, as well as how it is resisted by these institutions, offers important lessons for the transitional justice field. Meaningfully inclusive institutional participation is necessary for the success of reconciliation practices. As demonstrated below and throughout this book the exclusion of young people's voices and the use of their stories solely to further a state's political agenda creates blind spots in transitional justice policy. As such, this chapter considers the relationship between youth, conflict, and reconciliation in the Solomon Islands to reveal the institutionalization of these exclusions but also to highlight how youth through their political will and agency are challenging the marginalizing participatory parameters often prescribed to their stories. It explores the diverse ways in which youth resist the victim/perpetrator binary that has come to define young people's engagement in transitional justice practice.

Like the reconciliation practices before it, the Solomon Islands TRC demonstrates the dominance of institutional slippages between children and youth when representing their role in the conflict. Displays of political agency by young people during the TRC process, however, reveal that substantive inclusion produces opportunities for diverse representations within the reporting mechanisms of reconciliation processes. Despite this, the chapter argues that a fundamental tension exists between the self-reflections of youth who participate in the process and the beliefs of other agents regarding the place of young people in post-conflict practices. This tension has implications for the legitimacy of reconciliation processes amongst young people and thus their willingness to buy into the process and its mandates. When youth are denied opportunities to be heard and to assert meaning and ownership over their own stories within formal institutions, inclusive reconciliation remains elusive.

Given the embedded nature of meaning, before examining young people's participation at the Solomon Islands TRC and their representation in the narratives produced by this process, this chapter considers the position of youth in the Solomon Islands more broadly. In doing so, it demonstrates the importance of acknowledging their status as political actors and their capacity to act as knowledge producers. While placing the participation of Solomon Islander youth in local and national context, the chapter also seeks to situate the firsthand voices of Solomon Islander youth within the evolution of conceptual debates about the contributions of reconciliation practices to the successful realization of transitional justice. Following this, the chapter surveys discourses on collective representations to reveal how the stories of youth in the Solomon Islands demonstrate the challenges associated with prioritizing socialized and politicized constructions of children and youth. Finally, the chapter turns to an examination of different representations and stories of young people in the Solomon Islands TRC context to reveal how this institutionalized process engaged with the political agency and human rights claims of youth.

Centering Stories: Hearing the Solomon Islander Youth of the Past and Today.

Stories (re)told throughout this chapter are constructed from three months fieldwork in the Solomon Islands, as well as a discourse analysis of the transcripts from the TRC (approximately one hundred firsthand testimonies), the final report, and multiple National Youth Policies. Fieldwork took place between September and November 2015 and included thirty semi-structured interviews with key stakeholders to the Solomon Islands TRC process (including those who self-identified as youth during the Tensions), ethnographic observation, and two focus groups with twelve youth peacebuilders (six who were youth during the Tensions and six who self-identified as youth during 2015 and participated in community programs set up as a result of the violence that occurred between 1998 and 2004). Capturing the voices of youth from the time of reconciliation and in 2015 allows for the construction of a narrative that is rich and fluid, thus acknowledging and reflecting the enduring legacies of youth participation during the Solomon Islands TRC process. In this way, the stories told, reconstructed from reflections of past and present interactions and experiences, provide important insights from diverse voices that are imbued with social, political, and cultural contextual meaning.

The narratives constructed and analyzed from this diverse and expansive data set demonstrate that the reconciliation narratives of youth in the Solomon Islands are more fluid and complex than their representations in the final report suggest. This disconnect between reporting and the actual stories indicates that the pursuit of meaningfully inclusive reconciliation requires that youth be enabled to lead and contribute to decision-making practices for reconciliation. By revealing and analyzing the formal narrative generated from youth's stories by the TRC, in the context of their own retellings and the political institutions that inform their participation in the community, we can better understand the conditions that enable and constrain the realization of reconciliation practices that are substantively inclusive of youth as political actors. Adopting an interpretive approach,[2] which prioritizes the construction of narratives using multiple data sources, this chapter sheds light on the different webs of meaning that inform our understandings inclusive and interpersonal reconciliation.

An examination of how meaning was ascribed and enacted during the Solomon Islands TRC process offers significant insights regarding the potential contributions of youth as political actors, distinct from children. More broadly, the analysis contained in this chapter, coupled with the preceding discussions of young people's participation and representation during other TRCs, provides an alternative theoretical framework that centers the contributions of youth voices for the realization of holistic and interpersonal peace, reconciliation, and justice, which could be applied to other groups and individuals traditionally marginalized by transitional justice processes. In doing so, the analysis central to this book challenges more technocratic and marginalizing notions of who participates in these institutional justice processes, how, and to what end.

Consultation or Attribution: To Speak For or Speak To

Young people's need for independence, community, and visibility underpinned calls for understanding their participation not just in violence but also in development. These opportunities for agency are revealed through the collective, public storytelling of reconciliation practices, which demonstrate the value of these forums in the pursuit of reconciliation *as* understanding. As one young person explained during the TRC hearings, "We should appreciate the youths' achievements in our communities. . . . Lots of times, youths come up with very good proposals . . . but we do not seem to appreciate their contributions."[3] Attention to the voices of youth also made visible the need "to recognize [them] as very special and unique in their talents and capabilities" while also highlighting the imperative to move beyond understanding to actions that empower youth as political agents. Throughout, the storytelling of youth calls for "skilled young people to balance [the Solomon Islands] growth and development were prominent" as was the recognition that it was "time for [youth] to voice out [their] concerns."[4] Collective, visible modes of storytelling as such are critical for the realization of youth's agency, as these sites empower them to recover, articulate, formulate, and claim their contributions in ways that establish their past, present, and future.

Furthermore, beyond the more prescriptive functions of formalized reconciliation these stories also demystify the experiences and contributions of young people. Through young people's storytelling, Solomon Islanders are shown the value of nurturing partnerships with youth for collective growth. Within the TRC report this is best reflected by the story of the papaw tree. As one young person explained, "A papaw tree, if it is planted on infertile land, *we* will not harvest it; but if *we* plant it on fertile land it will bear fruit over and over again when its replanted" (emphasis added).[5] When empowered to speak and be heard, youth tell stories that contribute to the fulfillment of reconciliation *as* understanding at the community level, an important first step toward overcoming tension between youth's self-reflections of their capacities and those ascribed to them by institutional narratives. Within the Solomon Island context, however, the failure to take seriously the meaning assigned to these stories by youth throughout the final report is illustrative of the complexities associated with ensuring substantive participation in institutionalized reconciliation processes.

Consultation processes for the establishment of TRCs, as well as hearings and focus group testimony, have at their core a commitment to healing through narrative, as "we all live for stories . . . without stories the stuff that happens would float around . . . and none of it would mean anything."[6] Where youth are concerned, the different layers of institutionalized storytelling associated with TRCs are integral to their substantive participation as they facilitate a continual process of engagement where youth navigate how their stories are received and translated. By speaking and through the construction of meaningful stories, youth challenge structural and social boundaries placed on their agency and subjecthood. With respect to subjecthood, this facilitates a (re)claiming of youth's autonomy over their choices and actions, while also revealing to the post-conflict community a "mastery" of their agency.[7] For example, within the story of the pawpaw tree, by invoking the collective through the use of "we" the participant is presenting a call to action for the Solomon Islands community to engage substantively with youth as subjects of political action and healing. In addition, by drawing on symbols from nature the story spoken and constructed by this young person highlights the potential productive and positive growth that comes from engaging with youth as substantive political agents.

At the same time, the Solomon Islands TRC process reveals the persistence of structural and social boundaries that restrict attempts to (re)claim subjecthood during the consultation process. These boundaries (including narrow classifications of who youth are and the roles their occupy) silence their autonomy by prioritizing a linear narrative of their conflict experiences and participation during peacebuilding and reconciliation in the institutionalized retelling of their experiences throughout the final report. During interviews in 2015 with Solomon Islanders who self-identified as youth during the Tensions and the TRC process, many reflected on the unevenness of the participatory process. While the organizers of the TRC went to great lengths during the consultation process to ensure political buy-in and support for the TRC bill from youth across the provinces, the report and hearing process demonstrated backsliding into exclusionary practices as "leaders were talking for them" and prioritizing a particular "type of youth" rather than prioritizing narrative constructions that would reflect the voices and concerns of youth represented in their stories, most notably "program and resource distribution" between the regional provinces and Honiara. Despite positive reflections by Solomon Islander youth that storytelling through the TRC could empower them and their peers to speak and be heard, the disconnect between how stories told by youth and those spoken about youth were received produced a deep mistrust in institutionalized reconciliation as a productive and enabling process. As such, amongst the Solomon Islander youth communities growing disinterest and a refusal to push for the TRC and its outcomes emerged and has persisted in the years following. Mistrust and disinterest were further compounded by the refusal of subsequent governments to table the report in parliament, meaning that the formal reconciliation process and its aims remain unrealized.

The focus group with current Solomon Islander youth revealed that while many had a basic knowledge of the Tensions and youth's participation in this conflict, none knew about the formal TRC process that took place. When asked during their focus group, only one had heard the term "truth commissions." Furthermore, they understood it as an abstract idea occurring in other places and holding no relevance to their current experiences of political participation. Similarly, during the focus group with those who were youth during the Tensions, all participants agreed that while the TRC process facilitated a forum for peer solidarity and visibility for their voices and stories, there remained a lack of clarity around its purpose for fulfilling their specific transitional justice needs, most notably their pursuit of more substantive political participation in the years following.

The common sentiment expressed during the focus group was that while their participation was expected by the "big men" in their community, the reconciliation process wasn't for or about them; it was a tool to "show the international community the Government was serious" rather than about genuine commitment to their needs.[8] Likewise, amongst those who were youth during the Tensions, many expressed frustrations at how the focus on reconciliation had stolen focus from development and jobs. Many reflected that by prioritizing the formal TRC, the government and international community had created a divide between those in the provinces and those in urban Honiara where the violence of the Tensions was most prominent. As one youth explained, "We have a voice, we have ideas . . . but [the ideas] are about moving forward and all the TRC did was ask us to look backward . . . and for what?"[9] Perceptions amongst Solomon Islander youth that the TRC was solely about looking backward without a sense of purpose or representation has produced deeply embedded frustration, as many sought opportunities, change, and genuine political engagement from government representatives that never eventuated.

Frustrations about representation revealed during interviews and focus groups in 2015 were echoed in the TRC testimony, as one youth highlighted the tenuous relationship between youth and those seeking government office. Specifically they noted, "During your campaigns, you promised lots of things to us and we accepted your promises and voted for you. When you got Parliament, you forgot about us. We are the resources of Solomon Islands. I appeal to you to play your role in assisting the youth."[10] Realizing the reconciliation mandates of TRCs requires attention to how stories are told *and* received by those most impacted. Youth in particular "face and create unique reconciliation challenges" for these institutionalized transitional justice mechanisms.[11] Structural and cultural barriers, alongside misaligned expectations, create conditions where "post-conflict programmes fail to incorporate youth appropriate stance[s] during transitional justice."[12] In addition, as indicated above, the incorporation of youth as political storytellers enables opportunities for them to "subvert macro-level responses for reconciliation" in ways that compel post-conflict communities to take seriously their agency and subjecthood.[13] As such, formalized practices that empower meaningful storytelling, as well as listening and substantive responses, are central to the realization of youth's post-conflict needs both immediately after conflict and for future generations.

Across both focus groups, self-awareness of the capabilities of youth and the importance of collective storytelling for revealing these capacities emerged as a central theme of the discussion. However, the majority were reluctant to attribute any substantive impact to the visibility of their voices and stories. Solomon Islander youth during the Tensions, the TRC, and today share a profound commitment to their voices (collectively and as individuals), and they share the capacity of storytelling to demonstrate agency and challenge claims to their subjecthood. Yet these youth are also deeply aware of the limitations of voice and narrative, particularly with respect to its capacity to facilitate more meaningful institutionalized political participation by youth. The complexities revealed in the participatory processes and responses from youth reflect the conceptual nuances and challenges of institutionalized reconciliation and political participation for youth more broadly. While reconciliation processes attempt to shatter the "conspiracy of silence" arising from the harms experienced by individuals whose stories exist on the margins, the meaning attributed to these stories, and how they are appropriated by those with institutional power, often determines whether these individuals are truly seen and heard and how their contributions are valued.[14]

Reconciliation practices have the potential to expose the narratives of the traditionally silenced and thus create a more holistic and inclusive representation of the conflict if they meet individuals where they are and respect the self-attributed meanings of their stories. In these instances, TRC processes are a participatory platform for traditionally excluded individuals, such as youth, to exert ownership and claim agency and citizenship through the telling of stories and participation in the development and implementation of the TRC. Simply put, the Solomon Islands case demonstrates the challenges *and* the opportunities that arise when institutionalized reconciliation practices such as TRCs pursue a youth-inclusive approach. Representing the voices of this complex and diverse group of actors requires more than an "add and stir" approach. To truly represent their experiences, a ceding of power is needed to enable interactions with youth where their stories can exist free from political influence or appropriation. When meaning is assigned to tales of participation it should be self-directed and owned by youth rather than assigned or co-opted. Participatory processes that empower youth to tell their own stories and that hear and take seriously the self-ascribed significance of these narratives are critical to the realization of sustained, interpersonal reconciliation where the most marginalized members of the community perceive that justice as acknowledgment has been fulfilled.

Situating Solomon Islander Youth in Broader Reconciliation Debates

Advocates of TRCs contend that "revealing is healing" as it legitimates the stories of those involved in the conflict, most importantly the victims, and creates a formalized narrative of events.[15] They suggest that "the truth-finding dimension that accompanies and results from the telling . . . is empowering, dignifying and healing."[16] For proponents, the telling and reporting of truths exposes and legitimizes not only the voices of victims but the motivations of combatants, as well as the social, cultural, and political implications of violence and instability. TRCs as the primary mechanisms for these stories have the capacity to provide public acknowledgment of community experiences. Yet as the cases discussed in this book thus far demonstrate, and is further reinforced by the stories of Solomon Islander youth, the capacity to acknowledge does not exist is a vacuum and thus is often complicated by the contentious relationships that transitional states have with their citizens, particularly those whose marginalization is perpetuated or exacerbated during conflict, such as youth. As participants in both focus groups explained, the divide between generations in the Solomon Islands revealed during the reconciliation process remains in 2015. Participants note that this disconnect between generations is a challenge to the political agency youth possess today as it sustains historical "pervasive," "limiting," and "dismissive" perceptions of their capacity for ownership and leadership. Participants overwhelmingly concluded that rhetoric, which cast youth as "leaders for tomorrow," was "damaging" and "exclusionary" as it limited opportunities for their voices and ideas to be heard. Consistent amongst the interviews and focus groups was also the belief that this future rhetoric is largely "lip service" because despite talk of youth's importance, successive governments have been unwilling to implement youth programs or to take the time to understand their interests. When asked directly if political representatives "understood their reconciliation interests" and "motivations to participate in politics and reconciliation practices," most participants either laughed or sighed, demonstrating a frustration with those in power.

Ownership, recognition, and representation are essential elements for achieving inclusive reconciliation. The measure of a successful TRC process therefore is not solely its capacity to acknowledge the voices of those most affected but also its contribution to representing the self-identified, meaning traditionally marginalized individuals such as youth attribute to narratives about their conflict participation.[17] To that end, while TRCs have the potential to restore human dignity, reframe relationships, give a voice to the needs and interests of the most marginalized, and impact the realization of transitional justice, their capacity to empower youth participation must be considered in the context of the political on-the-ground realities where the TRC is embedded.

Opponents' claims, however, which challenge the capacity of TRCs to provide widespread reconciliation in the context of youth participation, also warrant further critical engagement. In particular, critiques that the public processes, which TRCs rely on, such as open forums retraumatize victims, when assessed through a youth agency lens reveals an important counter narrative.[18] As the stories from youth in the Solomon Islands demonstrate, however, openness is critical for the transparency and legitimacy of the process because it ensures that stories are told in ways that reflect the character of the contribution and its reflexive meaning. Among the youth interviewed there was broad agreement that substantive public participation requires that "their stories are visible and heard through their voices," which is the only way they can be truly empowered to problem solve and engage politically. In addition, these interviews revealed that the collective nature of these processes for youth created space for healing rather than retraumatization by fostering peer solidarity, trust, community, and a place where they could lean on each other. Reconciliation processes have an ethical duty of care to ensure that they do not further contribute to harm, yet as the stories of Solomon Islander youth demonstrate it is critical that these processes also consider how that duty extends to minimizing exclusion practices that can exacerbate harms, particularly for individuals who play central roles in the conflict, such as youth.

Critics also contend that victims and the broader community often feel "disappointment and anguish" when they perceive "that perpetrators appear to get off scot-free."[19] They argue that transitional communities feel a sense of "unfinished business" when governments do not fulfill their reporting obligations or implement the commission's recommendations.[20] For Solomon Islander youth "the one Solomon Islands unity strategy" that dominated the TRC discourse created frustration and disappointment because "while unity was important for bringing the country together, they needed to look first at their own Provinces, and what resources were being provided there, not just in Honiara." In addition, balancing the need for justice and healing with engagement was a key concern for youth, which is reflected in their concerns about "how amnesties would work" during the consultation process establishing the TRC bill. As one youth leader explained, "Many wanted justice and resources to rebuild," particularly education, and viewed "participation in the TRC" as an entry point to this, but "they were also concerned for their peers who fought and did not want to testify." As such, efforts to balance the politics of reconciliation with substantive participation for young people highlight the importance of not only hearing and taking seriously their needs but also prioritizing an enabling environment for reconciliation processes where all youth stories are visible.

The cases in this book demonstrate sentiments of unfinished business; amongst the youth demographics. Although they manifest in different ways, all reflect the challenges of traditionally marginalized individuals, such as those youth face in their pursuit for accurate representation in the institutionalized narratives of conflict. The politics of TRCs, which constrain a state's capacity to follow through on recommendations, or as was the case in the Solomon Islands to officially table and release the report, also produce narrow politically derived "truths" and reproduce stories that often fail to speak directly to the experiences of those they seek to include. Given this, the following discussion considers the barriers to producing a responsive institutionalized narrative of young people's conflict participation where they are both visible and heard. It explores the ongoing tension that informed how youth's stories were told within the final report of the Solomon Islands TRC and considers the role of youth advocates in challenging these reflections. Historical beliefs and traditions about young people's role in the Solomon Islands community have an enduring legacy that permeated and informed the construction of the youth narrative in the dedicated chapter of the final report.

As transcripts of the TRC hearings demonstrate and interviews and focus groups with youth reinforce, when young people are given space to tell their own stories, in their words, the narrative of their participation reflects a more diverse and nuanced tapestry of conflict and reconciliation experiences. Creating enabling reconciliation environments that support and nurture this representative complexity is crucial to the realization of holistic and inclusive justice that is underpinned by productive interpersonal relationships. Institutional processes silence youth's distinctive voices and mediate the boundaries of their participation to maintain the politicized status quo, regardless of the effects on the reconciliation agenda and thus sustainable peace. Barriers and opportunities exogenous and endogenous to the Solomon Islands informed how youth participated in the TRC. Furthermore, the contributions of Solomon Islanders to the realization of inclusive reconciliation agendas for local and international communities are not siloed; instead they exist on an evolutionary spectrum that is defined by slippages and turning points.

How Have We Gotten Here? Turning Points in Youth Participation

Young people's political participation in transitional justice environments is steeped in historical, discursive, and cultural complexity. At the same time, persistent representations of young people as fixed, homogenous, or binary identities in the institutional reporting processes of TRCs means there are limited opportunities to make visible the ambiguities of this participation or to take seriously its implications on sustainable and inclusive reconciliation. Instead, these representations reveal a disconnect between truth and the politics that underpin how meaning is ascribed and enacted when stories don't align to fulfill the political agendas of those with power and influence. These institutionalized narratives reflect what Jana Tabak describes as a "muting" of the "messy, ambiguous, and sometimes paradoxical experiences" of young people (whether child, adolescent or youth)."[21] By institutionalizing these linear constructions these international discourses legitimize artificial boundaries that distinguish the normal child from the soldier. Extending this understanding to the reconciliation context, the singular narrative about young people that TRCs prioritize in their (re)telling of youth experiences produces discursive boundaries that disregard completely the fluidity between child, adolescent, and youth. This presents challenges for how we understand youth's capacity for political participation, as it often results in a conflation of narratives about their experiences along simplified participatory and agential boundaries. Institutionalized (re) tellings made visible through TRC transcripts often reflect politicized, externally constructed beliefs about who young people are or need to be to fulfill the positive potential of the transitional community rather than the on-the-ground realities. Starkly, the relegation of these ideas to the annex of the Solomon Islands TRC report, instead of the main report alongside the chapter on children, reflects the complexities associated with making visible the messiness of diverse experiences within institutionalized reconciliation.

Youth's reflections on how the government interacts with them in contrast to their own ideas about their situatedness reveals a paradox regarding the external construction of young people's participation. As one young person explains in their submission to the TRC, "When we talk about youths, I see [them] in three types: (1) school leavers; (2) church youths; (3) street youths," thus revealing an important relationship between youth's self-constructions of their identities, everyday experiences, and sense of place within the community.[22] He continues, "The Government concentrates more to assist youths who join up with sports clubs but it do[es] not pay attention to the church and street youth."[23] The contrasts revealed here indicate that the government's engagement with Solomon Islander youth was limited to a socially constructed "ideal" type; one informed by beliefs about how they *should* participate in community, rather than the diverse realities of their everyday interactions. Despite this, youth's own stories at the TRC hearings revealed that "in every community or village and in urban areas you can find young people . . . engaged in schools, employment; running a formal or informal business or hav[ing] no job opportunity."[24]

One of the key evolutions regarding youth's political participation revealed through an examination of firsthand stories from the Solomon Islands TRC is the value of youth voices in framing narratives of their agency and subjecthood post conflict. When youth's voices are heard and taken seriously, potential empowerment opportunities emerge from the messiness of seeing youth and their hard-fought efforts to challenge perceptions of who they are or are destined to be within the post-conflict community. Substantive participation for youth in transitional justice contexts, particularly in formal processes like TRCs, is informed by a constant series of push-and-pull factors, most notably identity constructs, political agendas, and the everyday hierarchies of community, which align advanced age with power and respect. Thus, tangible reconciliation efforts are often stymied by narrow, externally derived discursive constructions that inform the tenor of the relationship between governments and members of the community.

Where Solomon Islander youth are concerned, external discursive constructions, coupled with "state thinness," produce programmatic challenges and implementation gaps.[25] As such, to understand the participation of Solomon Islander youth in the Tensions and their subsequent motivations to be "heard" by the TRC it is useful to briefly reflect on the historical relationship youth have had with the state. Institutional youth policies in the Solomon Islands have a long legacy of unfulfilled potential, with the imperative of consultation and policy development "becom[ing] ends unto themselves."[26] Although the Tensions stalled government efforts to empower youth's political participation through inclusive policies, deeply embedded, exclusionary perceptions of youth's political role preceded the outbreak of violence and persisted during multiple attempts to pursue transitional justice. The 2010 Youth Policy demonstrated this shallow relationship with the state, revealing that youth were a "low priority for governments" from 2000 to 2008, resulting in no institutional ownership of or for youth programming.[27] Similar concerns about government indifference to the realization of an enabling environment were raised again in the 2017 National Youth Policy, which notes that political will for the implementation of programs to empower youth's civic participation was "found wanting."[28] As such, the promise of government-supported youth programs to facilitate youth's substantive participation has remained largely unrealized.[29] The youth-state relationship in the Solomon Islands, both with respect to youth's participation in transitional justice and more broadly, reflects broader complexities with respect to the meaningful participation of youth with political processes, such as TRCs. Increasingly within formal reconciliation contexts youth pursue claims of ownership over their stories while also competing with and contesting external framings of their experiences that further political agendas and maintain the status quo.

Within the Solomon Islands context, for example, the government's reliance on a linear construction of the ideal youth acts as a primary push factor to their continued marginalization and the institutionalized denial of their subjecthood. Insights from youth participants at the TRC concerning how the government invests in youth programs are illustrative of this, as well as youth's frustration with how their experiences are constructed. As one youth explained, "When submissions came through the Ministry, where is the assistance given by governments to the church youths to assist in their programs? There is nothing. [However] whenever we talk about sports . . . the Government spent millions of dollars."[30] Similar concerns were echoed by the youth interviewed in 2015, who when asked to reflect on how the government invested in their diverse political and social participation following the TRC noted that governments' claims about the importance of investing in youth programming were shallow, empty, and largely unfulfilled in practice.[31] They highlighted, in contrast, the role NGOs and programs such as Youth@Work played in ensuring their diverse contributions and political participation. Broad consensus existed across the interviewees and focus groups that Youth@Work in particular was instrumental in helping them challenge the simplistic participatory boundaries constructed and perpetuated by the government's prioritizing of an ideal youth. As one youth interviewee explained, "By giving young people a place to go to sell their products and demonstrate their skills," Youth@Work enabled youth to interact with and learn from the community in diverse and sometimes "surprising" ways.[32] Thus, through visibility and engagement youth were afforded opportunities to challenge old-worn perceptions of who they are and their capacity to substantively participate in the political community.

Persistent external representations that sustain the victim/perpetrator binary deny youth ownership over their conflict stories. In addition, the paradox they produce within post-conflict communities such as the Solomon Islands, impact efforts to restore trust and rebuild the interpersonal relationships that are central to the maintenance of sustainable peace. As such, the characterizations of young people's participation found in the final reports, which are not freely chosen or spoken, serve the perceived interests of the state, the commissioners, and the international community. By defining the roles and identities of young people solely through the politicized reconciliation lens, these practices reinforce a "vision[ing] and di-vision[ing]" of their experiences, reproducing conditions of marginalization and exclusion typically associated with retributive forms of transitional justice. While youth participation in TRCs has evolved since the South African TRC, the character of this engagement often continues to reinforce artificial boundaries. Discursive representations of youth's participation in TRC contexts indicate turning points or "deflections in a long-term pathway" of meaning construction, and once revealed they are consistently reproduced and enacted in future TRC dialogues.[33] These turning points, however, are also sites of contestation, as while the diversity of the discourse is permanently altered by increased recognition of youth's voices and capacity to claim their agency, the old binary discourses persist and are reproduced, particularly within the institutional narratives of the TRC final reports.

The emerging plurality associated with these turning points and the subsequent tension that it creates highlight the embedded political nature of stories and participation for young people in these contexts. Notably, the discursive slippage between child, adolescent, and youth, coupled with the conscious evoking of narrow binary representations, highlights the role of "differential operations of power" that inform how young people's agency and participation is understood during reconciliation. A tension inevitably emerges between external representations of youth's conflict stories and self-reflections of youth's subjecthood and experiences, which reveals the turning points but also the structural factors that push back against these discursive evolutions and their enactment and institutional embeddedness.

It was not until the Sierra Leone TRC that the firsthand narratives of youth became an institutional focus for reconciliation practices. The Solomon Islands case marks the next turning point in the narrative of youth representation, as it is during this TRC that we see the contributions of youth to the process of reconciliation. The story of youth representation in reconciliation narratives is a complex one of incremental progress and frequent backsliding. Although multiple TRCs have sought to acknowledge their narratives, few have done so in a meaningful way that encouraged substantive participation. While TRCs in Peru, South Africa, and Timor-Leste have considered the implication of conflict on children by including chapters on their experiences in the final reports, the distinct stories of youth have not been afforded the same consideration within the reconciliation process. Furthermore, while children are acknowledged as legitimate beneficiaries of reparations, in the recommendations there is no separate mention of the divergent needs of youth as a distinct demographic.[34] In each of these cases, normative perceptions of youth persist, as they have been considered only as children or cast as the perpetrators of heinous crimes. That is, their experiences have been represented and their stories told through a discursive lens that prioritizes the victim/perpetrator binary.

The Solomon Islands case represents a significant yet complex departure from this binary. While this dichotomy remains a central part of the reconciliation narrative about youth, it is merely one thread in a tapestry of stories. Indeed, the Solomon Islands case highlights the capacity of youth to challenge inaccurate assumptions about their experiences through engagement. Through substantive participation in the TRC process at all stages, youth were able to reframe their relationship with the broader Solomon Islands community despite the persistence of the victim/perpetrator binary at the institutional level. Solomon Islander youth demonstrated that the victim/perpetrator framework reflected only a small part of their conflict story. Their participation suggests that when the victim/perpetrator binary is used as the sole representation of youth it often fails to accurately embody their experiences or hear their voices.

Indeed, the Solomon Islands case reveals a tension between the stories *about* youth and the stories *by* youth. While previous TRCs have produced narratives where it is difficult to distinguish between the different interpretations of youth, in the Solomon Islands the divergent narratives are more pronounced. While the institutional narrative excluded representations of youth, which were multifaceted and unique, the interactions of youth with the TRC process ensured that the complex relationships between youth, justice, and reconciliation, as well as the contributions made by youth to post-conflict justice processes, are knowable. Furthermore, although the final report's chapter on children failed to recognize that the interests and experiences of youth often diverge significantly from those of children, preferring instead to conceive their identities as being inextricably connected, the process highlights their contributions as engaged political agents.

Youth in the Solomon Islands

The National Youth Policy of the Solomon Islands 2010–2015 represents the Solomon Islands as "a youthful nation . . . that demands action." Moreover, it explicitly acknowledges the capacity of youth to act as political actors.³⁵ Where reconciliation practices are concerned, the voices of Solomon Islander youth are essential for the development of an inclusive and holistic record of the conflict, as at that time youth comprised 32 percent of the population. Indeed, the 1999 census, which was conducted a year into the Tensions, found that 131,231 Solomon Islanders were between the ages of fourteen and twenty-nine years old.³⁶ To that end, youth were stakeholders with a unique investment in the production of a reconciliation narrative that accurately portrayed their experiences. That is, following the Tensions they were a demographic whose stories were an essential part of the national conversation regarding reconciliation.

Since the 1980s, the Solomon Islands government has sought to develop a series of policies and programs to encourage the meaningful participation of youth. Over time, these policies have come to inform the nature of youth representation, as well as youth engagement with the broader political structures. Indeed, the formation of both the National Youth Development Plan and National Youth Congress have been key focal points of the development agenda of the Solomon Islands.³⁷ Alongside the current National Youth Policy sits a series of provincial policies that aim to reveal the wide-ranging needs and experiences of youth across the Solomon Islands. These provincially targeted policies acknowledge the unique and diverse interest of the youth demographic and seek to capture their distinct voices through the creation of focused and responsive policy goals and objectives. For example, while the National Youth Policy focuses on macro issues, such as "career pathways . . . governance . . . wellbeing and development"; the policies of the Central Island and Guadalcanal prioritize specific community challenges, such as "youth enterprises . . . young parents . . . [and] sex workers in the Central Islands; and 'communication and music' in Guadalcanal."³⁸ Thus, the provincial youth strategy areas are targeted to the unique interests of the local community.

The engagement of young people in the development agenda of the Solomon Islands is indicative of a trend in post-conflict communities. For example, as Jeff Helsing et al. observe about the peace activism in Bosnia, "Getting politicians . . . to view youth development as an integral element of reconstructions, rehabilitation, and reconciliation" is essential for ensuring that their capacity and agency is represented.³⁹ In the Solomon Islands context, the 2010–2015 youth policies reflected the government's renewed commitment to youth engagement, which was stymied by the violence and instability associated with the Tensions.

Indeed, the final report of the TRC directly attributed the government's failure to implement the 2000 National Youth Policy to the instability brought about by the Tensions.[40]

The voices and agency of youth are a central concern of the Solomon Islands institutions. This is reflected in a mandate of the renewed National Youth Policy, as one of the cornerstones of the policy is "helping youths to help themselves."[41] Here, the emphasis on assisting and supporting youth acknowledges their capacity and political will to act when given the proper resources. The underlying normative claim evident here is that youth are "developing assets" and "resources that can be cultivated" to facilitate change and development.[42] Scholars such as McEvoy-Levy have observed that this form of youth representation recognizes "the *potential* that youth have to steward the growth and stability of their countries."[43] This lens is also significant because it takes into account the stake that youth have in development and reconciliation agendas of post-conflict states due to their status as future political leaders. In the Solomon Islands context, the strategic plan aims to provide youth, and those that work closely with them, with "a path to maximize the collective results of their individual actions."[44] In doing so, it places the needs and behaviors of youth at the center of planning and implementation projects for youth. In addition, it aims to act on a commitment to *hear* and *act* on their capacity.

Among the priorities of the youth policy was a commitment to increase the "number of young people participating in activities that promote peace building and conflict prevention."[45] That is, it recognizes the importance of youth and their voices to ensuring sustainable peace and development. This policy outcome seeks to meaningfully engage youth "at all levels" in decision-making and program development. Furthermore, it acknowledges that "addressing the challenges" that youth face requires "activities that will do more than just skills training and helping youth to do things."[46] Embedded in the peacebuilding outcomes of the Solomon Islands is the recognition that youth are political agents. This institutionalized commitment to engage with youth in the decision-making process supports emerging claims in the scholarship that "youth have the capability to effect change independent of outside actors."[47] In Mozambique, Kosovo, and the Democratic Republic of Congo scholars have observed that acknowledging the agency of youth exposes the "complex reality where victim and perpetrator are often blurred."[48] Applying a youth agency lens to the challenges faced by youth post conflict, therefore, allows us to better understand and represent their needs, interests, and experiences. The voices of youth have historically received institutional consideration in the Solomon Islands, and as such the government was perfectly positioned to recognize the potential value of youth engagement in the reconciliation process. Far more surprising, however, is the absence of diverse representation within the institutional narrative.

Youth agency and substantive participation are evident in the mandate of the Solomon Islands TRC and throughout the recommendations of the final report. Specifically, the inclusion of youth as thematic stakeholders—alongside women, ex-combatants and, children—fulfills the broader reconciliation agenda of inclusion and acknowledgment and thus aims to elicit a more accurate representation of their experiences. Indeed, as Quinn observes, "Acknowledgement is responsible for the creation of the bonds of social capital and social trust."[49] To that end, recognizing the needs and interests of these individuals, and providing opportunities for substantive participation, facilitates a more inclusive reconciliation process.

Although the chapter on children failed to hear youth, the recommendations for reforms suggested by the commission demonstrate that youth were present in the dialogue on reconciliation. In particular, the recommendations included in the final report indicate that youth agency was visible and acknowledged in the Solomon Islands, as the commissioners described youth as "productive citizens of th[e] nation."[50] Complicating the visibility of youth, however, in this section of the report, is the use of the combined classifications "children and youth" in the discussion on why targeted recommendations were developed.[51] While the recommendations chapter employed the combined classification to label the discussion, its substance emphasized predominately the ways in which the Tensions affected youth, *not* children. Indeed, throughout this section there is only one mention of child soldiers. Instead, this section of the final report highlights the issue of "youth unemployment" by providing a table of unemployment statistics for ages fifteen to twenty-nine years. Moreover, the recommendations chapter of the Solomon Islands final report notes "address[ing] feelings of marginalization in the youth population of the country" as a key reform priority.[52] That is, while the substantive discussion emphasizes the distinct interests of youth, the rhetorical classifications frame their experiences alongside those of children, thus blurring the lines of representation.

The visibility of youth in the recommendations chapter is a direct contrast to youth visibility in the chapter on children. The chapter on children uses the child and youth classifications interchangeably, yet here these descriptions denote the experiences of children, and the youth label is absent. Indeed, the Solomon Islands TRC report's chapter on children uses these classifications without acknowledging the underlying nuances associated with them, the political and social implications, or the fluid and dynamic nature of this period in an individual's life. This is due in part to the Solomon Islands' adherence to the internationally recognized classification of the "child" throughout the children's chapter. Specifically, the findings in the chapter were informed by standards established in the Convention on the Rights of the Child (CRC), which defines a child as any individual "below the age of 18 years unless under the law applicable to the child, majority is attained earlier."[53] This definitional boundary, which prioritizes a legalistic, protectionist, and age-contingent notion of the child, unconsciously facilitated the institutional silencing of Solomon Islander youth. In doing so, their unique and diverse voices were lost in the document that was intended as the official, complete, and inclusive record of the conflict. Broadly speaking, the case of the Solomon Islands suggests that governments and international organizations need to reimagine the ways in which the stories of youth are represented in their formal conflict narratives.

The recommendations acknowledge the agency of youth, highlighting their capacity to meaningfully collaborate on development programs that directly address their needs and interests. The TRC commissioners recommend that "the government promotes and encourages maximum youth participation in decision-making and leadership at all levels of government, that is real and meaningful, as a means to take seriously the concerns, aspirations, and wishes of the youth."[54] Similarly, the second recommendation promotes the agency and engagement of youth by encouraging the government to "create a fund . . . to develop jobs for youth."[55] These recommendations are underpinned by the belief that youth have the capacity to influence, through interaction, the social structures of the Solomon Islands community. Claims of influence are central to understandings of agency within the scholarly literature, which examines the contributions of youth as empowered political actors.[56] This is due to the underlying assumption inherent in this belief that a mutual and reciprocal relationship is possible between youth and the community, particularly in the formation of development initiatives.

Recognition by the commission that youth could contribute productively to the creation of policies, as well as their implementation, indicates that the stories of youth were heard in the consultation process. Indeed, the core belief evident in this recommendation is that youth are active agents with a significant stake in the outcomes of reconciliation and its capacity to contribute to a productive future for the Solomon Islands. Moreover, this acknowledgment of their capacity to engage substantively in the development of programs and to voice concerns about proposed practices reinforces the current scholarly trend in the peacebuilding field that reveals youth to be "very effective agents of social change," most commonly on the fringes of transitional societies.[57] Despite this, representing the ownership of youth at the institutional level remains a significant challenge for reconciliation practices.

In the Solomon Islands, for example, the recognition of youth's capacity demonstrated a departure from scholarly and popular depictions of youth that rarely represented the ownership and empowerment youth displayed over their conflict narratives. Indeed, dominant representations of youth's role in the conflict relied on a deeply rooted cultural understanding of youth as *Masta Liu*.[58] Representations of youth that rely on this classification denote ignorance, delinquency, and a tendency to succumb to manipulation. In doing so, they perpetuate narrow dichotomous frames common to understandings of youth in peace and conflict more broadly.[59] Overreliance on the deviant classifications obscures the voices and stories of empowered young people. Moreover, this representation creates inaccurate normative assumptions about why individuals engage with conflict and reconciliation. Mathew Allen's work with ex-combatants in the Solomon Islands, which considers their motivations for participating in the conflict, challenges the negative imagery associated with the *Masta Liu* characterization. Specifically, he observes that the motivations of youth extended beyond feelings of helpless and aimlessness to a belief that they were "fighting for something."[60] Taken together, the reconciliation narratives of youth evident in the Solomon Islands TRC final report, as well as in the commission transcripts and interviews, reveal a complex story about the experiences of youth that is neither linear nor one-dimensional.

When we consider only the chapter on children in the final report, however, the representations published prioritized a narrow dichotomy that portrayed the stories, and thus experiences of youth, as static and unresponsive. Indeed, the chapter on children reported one set of beliefs conceived through a normative framework that casts young people as either vulnerable and innocent or disinterested, lazy, and self-involved. This is problematic for the reconciliation agenda of the Solomon Islands because it created a public and formal record of the conflict that perpetuates stereotypes rather than recounting the experiences of youth through their voices and stories. In doing so, the institutionalized reconciliation narrative diminishes the sense of ownership young people displayed in the reconciliation process. Moreover, it creates an incomplete representation of youth that fails to meet the central reconciliation goal of facilitating acknowledgment to restore and rebuild community relationships.

AGENCY, OWNERSHIP, AND THE SOLOMON ISLANDS TRC

The story of the youth engagement with the TRC began in 2006 with the formulation of a Truth and Reconciliation Steering Committee. Guided by advocacy efforts from civil society groups, in particular the Solomon Islands Christian Association and the Grand Coalition for Change, the government adopted the development of a TRC as a key policy objective. The Grand Coalition sought to start a national conversation about peace and social justice by "putting in place legal and other instruments" that would "maintain peace and normalcy" within the community and thus encourage prosperity. The goal was to ensure that the measures put in place were responsive to the national dialogue and therefore inclusive of a wide range of responses. Given this, the consultation process undertaken by the steering committee required the engagement of a cross section of the community, including youth.

The Steering Committee was responsible for consulting with these stakeholders about the design and implementation of a potential TRC. It was "directed to explore and plan the structure, functions and powers of a Commission."[61] In this respect, the purpose of the committee was to ensure that the potential TRC reflected the needs and experiences of a cross section of the Solomon Islands community. The members of this committee were representatives from key organizations in the Solomon Islands, as well as those groups identified as having a significant stake in the outcome of the reconciliation process. Amongst those represented were the youth demographic. The youth representative of this committee was responsible for gathering the opinions of youth and ensuring that they were represented throughout the design and consultation process for the creation of the TRC. They conducted focus groups and town halls across the provinces for the youth demographic, which facilitated comprehensive engagement and provided information about the proposed reconciliation process.[62] Central to the responsibilities of the youth representative was the implementation of forums that would engage youth from all provinces in fact-finding sessions to assess their interest in participating in the proposed formal reconciliation process.[63] It appears, therefore, that in the early stages of the reconciliation process youth were active and empowered actors whose voices were impactful. Maintaining this level of engagement, however, in the creation of the conflict narrative proved to be a significant challenge. The contrast between youth engagement in the development process of the TRC and their institutionalized stories reveals the impact of political agendas on the creation of formalized reconciliation narratives. The tension between these two representations suggests that the external beliefs and political will of powerful actors and institutions often act as significant barriers to the production of holistic and inclusive conflict narratives that acknowledge the voices of youth.

Barriers and Gateways to Agency: Collective Social Representation

Children and youth occupy a unique space in both scholarship and practice as they exercise "a form of passive political agency."[64] Indeed, recent empirical work on youth and children in conflict and post-conflict environments demonstrates the political symbolism associated with the visibility of children in these environments. Therefore, collectively the stories of young people help to advance the political agendas and causes of young people, particularly when it comes to issues of rights. When young people are conceived only in this way, however, these representations act as significant barriers to agency, empowerment, and ownership over their own stories.

Collective identities "denote membership in social groups, whether that membership is chosen by them or ascribed to them by others."[65] Specifically, classifications, such as *children* and *youth*, are descriptive frames that reveal their relationship to the political environment as well as with their family and the community. These depictions often reflect social expectations and impose characteristics on individuals based on "historical practices, cultural norms, social attitudes, religious values, legal dictates or the needs of the society."[66] Indeed, these outside influences produce complex webs of "interactions and meaning" that inform and are produced by young people as they move between relationships, networks, and institutions.[67] These socially produced representations have proven problematic for the development of a comprehensive reconciliation narrative of youth's experiences because they rely largely on the community perception and therefore leave little room for self-identification and the voices of youth. For example, as McEvoy-Levy observes, "A fourteen-year-old who has been a combatant, or who has experienced power and independence as a member of an armed group, may not want to be seen as a child," yet their biological age ascribes automatic classification under the dominant normative framework established by the international community and codified within the CRC.[68] Children who have experienced war, however, challenge this representation, as it denotes a level of vulnerability, as well as a lack of control and a need to be managed, that does not reflect the reality of their experiences.

As the following discussion of the Solomon Islands TRC demonstrates, the same dynamic exists amongst this youth population, and through participation in the TRC process they sought to challenge their collective social representations. Collective representations challenge the capacity of youth to have their stories acknowledged because prominent social classifications often rely on "identities of exclusions," which obscure displays of agency and ownership often evident in TRC processes.[69] Furthermore, as Jacobs observes, representations of young people are not value neutral, rather they are often constructed to "influence domestic and international politics."[70] Collective and institutionalized representations, therefore, rarely capture the ambiguous and complicated nature of youth's engagement with conflict and reconciliation processes.

Complicating the collective representation process with respect to youth is the fluid and transitional nature of this development phase. Specifically, individuals within these broadly defined constructs often take on multiple and shifting roles, which produce crosscutting identities. Given this, local and global representations and prominent normative frameworks rarely reflect the true nature of young people's experiences and interests. Gready observes this phenomenon in the case of South Africa, as he describes youth as "both victims *and* perpetrator, or political activists *and* criminals" (emphasis in the original).[71] Social group representations, therefore, present a significant challenge to the production of an inclusive reconciliation narrative that hears, represents, and responds to the firsthand stories of youth. Indeed, as the Solomon Islands TRC process demonstrates, while we are now able to conceive of youth engagement as fluid and dynamic, the victim and deviant dichotomies remain prominent in the institutional representations of youth as a collective, social group.

Displays of Agency: Stepping Stone to Representation at the TRC

The conflict in the Solomon Islands was a low-level, ethnic conflict waged between the Malaita Eagle Force (MEF) and the Guadalcanal Isatabu Freedom Movement (IFM) in their provinces and the capital city of Honiara. By the time the conflict reached its peak in June 2000, young men, particularly those from Malaita, needed little convincing to join the resistance. Motivated by a desire to "defend and protect their people," these youths were ready for change.[72] Driven from their villages and their jobs by Guale militants (a term used to describe combatants from the Guadalcanal Province in the Solomon Islands), most of whom were also young men, Malaitan youth sought refuge with their families in temporary shelters around Honiara. Motivated by these forced evictions, as well as a wide range of human rights abuses committed by both sides, "Malaitan men began to form vigilante groups to 'secure' the outskirts of Honiara" and to protect themselves and their families.[73] To that end, Malaitan youth were highly visible and key contributors to the violence, perceiving it to be a necessary act of resistance against a corrupt and unjust system.

In contrast, the youth of Guadalcanal played a key role in the Tensions from the beginning. Among their key grievances was the perception that the mass migration of Malaitans had resulted in the loss of already scarce job prospects and that those who had migrated had little respect for local *Kastom*. Young Gual's participation in the violence was born largely out of frustration that their voices and the voices of their community were not being acknowledged.[74] Specifically, following a lack of institutional action on a 1999 submission to the central government titled "Demands by the Bona Fide and Indigenous People of Guadalcanal,"[75] which detailed claims for compensations with respect to land and other grievances, many young Guals joined the IFM to voice their dissatisfaction. Political and cultural factors, therefore, played a significant role in motivating these young Solomon Islanders to engage in the violence associated with the Tensions.

These factors acted as a catalyst for action rather than, as the final report suggested, a means of coercion. Rather than hearing and believing youth when they exerted agency over their decision to participate in the conflict, the final report drew on policy research to highlight the victim narrative, which assigned narrow normative assumptions about young people to their experiences. To that end, the institutional narrative of the final report relied on information and data collected by organizations with a specific mandate. These types of policy reports, while valuable in their capacity to further the needs and interests of young people, prioritize a protectionist lens that represents the experiences of children and youth together to further the political cause.[76] Indeed, scholars have observed that children "are often represented in isolation, victimized and vulnerable" in order to evoke an emotional response in the global and local political community.[77] The same is true for youth, particularly where their stories are combined with children. In the Solomon Islands' chapter on children, the narrative produced used details from the *Global Report on Child Soldiers* to highlight the vulnerability of young people, prioritizing their status as victims. The final report contended that "the line between free will and coercion is quite flimsy . . . voluntary recruitment is often a choice not exercised freely; it is rarely based exclusively on the volition of the child but tends to be conditioned by factors beyond his/ her control."[78]

While the coercive framework described above explained the participation of Solomon Islander youth in some instances, it also relied on a one-dimensional and linear understanding of why young people fight, which is imbued with institutional bias. For example, the stories included in the chapter on children emphasize only the behaviors of young people that fit the victim/perpetrator binary. For example, the report observes that "the ethnic tension pushed a lot of young people out from their normal activities. Most got involved in drinking, smoking, and all sorts of criminal activities even today."[79] Similarly, it notes that "youth gangs, some ethnically based, appeared in areas of the town such as Burns Creek and Fulisango Zion and started to fight each other to establish territories. Marijuana and kwaso, the home brewed distilled alcohol made with yeast, became readily available at prices that were lower than that of beer."⁸⁰ Finally, the report focuses on the material motivations of youth fighters, emphasizing the possessions and opportunities available to young militants. As one militant's submission included in the final report explains, "During the tensions, everyone had a car."⁸¹ While these stories are a vital component of the conflict experiences of youth, the institutionalized narrative of the TRC seems to suggest that they were the only experiences. Yet as this chapter demonstrates, this is only part of youth's conflict narrative in the Solomon Islands. Indeed, by including these stories but not acknowledging displays of agency and ownership, which are also evident in the TRC process, the report created a hierarchy of experiences that reflected institutional ideas about youth and the beliefs of external actors rather than youth themselves. Employing this framework in the formal record of the conflict explained the motivations of young people by prioritizing the beliefs and interpretations of external stakeholders, which challenged the stories and claims of youth. Reliance on the coercion narrative to question young people's claims that their participation was voluntary furthered the agenda of the state and the international community, while silencing the firsthand stories of youth. The challenge inherent in this coercive representation is evident in the report itself, which after applying this narrative to five submissions from young people goes on to demonstrate that "Malaitans were emphatic in claiming they joined voluntarily."⁸² That is, the authors of the final report appeared to grapple with the complexity of the stories of youth and the inherent normative tension exposed between external and firsthand interpretations of youth's experiences. Although the institutional narrative prioritized a homogenous representation of young people embedded in stories of vulnerability, intermittent displays of ownership are included throughout the chapter. The willingness of children and youth to fight to protect their rights and to publicly and emphatically expose their grievances demonstrated their capacity to act as political stakeholders. In addition, their heightened engagement with the Guadalcanal Revolutionary Army and later the IFM challenged dominant understandings of youth in the Solomon Islands, which framed their public identity as subordinate to the "big men" in the community.

Displays of agency, responsibility, and choice are prominent features of the conflict narratives of Malaitan and Guadalcanal youth. Although the final report sporadically acknowledges that young soldiers "insist that their involvement was voluntary," it includes the caveat that "the adult members of their respective militant groups failed in their responsibility to protect them."[83] That is, when the choices and agency of youth are occasionally recognized, they are displayed within a broader "protectionist" narrative, which places the final ownership of their experiences in the hands of adults. Moreover, the chapter on children uses the term "child soldiers" to represent all "young people caught up in a militant group."[84] The lack of differentiation between children and youth created a static and homogenous representation of their experiences. In doing so, the institutional narrative of the final report mitigated displays of agency and responsibility. The characterization of all young militant fighters as child soldiers denotes passivity and vulnerability, which obscured the diversity evident in their actual stories throughout the formal conflict narrative produced by the commission. As a result, the final report of the Solomon Islands TRC perpetuated the common assumptions from the literature that young people, in particular child soldiers, are either "dangerous and disorderly" or in this case the "hapless victim."[85]

The foot soldiers of the MEF and the IFM consisted largely of young men who often self-identified with many of the cultural characteristics of *Masta Liu*.[86] These young men have actively sought to claim ownership over the aspects of this collective representation that denotes their experiences growing up in the Solomon Islands, most notably the heightened tendency of young people to drop out of the education system and the "transient or non-existent employment histories."[87] Typically used by external agents, the term *Masta Liu* portrays youth as ignorant and naive individuals who are highly susceptible to manipulation by the "big men" of the community.[88] The term is associated predominately with deviance and denies ownership, thus ultimately neglecting the perceptions of those it seeks to describe. Indeed, the final report relies on the *Masta Liu* classification to indicate a "twilight zone between children as victims and children as perpetrators."[89] In doing so, the chapter creates an either/or representation of the stories of young people that overlooks the dynamic nature of their engagement, as well as the instances of youth asserting agency over this deviance classification. Indeed, as one youth explained, "I joined the militants because most of them were my *wantoks* and relatives. No one asked me to join them. I just followed them, following my own decision. I had relatives in the MEF, so I was not scared of joining them. I also joined them just to get drunk and hang around with them." While this submission acknowledges deviance and the power structures that enabled the participation of youth in the conflict, it also demonstrates the willingness of youth to take responsibility for their participation in the Tensions. Given this, the report's conclusion that this submission represents trivial motivations obscures the agency inherent to this story, most notably that the youth was making his "own decision[s]." Similarly, another youth ex-combatant describes, "There was no school attendance and there was nothing to do at home, so you could see different types of grouping, youths, children, and elderly. If you saw some of the boys smoking you wanted to join in too; like smoking marijuana or *savusavu* [local tobacco], everyone would like to do that."[90] Again, the narrative in this submission demonstrates choice and empowerment over deviant behavior. Yet by assigning a classification to this story that represents these motivations as trivial, the final report perpetuated static ideas about youth that reflect narrow beliefs regarding who youth are. By asserting ownership over the experiences associated with this deeply rooted cultural depiction, Solomon Islander youth unconsciously reframed their public narrative and their relationship with the broader Solomon Islands community. This demonstrates that for young people in transitional contexts representation is dynamic, fluid, and reflected in the behaviors of those who participated in the reconciliation process, as researchers, statement takers, transcribers, and grave diggers. That is, the actions and behaviors of youth challenge the boundaries of externally constructed representations through practice. While on the surface the participation of youth in the Tensions can be viewed as an attempt by "unemployed . . . youth to wreak havoc," it may also be interpreted as a manifestation of their "growing sense of frustration and grievance" at the government's inaction.[91] Missing from this narrow understanding of the *Masta Liu* is an acknowledgment of the ways in which young people utilize their experiences to assert agency and build political capital.

Self-representation as *Masta Liu* is significant because it highlights the capacity of young people in the Solomon Islands to reclaim and reappropriate externally derived representations through action. Moreover, interview participants suggested that youth engagement with the TRC process indicated their willingness to challenge deep-seated cultural assumptions. Specifically, according to one participant, "Youth are important, especially in the villages as they provide guidance. Progress is being made, change is happening, and youth are important for that change, but it is not driven by the TRC."[92] Furthermore, according to another interview participant, "We gave them the space to talk, and they choose to forgive, [but the] problem with the children and youth section is that it does not match the actual experiences. It presents a common international understanding."[93]

The actions and participation of youth in the reconciliation process challenged and reframed, albeit subconsciously, the descriptive, cultural framework often associated with ignorance and aimlessness in the Solomon Islands context. Not only were youth highly visible during the conflict, but their motivations were also underpinned by a specific political discourse and a perceived obligation to act as protectors of their *Kastom* and their future. As Louise Vella explains, *Kastom* "encompasses indigenous ideologies, relationship to and management of the land, moral frameworks, dispute management, gender relations and social organizations."[94] *Kastom* is thus a structural and cultural model that guides actions and relationships throughout the Solomon Islands. Where youth are concerned, *Kastom* denotes the relationship between youth and their communities, in particular the "big men" and chiefs. To attribute their participation in the Tensions to narrow binaries, which despite a few exceptions has commonly been the case, fails to consider their underlying motivations and underrepresents the level of agency they displayed throughout the Tensions. In addition, these binary representations do not represent the unique interpretations of Solomon Islander youth with respect to the external events that facilitated their participation in the conflict. With this in mind, this book aims to explore the ways in which TRCs have, over time, become an increasingly useful public forum for young people to reflect on their conflict experiences.

Broadly speaking, the lives of young people in the Solomon Islands were uniquely impacted by the series of events that exacerbated the Tensions. Specifically, the closure of major exporting companies, the collapse of the tourism industry, and the withdrawal of international NGOs and foreign aid significantly increased the number of frustrated unemployed youth on the streets in Honiara.[95] In addition, the widespread shutdown of schools left "two-thirds of the nation's teachers . . . on unpaid leave during the conflict," further exacerbating a growing sense of idleness amongst the youth of the Solomon Islands.[96] Frustrated and looking to break away from "the constraints of traditional village life," but with limited opportunities in the urban center of Honiara, youth found in the Tensions a space to engage in the politics of the nation.[97] Indeed, amongst the motivations for youth participating in the conflict was a desire to shift their relationship with the political world in a manner that increased their visibility. Their participation, therefore, can be interpreted as an attempt to reframe their relationship with the broader community. In this way, restorative justice and reconciliation can be viewed as a way of building social trust and political capital.

Although misguided, the participation of youth in these militia groups ensured that they were involved in efforts to challenge what was widely perceived to be a corrupt and unfair system. Indeed, youth on both sides of the conflict had legitimate grievances that motivated their willingness to take up arms. According to one submission, "My heart was definitely with the MEF militants. I joined them because I am Malaitan. I joined voluntarily just like others who wanted to support the militants. I was motivated because I am Malaitan, the killing and harassment done to Malaitans was like hurting me and my family."[98] Similarly, as a Gual youth explains, "At that time, I really hated some of those Malaitans . . . I was threatened by some of the Malaitan students and that same year one of my cousins was murdered by Malaitans too."[99] Solomon Islander youth, therefore, were key stakeholders in the conflict. As their submissions to the TRC highlight, they had a unique and diverse stake in the outcomes of the transitional justice processes undertaken following the conflict. Given this, the voices of youth were essential to the design and implementation of these post-conflict processes. Their heightened participation in the violence required consideration at all stages of the reconciliation process to ensure that their needs and experiences were represented in a responsive and meaningful way.

Challenging the Victim/Perpetrator Binary through Engagement

The case of the Solomon Islands reveals a dynamic youth demographic that is not represented in the prominent narratives told in the TRC's final report. Their complex and at times ambiguous relationship with reconciliation and conflict is largely excluded from this formal institutionalized narrative. Missing from this narrative are the stories of youth who were both victims and perpetrators, as well as those who resisted engaging with the conflict or who worked as peace negotiators and activists.[100] Moreover, notions of youth engagement derived solely from the final report miss demonstrations of agency by youth displayed throughout the TRC process. For example, the youth of the Solomon Islands participated in reconciliation not only by providing statements and participating in focus groups but also by taking on roles as statement takers, grave diggers, researchers, and transcribers.[101] Rather than presenting a narrative of children and youth that reflects this diversity, the final report reduced their experiences to binary representations. Specifically, the final report emphasized their vulnerability, detachment, and apathy and represented their experiences as victims and deviants. The narratives are presented in the chapter under the headings of "Children as Victims" and "'Raskols' and Militants: Children as Perpetrators"; thus the model used to tell their stories perpetuated discursive binaries rather than seeing and acknowledging their diverse experiences.[102] In addition, these normative representations excluded youth from the formalized narratives because they challenged the homogenous classification of all young people. While children and youth were considered separately during the collection of testimony, this distinct engagement is not acknowledged in the institutionalized narrative. Moreover, although youth were afforded separate considerations in the decision-making process and the outline of the mandate and the recommendations uses the term "youth" either distinct from children or interchangeably, this degree of recognition and representation does not carry through to the institutionalized narrative.

In contrast, interviews conducted in the Solomon Islands, statements by youth presented to the commission, and transcripts of the thematic hearing on youth represent youth as highly motivated, driven, and empowered individuals. These representations are significant as they lend legitimacy to claims that understanding the engagement of youth in transitional justice contexts requires an examination of their experiences through the "youth as political agents" model. For example, as one participant notes, "We gave the youth the jobs, because they were hungry, they wanted to be part of the reconciliation—as they saw this as the future."[103] This sentiment is echoed by a trauma counselor working with the youth demographic who concludes, "The youth—they mobilized. Fieldworkers mostly were youth and Statement takers, mostly were youth. Most of them were graduates from the university here."[104]

The stories of youth evident in these statements highlight their willingness to engage substantively with the reconciliation process. Beliefs concerning the agency and empowerment of youth are central to these narratives. These submissions demonstrate the capacity of the youth agency lens to represent the complexity of youth engagement with the reconciliation process. Starting from the position of youth themselves exposes their capacity to contribute to the political structures and institutions of reconciliation by revealing their voices and ideas and deconstructing their actual behavior. In doing so, representations of youth, which acknowledge their stories firsthand, amplify their voices and create a more accurate reflection of their interests and experiences. This is significant for our understanding of the political agency of youth in the Solomon Islands, as well as their capacity to contribute to reconciliation and development, because these stories represent a significant departure from the beliefs evident in the construction of the final report.

Interview participants emphasized the logistical significance of youth engagement in the reconciliation process. As one interviewee notes, "The youth, they came when we called, we used them in every area of the TRC."[105] Indeed, their widespread engagement with the TRC process challenged normative assumptions of youth as disengaged and uninterested. The case of the Solomon Islands lends credence to an emerging body of empirical work in the peacebuilding field that demonstrates youth's capacity to act as entrepreneurs of peace.[106] This research reveals the positive impact of engaging with the voices of youth in social and political structures. Scholars such as Drummond-Mundal and Cave suggest that this inclusion "makes pragmatic and constructive sense" because they have ideas and experience that "can work either for or against new social and political constructions."[107] Similarly, Claire O'Kane, Clare Feinstein, and Annette Giertsen conclude that sustainable peace requires "the adults of tomorrow . . . to feel a sense of ownership and responsibility for the creation and maintenance of a climate of peace."[108] Where reconciliation practices are concerned, the same underlying principle applies because including the stories of youth creates legitimacy and ownership over the outcome of reconciliation.

The scholarly claim that youth have the capacity to act as "agents of change" is further supported by the Solomon Islands case. As a researcher at the TRC highlights, one of the benefits of engaging young people in the TRC process was that "youth talking to youth, it is very powerful, they bring each other in to the process, their friends, youth have chains of networks . . . they want to share their stories with each other."[109] Similarly, as the quote at the beginning of this chapter highlights, widespread youth engagement in the reconciliation process encouraged others to share their narratives. Reconciliation narratives, therefore, that acknowledge and disseminate the diverse, fluid, and complex self-reflections of youth ensure that youth are not only visible but also heard by the broader community. To that end, the more stories of youth that are represented in the reconciliation process, the greater the likelihood that a state will fulfill the acknowledgment and healing mandate central to most TRCs. Taken together, the above interviews indicate the importance of directly engaging with the narratives of youth and ensuring their substantive participation in the process. Significantly, the open and inclusive nature of the TRC process creates space for youth to actively engage as political agents.

Moreover, interviews reveal the importance of using a youth agency lens when constructing reconciliation narratives for youth. It is evident in the Solomon Islands context that when institutions rely purely on the assumptions and the beliefs of external agents, the voices of youth are obscured by narrow representative frameworks. When community members were asked to describe the engagement of youth with the TRC and during the conflict, the general sentiment reflected the deviance framework. For example, many of the interview participants concluded that youth were "too focused on smoking, drinking, chewing the beetle nut" to actively participate in the TRC.[110] Furthermore, many represented youths as irresponsible and untrustworthy by suggesting that "the youth, they are babies having babies."[111] In addition, external representations of youth highlight a skepticism surrounding the motivations of youth and the genuineness of their commitment to reconciliation and development. As one participant suggests, "The youth . . . they participate in reconciliation to get the money that is all."[112] External representations indicate a belief that youth were driven to participate by the possibility of material gain rather than a sense of national and political responsibility, as the firsthand submissions by youth described earlier in this chapter reveal. That is, the different interpretations of the motivations for youth participation exposed a tension between the stories of youth and the stories by youth. This tension suggests that while external actors were able to see youth throughout the Solomon Islands reconciliation process, their voices remained unheard and silenced, particularly at the institutional level. Finally, the stories told *about* youth's participation in the conflict use terms such as "lost," "manipulated," and "vulnerable to the big boys."[113] In doing so, they reveal a narrative about the roles youth occupied in the conflict that neglects or mischaracterizes displays of ownership, agency, and empowerment by youth.

These interview responses support claims that reconciliation narratives that rely only on the voices of the most powerful actors and institutions fail to see those they seek to represent. The contrast evident in these representations highlights the importance of gathering a wide range of beliefs and ideas when constructing formal conflict narratives. Indeed, when the voices of individuals are marginalized, their representation in these narratives fails to reflect the diversity of their experiences or to acknowledge the complexity of their stories. Hearing and responding to the stories of youth, alongside the perspectives of other stakeholders within the Solomon Islands, ensures a balanced and holistic narrative of their experience. Broadly speaking, responses by youth reveal significant gaps in the formal representations of young people in reconciliation narratives. A disconnect persists between the narrow picture of youth reflected in the TRC report and the stories and actions of youth revealed throughout the reconciliation process. These differences indicate that collective representations ascribed by institutions often fail to capture who youth are and fail to truly hear their voices.

Social Representations: Motivation, Ownership, and Agency

Social representations are not fixed or static, as they are informed and produced by webs of meaning that are embedded in cultural values, social interactions, beliefs, and norms. However, representations of youth in the final report, which adhered to the youth as victims and youth as perpetrators classifications, were not responsive to the fluidity of youth's interactions with the social and political environment. Relying on the victim/perpetrator binaries when representing the experiences of youth ensures that the stories told about youth remain unresponsive and thus misrepresent or overlook elements of their stories that do not fit within these frameworks. In contrast, when the voices of youth are placed front and center, through the application of a youth agency lens we are better able to see the numerous ways in which this traditionally marginalized group challenge these narrow collective representations. Representations of youth that consider substantive participation as an indicator of agency and empowerment provide an opportunity for the reconciliation community to see the often surprising ways in which young people interpret their surroundings.

Understanding youth engagement in reconciliation processes requires an acknowledgment that they often experience a range of crosscutting issues and assume constantly changing and concurrent roles. Indeed, acknowledging the agency of youth in these contexts does not disconnect the interests and belief of external actors. In contrast, the youth agency lens seeks to understand how youth interact with, use, and respond to outside influences, in particular their relationships with the transitional community. In the Solomon Islands, young people utilized these external representations to reframe the dominant narratives about their role in the community and to challenge misrepresentations about their capacity and motivation to engage in reconciliation and development. For example, as one participant explains, "The adults they viewed us as puppets; we were the victims and the ones thrown in jail, but we are also the ones with the knowledge and the future."[114] Evident in this submission is a recognition that youth can harness knowledge and their position as future leaders to rebuild their relationships within the community. This sentiment was echoed by another interview participant who suggests that "it is very evident that young people are involved they are the ones visibly doing the looting in the crisis they were also the victims. But to see them wanting to be involved in the reconciliation, in making the future that is also positive for me."[115] These responses suggest that the stories of youth are complex, fluid, and constantly being rewritten. This has implications for the ways in which they are represented; an overreliance on static, dichotomous frames will miss the multiple ways in which youth are constantly challenging and changing their narratives. Indeed, many interview participants that had direct contact with youth during the process reinforce this complexity. They highlight the contributions of youth, noting the distinct and vital roles they played in the TRC process. These interview responses challenge the institutional narrative presented by the final report of the TRC, which represents youth as "children" and passive subjects of other's experiences. That is, unlike the firsthand stories of youth, which emphasize their active role in conflict narratives, the institutional narrative of the TRC suggests that young people were primarily participants or pawns in the conflict stories of other older individuals.

In addition, many suggest that the unique and intricate relationship youth had with the conflict ensured that they were key assets to the Solomon Islands transitional justice process. As one TRC employee describes, "These youths they were witnesses they were witnesses to murder. They did not feel good about holding onto these secrets for all these years, they believed in reconciliation. The elder people did not realize that these young people witnessed these things, they helped us solve a lot of questions, murders, and disappearance."[116] Amongst those who directly engaged with youth during the TRC process, the general sentiment about youth representation was that youth were political and active agents, not passive subjects. Most surprising, however, were the interpretations by these interview participants that youth yielded significant power over the reconciliation process. For example, when asked to describe the interactions of youth with the TRC, one commissioner responded:

> During the conflict, they were militants, but in the TRC, youth's response is that they were very willing to come forward, they want to reconcile, they want to forgive. They were victims but many of them were also perpetrators, they were used to take the messages across the rivers to the Islands, they went through a lot of hard time, some were killed, some were shot. The tension was mainly around youth, first they carried the messages, carried it across the river, they could run fast. They were witnesses, who was talking to who, who was in which area, they relayed these messages. Now in the TRC we found that information out and the Youth they were very willing to tell the stories, to talk, to participate.[117]

These statements reflect the beliefs of those who had worked directly with youth during the reconciliation process, including church and youth leaders, trauma counselors, and statement takers. They highlight the need to represent youth in the Solomon Islands in a more open and dynamic way. More broadly, they indicate a need to engage with and reflect upon youth's relationship with reconciliation practices in a more nuanced way that acknowledges their active role in conflict and transitional environments.

SHIFTING THE NARRATIVE: REPRESENTATION AS OWNERSHIP

In the Solomon Islands, the roles played by youth in the reconciliation process were inextricably tied to the future. In fact, many interview participants reinforced the notion that youth's relationship with the transitional justice process was forward-looking and development-focused. The self-reflective narratives of youth highlight a capacity-building response to transitional justice. According to one interviewee, "We participate because we need a future . . . and reconciliation may give us the future."[118] Similarly, a representative of the National Youth Parliament observes that "we inherit the unfinished business of truth and reconciliation. But with the right support, things can improve for us."[119] At the center of these stories is the notion that youth have the capacity to participate in transitional processes in a manner that is mindful of the nexus between justice, reconciliation, and development.

In addition, the responses of youth challenged the common perception that young people are all pre-political or that they are "yet to develop an individual political consciousness and the capacity to bear the burdens" of participation and agency.[120] In the Solomon Islands context, this was evident when youth were asked to describe their role in the TRC process. Terms and phrases such as "opportunity," "important for the future," "empowered," and "having a voice" dominated the discussion.[121] Specifically, many emphasized "the need to express themselves" as a key motivation for their participation in the TRC focus groups and special hearings that took place. These identity constructions are significant as they illustrate potential, responsiveness, and ownership, all of which are key indicators of agency and empowerment when youth's stories are examined through a youth agency lens. Furthermore, these self-reflections are meaningful because they challenge the simple identity constructions traditionally ascribed to them by other actors in transitional contexts, namely the victim/perpetrator classifications.

These interview responses are indicative of the belief amongst Solomon Islander youth that they are uniquely positioned to engage with the TRC process because the outcome of the process is tied to their future. According to one participant, "The youth, we know what is happening, we have ideas for policies, policies that will heal and help us move forward. We want the education, and we want the resources."[122] In addition, these interviews reveal the importance of citizenship and belonging to youth in the Solomon Islands. In doing so, they provide credence to scholarship throughout the transitional justice field, which suggests that TRCs are instrumental because they allow marginalized individuals to claim citizenship through the process of having their voices heard.[123] These responses reinforce the emerging body of research that contends that the true value of TRCs is their capacity to allow traditionally marginalized individuals the opportunity to claim ownership over their conflict and reconciliation narrative. Yet, this book contends that it is the process, rather than the end product, that facilitates this capacity.

This sentiment was also echoed throughout the youth hearings at the Solomon Islands TRC. For example, Mr. Kwainao remarked "[Youth] can do anything whatever mountain is there, what road there [is], we can jump, and we can climb because that is the spirit of young people."¹²⁴ Another explained, "When you talk about young people, they are powerful just like nature. . . . When young people decide to do things, they can do it without anyone stopping them."¹²⁵ These responses indicate youth's willingness to take ownership over their future. Youth participation in the TRC process in the Solomon Islands revealed the political will, agency, and capacity of a demographic traditionally excluded or marginalized by transitional justice, particularly at the institutional level. TRCs tend to challenge traditional representations and understandings of youth in transitional contexts by exposing their capacity and determination to act, engage with, and reform the social and political structures of the community. The contributions of youth, both in interviews and submissions to the TRC, highlight their unique stories and indicate a sense of ownership over the reconciliation process, which derived from the belief that without their voices the Solomon Islands cannot effectively move forward and heal. Among the firsthand stories of youth is a heightened awareness of the development deficit produced by the Tensions. Yet rather than interpret these as symbols of their vulnerability (as was done in the final report), the actual submissions of youth offer practical and development-focused initiatives that shift the focus to their agency. Although young people highlight their suffering and victim status in their stories, they do not use these classifications to denote vulnerability and helplessness. Thus, while many emphasize the disruption to their schooling and a lack of services, they also produce solutions and a willingness to participate in the processes required to address these issues. At the local level, the tension between the institutional narratives of young people and their self-representations reflected a broader societal struggle between the "old big man system and the new development culture."¹²⁶ Indeed, the representations of youth in the final report reveal a country still grappling with hearing and understanding the voices of its youth demographic.

Conclusion

The Solomon Islands TRC process provided youth with the opportunity to demonstrate their capacity to contribute meaningfully to reconciliation. Their meaningful and substantive participation in the development and implementation processes of the TRC reflected the capacity of young people and illustrated the dynamic nature of youth's capacity in transitional justice contexts. As this chapter demonstrates, representations of youth need to be informed by the lived experiences of youth rather than conceptual frameworks. When national and international policymakers responsible for transitional justice genuinely consider and center youth's voices, they create space for their substantive inclusion as leaders and decision makers for reconciliation.

As observed in the Solomon Islands, the responses of children and youth to conflict and to reconciliation practices are diverse, unique, and responsive to their environment. Narrow, normative classifications thus produce inadequate depictions of youth that often misrepresent their experiences and interests. Indeed, it is evident in the Solomon Islands case that youth have the capacity to demonstrate agency through their engagement with the process of reconciliation. Yet as the TRC in the Solomon Islands also demonstrates, these stories and representations are often missing from the institutional narratives produced to acknowledge the harms associated with the conflict. This is particularly apparent when the broader community continues to rely on culturally embedded notions to describe youth and their place in the community.

Youth participation in the Solomon Islands TRC represents a trend in transitional justice toward practices that are inclusive and focused on the fringes of society. In this chapter I have argued that while TRCs must be inclusive and represent the needs of traditionally marginalized individuals to ensure that they fulfill their reconciliation mandate, political and social limitations exist that prevent the formal narratives of TRCs from reflecting the dynamic nature of youth's voices. This chapter demonstrated that the narratives presented throughout the children's chapter of the Solomon Islands TRC report perpetuate a static and one-dimensional portrait of young people. These dominant binary representations are problematic for our understanding of the roles youth occupy in conflict and reconciliation because they fail to account for the constantly evolving nature of young people's interactions with their surroundings.

Conclusion

Considering the Legacy of Young People's Participation and Adopting a Way Forward

> The youth were fast learners . . . they integrate very well.
>
> —Interview, Solomon Islands, Oct. 2015

> Unity and youth programs were a big concern . . . they are young ambassadors for peace who everyday raise issues on social media . . . but the leaders are not connected to their issues . . . so they establish forums between themselves.
>
> —Interview, Solomon Islands, Nov. 2015

For communities grappling with legacies of past human rights violations and seeking to build peaceful futures, young people are essential stakeholders. Yet within the institutional architecture created to pursue accountability, including TRCs, their contributions are often underappreciated or misappropriated. Tensions emerge when young people's stories challenge the construction of a linear conflict narrative and when they are excluded from efforts to end the culture of impunity. Heightened attention on youth's advocacy in these contexts demonstrates that "the same young people who" are leading "demand[s] for change are later marginalized from" the practices and "negotiations about addressing and preventing the injustice of the past and present."[1] When transitional justice practices fail to substantively engage with young people, this has implications for the capacity of the process to achieve its mandate and to contribute to sustainable peace. Transitional justice processes that fail to enable young people "to talk to each other and their leaders about a violent and often controversial past, and to face and reflect on uncomfortable truths and realities"[2] leave communities fractured. Excluding or failing to reflect their diverse stories, therefore, often leaves young people disconnected and uninterested in the outcome of the transitional justice process.

Young people engage widely as political and social actors during conflict, yet their participation in transitional justice is mediated by external actors. As the cases in this book illustrate, this is particularly evident in reconciliation practices, where how young people participate is often predetermined without their consultation. Gains made toward more deliberate and meaningful participation for both children and youth in TRC processes have been hard fought, piecemeal, and driven by the sustained advocacy of youth themselves. Going forward, transitional justice practitioners must carve out more spaces to work *with* youth to center their voices in a way that respects their ownership over their stories.

With one in four young people globally affected by violence and instability, their voices are necessary and invaluable for holistic and meaningful reconciliation. Cast predominately as passive beneficiaries of formal reconciliation, young people have diverse leadership capacity that continues to be an untapped resource for the development of responsive and community-focused accountability strategies. Youth in particular are politically significant "as smaller-scale socio-cultural and ideological entrepreneurs bringing knowledge, perspectives, and hidden politics to the surface."[3] However, the use of their stories as the embodiment of a broader political idea neglects their agency and minimizes opportunities for youth to contribute as knowledge producers capable of challenging cultures of impunity within post-conflict states. When empowered to lead and to speak their truth, young people as "purveyors of historical memory"[4] can defy the status quo and reframe conversations about the past. In doing so, young people are invaluable for reconciliation processes seeking to rebuild the trust necessary for restoring meaningful interpersonal relationships. The above quotes echo many of the stories represented throughout this book, which suggest that despite being disconnected from the traditional power structures of TRCs young people are not dissuaded from advocating for participation or from pursing alternative avenues for making their voices heard. Within the formal reconciliation architecture, however, more must be done to normalize young people's substantive participation and acknowledge their agency. Before offering strategies for chartering a way forward for reconciliation practices, this chapter will examine the lessons learned from historical attempts by TRCs to engage young people.

Reconceptualizing and Reframing Young People

When young people are heard and taken seriously their voices have transformative potential. However, within formal transitional justice processes this capacity is often forgotten in favor of maintaining traditional power hierarchies and long-worn procedural expectations of whose voices *should* be prominent in the pursuit of reconciliation. Young people's activism in Tunisia, for example, began a revolution against Ben Ali's regime by mobilizing an expansive and inclusive social and political coalition.[5] Despite this, when the Truth and Dignity Commission was officially launched in December 2014, only limited and highly mediated space was carved out for young people's substantive participation and ownership of their conflict experience stories.[6]

The appropriation of young people's stories for political motivations in Tunisia resulted in a denial of agency and has proven to be a notable source of frustration for youth activists. As Rim El Gantri explains, even though Tunisia was "showing [itself to be] a country favoring youth . . . that [they] were the pillar of the country—in fact, it was not true." She continues, "Youth were used during the elections to create an image, but they didn't benefit from their 'rights' especially not in marginalized regions."[7] This quote reflects the consensus amongst youth activists who highlight that their political agency continues to be denied within institutions through the co-opting of their stories. Charfeddine El Kellil, member of the I Will Not Forgive youth-led coalition explains that "the political attitude towards youth have not changed. They saw youth as an electoral reservoir, as objects not subjects." In addition, another youth activist concluded that in the formal reconciliation process institutionalization has marginalized young people who "have a specific relationship with institutions"[8] brought about by the revolution. Like the other cases presented throughout this book, the Tunisian TRC reveals a deeply embedded tension between the meaning assigned to stories *of* youth and stories *by* youth. In addition, it highlights the impact of long-worn political structures on who has the capacity to decide how stories of violence, instability, and political revolution are told and understood during formal reconciliation processes. Inclusive participation for young people in TRCs that recognizes their political agency and respects how they navigate the social and political landscape requires that policymakers responsible for developing reconciliation mandates cede decision-making spaces within these institutions to young people from a diverse range of backgrounds.

Without these compromises the stories of young people will continue to be imbued with external politics, and youth will continue to be an embodiment of normative ideals that do not necessarily reflect their needs or experiences. Unless international and national actors take seriously the lessons revealed from previous attempts at engaging with young people during formal reconciliation processes, they will continue to contribute to the cycles of exclusion and marginalization that have led young people to feel disconnected from the aims of transitional justice. Young people have the capacity as knowledge producers to connect the stories of the past with the future in ways that legitimize the accountability within TRCs. This process, however, should not be passive or elite driven. When empowered to take ownership over their conflict stories, and when enabled to learn from the stories of others through substantive inclusion, young people play an instrumental role in rebuilding relationships and fulfilling the "never again" mandate of transitional justice.

This transformative potential was evident during the Canadian TRC process. Unlike the Tunisian process, the Canadian TRC demonstrated a responsiveness to the active participation of young people. Established in 2008 to investigate and acknowledge the human rights abuses that occurred within residential school systems, the process did not initially have a specific focus on youth until their participation in the first hearing demonstrated their agency. When heard, youth's stories exposed the importance of considering intergenerational trauma in the pursuit of holistic reconciliation. Furthermore, their level of engagement highlighted the significance of knowledge for empowering young people's connectedness to the truths revealed.[9] This connectedness to past truths amongst the youth demographic is essential for ensuring that future leaders are invested in the implications of these truths and in creating social and political conditions that can guarantee that the human rights violations revealed are not repeated. As one Canadian youth activist explains, "We are the next generation; after ten years we are going to be the adults, the lawyers, the prime ministers. We have to know when we are young, and when we are older, we can make sure this doesn't happen."[10] Inclusive practices that enable the retelling and acknowledgment of past trauma present opportunities for young people to feel linked with the past in a way that facilitates the creation of a sustainable peace for the future. In this way, young people when empowered to substantively engage with transitional justice processes such as TRCs possess the political will not only to embody aspirations for a prosperous future but also to actively build a peaceful and sustainable future as political actors.

The Canadian TRC was an integral part of "an overall holistic and comprehensive response to the Indian Residential School legacy."[11] As stated in the mandate, the aim was to provide a "sincere [recognition] of the injustices and harms experienced by Aboriginal people and the need for continued healing."[12] To that end, the commission sought to recast and renew the relationship between Indigenous and non-Indigenous Canadians that had been fractured by the human rights abuses committed against young people in the school systems. Although youth were not initially centered in this reconciliation process, their substantive participation in the first hearings to the committee demonstrated their capacity to contribute important yet unexplored perspectives to the reconciliation narrative. Unlike previous TRCs the Canadian process adopted a responsive approach to young people's demonstrations of agency and ownership at this first hearing, creating "education days" at all remaining national events. These education days provided opportunities for young people to actively engage with the reconciliation process through attendance at cultural ceremonies, hearings, and an exhibit about the history and impact of the Indian residential schools.[13] They were also empowered with knowledge through the development of a complementary teaching unit that furthered principles of shared storytelling for ownership and political buy-in.[14] The Canadian TRC process offers important lessons regarding the importance of addressing gaps in the inclusiveness of truth-telling and acknowledgment processes. While progress is evident, formal reconciliation processes must continue to evolve in ways that ensure substantive participation is normalized and youth are valued as knowledge producers.

The notion that young people have transformative potential underpins recent developments in international policy, specifically the institutionalization of the youth, peace, and security (YPS) agenda through UN Resolution 2250 and subsequent resolutions 2249 (2018) and 2535 (2020). As the Secretary General noted in 2015, the codification of the YPS agenda demonstrates a welcome "shift in the way the world seeks to prevent and end violence by acknowledging the positive and constructive roles that youth play in building sustainable peace and preserving international security."[15] In the transitional justice field the adoption of this normative shift has been slower and, as demonstrated in the preceding chapters, marred by institutional backsliding. Despite overwhelming evidence of their weaknesses, particularly their inability to capture marginalized voices, there remains a reliance on elite-driven, institutionalized approaches in states transitioning from violence and instability. These formal approaches rely on strict procedural rules and power structures that crowd out the distinct voices of young people. However, the solution is not to abandon these formal transitional justice institutions but to create conditions within them that enable and empower young people and their stories. Moreover, national and international actors involved in the design and implementation of transitional justice practices should consider the contributions of strategies that young people are adopting on the margins of these formal mechanisms to transform reconciliation discourses and reestablish interpersonal relationships.

Reframing young people's engagement with transitional justice mechanisms such as TRCs to enable substantive participation offers opportunities to create more inclusive justice practices. As Simpson explains, including young people "can help move truth-seeking and other transitional justice tools away from elite-led and externally driven processes and approaches,"[16] thus ensuring they are more responsive to the needs of the community. For young people, transitional justice practices have the potential to offer a mechanism through which to feel more connected to their social, political, and cultural history; a vehicle for active political and community engagement; and an opportunity to heal and rebuild relationships. Yet to ensure this potential is fulfilled it is necessary to understand how young people's participation has evolved.

Taken together, the chapters in this book reveal the relationship between young people and TRCs and explore the conditions that inform the character of this relationship. It provides an examination of how their conflict stories are utilized in the formal narratives produced by TRCs. This analysis demonstrates that despite widespread recognition in post-conflict states that young people are key actors with a unique stake in the outcome of TRCs, formal reconciliation narratives continue to silence their diverse and dynamic voices. Central to these claims are two overarching concerns. First, representations of children and youth across all TRCs reveal institutional classification slippages that were due in part to the prolonged nature of TRC processes. Second, emphasis on creating a singular reconciliation narrative that fulfills political agendas produces storytelling conditions where young people's voices are appropriated by external actors to reflect aspirational ideas about the transitional state's productive future potential. These claims indicate that TRCs, particularly at the institutional level, fail to meaningfully represent the experiences of young people and thus to realize the broader reconciliation mandate of accountability through acknowledgment.

Youth are complex individuals, highly responsive to external social and political pressures. They are also innovative and motivated individuals who are uniquely positioned to meaningfully influence reconciliation due to their status as the future leaders of transitional states. Yet normative representations of youth within the transitional justice field reflect an understanding of their roles as passive objectives caught between two socially and politically constructed worlds. An overreliance on classifying youth as a group of individuals in flux, not adults but not children either, facilitates inaccurate or unhelpful positionings of youth within the reconciliation discourse.

To overcome the ambiguity associated with framing the roles and experiences of young people from their perspective, transitional justice discourses rely on static binary classifications to inform the ways in which they are represented at TRCs. On the one hand, they are perceived as passive and innocent individuals in need of protection. On the other hand, they are often cast as the instigators of challenges to the peace and stability of transitional states, thus capable of spoiling reconciliation efforts.[17] While it is true that young people occupy these roles, the perception that this positioning is an either/or proposition, and that these roles are static, mischaracterizes and politicizes their stories. When the reconciliation narratives presented in the final reports of TRCs prioritize this binary, the distinctive voices of youth are silenced. This presents a challenge for attempts to create more responsive and inclusive transitional justice mechanisms, as while young people are increasingly visible in formal processes, they are not necessarily heard.

Balancing Political Agendas and Youth Agency: The Institutional Silencing of Youth

The evolution of young people's engagement with formal reconciliation mechanisms reveals overt and covert institutional silencing of their voices. This silencing is produced by a tension associated with balancing the political agendas of traditionally powerful actors with emerging notions of inclusivity that recognize the peace dividend produced by the substantive participation of young people. While TRC processes have increasingly carved out a space for youth, separate from children, the most visible outcome of TRCs, namely the final report, fails to hear and most importantly respond to the voices of youth. Misrepresentations within the reports challenge the pursuit of sustainable peace as these institutional documents are used to guide the future political agendas of transitional states. The reporting mandate of TRCs is significant because acknowledgment provides legitimacy to the conflict stories of traditionally marginalized individuals. Moreover, the inclusion of their voices in the formal state-endorsed narrative provides those typically excluded from transitional justice the opportunity to reclaim agency and ownership over their experiences. While the TRC processes of transitional states have shown youth to be active and politically engaged, youth are often silenced in the reports produced by these institutions. The current processes and norms that inform how conflict narratives are reported through TRCs demonstrate an inability to account for or acknowledge the diversity of young people's experiences. This has implications for the pursuit of substantive inclusion within this reconciliation process and threatens to undermine their legitimacy for young people.

The practice of transitional justice has evolved significantly from its restrictive, legal origins. However, the expansive and inclusive parameters that have come to define transitional justice are often purely conceptual, particularly where youth and their substantive participation are concerned. Contemporary notions of transitional justice espouse its global reach and capacity to be more representative and holistic. Yet the interactions of youth within TRCs challenge this notion, as their capacity to assign meaning to their own experiences rarely breaks through the political hierarchies endemic to these structures. Representations of young people within formal transitional justice practices challenge claims of inclusivity as this architecture often fails to accurately account for the impact of institutional slippage between children and youth.

The institutional structures of TRCs, specifically the reporting mandate, either rely on dichotomous and narrow representations of young people or more troubling still do not represent the distinct experiences of youth and children at all.

When the voices of youth are represented during the reconciliation process the result is a more responsive and holistic conflict narrative. The capacity of transitional states to achieve this, however, is often constrained by competing understandings of who youth are and the roles they play in conflict and transitional justice amongst the wide range of actors with a stake in the final outcomes of reconciliation processes. As the cases in this book demonstrate, there have been significant developments in the scope of youth engagement with the formal reconciliation processes of transitional states. Yet the nature of their participation, as well as recognition of their contributions to transitional justice more broadly, continues to provide significant challenges to the operationalization of practices that respond to the shifting discourse that youth are important political actors with agency. This is due in part to the persistence of dichotomous classifications in the understandings of youth communicated by external stakeholders. Drawing on the cases of South Africa, Sierra Leone, and the Solomon Islands, the analysis in this book illustrates that these narrow and dichotomous representations continue to inform understandings of youth in reconciliation because they tell a particular story about youth that fits the political agendas of national and international policymakers.

Claims that youth are either vulnerable or deviant continue to inform youth representation in the final reports of TRCs. These dichotomous depictions of youth are problematic as they often deny youth agency and ownership over their reconciliation stories. In addition, when TRCs conceive and cast youth through only this lens they silence the fluid and dynamic voices of youth that do not fit this largely static description. Youth occupy a multitude of roles in conflict and reconciliation practices that are not depicted through the victim/perpetrator binary lens. Both these models obscure their leadership and the other often overlapping roles that young people take on in conflict and reconciliation, namely as peacemakers, statement takers, researchers, transcribers, mediators, activists, and storytellers. What distinguishes these roles from the dominant victim/perpetrator classifications is the underlying acknowledgment that youth have agency and ownership over how they engage with justice and reconciliation for sustainable peace. Emerging recognition that youth occupy substantive decision-making roles is informed by their firsthand advocacy. In addition, efforts to engage with youth rather than for them are supported by normative claims that they have a unique and dynamic capacity to influence social and political systems and structures.

Acknowledging that youth have a distinct voice and agency does not discount that youth also occupy the roles of victim and perpetrator. Instead, it demonstrates that the roles of youth are constantly shifting based on their interactions and relationships. This diversity also demonstrates the importance of ensuring that youth have opportunities for self-representation through ascribing meaning to their own conflict narratives during reconciliation. Classifying youth experiences only through the victim/perpetrator binary lens, therefore, offers an incomplete representation of the relationship between youth, reconciliation, and TRCs. The youth agency lens used to examine their participation in TRC processes offers an alternative way of thinking about youth in transitional justice contexts, one that is more inclusive and responsive to their substantive participation and mindful of institutional slippages between classifications of children and youth. It does not, however, conflate their role or influence, nor does it romanticize their participation. The analysis in this book exposes the voices of young people and demonstrates the differences between their self-reflections and external notions of their engagement. In doing so, it aims to highlight the complexity associated with incorporating the dynamic and diverse stories of young people into the institutional frameworks of a TRC's final report.

Moreover, the representative limitations revealed by stories of individuals who exist on the margins challenge the stated inclusive and representative objectives of TRCs. As the cases in this book demonstrate, TRCs fail to balance representations of young people's lived experiences with the perceptions of other actors. Despite claims and displays of agency, enthusiasm, and political will by youth in each of the cases, external political agendas and the structures of TRCs limited their capacity to represent the differences in how young people interpret and participate in conflict. The emphasis on producing a clear and linear explanation of human rights violations, as well as the causes of the conflict, resulted in representations of youth that fulfilled the agenda of the state, rather than reflecting their diverse interests and the unique nature of their conflict experiences. The tension between these two positions occurred, as rarely did the experiences and interests of youth fit the institutional structures of TRCs, and therefore young people's stories were appropriated and reduced to a single, linear narrative.

Tales of Progress and Backsliding

The participation of youth in the development of TRC mandates and conditions provides a space for them to claim ownership and agency over their stories. The evolution of youth engagement from South Africa to Sierra Leone and finally the Solomon Islands has contributed to a global trend of young people participating more substantively in reconciliation practices. Transitional justice is responsive to shifts in social and political norms. TRCs in particular have a history of adapting the lessons learned at previous institutions to the current transitional contexts in which they are situated. The cases in this book demonstrate the evolutionary nature of TRCs with respect to young people's participation. While the reports of each case study present a nonlinear narrative of the development of youth representation, the scope of youth engagement was shaped by the practices of the preceding TRC.

Today there is greater recognition that youth is a period distinct from childhood and that the experiences associated with these stages should be represented. The chapters in this book highlight the contributions of the emerging global norm, which recognizes youth's leadership in the political spaces they occupy and values their role as empowered political agents. Yet the relationships between young people and formal institutions such as TRCs also reveal persistent tensions within the transitional justice field with respect to how meaning is assigned to the stories of young people. Representations and the engagement of young people across five truth commissions were explored to reveal important turning points in the normative discourse surrounding inclusive participation for young people. The result is a complex tapestry of engagement where political concerns and aspirations intertwine to inform how meaning is assigned to the conflict narratives of young people. In the South African case, the TRC process established a precedent of problematic institutional slippage between representations of children and youth. While the protracted nature of TRC processes makes avoiding this normative discourse complex, an overreliance on simplistic, externally derived binaries for classifying young people's role in conflict ensured that limited space existed for nuanced and diverse stories within the formal reconciliation narrative that would challenge and reveal this slippage. This institutional slippage was exacerbated by the prioritizing of the Convention on the Rights of the Child (CRC) as the normative framework to inform the commission's interactions with young people. Coupled with the limited mandate and strict rules about participation for young people, the TRC produced conditions that excluded the direct participation of children and recognition of their distinct experiences. Youth thus became a proxy for children and their stories were institutionally homogenized, despite opportunities to testify at the public hearings. Once compiled in the final report youth's voices were often appropriated to explain the ways in which children experienced conflict. This resulted in a blurring of the representative boundaries between children and youth.

In the South African TRC, while young people were visible for the first time in the reconciliation narratives the nature and scope of this visibility had significant limitations that resulted in a silencing of political agency and an inability of young people to buy into the process. Broadly speaking, the engagement of young people with the South African TRC laid the foundation for future interactions. It produced a normative framework for understanding young people that reduced their experiences to narrow binaries and thus crowded out representations and stories that sit outside the victim/perpetrator construct.

The Sierra Leone TRC presents a turning point in the narrative of engagement because it remains the only reconciliation process to separate the stories of children and youth. Representations at this TRC deviated from other cases as youth agency was prominent throughout both the final report and the process. A focus on young people during the TRC process created space for youth's substantive inclusion. This was reflected in the creation of the Accountability Now clubs, which were established by the Specifical Court of Sierra Leone to empower youth to participate in peer-to-peer human rights education.[18] By empowering youth to participate in knowledge development and dissemination, this program recognized their capacity to productively navigate political and social relationships to create conditions for meaningful justice and accountability.

Although the deviance classification persisted, youth claimed ownership over this deviance. The Sierra Leone TRC clearly demonstrates the tension between representations *of* youth and representations *by* youth. Deviance when employed by youth to represent their experiences reflects empowerment and ownership. In contrast, when utilized by external agents, youth and their experiences become resources and reflections of the reconciliation agenda rather than knowledge producers and political actors. Therefore the TRC process in Sierra Leone denotes a significant departure in how youth are conceived and cast during reconciliation. In this way, it lends credence to the argument that when the voices of youth are heard and applied, those voices contribute to a more complete representation of the conflict.

Finally, the Solomon Islands case highlights the capacity of youth to contribute meaningfully to the development of TRCs. The interactions of youth with the TRC in the Solomon Islands denote a more interpersonal notion of reconciliation that focuses attention on the needs of individuals. This interpersonal style of reconciliation allowed youth to engage extensively with the process of reconciliation and to reframe their position within the Solomon Islands community. As the opening quotes of this chapter demonstrate, through close engagement with the reconciliation process youth positioned themselves as leaders of the development and reconciliation movement. Despite well-intentioned efforts to be inclusive and responsive, the final report of the TRC rendered meaningless their substantive participation due to the pervasiveness of the victim/perpetrator binary.

Taken together, this evolution of youth engagement suggests a tension between representations *of* youth and *by* youth. Youth engagement with reconciliation can be characterized by instances of backsliding in the global norm. What is clear is that the dynamic nature of young people and their conflict roles is never the dominant reconciliation narrative due to the underlying politics associated with TRCs. Youth are knowledge producers who navigate the social and political landscape to demonstrate political agency. Despite this, the formal reconciliation architecture of post-conflict states fails to genuinely consider their stories or to enable their substantive participation in the development of TRC mandates, the final reports, and the recommendations.

Understanding the Past to Create More Responsive Reconciliation Futures

The youth agency model is central to the discussions in the book. Drawing on this model to understand how young people engage with transitional justice processes provides a framework for evaluating the capacity of these institutions to facilitate inclusive participation. Truth telling as a process provides a space for youth to claim agency, particularly when their narratives are heard and taken seriously. Reconciliation and restorative justice offers opportunities to empower youth in ways that recognize that they are knowledge creators capable of restoring and owning their relationships with the community. Similar normative ideas about inclusive participation have emerged in the peacebuilding discourse, which concludes that young people "may be more inclined to trust in and further" institutional practice if their voices are centered and taken seriously.[19] This has implications for their engagement in the political structures and future development programs of transitional states, as it highlights the importance of ensuring that youth have a seat at the table, particularly when discussing practices that will directly impact their present and future.

Furthermore, the findings of this book have implications for how we understand the contributions of TRCs to the goal of reconciliation. It suggests that measures of success should be reappropriated to emphasize the importance of the process rather than the outcome. In looking at the process, national and international policymakers are better able to determine whether the reconciliation practices implemented meet the primary goals of inclusion and acknowledgment. This book also contributes to the growing yet still underdeveloped body of work on youth in transitional justice. It provides insights regarding the relationship between youth, reconciliation, and transitional justice and offers an alternative way for conceiving and casting the nature of this relationship. Where TRCs are concerned, these findings suggest that there is a need for institutional structures to be more inclusive and fluid when producing representations of youth and their experiences. As such, greater attention needs to be given to the perceptions and voices of youth so that we can better hear and quantify their interests and experiences as well as distinguish them from children.

Finally, I suggest that policymakers responsible for the operationalization of TRCs need to find a way to balance the political goals of producing a cohesive conflict narrative with the often divergent, dynamic, and unique perspectives of youth. This has broader implications for how we hear and interact with other groups traditionally excluded from transitional justice practices. It suggests that where TRCs are concerned, a move away from political reconciliation and toward the interpersonal approach will provide a more inclusive space for the voices of marginalized groups. Indeed, TRCs that emphasize interpersonal reconciliation when engaging with the voices of marginalized individuals are more capable of acknowledging and addressing their interests and experiences. Claims that TRCs are inclusive and representative have proven to be largely conceptual, as in practice the voices of youth, women, and children often fail to break through international and local normative frameworks that emphasize vulnerability (manifested through either deviance or innocence). The findings in this book suggest that it is not sufficient to simply make these groups more visible in the reconciliation process, but national and international policymakers responsible for the development of TRCs must also take seriously the content of their stories and how they are interpreting their meaning.

Acknowledging a Way Forward for Reconciliation Practices

The stories presented in this book evidence the urgent need to develop new strategies for the substantive inclusion of young people in formal reconciliation practices, specifically TRCs. Greater coordination is also required between formal TRCs and the informal practices led by young people designed to bring about reconciliation. Avenues for participation must be expanded within TRCs. At the same time, support must be given to youth-led strategies that occur on the margins of formal reconciliation processes. The closing section offers some key considerations for the design and implementation of TRCs that are substantively inclusive of young people.

One: *Create practices that capitalize on young people's political agency, and their capacity for autonomous decision-making and leadership to value their contributions as knowledge producers.* Transitional justice practices, particularly those with expansive participatory parameters such as TRCs, must support mandates, which situate young people as active storytellers capable of owning and producing knowledge. This will ensure that the outputs of TRCs, namely the final report and its recommendations, acknowledge that young people are experts in the meaning of their own experiences. Empowering young people as knowledge producers also requires that TRCs capture and take seriously the stories of young people in ways that reflect how they self-identify. This is particularly important in post-conflict states where classifications of young people are fluid, expansive, and highly subjective.

Young people's interactions with reconciliation practices should not be mediated by external actors. Young people should be enabled to engage and be provided with resources to facilitate this participation, but how this engagement occurs needs to be determined by young people themselves. Support for young people's participation in TRCs should prioritize capacity building. Their contributions to reconciliation outside institutions should also be enabled through the provision of sustainable funding. Capacity building practices and funding models should be developed with young people and should be flexible and widely accessible.

Two: *Prioritize partnerships at the decision-making level.* Substantive inclusion requires that national and international policymakers see young people as partners in reconciliation. TRC mandates, recommendations, and the arrangement of the commission should be constructed *with* youth. Current evolutions of the TRC process have produced more consultative processes, most notably the Solomon Islands TRC (chapter 5). Yet often this process does not result in meaningful change or the adoption of young people's ideas. While efforts to create more gender-balanced TRC commissions have occurred, young people have yet to be empowered to participate in this way. Youth have the capacity to serve on TRC commissions, as well as in active roles as mediators, researchers, and focus group facilitators. Thus, evolutions in participation that value partnerships must also be meaningful and look beyond tokenistic participation that amounts to an add-youth-and-stir approach. TRC processes should enable youth to participate *as* policymakers. This will involve powerful actors ceding space to young people.

Three: *Formal TRC processes need to acknowledge the role of informal practices led by youth in facilitating reconciliation.* Reconciliation stories span across generations and transitional communities. Yet the preoccupation with developing a linear conflict narrative often ensures that the voices holding these stories continue to be silenced, despite best intentions by the architects of these institutions to remain inclusive. While young people may struggle to be heard in formal reconciliation practices, examples throughout this book demonstrate that they are maintaining ownership of their stories through informal practices. The pursuit of meaningful accountability for human rights abuses requires an acknowledgment of all strategies for reconciliation. Formal reconciliation processes need to do more to enable networks within diverse communities that connect formal and informal reconciliation strategies.

International and national actors can play a significant role in facilitating cooperation between these networks by creating space for all youth and supporting existing youth-led strategies. It is also integral that inclusion for young people be democratized to recognize how intersecting factors, such as location, gender, socioeconomic status, and race, inform their conflict stories and the meaning assigned to them. Reconciliation practices as such must encourage and reveal dissenting voices that may challenge the political conflict narrative and upend the status quo of institutional reconciliation.

Notes

Introduction

1. The Tensions was the name given to the ethnic conflict that took place between 1994 and 2004 in the Solomon Islands. For a detailed examination of the Tensions, see Matthew G. Allen, *Greed and Grievance: Ex-Militants' Perspectives on the Conflict in Solomon Islands, 1998–2003* (Honolulu: University of Hawaii Press, 2013).

2. Nelson Rodridge Legua, "Youth@Work Solomon Islands," Pacific Community, YouTube video, June 7, 2017, https://www.youtube.com/watch?v=jl21TnOGM98.

3. Sandra Bartlett, "Youth@Work Solomon Islands," Pacific Community, YouTube video, June 7, 2017, https://www.youtube.com/watch?v=jl21TnOGM98.

4. Toito'Ona, "Youth Market is Back," *Solomon Star*, Oct. 31, 2016.

5. Anonymous Thirteen, interview with the author in Solomon Islands, Nov. 2015. All interviews have been anonymized per ethics requirements unless participants have consented to be identified.

6. Anonymous Seventeen, interview with the author in Solomon Islands, Nov. 2015.

7. Anonymous Fourteen, interview with the author in Solomon Islands, Nov. 2015.

8. Bartlett cited in Aiden Craney, *Youth in Fiji and Solomon Islands: Livelihoods, Leadership and Civic Engagement* (Canberra, AU: ANU Press, 2022), 16.

9. Anonymous Eighteen, interview with the author in Solomon Islands, Nov. 2015.

10. For information about UN Resolution 2250 and the Youth, Peace and Security agenda, see Helen Berents and Saji Prelis, *More than a Milestone: The Road to UN Security Council Resolution 2250 on Youth, Peace and Security*, Search for Common Ground and the Global Coalition on Youth Peace and Security, Dec. 2020, https://www.youth4peace.info/system/files/202012/The%20Story%20of%202250_FINAL%20Dec%209%202020.pdf.

11. UN Security Council, Resolution 2250, S/RES/2250 (Dec. 9, 2015), https://undocs.org/en/S/RES/2250(2015).

12. UN Security Council, Resolution 2250.

13. Ali Altiok and Irena Grizelj, "We Are Here: An Integrated Approach to Youth-Inclusive Peace Processes," United Nations Office of the Secretary-General's Envoy on Youth, March 2019, https://www.youth4peace.info/book-page/global-policy-paper-we-are-here-integrated-approach-youth-inclusive-peace-processes.

14. UN Secretary-General, *Youth and Peace and Security*, UN Doc S/2020/167, March 2, 2020, https://undocs.org/en/S/2020/167.

15. Helen Berents, "Power, Partnership, and Youth as Norm Entrepreneurs: Getting to UN Security Council Resolution 2250 on Youth, Peace, and Security," *Global Studies Quarterly* 2, no. 3 (2022): 1–11.

16. Savannah Spalding et al., "Making Noise and Getting things Done: Youth Inclusion and Advocacy for Peace: Lessons from Afghanistan, South Sudan and Myanmar" (2012) Queensland: QUT Centre for Justice, https://research-repository.griffith.edu.au/bitstream/handle/10072/421260/Berents5114457-Accepted.pdf?sequence=2.

17. UN Security Council, Resolution 2250.

18. Altiok and Grizelj, "We Are Here," 8.

19. Altiok and Grizelj, 8.

20. UN Secretary-General, *Youth and Peace and Security*, UN Doc S/2020/167.

21. Jana Tabak and Letícia Carvalho, "Responsibility to Protect the Future: Children on the Move and the Politics of Becoming," in *Children and the Responsibility to Protect*, eds. Bina D'Costa and Luke Glanville (Leiden, NL: Brill Nijhoff, 2019), 115–38.

22. Helen Berents and Siobhán McEvoy-Levy, "Theorising Youth and Everyday Peace (Building)," *Peacebuilding* 3, no. 2 (2015): 115–25.

23. Altiok and Grizelj, "We Are Here," 9.

24. Graeme Simpson, *The Missing Peace: Independent Progress Study on Youth, Peace, and Security*. Progress Study on Youth, Peace and Security, New York: UN Peacebuilding Support Office, 2018, https://digitallibrary.un.org/record/3846611?ln=en.

25. Altiok and Grizelj, "We Are Here," 33.

26. Karen Brounéus, *Reconciliation: Theory and Practice for Development Cooperation*, Swedish International Development Cooperation Agency (SIDA), Stockholm, 2003; Simpson, *The Missing Peace*, 46–53.

27. Altiok and Grizelj, "We Are Here," 32.

28. Catherine Bennett, "Letters of Reconciliation Sent to Ex-FARC Fighters," *Observers*, July 7, 2017; María José Carmona, "Lessons in Tolerance: The Colombian Letters Sent to Former FARC Fighters," *El País*, June 2, 2017.

29. Asli Ozcelik et al., "Youth-Led Peace: The Role of Youth in Peace Processes," SSRN Scholarly Paper (Rochester, NY: Social Science Research Network, 2021), https://papers.ssrn.com/abstract=3853760.

30. Altiok and Grizelj, "We Are Here," 51.

31. Altiok and Grizelj, 51.

32. Virginie Ladisch and Joanna Rice, "Cote d'Ivoire Youth Find Voice Through Storytelling," International Center for Transitional Justice (Oct. 27, 2016), https://www.ictj.org/news/cote-divoire-youth-political-voice-stories-war.

33. Simpson, *The Missing Peace*, 104.

34. Helen Berents and Caitlin Mollica, "Youth and Peacebuilding," in *The Palgrave Encyclopedia of Peace and Conflict Studies*, eds. Oliver P. Richmond and Gëzim Visoka (Cham: Palgrave Macmillan, 2020), 95–91.

35. Elina Oinas, Henri Onodera, and Leena Suurpää, eds., *What Politics? Youth and Political Engagement in Africa* (Leiden, NL: Brill, 2018).

36. Berents and Mollica, *Youth and Peacebuilding*, 95.

37. Department of Economic and Social Affairs, *World Youth Report 2005: Young People Today and in 2015.* New York: United Nations, 2005, https://www.un.org/development/desa/youth/world-youth-report/world-youth-report-2005.html.

38. Alphaslan Özerdem and Sukanya Podder, *Youth in Conflict and Peacebuilding: Mobilization, Reintegration and Reconciliation* (London: Palgrave Macmillan, 2015), 6–7; see also Berents and Mollica, "Youth and Peacebuilding."

39. UN Security Council, Resolution 2250 (2015); Simpson, *The Missing Peace*, 9.

40. Altiok and Grizelj, "We Are Here," 13.

41. Simpson, *The Missing Peace*, 103–4.

42. Boyden, preface to *Years of Conflict: Adolescence, Political Violence and Displacement*, ed. Jason Hart (New York: Berghahn Books, 2010), ix.

43. UN Development Programme, "UNDP Youth Strategy 2014–2017: Empowered Youth, Sustainable Future," 11. The numerical classification of ten to twenty-four is the internationally recognized definition of youth endorsed by the United Nations. However, this book is mindful of cultural variations to this classification. For a detailed discussion of this classification and the complexities associated defining youth, see chapter 3; see also Yvonne Kemper, "Youth in War-to-Peace Transitions: Approaches of International Organisations," Berghof Research Center for Constructive Conflict Management, Jan. 1, 2005, 8.

44. Sinclair Dinnen, "State-Building in a Post-Colonial Society: The Case of Solomon Islands," *Chicago Journal of International Law* 9, no. 1 (2008): 60; Clifton, Donna, and Alexandra Hervish, "The World's Youth: 2013 Data Sheet," Washington, DC: Population Reference Bureau, 2013, 6–10, https://www.prb.org/wp-content/uploads/2013/04/youth-data-sheet-2013.pdf.

45. For Sierra Leone, see Sierra Leone Government, "Sierra Leone National Youth Policy," June 30, 2003, 3. For Timor-Leste see, Democratic Republic of Timor-Leste, "National Youth Policy of Timor-Leste," Secretary of State for Youth and Sport, Balide, Díli, Nov. 14, 2007, 7.

46. Brounéus, *Reconciliation*, 3.

47. For research on youth participation in peacebuilding, see Albrecht Schnabel and Anara Tabyshalieva, eds., *Escaping Victimhood: Children, Youth and Post-Conflict Peacebuilding* (New York: United Nations University Press, 2013); Stephanie Schwartz, *Youth and Post-Conflict Reconstruction: Agents of Change* (Washington, DC: United States Institute of Peace Press, 2010); Lesley J. Pruitt, *Youth Peacebuilding: Music, Gender, and Change* (Albany: State University of New York Press, 2013); Helen Berents, *Young People and Everyday Peace: Exclusion, Insecurity and Peacebuilding in Colombia* (New York: Routledge, 2018); Siobhán McEvoy-Levy, *Troublemakers or Peacemakers? Youth and Post-Accord Peacebuilding* (Notre Dame, IN: University of Notre Dame Press, 2006).

48. Bina D' Costa, ed., "Turtles Can Fly: Vicarious Terror and the Child in South Asia," in *Children and Violence: Politics of Conflict in South Asia* (Cambridge: Cambridge University Press, 2016), 5; Olga Nieuwenhuys, "Keep Asking: Why Childhood? Why Children? Why Global?" *Childhood* 17, no. 3 (Aug. 1, 2010): 291–96.

49. Norman Long cited in Krijn Peters, "Re-Examining Voluntarism: Youth Combatants in Sierra Leone," Pretoria, SA: Institute for Security Studies, April 1, 2004, 6.

50. Anna Holzscheiter, *Children's Rights in International Politics: The Transformative Power of Discourse* (Basingstoke, UK: Palgrave Macmillan, 2010), 2; see also Kirsten J. Fisher, *Transitional Justice for Child Soldiers: Accountability and Social Reconstruction in Post-Conflict Contexts* (Basingstoke, UK: Palgrave Macmillan, 2013).

51. Graça Machel, *Impact of Armed Conflict on Children*. UN Doc. A/51/306 (Aug. 26, 1996), https://undocs.org/A/51/306.

52. UN Children's Fund (UNICEF), "Cape Town Principles and Best Practices," UNICEF, April 27, 1997.

53. UNICEF, "The Paris Principles: Principles and Guidelines on Children Associated with Armed Forces or Armed Groups," UN Children's Fund (UNICEF), Feb. 2007, https://www.refworld.org/docid/465198442.html; UN Member States, "The Paris Commitments to Protect Children from Unlawful Recruitment or Use by Armed Forces or Armed Groups," UN Children's Fund (UNICEF), Feb. 2007.

54. UNICEF, "Paris Principles," para. 2.

55. D'Costa, "Turtles Can Fly," 17.

56. Vanessa Pupavac, "Misanthropy Without Borders: The International Children's Rights Regime," *Disasters* 25, no. 2 (2001): 95–112; Katrina Lee-Koo,

"Children and Armed Conflict: Mapping the Terrain," in *Children and Global Conflict*, eds. Kim Huynh, Bina D'Costa, and Katrina Lee-Koo (Cambridge: Cambridge University Press, 2015), 10–16.

57. Kim Huynh, "Children and Agency: Caretakers, Free-Rangers and Everyday Life," in Huynh, D'Costa, and Lee-Koo, *Children and Global Conflict*, 37–43; P. W. Singer, *Children at War* (Berkeley: University of California Press, 2006), 56–59; David Archard, *Children: Rights and Childhood*, 2nd ed. (London: Routledge, 2004); Allison James and Alan Prout, *Constructing and Reconstructing Childhood: Contemporary Issues in the Sociological Study of Childhood*, 3rd ed. (London: Routledge, 2015), 1.

58. Cecilia Jacob, *Child Security in Asia: The Impact of Armed Conflict in Cambodia and Myanmar* (London: Routledge, 2014), 34.

59. Fisher, *Transitional Justice for Child Soldiers*; Ilene Cohn and Guy S. Goodwin-Gill, *Child Soldiers: The Role of Children in Armed Conflict* (Oxford: Oxford University Press, 1994).

60. Rachel Brett and Margaret McCallin, *Children: The Invisible Soldiers*, 2nd ed. (Stockholm: Rädda Barnen, 1998); Mark A. Drumbl, *Reimagining Child Soldiers in International Law and Policy* (Oxford: Oxford University Press, 2012).

61. See for example Özerdem and Podder, "Youth in Conflict and Peacebuilding," chap. 4.

62. UNICEF Innocenti Research Centre and International Center for Transitional Justice, *Children and Truth Commissions* (Florence, IT: UNICEF, 2010), 46, 86, https://www.unicef-irc.org/publications/pdf/truth_commissions_eng.pdf.

63. Truth and Reconciliation Commission, *Truth and Reconciliation Commission of South Africa Report*, 7 vols., Truth and Reconciliation Commission, 1998, https://www.justice.gov.za/trc/report/.

64. *Truth and Reconciliation Commission (Comisión de La Verdad y Reconciliación [CVR])*, United States Institute of Peace, Truth Commissions Digital Collection, 2003, https://www.usip.org/publications/2001/07/truth-commission-peru-01.

65. Chega is Portuguese for "No more, stop, enough." It was chosen as the title of the report because it captures the main message given by victims to the CAVR. Timor-Leste Commission for Reception, Truth, and Reconciliation (CAVR). *Chega! The Final Report of the Timor-Leste Commission for Reception, Truth, and Reconciliation*. Dili, Timor-Leste: CAVR, 2005, http://chegareport.org/Chega%20All%20Volumes.pdf.

66. The English version of the report was edited by Pat Walsh and published in 2015. Pat Walsh, ed., *Chega! Book 1: What Happened and How to Stop It Happening Again*, trans. Mayra Walsh (Dili, Timor-Leste: INSIST Press, 2015), http://www.chegareport.org/download-chega-products-2/.

67. Truth and Reconciliation Commission, *Witness to Truth: Report of the Sierra Leone Truth and Reconciliation Commission*, 3 vols. (Freetown, Sierra

Leone: Sierra Leone Truth and Reconciliation Commission, 2004), http://www.sierraleonetrc.org/index.php/view-the-final-report/download-table-of-contents.

68. Truth and Reconciliation Commission, *Report for the Children of Sierra Leone* (Freetown, Sierra Leone: UNICEF, 2004).

69. Truth and Reconciliation Commission, *Report for the Children*, 5.

70. Solomon Islands Truth and Reconciliation Commission, *Solomon Islands Truth and Reconciliation Commission Final Report: Confronting the Truth for a Better Solomon Islands*, 5 vols., Honiara, Solomon Islands, 2012.

71. The Truth and Reconciliation Act 2008 (Act No. 5/2008) (Solom. Is.) § 17(1).

72. Tess Newton Cain, "Final Report of the Solomon Islands Truth & Reconciliation Commission Unofficially Released," *Devpolicy Blog from the Development Policy Centre* (blog), April 30, 2013, https://devpolicy.org/final-report-of-the-solomon-islands-truth-reconciliation-commission-unofficially-released-20130501-2/; Australian Network News, "Solomons Truth and Reconciliation Report Released," *ABC News (Online)*, April 29, 2013, https://www.abc.net.au/news/2013-04-29/solomons-truth-and-reconciliation-report-released/4658288; CathNews New Zealand, "Bishop Releases Truth and Reconciliation Report," *CathNews New Zealand*, May 3, 2013, https://cathnews.co.nz/2013/05/03/bishop-releases-truth-and-reconciliation-report/.

73. Philip Cook and Cheryl Heykoop, "Child Participation in the Sierra Leonean Truth and Reconciliation Commission," in *Children and Transitional Justice: Truth-Telling, Accountability and Reconciliation*, eds. Sharanjeet Parmar et al. (Cambridge, MA: Human Rights Program, Harvard Law School, 2010), 161; Bina D'Costa, "Children and Justice: Past Crimes, Healing and the Future," in Huynh, D'Costa, and Lee-Koo, *Children and Global Conflict*, 240.

74. Madeleine Fullard and Nicky Rousseau, "Truth Telling, Identities, and Power in South Africa and Guatemala," in *Identities in Transition: Challenges for Transitional Justice in Divided Societies*, ed. Paige Arthur (Cambridge: Cambridge University Press, 2010), 56.

75. Jessica Senehi and Sean Byrne, "From Violence Toward Peace: The Role of Storytelling for Youth Healing and Political Empowerment after Social Conflict," in McEvoy-Levy, *Troublemakers or Peacemakers?*, 238.

76. Siobhán McEvoy-Levy, *Peace and Resistance in Youth Cultures: Reading the Politics of Peacebuilding from Harry Potter to The Hunger Games* (London: Palgrave Macmillan, 2018), 41.

77. Katrina Lee-Koo, "Children and Peacebuilding: Propagating Peace," in Huynh, D'Costa, and Lee-Koo, *Children and Global Conflict*, 203.

78. Robert Atkinson, "The Life Story Interview as a Bridge in Narrative Inquiry," in *Handbook of Narrative Inquiry: Mapping a Methodology*, ed. D. Jean Clandinin (London: SAGE, 2007), 224.

79. Renée Jeffery, *Amnesties, Accountability, and Human Rights* (Philadelphia: University of Pennsylvania Press, 2014), 14.

80. Caitlin Mollica, "The Diversity of Identity: Youth Participation at the Solomon Islands Truth and Reconciliation Commission," *Australian Journal of International Affairs* 71, no. 4 (2017): 371–88.

81. Siobhán McEvoy-Levy, "Children, Youth and Peacebuilding," in *Critical Issues in Peace and Conflict Studies: Theory, Practice and Pedagogy*, eds. Thomas Matyók, Jessica Senehi, and Sean Byrne (Lanham, MD: Lexington Books, 2011), 168.

Chapter 1

1. Acknowledgment: this chapter is derived in part from an article published in *Australian Journal of International Affairs* on March 1, 2017, © 2017 Australian Institute of International Affairs, https://www.tandfonline.com/doi/10.1080/10357718.2017.1290045, reprinted by permission of Taylor & Francis Ltd, https://www.tandfonline.com, on behalf of Australian Institute of International Affairs. The Truth and Reconciliation Act 2008 (Act No. 5/2008) (Solom. Is.), Government of the Solomon Islands.

2. Solomon Islands Truth and Reconciliation Commission, *Solomon Islands Truth and Reconciliation Commission Final Report: Confronting the Truth for a Better Solomon Islands*, 5 vols., Honiara, Solomon Islands, 2012, 9.

3. *Solomon Islands Truth and Reconciliation Commission Final Report*, 631; see also, Matthew G. Allen, *Greed and Grievance: Ex-Militants' Perspectives on the Conflict in Solomon Islands, 1998–2003* (Honolulu: University of Hawaii Press, 2013).

4. Valerie Braithwaite et al., *Pillars and Shadows: Statebuilding as Peacebuilding in Solomon Islands* (Canberra: Australian National University Press, 2010), 127–28.

5. Christine Jourdan, "Masta Liu," in *Youth Cultures: A Cross-Cultural Perspective*, eds. Vered Amit-Talai and Helena Wulff (London: Routledge, 1995), 202. Introduced into Solomon Islands Pijin by the Malaitans, the term took on greater significance in the 1970s when the Masta Liu Project was established to provide training to unemployed youth in Honiara.

6. For a discussion of *Masta Liu* in the context of the Solomon Islands, see, for example, Jon Fraenkel, *The Manipulation of Custom: From Uprising to Intervention in the Solomon Islands* (Wellington, NZ: Victoria University Press, 2004), 113, 119; see also, Braithwaite et al., *Pillars and Shadows*, 99–100.

7. Allen, *Greed and Grievance*, 5.

8. The Truth and Reconciliation Act 2008 (Act No. 5/2008) (Solom. Is.) § 5(2)(c).

9. *Solomon Islands Truth and Reconciliation Commission Final Report*, 9.

10. *Solomon Islands Truth and Reconciliation Commission Final Report*, 723.

11. *Solomon Islands Truth and Reconciliation Commission Final Report*, 1214–15.

12. *Solomon Islands Truth and Reconciliation Commission Final Report*, 722.

13. On democratic transitions, see Jon Elster, *Closing the Books: Transitional Justice in Historical Perspective* (Cambridge: Cambridge University Press, 2004), 1; Neil Kritz, ed., *Transitional Justice: How Emerging Democracies Reckon with Former Regimes*, 3 vols. (Washington, DC: United States Institute of Peace Press, 1995), vol. 1; Paige Arthur, "How 'Transitions' Reshaped Human Rights: A Conceptual History of Transitional Justice," *Human Rights Quarterly* 31, no. 2 (2009), 329–31. For a detailed discussion on transitions from war to peace, see M. Cherif Bassiouni, ed., *Post-Conflict Justice* (Ardsley, NY: Transnational Publishers, 2002); Naomi Roht-Arriaza, "The New Landscape of Transitional Justice," in *Transitional Justice in the Twenty-First Century: Beyond Truth versus Justice*, eds. Javier Mariezcurrena and Naomi Roht-Arriaza (Cambridge: Cambridge University Press, 2006), 2; Tricia D. Olsen, Leigh A. Payne, and Andrew G. Reiter, *Transitional Justice in Balance: Comparing Processes, Weighing Efficacy* (Washington, DC: United States Institute of Peace Press, 2010), 10–11.

14. For a discussion of the development of the norms and debates of transitional justice, see Renée Jeffery, "Transitional Justice and the Tensions" in *Transitional Justice in Practice*, ed. Renée Jeffery (New York: Palgrave Macmillan, 2017), 2–3.

15. Renée Jeffery and Hun Joon Kim, "Introduction: New Horizons; Transitional Justice in the Asia-Pacific," in *Transitional Justice in the Asia-Pacific*, eds. Renée Jeffery and Hun Joon Kim (Cambridge: Cambridge University Press, 2014), 1; see also Kathryn Sikkink and Hun Joon Kim, "The Justice Cascade: The Origins and Effectiveness of Prosecutions of Human Rights Violations," *Annual Review of Law and Social Science* 9, no. 1 (2013), 270; Naomi Roht-Arriaza, "Civil Society in Processes of Accountability," in Bassiouni, *Post-Conflict Justice*, 97.

16. Kathryn Sikkink, *The Justice Cascade: How Human Rights Prosecutions Are Changing World Politics* (New York: W. W. Norton, 2011), 158–59; see also Hun Joon Kim and Renée Jeffery, conclusion to *Transitional Justice in the Asia-Pacific*, 301.

17. Chandra Lekha Sriram, "Revolutions in Accountability: New Approaches to Past Abuses," *American University International Law Review* 19, no. 2 (2003): 301–429; Ellen Lutz and Kathryn Sikkink, "The Justice Cascade: The Evolution and Impact of Foreign Human Rights Trials in Latin America," *Chicago Journal of International Law* 2, no. 1 (2001): 1–33.

18. Rosemary Nagy, "Transitional Justice as Global Project: Critical Reflections," *Third World Quarterly* 29, no. 2 (2008): 276; Dustin Sharp, "Development, Human Rights and Transitional Justice: Global Projects for Global Governance," *International Journal of Transitional Justice* 9, no. 3 (2015): 517.

19. Nagy, "Transitional Justice as Global Project," 276; Ruti G. Teitel, *Globalizing Transitional Justice: Contemporary Essays* (New York: Oxford University Press, 2014).

20. For a detailed discussion of these debates see Jeffery and Kim, "Introduction," 8–20.

21. Olsen, Payne, and Reiter, *Transitional Justice in Balance*, 9–13; Nagy, "Transitional Justice as Global Project," 276–79.

22. Jeffery and Kim, "Introduction," 8.

23. Elster, *Closing the Books*, 1.

24. Elster, 1.

25. Elster, 1.

26. Elster, 53.

27. Many scholars have written about Nuremberg's contribution to the human rights field. Two notable examples include Paul Gordon Lauren, *The Evolution of International Human Rights: Visions Seen*, 3rd ed. (Philadelphia: University of Pennsylvania Press, 2011), 202; and Michael Ignatieff, *Human Rights as Politics and Idolatry*, ed. Amy Gutmann (Princeton, NJ: Princeton University Press, 2001), 5–6.

28. Robert Jackson, Opening statement, Nov. 21, 1945, International Military Tribunal, *Trial of the Major War Criminals* 2:98–99, 130.

29. International Military Tribunal, 11:941.

30. For a detailed discussion of democratic transitions, see Samuel P. Huntington, *The Third Wave: Democratization in the Late Twentieth Century* (Norman: University of Oklahoma Press, 1991), 7.

31. Richard H. Solomon, preface to *Transitional Justice: How Emerging Democracies Reckon with Former Regimes*, ed. Neil Kritz (Washington, DC: United States Institute of Peace Press, 1995), xxiii.

32. Ruti G. Teitel, "Transitional Justice Genealogy," *Harvard Human Rights Journal* 16 (2003): 69.

33. Diane F. Orentlicher, "Settling Accounts: The Duty to Prosecute Human Rights Violations of a Prior Regime," *Yale Law Journal* 100, no. 8 (1991): 2541.

34. Orentlicher, 2551–53.

35. Dustin N. Sharp, "Interrogating the Peripheries: The Preoccupations of Fourth Generation Transitional Justice," *Harvard Human Rights Journal* 26 (2013): 155.

36. These tensions have been examined extensively in transitional justice scholarship. For a detailed discussion of this debate, see, for example, Jeffery and Kim, "Introduction," 9–13; Luc Huyse, "Justice after Transition: On the Choices Successor Elites Make in Dealing with the Past," *Law and Social Inquiry* 20, no. 1 (1995): 54–55; Orentlicher, "Settling Accounts"; Naomi Roht-Arriaza, "State Responsibility to Investigate and Prosecute Grave Human Rights Violations in International Law," *California Law Review* 78, no. 2 (1990): 449–514.

37. Naomi Roht-Arriaza, "The New Landscape of Transitional Justice," in *Transitional Justice in the Twenty-First Century: Beyond Truth versus Justice*, eds. Javier Mariezcurrena and Naomi Roht-Arriaza (Cambridge: Cambridge University Press, 2006), 2.

38. Dustin N Sharp, "Beyond the Post-Conflict Checklist: Linking Peacebuilding and Transitional Justice Through the Lens of Critique," *Chicago Journal of International Law* 14, no. 1 (2013): 165.

39. Michael Barnett et al., "Peacebuilding: What Is in a Name?," *Global Governance* 13, no. 1 (2007): 44; John Paul Lederach, *Building Peace: Sustainable Reconciliation in Divided Societies* (Tokyo: United Nations University Press), 1994, 14.

40. Sikkink, *The Justice Cascade*, 5.

41. Jeffery and Kim, "Introduction," 5.

42. Antje du Bois-Pedain, *Transitional Amnesty in South Africa* (Cambridge: Cambridge University Press, 2007), 176; Renée Jeffery, "Transitional Justice and the Tensions," in Jeffery, *Transitional Justice in Practice*, 9.

43. Jeffery, "Transitional Justice and the Tensions," 9.

44. Joanna R. Quinn, *The Politics of Acknowledgement: Truth Commissions in Uganda and Haiti*, Law and Society Series (Vancouver, BC: UBC Press, 2010), 38–39.

45. Howard Zehr, "Restorative Justice: The Concept," *Corrections Today* 59, no. 7 (Dec. 1997): 68–70; Paul Gready and Simon Robins, "From Transitional to Transformative Justice: A New Agenda for Practice," *International Journal of Transitional Justice* 8, no. 3 (2014): 340.

46. John Braithwaite, "Setting Standards for Restorative Justice," *British Journal of Criminology* 42, no. 3 (2002): 565; Kerry Clamp, *Restorative Justice in Transition* (London: Routledge, 2014), 4.

47. Clamp, 6.

48. Quinn, *The Politics of Acknowledgement*, 38; Martha Minow, *Between Vengeance and Forgiveness: Facing History After Genocide and Mass Violence* (Boston: Beacon Press, 1998).

49. Kieran McEvoy, "Beyond Legalism: Towards a Thicker Understanding of Transitional Justice," *Journal of Law and Society* 34, no. 4 (2007): 411–40.

50. Kathleen Daly and Gitana Proietti-Scifoni, "Reparation and Restoration," in *Oxford Handbook of Crime and Criminal Justice*, ed. Michael Tonry (Oxford: Oxford University Press, 2011), 208; John Braithwaite, "Principles of Restorative Justice," in *Restorative Justice and Criminal Justice: Competing or Reconcilable Paradigms?*, eds. Andrew von Hirsch et al. (London: Hart Publishing, 2003), 17–18.

51. Gready and Robins, "From Transitional to Transformative Justice," 340.

52. Olsen, Payne, and Reiter, *Transitional Justice in Balance*, 24–25.

53. Rama Mani, "Dilemmas of Expanding Transitional Justice or Forging the Nexus between Transitional Justice and Development," *International Journal of Transitional Justice* 2, no. 3 (2008): 253–65.

54. Wendy Lambourne, "Transitional Justice and Peacebuilding after Mass Violence," *International Journal of Transitional Justice* 3, no. 1 (2009): 29.

55. Daniel Philpott, "Beyond Politics as Usual: Is Reconciliation Compatible with Liberalism?," in *The Politics of Past Evil: Religion, Reconciliation, and the Dilemmas of Transitional Justice*, ed. Daniel Philpott (Notre Dame, IN: University of Notre Dame Press, 2006), 22.

56. Philpott, 23.

57. Philpott, 23.

58. Joanna Quinn, introduction to *Reconciliation(s): Transitional Justice in Postconflict Societies*, ed. Joanna Quinn (Montreal, QC: McGill-Queen's University Press, 2009), 5; Brandon Hamber and Gráinne Kelly, "A Working Definition of Reconciliation," Belfast, IR: Democratic Dialogue, Sept. 2004.

59. John Paul Lederach, "Civil Society and Reconciliation," in *Turbulent Peace: The Challenges of Managing International Conflict*, eds. Chester A. Crocker et al. (Washington, DC: United States Institute of Peace Press, 2001), 842.

60. Susan Dwyer, "Reconciliation for Realists," *Ethics and International Affairs* 13, no. 1 (1999): 89.

61. Daniel Philpott, "Reconciliation: An Ethic for Responding to Evil in Global Politics," in *Confronting Evil in International Relations: Ethical Responses to Problems of Moral Agency*, ed. Renée Jeffery (New York: Palgrave Macmillan, 2008), 126.

62. Priscilla B. Hayner, *Unspeakable Truths: Confronting State Terror and Atrocity* (New York: Routledge, 2002), 161.

63. Joanne Wallis, Renée Jeffery, and Lia Kent, "Political Reconciliation in Timor Leste, Solomon Islands and Bougainville: The Dark Side of Hybridity," *Australian Journal of International Affairs* 70, no. 2 (2016): 159.

64. Rosalind Shaw and Lars Waldorf, "Introduction: Localizing Transitional Justice," in *Localizing Transitional Justice: Interventions and Priorities after Mass Violence*, eds. Rosalind Shaw, Lars Waldorf, and Pierre Hazan (Stanford, CA: Stanford University Press, 2010), 4.

65. Shaw and Waldorf in Wallis, Jeffery, and Kent, "Political Reconciliation," 160.

66. Wallis, Jeffery, and Kent, "Political Reconciliation," 161; Colleen Murphy, *A Moral Theory of Political Reconciliation* (Cambridge: Cambridge University Press, 2010), 10.

67. Murphy, *A Moral Theory of Political Reconciliation*, 13, 20; Wallis, Jeffery, and Kent, "Political Reconciliation," 161.

68. Quinn, *The Politics of Acknowledgement*, 15.

69. Quinn, "Introduction," 7.

70. Joanna Quinn, "What of Reconciliation? Traditional Mechanisms of Acknowledgment in Uganda," in *Reconciliation(s)*, 177; see also William Bole et

al., *Forgiveness in International Politics: An Alternative Road to Peace* (Washington, DC: United States Conference of Catholic Bishops, 2004).

71. For a detailed critical discussion of the "revealing is healing" debate, see Renée Jeffery, "The Forgiveness Dilemma: Emotions and Justice at the Khmer Rouge Tribunal," *Australian Journal of International Affairs* 69, no. 1 (2015): 35–52.

72. Brandon Hamber, "Does the Truth Heal? A Psychological Perspective on Political Strategies for Dealing with the Legacy of Political Violence," in *Burying the Past: Making Peace and Doing Justice After Civil Conflict*, ed. Nigel Biggar (Washington, DC: Georgetown University Press, 2003), 158.

73. Quinn, *The Politics of Acknowledgement*, 16.

74. Rajeev Bhargava, "Restoring Decency to Barbaric Societies," in *Truth v. Justice: The Morality of Truth Commissions*, eds. Robert I. Rotberg and Dennis Thompson (Princeton, NJ: Princeton University Press, 2000), 54.

75. Philpott, "Beyond Politics as Usual," 21.

76. Philpott, 21.

77. Alex Boraine, "Truth and Reconciliation in South Africa: The Third Way," in Rotberg and Thompson, *Truth v. Justice*, 151–53; André Du Toit, "The Moral Foundations of the South African TRC: Truth as Acknowledgment and Justice as Recognition," in Rotberg and Thompson, *Truth v. Justice*, 132; Thomas M. Antkowiak, "Truth as Right and Remedy in International Human Rights Experience," *Michigan Journal of International Law* 23, no. 4 (2002): 977–1013.

78. Philpott, "Beyond Politics as Usual," 21.

79. Madeline Fullard and Nicky Rousseau, "Truth Telling, Identities, and Power in South Africa and Guatemala," in *Identities in Transition: Challenges for Transitional Justice in Divided Societies*, ed. Paige Arthur (Cambridge: Cambridge University Press), 56.

80. Fullard and Rousseau, 56.

81. Jessica Senehi and Sean Byrne, "From Violence Toward Peace: The Role of Storytelling for Youth Healing and Political Empowerment after Social Conflict," in *Troublemakers or Peacemakers?*, ed. Siobhán McEvoy-Levy (Notre Dame, IN: University of Notre Dame), 236.

82. Senehi and Byrne, 238.

83. Renée Jeffery and Caitlin Mollica, "The Unfinished Business of the Solomon Islands TRC: Closing the Implementation Gap," *Pacific Review* 30, no. 4 (2017): 538.

84. For a critical assessment of the challenges associated with the inclusion of women in transitional justice practices, see, for example, Louise Vella, "Documenting Women's Experiences of Conflict and Sexual Violence: On the Ground with the Solomon Islands Truth and Reconciliation Commission," in Jeffery, *Transitional Justice in Practice*, 141–69; Tristan Anne Borer, "Gendered War and Gendered Peace: Truth Commissions and Postconflict Gender Violence: Lessons from South Africa," *Violence Against Women* 15, no. 10 (2009):

1169–1193; Alessandra Dal Secco, "Truth and Reconciliation Commissions and Gender Justice," in *Gendered Peace: Women's Struggles for Post-War Justice and Reconciliation*, ed. Donna Pankhurst (New York: Routledge, 2012). For a discussion of the challenges faced by refugees, see Laura A. Young and Rosalyn Park, "Engaging Diasporas in Truth Commissions: Lessons from the Liberia Truth and Reconciliation Commission Diaspora Project," *International Journal of Transitional Justice* 3, no. 3 (2009): 341–61.

85. Sharp, "Interrogating the Peripheries," 149.

86. Olsen, Payne, and Reiter, *Transitional Justice in Balance*, 23; Jeffery, "The Forgiveness Dilemma," 36; Audrey R. Chapman, "Truth Commissions as Instruments of Forgiveness and Reconciliation," in *Forgiveness and Reconciliation: Religion, Public Policy, and Conflict Transformation*, eds. Raymond G. Helmick and Rodney L. Petersen (Philadelphia: Templeton Foundation Press, 2001), 258.

87. Kirsten Ainley et al., *Evaluating Transitional Justice: Accountability and Peacebuilding in Post-Conflict Sierra Leone*, Rethinking Peace and Conflict Studies (Basingstoke, UK: Palgrave Macmillan, 2015); Eric Brahm, "Uncovering the Truth: Examining Truth Commission Success and Impact," *International Studies Perspectives* 8, no. 1 (2007): 16–35; Hayner, *Unspeakable Truths*; Onur Bakiner, "Truth Commission Impact: An Assessment of How Commissions Influence Politics and Society," *International Journal of Transitional Justice* 8, no. 1 (2014): 6–30.

88. Holly L. Guthrey and Karen Brounéus, "Peering into the 'Black Box' of TRC Success: Exploring Local Perceptions of Reconciliation in the Solomon Islands TRC," in Jeffery, *Transitional Justice in Practice*, 85.

89. Hayner, *Unspeakable Truths*, 604; Teitel, "Transitional Justice Genealogy," 78.

90. Hayner, 14; Geoff Dancy et al., "The Turn to Truth: Trends in Truth Commission Experimentation," *Journal of Human Rights* 9, no. 1 (2010): 49.

91. Daan Bronkhorst, *Truth Commissions and Transitional Justice: A Short Guide*. Amsterdam: Amnesty International Dutch Section, 2004; Jeffery and Mollica, "The Unfinished Business of the Solomon Islands TRC," 538.

92. Jeffery and Mollica, 533.

93. Jeffery and Mollica, 533; Borer, "Reconciling South Africa or South Africans?"

94. Brahm, "Uncovering the Truth," 24; Priscilla B. Hayner, "Fifteen Truth Commissions—1974 to 1994: A Comparative Study," *Human Rights Quarterly* 16, no. 4 (1994): 597–655.

Chapter 2

1. UN Secretary-General, *The Rule of Law and Transitional Justice in Conflict and Post-Conflict Societies*, UN Doc. S/2004/616 (Aug. 23, 2004).

2. Holly L. Guthrey and Karen Brounéus, "Peering into the 'Black Box' of TRC Success: Exploring Local Perceptions of Reconciliation in the Solomon Islands TRC," in *Transitional Justice in Practice*, ed. Renée Jeffery (New York: Palgrave Macmillan, 2017), 91; Kirsten Ainley, Rebekka Friedman, and Chris Mahony, "The Potential and Politics of Transitional Justice: Interactions Between the Global and the Local in Evaluations of Success," in *Evaluating Transitional Justice: Accountability and Peacebuilding in Post-Conflict Sierra Leone*, eds. Kirsten Ainley et al. (London: Palgrave Macmillan, 2015), 265–79; Chris Mahony and Yasmin Sooka, "The Truth About the Truth: Insider Reflections on the Sierra Leonean Truth and Reconciliation Commission," in Kirsten Ainley et al., *Evaluating Transitional Justice*, 35–54.

3. For empirical research on the contributions of the youth agency lens in the African context, see Stephanie Schwartz, *Youth and Post-Conflict Reconstruction: Agents of Change* (Washington, DC: United States Institute of Peace Press, 2010); for a general overview of the youth agency lens, see Siobhán McEvoy-Levy, "Introduction: Youth and the Post-Accord Environment," in *Troublemakers or Peacemakers? Youth and Post-Accord Peacebuilding*, ed. Siobhán McEvoy-Levy (Notre Dame, IN: University of Notre Dame Press, 2006), 1–26; Helen Berents, *Young People and Everyday Peace: Exclusion, Insecurity and Peacebuilding in Colombia* (New York: Routledge, 2018).

4. Siobhán McEvoy-Levy, "Children, Youth and Peacebuilding," in *Critical Issues in Peace and Conflict Studies: Theory, Practice and Pedagogy*, eds. Thomas Matyók, Jessica Senehi, and Sean Byrne (Lanham, MD: Lexington Books, 2011), 173.

5. McEvoy-Levy, 173.

6. Alan Prout and Allison James, "A New Paradigm for the Sociology of Childhood? Provenance, Promise and Problems," in *Constructing and Reconstructing Childhood: Contemporary Issues in the Sociological Study of Childhood*, 3rd ed. (London: Falmer Press 1990), 13.

7. Siobhán McEvoy, *Peace and Resistance in Youth Cultures: Reading the Politics of Peacebuilding from Harry Potter to The Hunger Games* (London: Palgrave Macmillan, 2018); Helen Berents and Siobhán McEvoy-Levy, "Theorizing Youth and Everyday Peace (Building)," *Peacebuilding* 3, no. 2 (2015): 119.

8. Schwartz, *Youth and Post-Conflict Reconstruction*, 16.

9. Schwartz, 17; see also Jeannie Annan et al., "The State of Youth and Youth Protection in Northern Uganda: Findings from the Survey for War Affected Youth," UNICEF Uganda, Sept. 2006, viii; Yvonne Kemper, "Youth in War-to-Peace Transitions: Approaches of International Organisations," Berghof Research Center for Constructive Conflict Management, Jan. 1, 2005, https://shorturl.at/aIPV4.

10. Cynthia Enloe, "WomenandChildren: Making Feminist Sense of the Persian Gulf Crisis," *Village Voice* 25, no. 9 (1990): 32.

11. Erica Burman, "Beyond 'Women vs. Children' or 'WomenandChildren': Engendering Childhood and Reformulating Motherhood," *International Journal of Child Rights* 16, no. 2 (2008): 181.

12. Notable examples of these reports include Clara Ramírez-Barat, "Engaging Children and Youth in Transitional Justice Processes: Guidance for Outreach Programs," New York: International Center for Transitional Justice, Nov. 2012, https://shorturl.at/iIX14; UNICEF Innocenti Research Centre and International Center for Transitional Justice, *Children and Truth Commissions* (Florence: UNICEF, 2010), https://www.unicef-irc.org/publications/pdf/truth_commissions_eng.pdf.

13. Katrina Lee-Koo, "Children and Armed Conflict: Mapping the Terrain," in *Children and Global Conflict*, eds. Kim Huynh, Bina D'Costa, and Katrina Lee-Koo (Cambridge: Cambridge University Press, 2015), 13.

14. Lee-Koo, 13.

15. McEvoy-Levy, "Children, Youth and Peacebuilding," 159.

16. Bina D' Costa, "Turtles Can Fly: Vicarious Terror and the Child in South Asia," in *Children and Violence: Politics of Conflict in South Asia*, ed. Bina D' Costa (Cambridge: Cambridge University Press, 2016), 10–11.

17. McEvoy-Levy, "Children, Youth and Peacebuilding," 176. For a detailed discussion of the youth bulge theory, see Henrik Urdal, "The Demographics of Political Violence: Youth Bulges, Insecurity and Conflict," in *Too Poor for Peace? Global Poverty, Conflict, and Security in the 21st Century*, eds. Lael Brainard and Derek Chollet (Washington, DC: Brookings Institution Press, 2007).

18. For empirical scholarly research that challenges the legitimacy of the youth bulge thesis, see Marc Sommers, "In the Shadow of Genocide: Rwanda's Youth Challenge," in McEvoy-Levy, *Troublemakers or Peacemakers?*, 81–98; see also Lesley Pruitt, "Youth, Peace & Security: Gender Matters in Asia and the Pacific," *Global Change, Peace & Security* 33, no. 3 (2021): 241–57; Ali Altiok, "Squeezed Agency: Youth Resistance to the Securitization of Peacebuilding," in *Securitizing Youth: Young People's Role in the Global Peace & Security Agenda*, ed. Marisa O. Ensor (New Brunswick, NJ: Rutgers University Press, 2021).

19. Berents, *Young People and Everyday Peace*, 57.

20. Berents, 57; see also Vanessa Pupavac, "Misanthropy Without Borders: The International Children's Rights Regime," *Disasters* 25, no. 2 (2001): 96.

21. Paul Gready, *The Era of Transitional Justice: The Aftermath of the Truth and Reconciliation Commission in South Africa and Beyond* (New York: Routledge, 2011), 150.

22. Alison Smith, "Basic Assumptions of Transitional Justice and Children," in *Children and Transitional Justice: Truth-Telling, Accountability and Reconciliation*, eds. Sharanjeet Parmar et al. (Cambridge, MA: Human Rights Program, Harvard Law School, 2010), 33.

23. Albrecht Schnabel and Anara Tabyshalieva, eds., *Escaping Victimhood: Children, Youth and Post-Conflict Peacebuilding* (New York: United Nations

University Press, 2013); see also Alpaslan Özerdem and Sukanya Podder, *Youth in Conflict and Peacebuilding: Mobilization, Reintegration and Reconciliation* (London: Palgrave Macmillan, 2015); McEvoy-Levy, *Troublemakers or Peacemakers?*

24. Özerdem and Podder, *Youth in Conflict and Peacebuilding*; Schwartz, *Youth and Post-Conflict Reconstruction*; Jason Hart, ed., introduction to *Years of Conflict: Adolescence, Political Violence and Displacement* (New York: Berghahn Books, 2010), 20; Lesley J. Pruitt, *Youth Peacebuilding: Music, Gender, and Change* (Albany: State University of New York Press, 2013); Kemper, "Youth in War-to-Peace Transitions."

25. For a critical examination of this scholarship see Altiok, "Squeezed Agency"; Berents and McEvoy-Levy, "Theorizing Youth"; Lesley J. Pruitt, "Gendering the Study of Children and Youth," *Peacebuilding* 3, no. 2 (2015): 157–70.

26. Anna Holzscheiter, "Children as Agents in International Relations? Transnational Activism, International Norms, and the Politics of Age," in *Discovering Childhood in International Relations*, ed. J. Marshall Beier (Cham: Palgrave Macmillan, 2020), 70. For further scholarship critiquing this characterization, see also Helen Berents and Caitlin Mollica, "Reciprocal Institutional Visibility: Youth, Peace and Security and 'Inclusive' Agendas at the United Nations," *Cooperation and Conflict* 57, no. 1 (2022): 65–83.

27. Lee-Koo, "Children and Armed Conflict," 10–11. For a discussion of children as subjects in the context of South Asia, see Duncan McDuie-Ra, "Children and Civil Society in South Asia: Subjects, Participants and Political Agents," in D'Costa, *Children and Violence*, 46–61.

28. Jo Boyden, "Children's Experience of Conflict Related Emergencies: Some Implications for Relief Policy and Practice," *Disasters* 18, no. 3 (1994): 256.

29. Nick Lee, "The Challenges of Childhood: Distributions of Childhood's Ambiguity in Adult Institutions," *Childhood* 6, no. 4 (1999): 465.

30. Chris Jenks, *Childhood*, 2nd ed. (London: Routledge, 2005), 9.

31. Alberto Munari, "Jean Piaget," *Prospects* 24, no. 1 (1994): 311–27. *Becomings* is a term used by Piaget to denote the intellectual immaturity of children and thus their nonpolitical, social status. Moreover, the term acknowledges that children are in the process of developing the cognitive skills necessary for participation in the adult world.

32. Jenks, *Childhood*, 104; Alan Prout, "Participation, Policy and the Changing Conditions of Childhood," in *Hearing the Voices of Children: Social Policy for a New Century*, eds. Christine Hallett and Alan Prout (London: Routledge Falmer, 2003), 11–25.

33. David Archard, *Children: Rights and Childhood*, 2nd ed. (London: Routledge, 2004), 22.

34. David Nelken, "Afterword: Choosing Rights for Children," in *Children's Rights and Traditional Values*, eds. Gillian Douglas and Leslie Sebba (Aldershot, UK: Ashgate Publishing, 1998), 315.

35. Michael D. A. Freeman, *The Rights and Wrongs of Children* (London: Pinter, 1983), 37.

36. Matías Cordero Arce, "Towards an Emancipatory Discourse of Children's Rights," *International Journal of Children's Rights* 20, no. 3 (2012): 365–421; Ann Sheppard, "Child Soldiers: Is the Optional Protocol Evidence of an Emerging 'Straight-18' Consensus," *International Journal of Children's Rights* 8, no. 1 (2000): 37–70; Andrew Mawson, "Children, Impunity and Justice: Some Dilemmas from Northern Uganda," in Boyden and Berry, *Children and Youth on the Front Line*, 130–41.

37. Jo Boyden, "Childhood and the Policy Makers: A Comparative Perspective on the Globalization of Childhood," in James and Prout, *Constructing and Reconstructing Childhood*, 2nd ed. (New York: Routledge Falmer, 1997), 183.

38. Michael Wyness, *Childhood and Society: An Introduction to the Sociology of Childhood* (Basingstoke, UK: Palgrave Macmillan, 2006), 94; see also Boyden and Berry, *Children and Youth on the Front Line*, x–xxvii.

39. The scholarship on child soldiers is extensive; see, for example, P. W. Singer, *Children at War* (Berkeley: University of California Press, 2006); Michael Wessells, "Child Soldiers, Peace Education, and Postconflict Reconstruction for Peace," *Theory Into Practice* 44, no. 4 (2005): 363–69; Rachel Brett and Margaret McCallin, *Children: The Invisible Soldiers*, 2nd ed. (Stockholm: Rädda Barnen, 1998); Rachel Brett and Irma Specht, *Young Soldiers: Why They Choose to Fight?* (Boulder, CO: Lynne Rienner Publishers, 2004); Kirsten J. Fisher, *Transitional Justice for Child Soldiers: Accountability and Social Reconstruction in Post-Conflict Contexts* (Basingstoke, UK: Palgrave Macmillan, 2013).

40. Berents, *Young People and Everyday Peace*, 56.

41. UNICEF Innocenti Research Centre and International Center for Transitional Justice, *Children and Truth Commissions*, 8; see also Parmar et al., *Children and Transitional Justice*.

42. US Agency for International Development (USAID), "Youth and Conflict: A Toolkit for Intervention," USAID, 2005, https://resourcecentre.savethechildren.net/document/youth-and-conflict-toolkit-intervention; Henrik Urdal, "A Clash of Generations? Youth Bulges and Political Violence," *International Studies Quarterly* 50, no. 3 (2006): 607–29.

43. McEvoy-Levy, "Introduction: Youth and the Post-Accord Environment."

44. Schwartz, *Youth and Post-Conflict Reconstruction*, 11.

45. Berents, *Young People and Everyday Peace*, 58.

46. James and Prout, *Constructing and Reconstructing Childhood*, 3rd ed., 51, 178–84.

47. Alison M. S. Watson, The *Child in International Political Economy: A Place at the Table* (London: Routledge, 2009).

48. Alison M. S. Watson, "Children and International Relations: A New Site of Knowledge?" *Review of International Studies* 32, no. 2 (2006): 237–50.

49. Smith, "Basic Assumptions," 33.

50. Kemper, "Youth in War-to-Peace Transitions," 14.

51. United Nations Secretary-General, *International Youth Year: Participation, Development, Peace*, UN Doc. A/40/256 (May 6, 1985).

52. Kemper, "Youth in War-to-Peace Transitions," 8.

53. Alice Schlegel, "A Cross-Cultural Approach to Adolescence," *Ethos* 23, no. 1 (1995): 16.

54. Helen Brocklehurst, *Who's Afraid of Children? Children, Conflict, and International Relations* (Aldershot, UK: Ashgate Publishing, 2006), 171–72; see also Watson, "Children and International Relations."

55. Brocklehurst, *Who's Afraid of Children?*, 171–72.

56. Charli R. Carpenter, *Forgetting Children Born of War: Setting the Human Rights Agenda in Bosnia and Beyond* (New York: Columbia University Press, 2010).

57. McEvoy-Levy, "Introduction: Youth and the Post-Accord Environment," 2.

58. Karen Wells, *Childhood in a Global Perspective* (Cambridge: Polity Press, 2009), 34.

59. Katrina Lee-Koo, "Horror and Hope: (Re)Presenting Militarised Children in Global North–South Relations," *Third World Quarterly* 32, no. 4 (2011): 731.

60. McEvoy-Levy, "Introduction: Youth and the Post-Accord Environment," 2; Cecilia Jacob, *Child Security in Asia: The Impact of Armed Conflict in Cambodia and Myanmar* (London: Routledge, 2014), 35–36.

61. David M. Rosen, *Armies of the Young: Child Soldiers in War and Terrorism* (New Brunswick, NJ: Rutgers University Press, 2005), 2.

62. Jenny Kuper, *International Law Concerning Child Civilians in Armed Conflict* (Oxford: Clarendon Press, 1997), 15.

63. D'Costa, *Children and Violence*.

64. J. J. Rousseau, *Emile, or Education*, trans. Barbara Foxley (London: J. M. Dent & Sons, 1911), 1.

65. Nancy Scheper-Hughes and Carolyn Fishel Sargent, "Introduction: The Cultural Politics of Childhood," in *Small Wars: The Cultural Politics of Childhood*, eds. Nancy Scheper-Hughes and Carolyn Fishel Sargent (Berkeley: University of California Press, 1998), 13.

66. Archard, *Children*, 22.

67. Lee-Koo, "Children and Armed Conflict," 11.

68. Jenks, *Childhood*, 104; Harry Hendrick, "Constructions and Reconstructions of British Childhood: An Interpretive Survey, 1800 to the Present," in James and Prout, *Constructing and Reconstructing Childhood*, 2nd ed., 36.

69. Rousseau, *Emile, or Education*, 5.

70. Peter Coveney, "The Image of the Child," in *The Sociology of Childhood: Essential Readings*, ed. Chris Jenks (London: Batsford Academic and Educational, 1982), 45.

71. Brocklehurst, *Who's Afraid of Children?*, 11.
72. Paige Arthur, ed., introduction to *Identities in Transition: Challenges for Transitional Justice in Divided Societies* (Cambridge: Cambridge University Press, 2010), 6.
73. Lee-Koo, "Children and Armed Conflict: Mapping the Terrain," 12.
74. Harris cited in Gready, *The Era of Transitional Justice*, 150.
75. Jacob, *Child Security in Asia*, 35.
76. Boyden, "Preface," ix.
77. Boyden, ix.
78. Jacob, *Child Security in Asia*, 32; Brocklehurst, *Who's Afraid of Children?*, 55.
79. Jacob, *Child Security in Asia*, 34.
80. James and Prout, *Constructing and Reconstructing Childhood*, 12.
81. Berents, *Young People and Everyday Peace*, 4.
82. Karen Hein, "Young People as Assets: A Foundational View," *Social Policy* 30, no. 1 (1999), 23; Siobhán McEvoy-Levy, "Youth as Social and Political Agents: Issues in Post-Settlement Peace Building," Kroc Institute Occasional Paper, Joan B. Kroc Institute for International Peace Studies, University of Notre Dame, Dec. 2001, 23; Pruitt, *Youth Peacebuilding*; Celina Del Felice and Andria Wisler, "The Unexplored Power and Potential of Youth as Peacebuilders," *Journal of Peace Conflict and Development* 11 (2007): 13–20; Schwartz, *Youth and Post-Conflict Reconstruction*.
83. Mona J. Macksoud et al., "Assessing the Impact of War on Children," in *Minefields in Their Hearts: The Mental Health of Children in War and Communal Violence*, eds. Roberta J. Apfel and Bennett Simon (New Haven, CT: Yale University Press, 1996); Mona S. Macksoud and J. Lawrence Aber, "The War Experiences and Psychosocial Development of Children in Lebanon," *Child Development* 67, no. 1 (1996): 70–88.
84. Jo Boyden and Joanna de Berry, eds., *Children and Youth on the Front Line: Ethnography, Armed Conflict and Displacement* (New York: Berghahn Books, 2004); Hart, *Years of Conflict*.
85. Carola Eyber and Alastair Ager, "Researching Young People's Experiences of War: Participatory Methods and the Trauma Discourse in Angola," in Boyden and Berry, *Children and Youth on the Front Line*, 190–94, 205–6; Mats Utas, "Fluid Research Fields: Studying Ex-Combatant Youth in the Aftermath of the Liberian Civil War," in Boyden and Berry, *Children and Youth on the Front Line*, 227–31.
86. On child soldiers, see Mark A. Drumbl, *Reimagining Child Soldiers in International Law and Policy* (Oxford: Oxford University Press, 2012); P. W. Singer, "Talk Is Cheap: Getting Serious about Preventing Child Soldiers," *Cornell International Law Journal* 37, no. 3 (2004): 561–86; Krijn Peters, "Re-Examining Voluntarism: Youth Combatants in Sierra Leone," Pretoria, SA: Institute for Security Studies, April 1, 2004; Krijn Peters and Paul Richards, "'Why We

Fight': Voices of Youth Combatants in Sierra Leone," *Africa* 68, no. 2 (1998): 183–210. On the youth bulge theory: "The youth bulge refers to an unusually large population of 15–24-year old's relative to the adult population . . . who predominately live in the Global South." Alice Macdonald, "'New Wars: Forgotten Warriors': Why Have Girl Fighters Been Excluded from Western Representations of Conflict in Sierra Leone?," *Africa Development* 33, no. 3 (2008): 140; Joshua S. Goldstein, *War and Gender: How Gender Shapes the War System and Vice Versa* (Cambridge: Cambridge University Press, 2001), 11.

87. Graça Machel, *Impact of Armed Conflict on Children*, UN Doc. A/51/306 (Aug. 26, 1996), https://undocs.org/A/51/306.

88. Machel, 30.

89. Machel.

90. Lee-Koo, "Children and Armed Conflict," 15.

91. Berents, *Young People and Everyday Peace*, 12.

92. Pupavac, "Misanthropy Without Borders," 103.

93. Brett and McCallin, *Children: The invisible Soldiers*, 50; Wessells, "Child Soldiers, Peace Education," 367–68.

94. Edward Newman, "The 'New Wars' Debate: A Historical Perspective Is Needed," *Security Dialogue* 35, no. 2 (June 2004): 175.

95. Brett and Specht, *Young Soldiers*, 40–45; Singer, "Talk Is Cheap," 561.

96. Schwartz, *Youth and Post-Conflict Reconstruction*, 20.

97. Lee-Koo, "Children and Armed Conflict," 15.

98. Kemper, "Youth in War-to-Peace Transitions."

99. Goldstein, *War and Gender*, 11; see also, Macdonald, "'New Wars: Forgotten Warriors,'" 140.

100. Peters and Richards, "'Why We Fight.'"

101. Peters and Richards.

102. Urdal, "The Demographics of Political Violence," 92.

103. Urdal, "A Clash of Generations?," 612.

104. Samuel P. Huntington, *The Clash of Civilizations and the Remaking of World Order* (New Delhi: Penguin Books India, 1996); Howard B. Kaplan, "Deviant Behavior and Self-Enhancement in Adolescence," *Journal of Youth and Adolescence* 7, no. 3 (1978): 253–77.

105. Urdal, "A Clash of Generations?," 612–13.

106. Kelly M. Greenhill and Solomon Major, "The Perils of Profiling: Civil War Spoilers and the Collapse of Intrastate Peace Accords," *International Security* 31, no. 3 (2007): 10.

107. Greenhill and Major, 9–10.

108. Schwartz, *Youth and Post-Conflict Reconstruction*, 14.

109. Paul Collier and Anke Hoeffler, "Greed and Grievance in Civil War," *Oxford Economic Papers* 56, no. 4 (2004): 565.

110. Collier and Hoeffler, 565.

111. Collier and Hoeffler, 565.
112. Schwartz, *Youth and Post-Conflict Reconstruction*, 13.
113. Lesley Pruitt, "Rethinking Youth Bulge Theory in Policy and Scholarship: Incorporating Critical Gender Analysis," *International Affairs* 96, no. 3 (2020): 711–28; see also Lesley Pruitt, Helen Berents, and Gayle Munro, "Gender and Age in the Construction of Male Youth in the European Migration 'Crisis,'" *Signs: Journal of Women in Culture and Society* 43, no. 3 (2018): 687–709.
114. Pruitt, "Rethinking Youth Bulge Theory."
115. Christine Griffin, "Troubled Teens: Managing Disorders of Transition and Consumption," *Feminist Review* 55, no. 1 (Spring 1997): 19.
116. Andreana Clay, "'All I Need Is One Mic': Mobilizing Youth for Social Change in the Post-Civil Rights Era," *Social Justice* 33, no. 2 (2006): 108.
117. Berents, *Young People and Everyday Peace*; Berents and Mollica, "Reciprocal Institutional Visibility."
118. McEvoy-Levy, "Children, Youth and Peacebuilding," 159.
119. McEvoy-Levy, 168.
120. McEvoy-Levy, 168.
121. Schwartz, *Youth and Post-Conflict Reconstruction*.
122. Pruitt, *Youth Peacebuilding*, 2.
123. See, for example, Helen Berents, "'It's About Finding a Way': Children, Sites of Opportunity, and Building Everyday Peace in Columbia," *International Journal of Children's Rights* 22, no. 2 (2014): 361–84; Berents and Mollica, "Reciprocal Institutional Visibility"; Ali Altiok et al., "Youth, Peace, and Security," in *Routledge Handbook of Peace, Security and Development*, eds. Fen Osler Hampson, Alpaslan Özerdem, and Jonathan Kent, 433–47. London: Routledge, 2020.
124. John Paul Lederach, *Building Peace: Sustainable Reconciliation in Divided Societies* (Tokyo: United Nations University Press, 1994), 122.
125. Berents, *Young People and Everyday Peace*.

Chapter 3

1. Alpaslan Özerdem and Sukanya Podder, *Youth in Conflict and Peacebuilding: Mobilization, Reintegration and Reconciliation* (London: Palgrave Macmillan, 2015), 5.
2. Truth and Reconciliation Commission, *Truth and Reconciliation Commission of South Africa Report*, vol. 2, chap. 7, 85. South Africa's National Youth Policy defines youth as fourteen to thirty-five years of age. See Republic of South Africa, *National Youth Policy (NYP)*, 2009, https://www.youthpolicy.org/national/South_Africa_2009_National_Youth_Policy.pdf. Peru's Nation Youth Strategy defines youth as people fifteen to twenty-nine, and it also makes distinctions

between ages fifteen to nineteen, twenty to twenty-four, and twenty-five to twenty nine. See Government of Peru, *National Youth Strategy Plan 2012–2021*, https://www.youthpolicy.org/national/Peru_National_Youth_Strategy_2012_2021.pdf.

3. Piers Pigou, "Children and the South African Truth and Reconciliation Commission," in *Children and Transitional Justice: Truth-Telling, Accountability and Reconciliation*, eds. Sharanjeet Parmar et al. (Cambridge, MA: Human Rights Program, Harvard Law School, 2010), 117.

4. *Truth and Reconciliation Commission Report*, vol. 4, chap. 8, 22–23.

5. *Truth and Reconciliation Commission Report*, vol. 5, chap. 1, 23.

6. Soo Ah Kwon, "The Politics of Global Youth Participation," *Journal of Youth Studies* 22, no. 7 (Aug. 9, 2019): 928.

7. For a comprehensive examination of this dialogue, see Anna Holzscheiter, *Children's Rights in International Politics: The Transformative Power of Discourse* (Basingstoke, UK: Palgrave Macmillan, 2010), 159–96.

8. UN General Assembly, Resolution 34/4, International Year of the Child, A/RES/34/4 (Oct. 18, 1979), https://undocs.org/A/RES/34/4.

9. UN General Assembly, Resolution 34/4, A/RES/34/4.

10. UN General Assembly, Resolution 34/4, A/RES/34/4, ¶ 3(c).

11. Özerdem and Podder, *Youth in Conflict and Peacebuilding*, 94.

12. Holzscheiter, *Children's Rights in International Politics*, 103–4.

13. Maggie Black, *The Children and the Nations: The Story of UNICEF* (New York: UNICEF, 1986), 355.

14. Holzscheiter, *Children's Rights in International Politics*, 85.

15. Rachel Baker and Rachel Hinton, "Approaches to Children's Work and Rights in Nepal," *Annals of the American Academy of Political and Social Science* 575, no. 1 (2001): 190.

16. Kim Huynh, "Children and Agency: Caretakers, Free-Rangers and Everyday Life," in *Children and Global Conflict*, eds. Kim Huynh, Bina D'Costa, and Katrina Lee-Koo (Cambridge: Cambridge University Press, 2015), 41–42.

17. Huynh, 42; see also Harry Brighouse, "What Rights (If Any) Do Children Have?," in *The Moral and Political Status of Children*, eds. David Archard and Colin M. Macleod (Oxford: Oxford University Press, 2002), 38.

18. Holzscheiter, *Children's Rights in International Politics*, 86.

19. *Truth and Reconciliation Commission Report*, vol. 1, 148.

20. Özerdem and Podder, *Youth in Conflict and Peacebuilding*, 95.

21. Convention on the Rights of the Child, Nov. 20, 1989, 1577 U.N.T.S. 3, https://www.ohchr.org/en/instruments-mechanisms/instruments/convention-rights-child, Article 12.

22. Katrina Lee-Koo, "Children and Armed Conflict: Mapping the Terrain," in Huynh, D'Costa, and Lee-Koo, *Children and Global Conflict*, 15–16.

23. Bina D'Costa, "Turtles Can Fly: Vicarious Terror and the Child in South Asia," in *Children and Violence: Politics of Conflict in South Asia*, ed. Bina D'Costa (Cambridge: Cambridge University Press, 2016), 10–12.

24. Convention on the Rights of the Child, Nov. 20, 1989, 1577 U.N.T.S. 3, Article 12.

25. Holzscheiter, *Children's Rights in International Politics*, 87–88.

26. Michael D. A. Freeman and Philip Veerman, eds., *The Ideologies of Children's Rights* (Dordrecht: Martinus Nijhoff, 1992), 3; Carl M. Rogers and Lawrence S. Wrightsman, "Attitudes toward Children's Rights: Nurturance or Self-Determination?," *Journal of Social Issues* 34, no. 2 (1978): 59–68.

27. Holzscheiter, *Children's Rights in International Politics*, 114.

28. Michael D. A. Freeman, "The Limits of Children's Rights," in Freeman and Veerman, *The Ideologies of Children's Rights*, 31; see also Allison James and Alan Prout, eds., *Constructing and Reconstructing Childhood: Contemporary Issues in the Sociological Study of Childhood* (London: Falmer Press, 1990).

29. Michael D. A. Freeman, "Introduction: Children as Persons," in *Children's Rights: A Comparative Perspective*, ed. Michael D. A. Freeman (Aldershot, UK: Dartmouth, 1997), 1; D'Costa, "Turtles Can Fly," 8.

30. Anthony M. Platt, *The Child Savers: The Invention of Delinquency* (Chicago: University of Chicago Press, 1969), 51, 77, 161.

31. D'Costa, "Turtles Can Fly," 4–5.

32. *Geneva Declaration of the Rights of the Child of 1924*, League of Nations, adopted Sept. 26, 1924.

33. *Geneva Declaration of the Rights of the Child of 1924*.

34. Freeman, "Introduction: Children as Persons," 1. For additional discussion on the 1924 negotiations on the Geneva Declaration, see also Mark Ensalaco, "The Right of the Child to Development," in *Children's Human Rights: Progress and Challenges for Children Worldwide*, eds. Mark Ensalaco and Linda C. Majka (Lanham, MD: Rowman and Littlefield, 2005), 9–30; Bina D'Costa "The Rights of the Child: Political History, Practices and Protection," in Huynh, D'Costa, and Lee-Koo, *Children and Global Conflict*, 97–98.

35. For a detailed discussion of this debate, see Holzscheiter, *Children's Rights in International Politics*, 87–89.

36. Holzscheiter, 87–89.

37. Ensalaco and Majka, *Children's Human Rights*, 38.

38. UN General Assembly, Resolution 34/4, International Year of the Child, A/RES/34/4 (Oct. 18, 1979), https://undocs.org/A/RES/34/4.

39. D'Costa, "Turtles Can Fly," 8.

40. Sonia Harris-Short, "International Human Rights Law: Imperialist, Inept, and Ineffective? Cultural Relativism and the UN Convention on the Rights of the Child," *Human Rights Quarterly* 25, no. 1 (2003): 135.

41. D'Costa, "Turtles Can Fly," 8; D'Costa, "The Rights of the Child," 93; Katrina Lee-Koo, "Children and IR: Creating Spaces for Children," in Huynh, D'Costa, and Lee-Koo, *Children and Global Conflict*, 77–78.

42. Kim Huynh, "Children and Agency: Caretakers, Free-Rangers and Everyday Life," in Huynh, D'Costa, and Lee-Koo, *Children and Global Conflict*, 41–42.

43. Huynh, 41–42.
44. Huynh, 37–38; see also Harry Hendrick, "Constructions and Reconstructions of British Childhood: An Interpretive Survey, 1800 to the Present," in James and Prout, eds., *Constructing and Reconstructing Childhood*, 2nd ed. (New York: Routledge Falmer, 1997), 51.
45. Aisling Swaine and Thomas Feeny, "A Neglected Perspective: Adolescent Girls' Experiences of the Kosovo Conflict of 1999," in *Children and Youth on the Front Line: Ethnography, Armed Conflict and Displacement*, eds. Jo Boyden and Joanna de Berry (New York: Berghahn Books 2004), 63–84.
46. Swaine and Feeny, "A Neglected Perspective," 63.
47. Promotion of National Unity and Reconciliation Act 34 of 1995 §§ 2–11 (S. Afr.), South African Government.
48. Audrey R. Chapman, "Truth Recovery Through the TRC's Institutional Hearings Process," in *Truth and Reconciliation in South Africa: Did the TRC Deliver?*, eds. Audrey R. Chapman and Hugo van der Merwe (Philadelphia: University of Pennsylvania Press, 2008), 171.
49. Paul Gready, *The Era of Transitional Justice: The Aftermath of the Truth and Reconciliation Commission in South Africa and Beyond* (New York: Routledge, 2011), 148.
50. Gready, 148; *Truth and Reconciliation Commission Report*, vol. 1, para. 126.
51. Gready, 22; Desmond Tutu, *No Future Without Forgiveness* (New York: Random House, 2012), 35.
52. Howard Zehr, "Restorative Justice: The Concept," *Corrections Today* 59, no. 7 (Dec. 1997): 68–70; Howard Zehr, "Restorative Justice: When Justice and Healing Go Together," *Track Two: Constructive Approaches to Community and Political Conflict* 6, no. 3 (1997): 1–4.
53. Ann Skelton, "Restorative Justice as a Framework for Juvenile Justice Reform: A South African Perspective," *British Journal of Criminology* 42 (2002): 500.
54. *Truth and Reconciliation Commission Report*, vol. 4, 254.
55. South Africa Truth and Reconciliation Commission, "Special Hearings Transcripts," 336 (George Ndlozi, Children's Hearing, Johannesburg, June 12, 1997).
56. Desmond Tutu, "Foreword: The Voices of Our Children," in *Between Anger and Hop: South Africa's Youth and the Truth and Reconciliation Commission*, eds. Karin Chubb and Lutz van Dijk (Johannesburg, SA: Witwatersrand University Press, 2001), xi.
57. Gready, *The Era of Transitional Justice*, 147.
58. Promotion of National Unity and Reconciliation Act 34 of 1995 (S. Afr.).
59. Constitution of the Republic of South Africa Act 200 of 1993 § 30(3) (S. Afr.).

60. *Truth and Reconciliation Commission Report*, vol. 4, 251.

61. Albrecht Schnabel and Anara Tabyshalieva, eds., "Opportunities Missed: Sidelining Children and Youth in Post-Conflict Recovery and Reform Efforts," in *Escaping Victimhood: Children, Youth and Post-Conflict Peacebuilding* (New York: United Nations University Press, 2013), 12; Charli R. Carpenter, *Forgetting Children Born of War: Setting the Human Rights Agenda in Bosnia and Beyond* (New York: Columbia University Press, 2010); D'Costa, "The Rights of the Child," 96–98.

62. Yvonne Kemper, "Youth in War-to-Peace Transitions: Approaches of International Organizations," Berghof Research Center for Constructive Conflict Management, Jan. 1, 2005, 14, https://shorturl.at/aIPV4.

63. Geraldine Van Bueren, *The International Law on the Rights of the Child* (The Hague: Martinus Nijhoff, 1998), 341.

64. South Africa Truth and Reconciliation Commission, "Special Hearings Transcripts," 313 (Graça Machel, Children's Hearing, Johannesburg, June 12, 1997).

65. South Africa Truth and Reconciliation Commission, 202 (Dr. Simangele Magwaza, Children and Youth Hearing, Durban, May 14, 1997).

66. Children under the age of eighteen spoke privately about their experiences of apartheid to specially trained child counselors, who then relayed these stories and displayed these pictures to the commission at the hearings. The Durban hearing took place on May 14, 1997, and the Bloemfontein hearing occurred on the June 23, 1997.

67. South Africa Truth and Reconciliation Commission, "Special Hearings Transcripts," 215 (Children and Youth Hearing, Durban, May 14, 1997).

68. South Africa Truth and Reconciliation Commission, 215 (Bloemfontein Hearing, June 23, 1997).

69. Pigou, "Children and the South African Truth and Reconciliation Commission," 119.

70. South Africa Truth and Reconciliation Commission, "Special Hearings Transcripts," 401–2 (Mr. Mashalaba, Youth Submissions, Pietersburg, June 18, 1997).

71. *Truth and Reconciliation Commission Report*, vol. 4, 258.

72. South Africa Truth and Reconciliation Commission, "Special Hearings Transcripts," 233 (Ms. Sandra Adonis, Youth Hearings Submissions—Questions and Answers, Athlone, May 22, 1997).

73. Convention on the Rights of the Child, Nov. 20, 1989, 1577 U.N.T.S. 3, Article 12.

74. Michael Wyness, Lisa Harrison, and Ian Buchanan, "Childhood, Politics and Ambiguity: Towards an Agenda for Children's Political Inclusion," *Sociology* 38, no. 1 (2004): 90.

75. South Africa Truth and Reconciliation Commission, "Special Hearings Transcripts," 382 (Youth Submissions, Pietersburg, June 18, 1997).

76. Gready, *The Era of Transitional Justice*, 150.
77. *Comisión de La Verdad y Reconciliación (CVR): Informe Final*, Peru, vol. 1, 22, https://www.cverdad.org.pe/ifinal/.
78. Julia Paulson, "Truth Commissions and National Curricula: The Case of Recordándonos in Peru," in Parmar et al., *Children and Transitional Justice*, 340; see also Kenneth Bush and Diana Salarelli, eds., *The Two Faces of Education in Ethnic Conflict: Towards Peacebuilding Education for Children* (Florence: UNICEF Innocenti Research Centre, 2000).
79. *Comisión de La Verdad y Reconciliación (CVR)*, vol. 1, 22.
80. *Comisión de La Verdad y Reconciliación (CVR)*, vol. 6, 53.
81. *Comisión de La Verdad y Reconciliación (CVR)*, vol. 9, 23.
82. Paulson, "Truth Commissions and National Curricula: The Case of Recordándonos in Peru," 341.
83. South Africa Truth and Reconciliation Commission, "Special Hearings Transcripts," 277 (Letter from Rudie-Lee Reagan, Youth Hearings, Submissions—Questions and Answers, Athlone, May 22, 1997).
84. South Africa Truth and Reconciliation Commission, 277 (Letter from Rudie-Lee Reagan, Youth Hearings, Submissions—Questions and Answers, Athlone, May 22, 1997).
85. *Truth and Reconciliation Commission Report*, vol. 4, 260.
86. *Truth and Reconciliation Commission Report*, vol. 4, 251.
87. *Truth and Reconciliation Commission Report*, vol. 4, 251.
88. *Truth and Reconciliation Commission Report*, vol. 4, 251.
89. *Truth and Reconciliation Commission Report*, vol. 4, 271.
90. *Truth and Reconciliation Commission Report*, vol. 4, 270–1.
91. *Truth and Reconciliation Commission Report*, vol. 4, 255.
92. South Africa Truth and Reconciliation Commission, "Special Hearings Transcripts," 356 (Mr. Chris Van Eeden, Children's Hearing, Johannesburg, June 12, 1997).
93. *Truth and Reconciliation Commission Report*, vol. 4, 260–70.
94. South Africa Truth and Reconciliation Commission, "Special Hearings Transcripts," 360 (Mr. Chris Van Eeden, Children's Hearing, Johannesburg, June 12, 1997).
95. South Africa Truth and Reconciliation Commission, 300 (Dr. Coleman, Children's Hearing, Johannesburg, June 12, 1997).
96. Huynh, "Children and Agency," 41.
97. *Truth and Reconciliation Commission Report*, vol. 4, 251.
98. Siobhán McEvoy-Levy, "Youth as Social and Political Agents: Issues in Post-Settlement Peace Building," Kroc Institute Occasional Paper, Joan B. Kroc Institute for International Peace Studies (University of Notre Dame, Notre Dame, IN, Dec. 2001), 10.
99. Siobhán McEvoy-Levy, "Introduction: Youth and the Post-Accord Environment," in *Troublemakers or Peacemakers? Youth and Post-Accord Peace-*

building (Notre Dame, IN: University of Notre Dame Press, 2006), 10; see also Lauren Segal, Joy Pelo, and Pule Rampa, "Into the Heart of Darkness: Journeys of the Agents in Crime, Violence and Death," in *Crime Wave: The South African Underworld and Its Foes*, ed. Jonny Steinberg (Johannesburg, SA: Witwatersrand University Press, 2001), 96.

100. *Comisión de La Verdad y Reconciliación (CVR)*, 650.

101. Huynh, "Children and Agency," 41; see also David Archard, *Children: Rights and Childhood*, 2nd ed. (London: Routledge, 2004), 58.

102. *Truth and Reconciliation Commission Report*, vol. 1, 1.

103. *Truth and Reconciliation Commission Report*, vol. 1, 170.

104. Lee-Koo, "Children and Armed Conflict," 15.

105. *Truth and Reconciliation Commission Report*, vol. 1, 446.

106. *Truth and Reconciliation Commission Report*, vol. 1, 420.

107. *Comisión de La Verdad y Reconciliación (CVR)*, 670.

108. Graça Machel, *Impact of Armed Conflict on Children*, UN Doc. A/51/306 (Aug. 26, 1996), https://undocs.org/A/51/306.

109. *Comisión de La Verdad y Reconciliación (CVR)*, 960.

110. Machel, *Impact of Armed Conflict on Children*.

111. *Comisión de La Verdad y Reconciliación (CVR)*, 960.

112. *Comisión de La Verdad y Reconciliación (CVR)*, 940.

113. Kim Huynh, "Child Soldiers Causes, Solutions and Cultures," in Huynh, D'Costa, and Lee-Koo, *Children in Global Conflict*, 131.

114. UN General Assembly, *Convention on the Rights of the Child*, Res. 44/25 of Nov. 20, 1989, 1577 U.N.T.S.3, Article 1.

115. *Comisión de La Verdad y Reconciliación (CVR)*, 35.

116. *Comisión de La Verdad y Reconciliación (CVR)*, 50.

117. UNICEF Innocenti Research Centre and International Center for Transitional Justice, *Children and Truth Commissions* (Florence: UNICEF, 2010), https://www.unicef-irc.org/publications/pdf/truth_commissions_eng.pdf, 11.

118. Stephanie Schwartz, *Youth and Post-Conflict Reconstruction: Agents of Change* (Washington, DC: United States Institute of Peace Press, 2010), 47–50.

119. Helen Berents, *Young People and Everyday Peace: Exclusion, Insecurity and Peacebuilding in Colombia* (New York: Routledge, 2018).

120. Erica Burman, "Innocents Abroad: Western Fantasies of Childhood and the Iconography of Emergencies," *Disasters* 18, no. 3 (1994): 245.

121. *Truth and Reconciliation Commission Report*, vol. 4, 256.

122. Mr. Maxlesi's submission in Truth and Reconciliation Commission, 4:273.

123. McEvoy-Levy, "Introduction: Youth and the Post-Accord Environment," 5.

124. *Truth and Reconciliation Commission Report*, vol. 4, 241.

125. *Truth and Reconciliation Commission Report*, vol. 4, 240.

126. Huynh, "Children and Agency," 42; James and Prout, *Constructing and Reconstructing Childhood*, 1.

Chapter 4

1. Siobhán McEvoy-Levy, "Human Rights Culture and Children Born of Wartime Rape," in *Born of War: Protecting Children of Sexual Violence Survivors in Conflict Zones*, ed. R. Charli Carpenter (Bloomfield, CT: Kumarian Press, 2007), 162; David Nosworthy, "Children and Security Sector Reform in Post-Conflict Peacebuilding," Innocenti Working Paper 2010/09 (Florence: UNICEF Innocenti Research Centre, June 2010), https://doi.org/10.18356/1bcc1d1d-en. In Sierra Leone the National Youth Policy defines youth as being between ages fifteen and thirty-five, while also providing flexibility to accommodate those under fifteen if programming allows. See Government of Sierra Leone, *Draft National Youth Policy Review*, 2012, https://www.youthpolicy.org/wp-content/uploads/library/2012_review_Sierra_Leone_Youth_Policy_draft_Eng.pdf.

2. See, for example, Jenny Kuper, *International Law Concerning Child Civilians in Armed Conflict* (Oxford: Clarendon Press, 1997), 15.

3. Philip Cook and Cheryl Heykoop, "Child Participation in the Sierra Leonean Truth and Reconciliation Commission," in *Children and Transitional Justice: Truth-Telling, Accountability and Reconciliation*, eds. Sharanjeet Parmar et al. (Cambridge, MA: Human Rights Program, Harvard Law School, 2010), 160; Bina D'Costa, "Turtles Can Fly: Vicarious Terror and the Child in South Asia," *Children and Violence: Politics of Conflict in South Asia*, ed. Bina D'Costa (Cambridge: Cambridge University Press, 2016), 24.

4. Truth and Reconciliation Commission, *Witness to Truth: Report of the Sierra Leone Truth and Reconciliation Commission*, 3 vols. (Freetown, Sierra Leone: Sierra Leone Truth and Reconciliation Commission, 2004), http://www.sierra-leonetrc.org/index.php/view-the-final-report/download-table-of-contents, 3B:343.

5. Truth and Reconciliation Commission, *Witness to Truth*, 3B:343.

6. Truth and Reconciliation Commission, *Witness to Truth*, 3B:343.

7. Truth and Reconciliation Commission, *Witness to Truth*, 3B:358.

8. Siobhán McEvoy-Levy, "Children, Youth and Peacebuilding," in *Critical Issues in Peace and Conflict Studies: Theory, Practice and Pedagogy*, eds. Thomas Matyók, Jessica Senehi, and Sean Byrne (Lanham, MD: Lexington Books, 2011),161; Cecilia Jacob, *Child Security in Asia: The Impact of Armed Conflict in Cambodia and Myanmar* (London: Routledge, 2014), 34–36.

9. Helen Brocklehurst, "Doing IR: Securing Children," in *Discovering Childhood in International Relations*, ed. J. Marshall Beier (Cham: Palgrave Macmillan, 2020), 89–113; McEvoy-Levy, "Children, Youth and Peacebuilding," 162.

10. Alan Prout, "Participation, Policy and the Changing Conditions of Childhood," in *Hearing the Voices of Children: Social Policy for a New Century*, eds. Christine Hallett and Alan Prout (London: Routledge Falmer, 2003), 11–25.

11. Helen Brocklehurst, *Who's Afraid of Children? Children, Conflict, and International Relations* (Aldershot, UK: Ashgate Publishing, 2006), 140.

12. David M. Rosen, *Armies of the Young: Child Soldiers in War and Terrorism* (New Brunswick, NJ: Rutgers University Press, 2005), 2.

13. Rachel Brett and Irma Specht, *Young Soldiers: Why They Choose to Fight?* (Boulder, CO: Lynne Rienner Publishers, 2004); P. W. Singer, *Children at War* (Berkeley: University of California Press, 2006); Rachel Brett and Margaret McCallin, *Children: The Invisible Soldiers*, 2nd ed. (Stockholm: Rädda Barnen, 1998).

14. UNICEF Innocenti Research Centre and International Center for Transitional Justice, *Children and Truth Commissions* (Florence: UNICEF, 2010), https://www.unicef-irc.org/publications/pdf/truth_commissions_eng.pdf.

15. Susan Shepler, "The Rites of the Child: Global Discourses of Youth and Reintegrating Child Soldiers in Sierra Leone," *Journal of Human Rights* 4, no. 2 (2005): 198.

16. Helen Berents and Caitlin Mollica, "Youth and Peacebuilding," in *The Palgrave Encyclopedia of Peace and Conflict Studies*, eds. Oliver P. Richmond and Gëzim Visoka (Cham: Palgrave Macmillan, 2020), https://doi.org/10.1007/978-3-030-11795-5_95-1; Alison M. S. Watson, "Centralizing Childhood, Remaking the Discourse," in Beier, *Discovering Childhood in International Relations*, 243–61; Jeanette Rhedding-Jones, "Shifting Ethnicities: 'Native Informants' and Other Theories from/for Early Childhood Education," *Contemporary Issues in Early Childhood* 2, no. 2 (2001): 135–56.

17. See Shari Stone-Mediatore, *Reading Across Borders: Storytelling and Knowledges of Resistance* (New York: Springer, 2016). Shari Stone-Mediator's work examines these conditions of marginalization in the case of women.

18. Helen Berents, *Young People and Everyday Peace: Exclusion, Insecurity and Peacebuilding in Colombia* (New York: Routledge, 2018), 5.

19. Matías Cordero Arce, "Towards an Emancipatory Discourse of Children's Rights," *International Journal of Children's Rights* 20, no. 3 (2012): 15.

20. Berents, *Young People and Everyday Peace*, 92. Berents's chapter "Space, Power, and Terrains of Insecurity" provides a thoughtful and critical discussion of the distinction between childhood and adulthood.

21. Nick Lee, *Childhood and Society: Growing Up in an Age of Uncertainty* (Buckingham, UK: Open University Press, 2001), 43.

22. Erin K. Baines, "Complex Political Perpetrators: Reflections on Dominic Ongwen," *Journal of Modern African Studies* 47, no. 2 (2009): 183.

23. Mary Adams, "Stories of Fracture and Claim for Belonging: Young Migrants' Narratives of Arrival in Britain," *Children's Geographies* 7, no. 2 (2009): 162.

24. Truth and Reconciliation Commission, *Witness to Truth*, 3B:343–44.

25. Truth and Reconciliation Commission, *Witness to Truth*, 3B:343.

26. UN General Assembly, Resolution 40/14, International Youth Year: Participation, Development, Peace, A/RES/40/14 (Nov. 18, 1985).

27. UN General Assembly, Resolution 40/14.

28. World Youth Forum Delegates, *Dakar Youth Empowerment Strategy*. Transmitted by letter dated Oct. 4, 2001, from the Permanent Representative of Senegal to the United Nations to the Secretary-General. ¶ 4, N Doc. A/C.3/56/2 (Oct. 8, 2001).

29. World Youth Forum Delegates, *Dakar Youth Empowerment Strategy*, ¶ 48.

30. World Youth Forum Delegates, *Dakar Youth Empowerment Strategy*, ¶ 48(1).

31. Siobhán McEvoy-Levy, *Peace and Resistance in Youth Cultures: Reading the Politics of Peacebuilding from Harry Potter to The Hunger Games* (London: Palgrave Macmillan, 2018), 41.

32. World Youth Forum Delegates, *Dakar Youth Empowerment Strategy* ¶ 47–51(8).

33. World Youth Forum Delegates, *Dakar Youth Empowerment Strategy*, ¶ 18(3).

34. World Youth Forum Delegates, *Dakar Youth Empowerment Strategy*, ¶ 52.

35. World Youth Forum Delegates, *Dakar Youth Empowerment Strategy*, ¶ 53.

36. Jessica Senehi and Sean Byrne, "From Violence Toward Peace: The Role of Storytelling for Youth Healing and Political Empowerment after Social Conflict," in *Troublemakers or Peacemakers? Youth and Post-Accord Peacebuilding*, ed. Siobhán McEvoy-Levy (Notre Dame, IN: University of Notre Dame Press, 2006), 238; see also Madeleine Fullard and Nicky Rousseau, "Truth Telling, Identities, and Power in South Africa and Guatemala," in *Identities in Transition: Challenges for Transitional Justice in Divided Societies*, ed. Paige Arthur (Cambridge: Cambridge University Press, 2010) 54–86.

37. UN Secretary-General, *Policies and Programmes Involving Youth*, UN Doc. E/CN.5/2017/5 (Nov. 21, 2016).

38. UN Secretary-General, *Policies and Programmes Involving Youth*.

39. McEvoy-Levy, "Children, Youth and Peacebuilding," 165, 168–69.

40. Truth and Reconciliation Commission, *Witness to Truth*, 3B:343.

41. Truth and Reconciliation Commission, *Witness to Truth*, 2, 165.

42. Truth and Reconciliation commission, *Witness to Truth*, 3B:343.

43. UN General Assembly, Resolution 50/81, World Programme of Action for Youth to the Year 2000 and Beyond. A/RES/50/81 (Mar. 13, 1996), ¶ 25.

44. UN General Assembly, Resolution 50/81, ¶ 25.

45. UN General Assembly, Resolution 50/81, ¶ 104.

46. UN General Assembly, Resolution 56/117, ¶ 13.

47. Truth and Reconciliation Commission, *Witness to Truth*, 3B:360.

48. Truth and Reconciliation Commission, *Witness to Truth*, 3B:360.

49. Truth and Reconciliation Commission, *Witness to Truth*, 3B:358.

50. Truth and Reconciliation Commission, *Witness to Truth*, 3B:358.

51. Truth and Reconciliation Commission, *Witness to Truth*, 3B:359.
52. McEvoy-Levy, "Children, Youth and Peacebuilding," 2011, 165.
53. Truth and Reconciliation Commission, *Witness to Truth*, appendix 3, 701.
54. Truth and Reconciliation Commission, *Witness to Truth*, 3B:348.
55. Truth and Reconciliation Commission, *Witness to Truth*, 3B:358.
56. Truth and Reconciliation Commission, *Witness to Truth*, 3B:355.
57. Truth and Reconciliation Commission, *Witness to Truth*, 3B:343.
58. Truth and Reconciliation Commission, *Witness to Truth*, 3, 241.
59. Holly L. Guthrey and Karen Brounéus, "Peering into the 'Black Box' of TRC Success: Exploring Local Perceptions of Reconciliation in the Solomon Islands TRC," in *Transitional Justice in Practice*, ed. Renée Jeffery (New York: Palgrave Macmillan, 2017), 91; Chris Mahony and Yasmin Sooka, "The Truth About the Truth: Insider Reflections on the Sierra Leonean Truth and Reconciliation Commission," in *Evaluating Transitional Justice: Accountability and Peacebuilding in Post-Conflict Sierra Leone*, eds. Kirsten Ainley et al. (Basingstoke, UK: Palgrave Macmillan, 2015), 35–54.
60. Truth and Reconciliation Commission, *Witness to Truth*, 3B:358.
61. Truth and Reconciliation Commission, *Witness to Truth*, 3B:359.
62. Truth and Reconciliation Commission, *Witness to Truth*, 3B:359.
63. Truth and Reconciliation Commission, *Witness to Truth*, 3B:359.
64. Krijn Peters, *War and the Crisis of Youth in Sierra Leone* (Cambridge: Cambridge University Press, 2011).
65. Jo Boyden, preface to *Years of Conflict: Adolescence, Political Violence and Displacement*, ed. Jason Hart (New York: Berghahn Books, 2010), ix.
66. Peters, *War and the Crisis of Youth in Sierra Leone*, 9.
67. UNICEF Innocenti Research Centre and International Center for Transitional Justice, *Children and Truth Commissions*.
68. Truth and Reconciliation Commission, *Witness to Truth*, 1, 147.
69. Jack A. Goldstone, "Population and Security: How Demographic Change Can Lead to Violent Conflict," *Journal of International Affairs* 56, no. 1 (2002): 3–21.
70. Stephanie Schwartz, *Youth and Post-Conflict Reconstruction: Agents of Change* (Washington, DC: United States Institute of Peace Press, 2010), 12–15; Paul Collier and Anke Hoeffler, "Greed and Grievance in Civil War," *Oxford Economic Papers* 56, no. 4 (2004): 563–95.
71. Truth and Reconciliation Commission, *Witness to Truth*, 3B:344.
72. Kandeh cited in Truth and Reconciliation Commission, *Witness to Truth*, 3B:344.
73. Truth and Reconciliation Commission, *Witness to Truth*, 3B:343.
74. Truth and Reconciliation Commission, *Witness to Truth*, 3B:343.
75. Truth and Reconciliation Commission, *Witness to Truth*, 3B:344.

76. Berents, *Young People and Everyday Peace*.
77. David Car, "Narrative and the Real World: An Argument for Continuity," in *Memory, Identity and Community*, eds. Lewis P. Hinchman and Sandra Hinchman (Albany: State University of New York Press, 1997), 7–25.
78. Truth and Reconciliation Commission, *Witness to Truth*, 3B:239.
79. Truth and Reconciliation Commission, *Witness to Truth*, 3B:346.
80. Truth and Reconciliation Commission, *Witness to Truth*, 3B:343.
81. Truth and Reconciliation Commission, *Witness to Truth*, 3B:346.
82. Truth and Reconciliation Commission, *Witness to Truth*, 3B:346.
83. Truth and Reconciliation Commission, *Witness to Truth*, 3B:346.
84. Truth and Reconciliation Commission, *Witness to Truth*, 3B:348.
85. Truth and Reconciliation Commission, *Witness to Truth*, 3B:358.
86. Truth and Reconciliation Commission, *Witness to Truth*, 3B:351.
87. Truth and Reconciliation Commission, *Witness to Truth*, 3B:358.
88. Truth and Reconciliation Commission, *Witness to Truth*, 1, 20.
89. Ibrahim Bangura and Tejan Suma quoted in Truth and Reconciliation Commission, Witness to *Truth*, 3B:504.
90. Truth and Reconciliation Commission, *Witness to Truth*, 3B:513.
91. Truth and Reconciliation Commission, *Witness to Truth*, 3B:517.
92. Truth and Reconciliation Commission, *Witness to Truth*, 3B:499.
93. Ishmeal Harune Bangura in Truth and Reconciliation Commission, *Witness to Truth*, appendix 3, 34.
94. Peters, *War and the Crisis of Youth in Sierra Leone*, 10.
95. Truth and Reconciliation Commission, *Witness to Truth*, 2, 166.
96. Truth and Reconciliation Commission, *Witness to Truth*, 2, 166.
97. Truth and Reconciliation Commission, *Witness to Truth*, 2, 166.
98. Truth and Reconciliation Commission, *Witness to Truth*, 2, 166.
99. Fullard and Rousseau, "Truth Telling, Identities, and Power."
100. Truth and Reconciliation Commission, *Witness to Truth*, 3B:345.
101. Truth and Reconciliation Commission, *Witness to Truth*, 3B:346.
102. Truth and Reconciliation Commission, *Witness to Truth*, appendix 3, 17.
103. Truth and Reconciliation Commission, *Witness to Truth*, appendix 3, 17.
104. Truth and Reconciliation Commission, *Witness to Truth*, 3B:355.
105. Truth and Reconciliation Commission, *Witness to Truth*, 3B:355.
106. Berents, *Young People and Everyday Peace*, 2018; Helen Berents, "'It's About Finding a Way': Children, Sites of Opportunity, and Building Everyday Peace in Columbia," *International Journal of Children's Rights* 22, no. 2 (2014): 361–84; Alison M. S. Watson, "Children and International Relations: A New Site of Knowledge?," *Review of International Studies* 32, no. 2 (2006): 237–50.
107. McEvoy-Levy, *Peace and Resistance in Youth Cultures*; see also Helen Berents and Siobhán McEvoy-Levy, "Theorizing Youth and Everyday Peace (Building)," *Peacebuilding* 3, no. 2 (2015): 115–25.

108. Truth and Reconciliation Commission, *Witness to Truth*, 3B:355.
109. Truth and Reconciliation Commission, *Witness to Truth*, 3B:343.
110. Truth and Reconciliation Commission, *Witness to Truth*, 3B:343.
111. Katrina Lee-Koo, "Children and Peacebuilding: Propagating Peace," in *Children and Global Conflict*, eds. Kim Huynh, Bina D'Costa, and Katrina Lee-Koo (Cambridge: Cambridge University Press, 2015), 203.
112. Timor-Leste Commission for Reception, Truth, and Reconciliation (CAVR). *Chega! The Final Report of the Timor-Leste Commission for Reception, Truth, and Reconciliation* (Dili, Timor-Leste: CAVR, 2005), http://chegareport.org/Chega%20All%20Volumes.pdf, pt. 7.8. In Timor-Leste youth are defined as those aged from sixteen to thirty years old. See the Democratic Republic of Timor-Leste, *National Youth Policy of Timor-Leste*, Secretary of State for Youth and Sport Balide, Díli, Nov. 14, 2017, https://www.youthpolicy.org/national/Timor_Leste_2007_National_Youth_Policy.pdf.
113. Bina D'Costa, "Children and Justice: Past Crimes, Healing and the Future," in Huynh, D'Costa, and Lee-Koo, *Children and Global Conflict*, 243. For a detailed discussion of the role of the TBO in the conflict and their recruitment of child soldiers see, Timor-Leste Commission for Reception, Truth, and Reconciliation (CAVR), *Chega!* chaps. 7–8.
114. D'Costa, "Children and Justice," 244.
115. CAVR, *Chega!*, pt. 7.8, para. 22.
116. Kim Huynh, "Children and Agency: Caretakers, Free-Rangers and Everyday Life," in Huynh, D'Costa, and Lee-Koo, Children *and Global Conflict*, 42.
117. Huynh, 43–44.
118. CAVR, *Chega!*, pt. 11, para. 4.2.1.
119. CAVR, *Chega!*, pt. 11, para. 4.2.2.
120. CAVR, *Chega!*, pt. 11, para. 4.2.4.
121. Katrina Lee-Koo, "Children and Armed Conflict: Mapping the Terrain," in Huynh, D'Costa, and Lee-Koo, *Children and Global Conflict*, 14.
122. Lee-Koo, 16.
123. CAVR, *Chega!*, pt. 7.8, para. 421.
124. CAVR, *Chega!*, pt. 7.8, para. 61.
125. D'Costa, "Children and Justice," 244.
126. D'Costa, 245.
127. CAVR, *Chega!* pt. 7.8, para. 22.
128. CAVR, *Chega!*, pt. 7.8, para. 9.
129. CAVR, *Chega!*, pt. 7.8, para. 9.
130. Lee-Koo, "Children and Armed Conflict," 10.
131. Paige Arthur, *Identities in Transition: Challenges for Transitional Justice in Divided Societies* (Cambridge: Cambridge University Press, 2010), 35.
132. CAVR, *Chega!*, pt. 7.8, para. 44.
133. CAVR, *Chega!*, pt. 7.8, para. 429.

134. CAVR, *Chega!*, pt. 11, para. 4.2.8.
135. CAVR, *Chega!*, pt. 11, para. 4.2.
136. CAVR, *Chega!*, pt. 7.8, para. 156.
137. CAVR, *Chega!*, pt. 7.8, para. 226.
138. CAVR, *Chega!*, pt. 7.8, para. 149.
139. Tamar Schapiro, "What Is a Child?," *Ethics* 109, no. 4 (1999): 729.

Chapter 5

1. Acknowledgment: This chapter is derived in part from an article published in Australian Journal of International Affairs on March 1, 2017 © 2017 Australian Institute of International Affairs, available online: https://www.tandfonline.com/doi/10.1080/10357718.2017.1290045. Reprinted with permission of Taylor & Francis Ltd, https://www.tandfonline.com, on behalf of Australian Institute of International Affairs.

2. Mark Bevir, "How Narratives Explain," in *Interpretations and Methods: Empirical Research Methods and the Interpretive Turn*, eds. Dvora Yanow and Peregrine Schwartz-Shea (New York: M. E. Sharpe, 2003), 281–90.

3. Solomon Islands Truth and Reconciliation Commission, *Solomon Islands Truth and Reconciliation Commission Final Report: Confronting the Truth for a Better Solomon Islands*, 5 vols., Honiara, Solomon Islands, 2012, 4:1022.

4. Solomon Islands Truth and Reconciliation Commission, *Final Report*, 4:1015; 1023.

5. Solomon Islands Truth and Reconciliation Commission, *Final Report*, 4: 1015.

6. Benjamin Maiangwa and Sean Byrne, "Peacebuilding and Reconciliation through Storytelling in Northern Ireland and the Border Counties of the Republic of Ireland," *Storytelling, Self, Society* 11, no. 1 (2015): 85–110.

7. J. Marshall Beier, "Shifting the Burden: Childhoods, Resilience and Subjecthood," *Critical Studies on Security* 3, no. 3 (2015): 240–41.

8. Focus Group One and Two, September 26, 2015, Honiara: Solomon Islands. All focus groups and interviews have been anonymized per ethics requirements unless participants have consented to be identified.

9. Focus Group One and Two, September 26, 2015, Honiara: Solomon Islands.

10. Solomon Islands Truth and Reconciliation Commission, *Final Report*, 4:1016.

11. Alpaslan Özerdem and Sukanya Podder, *Youth in Conflict and Peacebuilding: Mobilization, Reintegration and Reconciliation* (London: Palgrave Macmillan, 2015), 78.

12. Özerdem and Podder, 78.

13. Özerdem and Podder, 78.

14. Anita Isaacs, "Truth and the Challenge of Reconciliation in Guatemala," in *Reconciliation(s): Transitional Justice in Postconflict Societies*, ed. Joanna Quinn (Montreal, QC: McGill-Queen's University Press, 2009), 120.

15. Martha Minow, *Between Vengeance and Forgiveness: Facing History After Genocide and Mass Violence* (Boston: Beacon Press, 1998), 72; Elizabeth Kiss, "Moral Ambition Within and Beyond Political Constraints," in *Truth v. Justice: The Morality of Truth Commissions*, eds. Robert I. Rotberg and Dennis Thompson (Princeton, NJ: Princeton University Press, 2000), 45–67.

16. Isaacs, "Truth and the Challenge of Reconciliation," 120.

17. Holly L. Guthrey and Karen Brounéus, "Peering into the 'Black Box' of TRC Success: Exploring Local Perceptions of Reconciliation in the Solomon Islands TRC," in *Transitional Justice in Practice*, ed. Renée Jeffery (New York: Palgrave Macmillan, 2017), 91; Rebekka Friedman, "The Potential and Politics of Transitional Justice: Interactions between the Global and the Local in Evaluations of Success," *Evaluating Transitional Justice: Accountability and Peacebuilding in Post-Conflict Sierra Leone*, Rethinking Peace and Conflict Studies, eds. Kirsten Ainley et al. (Basingstoke, UK: Palgrave Macmillan, 2015), 265–79.

18. Joanna R. Quinn, *The Politics of Acknowledgement: Truth Commissions in Uganda and Haiti*, Law and Society Series (Vancouver: UBC Press, 2010), 44.

19. Renée Jeffery, "The Forgiveness Dilemma: Emotions and Justice at the Khmer Rouge Tribunal," *Australian Journal of International Affairs* 69, no. 1 (2015): 35–36; Alex, Boraine, "Truth and Reconciliation in South Africa: The Third Way," in Rotberg and Thompson, *Truth v. Justice*, 147.

20. Renée Jeffery and Caitlin Mollica, "The Unfinished Business of the Solomon Islands TRC: Closing the Implementation Gap," *Pacific Review* 30, no. 4 (2017): 537–38.

21. Jana Tabak, "A Tale of a (Dis) Orderly International Society: Protecting Child-Soldiers, Saving the Child, Governing the Future," in *Discovering Childhood in International Relations*, ed. J. Marshall Beier (Cham: Palgrave Macmillan, 2020), 116.

22. Solomon Islands Truth and Reconciliation Commission, *Final Report*, 4:1009.

23. Solomon Islands Truth and Reconciliation Commission, *Final Report*, 4:1009.

24. Solomon Islands Truth and Reconciliation Commission, *Final Report*, 4:1013.

25. Daniel Evans, "Things Still Fall Apart: A Political Economy Analysis of State-Youth Engagement in Honiara, Solomon Islands," in *Pacific Youth: Local and Global Futures*, ed. Helen Lee (Canberra, AU: ANU Press, 2019), 85; Aidan Craney, *Youth in Fiji and Solomon Islands: Livelihoods, Leadership and Civic Engagement* (Canberra, AU: ANU Press, 2022), 130.

26. Evans, *Things Still Fall Apart*, 85.

27. Ministry of Women, Youth, and Children's Affairs, *Solomon Island National Youth Policy: 2010–2015* (Honiara: Solomon Islands Government, June 2010), 3.

28. Ministry of Women, Youth, Children and Family Affairs, *Solomon Islands National Youth Policy 2017–2030* (Honiara: Solomon Islands Government, 2017), 12.

29. For an extensive critical analysis of the implications substantive youth participation beyond reconciliation contexts, see also Evans, *Things Still Fall Apart*, 79–110; Craney, *Youth Leadership in the Solomon Islands and Fiji*, 137–58.

30. Solomon Islands Truth and Reconciliation Commission, *Final Report*, 4:1013.

31. Anonymous One, interview with the author in Solomon Islands, Oct. 2015.

32. Anonymous Four, interview with the author in Solomon Islands, Oct. 2015.

33. Robert J. Sampson and John H. Laub (2005) cited in Christoffer Carlsson, "Using 'Turning Points' to Understand Processes of Change in Offending Notes from a Swedish Study on Life Courses and Crime," *British Journal of Criminology* 52, no. 1 (2012): 3.

34. UNICEF Innocenti Research Centre and International Center for Transitional Justice, *Children and Truth Commissions* (Florence, IT: UNICEF, 2010), 86.

35. Ministry of Women, Youth, and Children's Affairs, "National Youth Policy," 1.

36. International Labour Organization, "Decent Work Country Programme: Solomon Islands (2009–2012)," ILO, Aug. 19, 2009, 5, http://www.ilo.org/wcmsp5/groups/public/—-asia/—-ro-bangkok/documents/publication/wcms_120555.pdf.

37. Hassall and Associates International, "Youth in Solomon Islands: A Participatory Study of Issues, Needs and Priorities," Final Report, 2003, 46, https://www.youthpolicy.org/national/Solomon_Islands_2003_Youth_Study.pdf.

38. Ministry of Women, Youth, and Children's Affairs, "National Youth Policy," 6; Central Islands Provincial Government, Solomon Islands, "Provincial Youth Policy," Central Islands Provincial Government, Sept. 15, 2009, 4–7; Guadalcanal Provincial Government, Solomon Islands, "Provincial Youth Policy," Guadalcanal Provincial Government, April 2010, 4–8.

39. Jeff Helsing, "Young People's Activism and the Transition to Peace: Bosnia, Northern Ireland and Israel," with Namik Kirlic, Neil McMaster, and Nir Sonnenschein, in *Troublemakers or Peacemakers? Youth and Post-Accord Peacebuilding*, ed. Siobhán McEvoy-Levy (Notre Dame, IN: University of Notre Dame Press, 2006), 197.

40. Solomon Islands Truth and Reconciliation Commission, *Final Report*, 3:646.

41. Ministry of Women, Youth, and Children's Affairs, "National Youth Policy," 1.

42. Siobhán McEvoy-Levy, "Children, Youth and Peacebuilding," in *Critical Issues in Peace and Conflict Studies: Theory, Practice and Pedagogy*, eds. Thomas Matyók, Jessica Senehi, and Sean Byrne (Lanham, MD: Lexington Books, 2011), 165.

43. McEvoy-Levy, "Children, Youth and Peacebuilding," 165; Making Cents International, "Youth Microenterprise and Livelihoods: State of the Field," Lessons from the 2007 Global Youth Microenterprise Conference, Making Cents International, Jan. 2008, 11, https://bettercarenetwork.org/sites/default/files/Youth%20 Microenterprise%20and%20Livelihoods%20-%20State%20of%20the%20Field.pdf.

44. Ministry of Women, Youth, and Children's Affairs, "National Youth Policy," 1.

45. Ministry of Women, Youth, and Children's Affairs, "National Youth Policy," 8.

46. Ministry of Women, Youth, and Children's Affairs, "National Youth Policy," 8.

47. McEvoy-Levy, "Children, Youth and Peacebuilding," 168.

48. McEvoy-Levy, 168; see also Stephanie Schwartz, *Youth and Post-Conflict Reconstruction: Agents of Change* (Washington, DC: United States Institute of Peace Press, 2010).

49. Quinn, *The Politics of Acknowledgement*, 1.

50. Solomon Islands Truth and Reconciliation Commission, *Final Report*, 3:722.

51. Solomon Islands Truth and Reconciliation Commission, *Final Report*, 3:768.

52. Solomon Islands Truth and Reconciliation Commission, *Final Report*, 3:768.

53. Convention on the Rights of the Child, Nov. 20, 1989, 1577 U.N.T.S. 3. Article 1. Solomon Islands ratified the United Nations Convention of the Rights of the Child on April 10, 1995.

54. Solomon Islands Truth and Reconciliation Commission, *Final Report*, 3:769.

55. Solomon Islands Truth and Reconciliation Commission, *Final Report*, 3:769.

56. Siobhán McEvoy-Levy, *Peace and Resistance in Youth Cultures: Reading the Politics of Peacebuilding from Harry Potter to The Hunger Games* (London: Palgrave Macmillan), 41–42; Katrina Lee-Koo, "Children and Peacebuilding: Propagating Peace," in *Children and Global Conflict*, eds. Kim Huynh, Bina D'Costa, and Katrina Lee-Koo (Cambridge: Cambridge University Press 2015), 203.

57. Helsing et al., "Young People's Activism," 196.

58. Christine Jourdan, "Masta Liu," in *Youth Cultures: A Cross-Cultural Perspective*, eds. Vered Amit-Talai and Helena Wulff (London: Routledge, 1995),

202; Jon Fraenkel, *The Manipulation of Custom: From Uprising to Intervention in the Solomon Islands* (Wellington, NZ: Victoria University Press, 2004), 113, 119.

59. Matthew G. Allen, *Greed and Grievance: Ex-Militants' Perspectives on the Conflict in Solomon Islands, 1998–2003*, Topics in the Contemporary Pacific (Honolulu: University of Hawaii Press, 2013), 6.

60. Allen, 5.

61. Solomon Islands Truth and Reconciliation Commission, *Final Report*, 5:1191.

62. Solomon Islands Truth and Reconciliation Commission, *Final Report*, 5:1206–1208.

63. Solomon Islands Truth and Reconciliation Commission, *Final Report*, 5:1214–1215.

64. Cecilia Jacob, *Child Security in Asia: The Impact of Armed Conflict in Cambodia and Myanmar* (London: Routledge, 2014), 34.

65. Paige Arthur, ed., "Introduction: Identities in Transition," in *Identities in Transition: Challenges for Transitional Justice in Divided Societies* (Cambridge: Cambridge University Press, 2010), 6.

66. Katrina Lee-Koo, "Children and Armed Conflict: Mapping the Terrain," in Huynh, D'Costa, and Lee-Koo, *Children and Global Conflict*, 10.

67. McEvoy-Levy, "Children, Youth and Peacebuilding," 170; for more detail on the ecological approach to youth, see Neil Boothby, Alison Strang, and Michael Wessells, eds., *A World Turned Upside Down: Social Ecological Approaches to Children in War Zones* (Bloomfield, CT: Kumarian Press, 2006).

68. McEvoy-Levy, "Children, Youth and Peacebuilding," 169.

69. Harris cited in Paul Gready, *The Era of Transitional Justice: The Aftermath of the Truth and Reconciliation Commission in South Africa and Beyond* (New York: Routledge), 150.

70. Jacob, *Child Security in Asia*, 35.

71. Gready, *The Era of Transitional Justice*, 150.

72. Valerie Braithwaite et al., *Pillars and Shadows: Statebuilding as Peacebuilding in Solomon Islands* (Canberra, AU: Australian National University Press, 2010), 29.

73. Allen, *Greed and Grievance*, 124–25.

74. Allen, 3. As Allen describes, "Gual" is a common abbreviation for Guadalcanal and is used to denote the identity of individuals from this Province.

75. Full text of these demands is available in Fraenkel, *The Manipulation of Custom*, 197–203.

76. Helen Brocklehurst, *Who's Afraid of Children? Children, Conflict, and International Relations* (Aldershot, UK: Ashgate Publishing, 2006), 55.

77. Jacob, *Child Security in Asia*, 32–34; Karen Wells, *Childhood in a Global Perspective* (Cambridge: Polity Press, 2009), 33–34.

78. Coalition to Stop the Use of Child Soldiers, cited in Solomon Islands Truth and Reconciliation Commission, *Final Report*, 3:638.

79. Solomon Islands Truth and Reconciliation Commission, *Final Report*, 3:636.
80. Solomon Islands Truth and Reconciliation Commission, *Final Report*, 3:637.
81. Solomon Islands Truth and Reconciliation Commission, *Final Report*, 3:637.
82. Solomon Islands Truth and Reconciliation Commission, *Final Report*, 3:639.
83. Solomon Islands Truth and Reconciliation Commission, *Final Report*, 3:646.
84. Solomon Islands Truth and Reconciliation Commission, *Final Report*, 3:646.
85. Myriam Denov, *Child Soldiers: Sierra Leone's Revolutionary United Front* (Cambridge: Cambridge University Press, 2010), 6–9.
86. Denov, 44; Kirsten J. Fisher, *Transitional Justice for Child Soldiers: Accountability and Social Reconstruction in Post-Conflict Contexts* (Basingstoke, UK: Palgrave Macmillan, 2013). As previously discussed, *Masta Liu* is a deeply rooted cultural depiction of youth that means "to wander aimlessly." For further examples, see Fraenkel, *The Manipulation of Custom*, 113, 119; Jourdan, "Masta Liu," 202.
87. Allen, *Greed and Grievance*, 44–45.
88. Allen, 6.
89. Solomon Islands Truth and Reconciliation Commission, *Final Report*, 3:634.
90. Solomon Islands Truth and Reconciliation Commission, *Final Report*, 3:634–35.
91. David Akin, "Compensation and the Melanesian State: Why the Kwaio Keep Claiming," *Contemporary Pacific* 11, no. 1 (Spring 1999): 58.
92. Anonymous Eight, interview with the author in Solomon Islands, Nov. 2015.
93. Anonymous Three, interview with the author in Solomon Islands, Oct. 2015.
94. Louise Vella, "'What Will You Do with Our Stories?' Truth and Reconciliation in the Solomon Islands," *International Journal of Conflict and Violence* 8, no. 1 (2014): 92.
95. Braithwaite et al., *Pillars and Shadows*, 30–31.
96. Clive Moore, *Happy Isles in Crisis: The Historical Causes for a Failing State in Solomon Islands, 1998–2004* (Canberra, AU: Asia Pacific Press, 2004), 14.
97. Braithwaite et al., *Pillars and Shadows*, 31.
98. Solomon Islands Truth and Reconciliation Commission, *Final Report*, 3:639.
99. Solomon Islands Truth and Reconciliation Commission, *Final Report*, 3:639.

100. Anonymous Two, interview with the author in Solomon Islands, Oct. 2015.

101. Anonymous One, interview with the author in Solomon Islands, Oct. 2015, and Anonymous Six, interview with the author in Solomon Islands, Nov. 2015.

102. Solomon Islands Truth and Reconciliation Commission, *Final Report*, 3:626–47. "Raskols" is a cultural term used throughout the Solomon Islands to denote the capacity of young people to cause disruptions in the community.

103. Anonymous Seven, interview with the author in Solomon Islands, Oct. 2015.

104. Anonymous Seven, interview with the author in Solomon Islands, Oct. 2015.

105. Anonymous Sixteen, interview with the author in Solomon Islands, Nov. 2015.

106. Schwartz, *Youth and Post-Conflict Reconstruction*; Helen Berents and Siobhán McEvoy-Levy, "Theorizing Youth and Everyday Peace (Building)," *Peacebuilding* 3, no. 2 (2015): 115–25.

107. Lori Drummond-Mundal and Guy Cave, cited in Claire O'Kane, Clare Feinstein, and Annette Giertsen, "The Active Role of Children and Young People in Post-Conflict Peace," in *Escaping Victimhood: Children, Youth and Post-Conflict Peacebuilding*, eds. Albrecht Schnabel and Anara Tabyshalieva (New York: United Nations University Press, 2013), 35.

108. O'Kane, Feinstein, and Giertsen, 35.

109. Anonymous Nine, interview with the author in Solomon Islands, Oct. 2015.

110. Anonymous Twenty, interview with the author in Solomon Islands, Nov. 2015.

111. Anonymous Four, interview with the author in Solomon Islands, Oct. 2015.

112. Anonymous Three, interview with the author in Solomon Islands, Oct. 2015.

113. Anonymous One, interview with the author in Solomon Islands, Oct. 2015.

114. Anonymous Three, interview with the author in Solomon Islands, Oct. 2015.

115. Anonymous Four, interview with the author in Solomon Islands, Oct. 2015.

116. Anonymous Four, interview with the author in Solomon Islands, Oct. 2015.

117. Anonymous Six, interview with the author in Solomon Islands, Oct. 2015.

118. Anonymous Seven, interview with the author in Solomon Islands, Oct. 2015.
119. Anonymous Sixteen, interview with the author in Solomon Islands, Nov. 2015.
120. Lee-Koo, "Children and Armed Conflict," 15.
121. Anonymous Nine, interview with the author in Solomon Islands, Nov. 2015.
122. Anonymous Nine, interview with the author in Solomon Islands, Nov. 2015.
123. Madeline Fullard and Nicky Rousseau, "Truth Telling, Identities, and Power in South Africa and Guatemala," in Arthur, *Identities in Transition*, 54–86.
124. Solomon Islands Truth and Reconciliation Commission, *Final Report*, 4:1016.
125. Solomon Islands Truth and Reconciliation Commission, *Final Report*, 4:1009.
126. Anonymous Sixteen, interview with the author in Solomon Islands, Nov. 2015.

Conclusion

1. Virginie Ladisch, "A Catalyst for Change: Engaging Youth in Transitional Justice," ICTJ Briefing, International Center for Transitional Justice, April 2018, 4.
2. Siobhán McEvoy-Levy, "Children, Youth and Peacebuilding," in *Critical Issues in Peace and Conflict Studies: Theory, Practice and Pedagogy*, eds. Thomas Matyók, Jessica Senehi, and Sean Byrne (Lanham, MD: Lexington Books, 2011), 173.
3. Siobhán McEvoy-Levy, "Youth," in *Routledge Handbook of Peacebuilding*, ed. Roger MacGinty (London: Taylor & Francis, 2013), 304.
4. Graeme Simpson, *The Missing Peace: Independent Progress Study on Youth, Peace, and Security* (New York: Progress Study on Youth, Peace and Security, UN, 2018), 103.
5. Alcinda Honwana, cited in Ladisch, "A Catalyst for Change," 2.
6. Truth and Dignity Commission, Tunisia. "Final Comprehensive Report: Executive Summary" (English trans.), May 2019, Tunisia: Avocats Sans Frontières, http://www.ivd.tn/rapport/doc/TDC_executive_summary_report.pdf.
7. Rim El Gantri, interviewed by Kate McCabe in McCabe, "Dreams of January," International Center for Transitional Justice, 2015.
8. Virginie Ladisch, interview by Virginie Ladisch, Jan. 2017, in Ladisch, "A Catalyst for Change," 6.

9. Ladisch, 13.

10. Ladisch, 13.

11. Truth and Reconciliation Commission of Canada, "Mandate for the Truth and Reconciliation Commission," Schedule N, Winnipeg, MB: Government of Canada, https://www.residentialschoolsettlement.ca/SCHEDULE_N.pdf.

12. Truth and Reconciliation Commission of Canada, "Mandate."

13. Ladisch, "A Catalyst for Change," 6.

14. "A Guide to Teaching and Learning about the History of Residential Schools," Legacy of Hope Foundation, accessed Oct. 14, 2023, https://legacyofhope.ca/.

15. Office of the Secretary-General's Envoy on Youth, "Global Reactions to Security Council Resolution 2250 on Youth, Peace and Security," United Nations, 2015.

16. Simpson, *The Missing Peace*, 103.

17. Helen Berents and Caitlin Mollica, "Youth and Peacebuilding," in *The Palgrave Encyclopedia of Peace and Conflict Studies*, eds. Oliver P. Richmond and Gëzim Visoka (Cham: Palgrave Macmillan, 2020), https://doi.org/10.1007/978-3-030-11795-5_95-1.

18. Clara Ramírez-Barat, "Engaging Children and Youth in Transitional Justice Processes: Guidance for Outreach Programs," International Center for Transitional Justice, New York, Nov. 2012, 14.

19. Stephanie Schwartz, *Youth and Post-Conflict Reconstruction: Agents of Change* (Washington, DC: United States Institute of Peace Press, 2010), 18; see also Helen Berents and Caitlin Mollica, "Reciprocal Institutional Visibility: Youth, Peace and Security and 'Inclusive' Agendas at the United Nations," *Cooperation and Conflict* 57, no. 1 (2021): 1–19.

Bibliography

Adams, Mary. "Stories of Fracture and Claim for Belonging: Young Migrants' Narratives of Arrival in Britain." *Children's Geographies* 7, no. 2 (2009): 159–71.

Ainley, Kirsten, Rebekka Friedman, and Chris Mahony. *Evaluating Transitional Justice: Accountability and Peacebuilding in Post-Conflict Sierra Leone.* Rethinking Peace and Conflict Studies. Basingstoke, UK: Palgrave Macmillan, 2015. See esp. "The Potential and Politics of Transitional Justice: Interactions between the Global and the Local in Evaluations of Success," 265–79.

Akin, David. "Compensation and the Melanesian State: Why the Kwaio Keep Claiming." *Contemporary Pacific* 11, no. 1 (Spring 1999): 35–67.

Allen, Matthew, Sinclair Dinnen, Daniel Evans, and Rebecca Monson. "Justice Delivered Locally: Systems, Challenges, and Innovations in Solomon Islands." Research Report. Washington, DC: World Bank, August 2013. https://www.dfat.gov.au/about-us/publications/Pages/justice-delivered-locally-systems-challenges-and-innovations-solomon-islands.

Allen, Matthew G. *Greed and Grievance: Ex-Militants' Perspectives on the Conflict in Solomon Islands, 1998–2003.* Topics in the Contemporary Pacific. Honolulu: University of Hawaii Press, 2013.

Altiok, Ali. "Squeezed Agency: Youth Resistance to the Securitization of Peacebuilding." In *Securitizing Youth: Young People's Role in the Global Peace & Security Agenda*, edited by Marisa O. Ensor. New Brunswick, NJ: Rutgers University Press, 2021.

Altiok, Ali, Helen Berents, Irena Grizelj, and Siobhán McEvoy-Levy. "Youth, Peace, and Security." In *Routledge Handbook of Peace, Security and Development*, edited by Fen Osler Hampson, Alpaslan Özerdem, and Jonathan Kent, 433–47. London: Routledge, 2020.

Altiok, Ali, and Irena Grizelj. "We Are Here: An Integrated Approach to Youth-Inclusive Peace Processes." New York: United Nations Office of the Secretary-General's Envoy on Youth, March 2019. https://www.youth4peace.

info/book-page/global-policy-paper-we-are-here-integrated-approach-youth-inclusive-peace-processes.

Annan, Jeannie, Christopher Blattman, and Roger Horton. "The State of Youth and Youth Protection in Northern Uganda: Findings from the Survey for War Affected Youth." UNICEF Uganda, Sept. 2006. https://archive.crin.org/en/docs/uni_avi_nuganda.pdf.

Antkowiak, Thomas M. "Truth as Right and Remedy in International Human Rights Experience." *Michigan Journal of International Law* 23, no. 4 (2002): 977–1013.

Arce, Matías Cordero. "Towards an Emancipatory Discourse of Children's Rights." *International Journal of Children's Rights* 20, no. 3 (2012): 365–421.

Archard, David. *Children: Rights and Childhood*. 2nd ed. London: Routledge, 2004.

Arthur, Paige. "How 'Transitions' Reshaped Human Rights: A Conceptual History of Transitional Justice." *Human Rights Quarterly* 31, no. 2 (2009): 321–67.

———, ed. *Identities in Transition: Challenges for Transitional Justice in Divided Societies*. Cambridge: Cambridge University Press, 2010.

———. "Introduction: Identities in Transition." In Paige, *Identities in Transition*, 1–14.

Atkinson, Robert. "The Life Story Interview as a Bridge in Narrative Inquiry." In *Handbook of Narrative Inquiry: Mapping a Methodology*, edited by D. Jean Clandinin, 224–45. London: SAGE, 2007.

Australian Network News. "Solomons Truth and Reconciliation Report Released." *ABC News (Online)*, April 29, 2013. https://www.abc.net.au/news/2013-04-29/solomons-truth-and-reconciliation-report-released/4658288.

Baines, Erin K. "Complex Political Perpetrators: Reflections on Dominic Ongwen." *Journal of Modern African Studies* 47, no. 2 (2009): 163–91.

Baker, Rachel, and Rachel Hinton. "Approaches to Children's Work and Rights in Nepal." *Annals of the American Academy of Political and Social Science* 575, no. 1 (2001): 176–93.

Bakiner, Onur. "Truth Commission Impact: An Assessment of How Commissions Influence Politics and Society." *International Journal of Transitional Justice* 8, no. 1 (2014): 6–30.

Barnett, Michael, Hunjoon Kim, Madalene O'Donnell, and Laura Sitea. "Peacebuilding: What Is in a Name?" *Global Governance* 13, no. 1 (2007): 35–58.

Bassiouni, M. Cherif, ed. *Post-Conflict Justice*. Ardsley, NY: Transnational Publishers, 2002.

Beier, J. Marshall. "Shifting the Burden: Childhoods, Resilience, Subjecthood." *Critical Studies on Security* 3, no. 3 (2015): 237–52.

Bennett, Catherine. "The Letters of Reconciliation Sent to Ex-FARC Fighters." *Observers*, July 7, 2017. https://observers.france24.com/en/20170707-letters-love-sent-ex-farc-combatants.

Berents, Helen. "'It's About Finding a Way': Children, Sites of Opportunity, and Building Everyday Peace in Columbia." *International Journal of Children's Rights* 22, no. 2 (2014): 361–84.

———. "No Child's Play: Recognizing the Agency of Former Child Soldiers in Peace Building Processes." *Dialogue e-Journal* 6, no. 2 (2009): 1–35. https://eprints.qut.edu.au/217204/1/HelenBerents.pdf.

———. *Young People and Everyday Peace: Exclusion, Insecurity and Peacebuilding in Colombia.* New York: Routledge, 2018. See esp. "Space, Power, and Terrains of Insecurity," 80–103.

———. "Power, Partnership, and Youth as Norm Entrepreneurs: Getting to UN Security Council Resolution 2250 on Youth, Peace, and Security." *Global Studies Quarterly* 2, no. 3 (2022): 1–11.

Berents, Helen, and Caitlin Mollica. "Reciprocal Institutional Visibility: Youth, Peace and Security and 'Inclusive' Agendas at the United Nations." *Cooperation and Conflict* 57, no. 1 (2022): 65–83.

———. "Youth and Peacebuilding." In *The Palgrave Encyclopedia of Peace and Conflict Studies*, eds. Oliver P. Richmond and Gëzim Visoka. Cham: Palgrave Macmillan, 2020). https://doi.org/10.1007/978-3-030-11795-5_95-1.

Berents, Helen, and Saji Prelis. "More than a Milestone: The Road to UN Security Council Resolution 2250 on Youth, Peace and Security." Search for Common Ground and the Global Coalition on Youth Peace and Security, Dec. 2020. https://www.youth4peace.info/system/files/2020-12/The%20Story%20of%202250_FINAL%20Dec%209%202020.pdf.

Berents, Helen, and Siobhán McEvoy-Levy. "Theorising Youth and Everyday Peace (Building)." *Peacebuilding* 3, no. 2 (2015): 115–25.

Bevir, Mark. *The Logic of the History of Ideas.* Cambridge: Cambridge University Press, 1999.

———. "How Narratives Explain." In *Interpretations and Methods: Empirical Research Methods and the Interpretive Turn*, edited by Dvora Yanow and Peregrine Schwartz-Shea, 281–90. New York: M. E. Sharpe, 2003.

Bevir, Mark, Oliver Daddow, and Ian Hall, eds. *Interpreting Global Security.* New York: Routledge, 2014.

Bhargava, Rajeev. "Restoring Decency to Barbaric Societies." In *Truth v. Justice: The Morality of Truth Commissions*, edited by Robert I. Rotberg and Dennis Thompson, 45–67. Princeton, NJ: Princeton University Press, 2000.

Black, Maggie. *The Children and the Nations: The Story of Unicef.* New York: Unicef, 1986.

Bois-Pedain, Antje du. *Transitional Amnesty in South Africa.* Cambridge: Cambridge University Press, 2007.

Bole, William, Drew Christiansen, and Robert T. Hennemeyer. *Forgiveness in International Politics: An Alternative Road to Peace.* Washington, DC: United States Conference of Catholic Bishops, 2004.

Boothby, Neil, Alison Strang, and Michael Wessells, eds. *A World Turned Upside Down: Social Ecological Approaches to Children in War Zones*. Bloomfield, CT: Kumarian Press, 2006.

Boraine, Alex. "Truth and Reconciliation in South Africa: The Third Way." In Rotberg and Thompson, *Truth v. Justice*, 141–57.

Borer, Tristan Anne. "Gendered War and Gendered Peace: Truth Commissions and Postconflict Gender Violence: Lessons from South Africa." *Violence Against Women* 15, no. 10 (2009): 1169–1193.

———. "Reconciling South Africa or South Africans? Cautionary Notes from the TRC." *African Studies Quarterly* 8, no. 1 (2004): 19–38.

Borer, Tristan Anne, John Darby, and Siobhán McEvoy-Levy. *Peacebuilding after Peace Accords: The Challenges of Violence, Truth, and Youth*. Notre Dame, IN: University of Notre Dame Press, 2006.

Boyden, Jo. "Childhood and the Policy Makers: A Comparative Perspective on the Globalization of Childhood." In James and Prout, *Constructing and Reconstructing Childhood*, 185–219.

———. "Childhood and the Policy Makers: A Comparative Perspective on the Globalization of Childhood." In James and Prout, *Constructing and Reconstructing Childhood*, 3rd ed., 167–201.

———. "Children's Experience of Conflict Related Emergencies: Some Implications for Relief Policy and Practice." *Disasters* 18, no. 3 (1994): 254–67.

———. Preface to Hart, *Years of Conflict*, ix–xii.

Boyden, Jo, and Joanna de Berry, eds. *Children and Youth on the Front Line: Ethnography, Armed Conflict and Displacement*. New York: Berghahn Books, 2004. See esp. the introduction, xi–xxvii.

Brahm, Eric. "Uncovering the Truth: Examining Truth Commission Success and Impact." *International Studies Perspectives* 8, no. 1 (2007): 16–35.

Braithwaite, John. "Principles of Restorative Justice." In *Restorative Justice and Criminal Justice: Competing or Reconcilable Paradigms?*, edited by Andrew von Hirsch, Julian V. Roberts, Anthony E. Bottoms, Kent Roach, and Mara Schiff, 1–20. London: Hart Publishing, 2003.

———. "Setting Standards for Restorative Justice." *British Journal of Criminology* 42, no. 3 (2002): 563–77.

Braithwaite, Valerie, Sinclair Dinnen, Matthew Allen, John Braithwaite, and Hilary Charlesworth. *Pillars and Shadows: Statebuilding as Peacebuilding in Solomon Islands*. Canberra, AU: ANU Press, 2010. https://doi.org/10.26530/OAPEN_459442.

Brett, Rachel, and Irma Specht. *Young Soldiers: Why They Choose to Fight?* Boulder, CO: Lynne Rienner Publishers, 2004.

Brett, Rachel, and Margaret McCallin. *Children: The Invisible Soldiers*. 2nd ed. Stockholm: Rädda Barnen, 1998.

Brighouse, Harry. "What Rights (If Any) Do Children Have?" In *The Moral and Political Status of Children*, edited by David Archard and Colin M. Macleod, 31–52. Oxford: Oxford University Press, 2002.
Brocklehurst, Helen. *Who's Afraid of Children? Children, Conflict, and International Relations*. Aldershot, UK: Ashgate Publishing, 2006.
———. "Doing IR: Securing Children." In *Discovering Childhood in International Relations*, edited by J. Marshall Beier, 89–113. Cham: Palgrave Macmillan, 2020.
Bronkhorst, Daan. *Truth Commissions and Transitional Justice: A Short Guide*. Amsterdam: Amnesty International Dutch Section, 2004.
Brounéus, Karen. *Reconciliation: Theory and Practice for Development Cooperation*. Stockholm: Swedish International Development Cooperation Agency (SIDA), 2003. https://publikationer.sida.se/contentassets/f831ec9a55b3443b94ee1e89d41f7158/13594.pdf.
Burman, Erica. "Beyond 'Women vs. Children' or 'WomenandChildren': Engendering Childhood and Reformulating Motherhood." *International Journal of Child Rights* 16, no. 2 (2008): 177–94.
———. "Innocents Abroad: Western Fantasies of Childhood and the Iconography of Emergencies." *Disasters* 18, no. 3 (1994): 238–53.
Bush, Kenneth, and Diana Salarelli, eds. *The Two Faces of Education in Ethnic Conflict: Towards Peacebuilding Education for Children*. Florence: UNICEF Innocenti Research Centre, 2000.
Cain, Tess Newton. "Final Report of the Solomon Islands Truth & Reconciliation Commission Unofficially Released." *Devpolicy Blog from the Development Policy Centre* (blog), April 30, 2013. https://devpolicy.org/final-report-of-the-solomon-islands-truth-reconciliation-commission-unofficially-released-20130501-2/.
Carlsson, Christoffer. "Using 'Turning Points' to Understand Processes of Change in Offending: Notes from a Swedish Study on Life Courses and Crime." *British Journal of Criminology* 52, no. 1 (2012): 1–16.
Carmona, María José. "Lessons in Tolerance: The Colombian Letters Sent to Former FARC Fighters." *El País*, June 2, 2017. https://english.elpais.com/elpais/2017/06/02/inenglish/1496399223_174779.html.
Carpenter, R. Charli. *Forgetting Children Born of War: Setting the Human Rights Agenda in Bosnia and Beyond*. New York: Columbia University Press, 2010.
Carr, David. "Narrative and the Real World: An Argument for Continuity." In *Memory, Identity and Community*, edited by Lewis P Hinchman and Sandra Hinchman, 7–25. New York: State University of New York Press, 1997.
CathNews New Zealand. "Bishop Releases Truth and Reconciliation Report." *CathNews New Zealand*, May 3, 2013. https://cathnews.co.nz/2013/05/03/bishop-releases-truth-and-reconciliation-report/.

Central Islands Provincial Government, Solomon Islands. "Provincial Youth Policy." Central Islands Provincial Government, Sept. 15, 2009.

Chapman, Audrey R. "Truth Commissions as Instruments of Forgiveness and Reconciliation." In *Forgiveness and Reconciliation: Religion, Public Policy, and Conflict Transformation*, edited by Raymond G. Helmick and Rodney L. Petersen, 257–77. Philadelphia: Templeton Foundation Press, 2001.

———. "Truth Recovery through the TRC's Institutional Hearings Process." In *Truth and Reconciliation in South Africa: Did the TRC Deliver?*, edited by Audrey R. Chapman and Hugo van der Merwe, 169–88. Philadelphia: University of Pennsylvania Press, 2008.

Chubb, Karin, and Lutz van Dijk. *Between Anger and Hope: South Africa's Youth and the Truth and Reconciliation Commission*. Johannesburg, SA: Witwatersrand University Press, 2001.

Clamp, Kerry. *Restorative Justice in Transition*. London: Routledge, 2014.

Clay, Andreana. "'All I Need Is One Mic': Mobilizing Youth for Social Change in the Post-Civil Rights Era." *Social Justice* 33, no. 2 (2006): 105–21.

Clifton, Donna, and Alexandra Hervish. "The World's Youth: 2013 Data Sheet," Washington DC: Population Reference Bureau, 2013. https://www.prb.org/wp-content/uploads/2013/04/youth-data-sheet-2013.pdf.

Cohn, Ilene, and Guy S. Goodwin-Gill. *Child Soldiers: The Role of Children in Armed Conflict*. Oxford: Oxford University Press, 1994.

Collier, Paul, and Anke Hoeffler. "Greed and Grievance in Civil War." *Oxford Economic Papers* 56, no. 4 (2004): 563–95.

Cook, Philip, and Cheryl Heykoop. "Child Participation in the Sierra Leonean Truth and Reconciliation Commission." In Parmar et al., *Children and Transitional Justice*, 159–92.

Coveney, Peter. "The Image of the Child." In *The Sociology of Childhood: Essential Readings*, edited by Chris Jenks, 42–47. London: Batsford Academic and Educational, 1982.

Craney, Aiden. *Youth in Fiji and Solomon Islands: Livelihoods, Leadership and Civic Engagement*. Canberra, AU: ANU Press, 2022.

Dal Secco, Alessandra. "Truth and Reconciliation Commissions and Gender Justice." In *Gendered Peace: Women's Struggles for Post-War Justice and Reconciliation*, edited by Donna Pankhurst, 65–106. New York: Routledge, 2012.

Daly, Kathleen, and Gitana Proietti-Scifoni. "Reparation and Restoration." In *Oxford Handbook of Crime and Criminal Justice*, edited by Michael Tonry, 207–53. Oxford: Oxford University Press, 2011.

Dancy, Geoff, Hunjoon Kim, and Eric Wiebelhaus-Brahm. "The Turn to Truth: Trends in Truth Commission Experimentation." *Journal of Human Rights* 9, no. 1 (2010): 45–64.

D'Costa, Bina. "Children and Justice: Past Crimes, Healing and the Future." In Huynh, D'Costa, and Lee-Koo, *Children and Global Conflict*, 212–48.
———, ed. *Children and Violence: Politics of Conflict in South Asia*. Cambridge: Cambridge University Press, 2016.
———. "The Rights of the Child: Political History, Practices and Protection." In Huynh, D'Costa, and Lee-Koo, *Children and Global Conflict*, 89–122.
———. "Turtles Can Fly: Vicarious Terror and the Child in South Asia." In D'Costa, *Children and Violence*, 1–42.
Del Felice, Celina, and Andria Wisler. "The Unexplored Power and Potential of Youth as Peacebuilders." *Journal of Peace Conflict and Development* 11 (2007): 1–29.
Democratic Republic of Timor-Leste. "National Youth Policy of Timor-Leste." Secretary of State for Youth and Sport, Balide, Díli, Nov. 14, 2007. http://www.youthpolicy.org/national/Timor_Leste_2007_National_Youth_Policy.pdf.
Denov, Myriam. *Child Soldiers: Sierra Leone's Revolutionary United Front*. Cambridge: Cambridge University Press, 2010.
Department of Economic and Social Affairs. *World Youth Report 2005: Young People Today, and in 2015*. New York: United Nations, 2005. https://www.un.org/development/desa/youth/world-youth-report/world-youth-report-2005.html.
Dinnen, Sinclair. "State-Building in a Post-Colonial Society: The Case of Solomon Islands." *Chicago Journal of International Law* 9, no. 1 (2008): 51–78.
Drumbl, Mark A. *Reimagining Child Soldiers in International Law and Policy*. Oxford: Oxford University Press, 2012.
Drummond-Mundal, Lori, and Guy Cave. "Young Peacebuilders: Exploring Youth Engagement with Conflict and Social Change." *Journal of Peacebuilding and Development* 3, no. 3 (2007): 63–76.
Du Toit, André. "The Moral Foundations of the South African TRC: Truth as Acknowledgment and Justice as Recognition." In Rotberg and Thompson, *Truth v. Justice*, 122–40.
Dwyer, Susan. "Reconciliation for Realists." *Ethics and International Affairs* 13, no. 1 (1999): 81–98.
Elliott, Heather, ed. *Children and Peacebuilding: Experiences and Perspectives*. Melbourne: World Vision Australia, 2002.
Elster, Jon. *Closing the Books: Transitional Justice in Historical Perspective*. Cambridge: Cambridge University Press, 2004.
Enloe, Cynthia. "WomenandChildren: Making Feminist Sense of the Persian Gulf Crisis." *Village Voice* 25, no. 9 (1990).
Ensalaco, Mark. "The Right of the Child to Development." In Ensalaco and Majka, *Children's Human Rights*, 9–30.

Ensalaco, Mark, and Linda C. Majka, eds. *Children's Human Rights: Progress and Challenges for Children Worldwide*. Lanham, MD: Rowman and Littlefield, 2005.

Evans, Daniel. "Things Still Fall Apart: A Political Economy Analysis of State-Youth Engagement in Honiara, Solomon Islands." In *Pacific Youth: Local and Global Futures*, edited by Helen Lee, 79–109. Canberra, AU: ANU Press, 2019.

Eyber, Carola, and Alastair Ager. "Researching Young People's Experiences of War: Participatory Methods and the Trauma Discourse in Angola." In Boyden and Berry, *Children and Youth on the Front Line*, 189–208.

Finlayson, Alan, Mark Bevir, R. A. W. Rhodes, Keith Dowding, and Colin Hay. "The Interpretive Approach in Political Science: A Symposium." *British Journal of Politics and International Relations* 6, no. 2 (2004): 129–64.

Fisher, Kirsten J. *Transitional Justice for Child Soldiers: Accountability and Social Reconstruction in Post-Conflict Contexts*. Basingstoke, UK: Palgrave Macmillan, 2013.

Fraenkel, Jon. *The Manipulation of Custom: From Uprising to Intervention in the Solomon Islands*. Wellington, NZ: Victoria University Press, 2004.

Freeman, Michael D. A. "Introduction: Children as Persons." In *Children's Rights: A Comparative Perspective*, edited by Michael D. A. Freeman. Aldershot, UK: Dartmouth, 1997.

———. "The Limits of Children's Rights." In Freeman and Veerman, *The Ideologies of Children's Rights*, 29–49.

———. *The Rights and Wrongs of Children*. London: Pinter, 1983.

Freeman, Michael D. A., and Philip Veerman, eds. *The Ideologies of Children's Rights*. Dordrecht: Martinus Nijhoff, 1992.

Friedman, Rebekka. "Restorative Justice in Sierra Leone: Promises and Limitations." In Ainley, Friedman, and Mahony, *Evaluating Transitional Justice*, 55–76.

Fullard, Madeleine, and Nicky Rousseau. "Truth Telling, Identities, and Power in South Africa and Guatemala." In Paige, *Identities in Transition*, 54–86.

Gates, Scott, and Simon Reich, eds. *Child Soldiers in the Age of Fractured States*. Pittsburgh, PA: University of Pittsburgh Press, 2009.

Goldstein, Joshua S. *War and Gender: How Gender Shapes the War System and Vice Versa*. Cambridge: Cambridge University Press, 2001.

Goldstone, Jack A. "Population and Security: How Demographic Change Can Lead to Violent Conflict." *Journal of International Affairs* 56, no. 1 (2002): 3–21.

Gready, Paul. *The Era of Transitional Justice: The Aftermath of the Truth and Reconciliation Commission in South Africa and Beyond*. New York: Routledge, 2011.

Gready, Paul, and Simon Robins. "From Transitional to Transformative Justice: A New Agenda for Practice." *International Journal of Transitional Justice* 8, no. 3 (2014): 339–61.

Greenhill, Kelly M., and Solomon Major. "The Perils of Profiling: Civil War Spoilers and the Collapse of Intrastate Peace Accords." *International Security* 31, no. 3 (2007): 7–40.

Griffin, Christine. "Troubled Teens: Managing Disorders of Transition and Consumption." *Feminist Review* 55, no. 1 (Spring 1997): 4–21.

Guadalcanal Provincial Government, Solomon Islands. "Provincial Youth Policy." Guadalcanal Provincial Government, April 2010.

Guthrey, Holly L., and Karen Brounéus. "Peering into the 'Black Box' of TRC Success: Exploring Local Perceptions of Reconciliation in the Solomon Islands TRC." In Jeffery, *Transitional Justice in Practice*, 85–111.

Hamber, Brandon. "Does the Truth Heal? A Psychological Perspective on Political Strategies for Dealing with the Legacy of Political Violence." In *Burying the Past: Making Peace and Doing Justice After Civil Conflict*, edited by Nigel Biggar, 155–74. Washington, DC: Georgetown University Press, 2003.

Hamber, Brandon, and Gráinne Kelly. "A Working Definition of Reconciliation." Belfast, IR: Democratic Dialogue, Sept. 2004. https://pure.ulster.ac.uk/ws/files/76832671/Paper_A_Working_Definition_of_Reconciliation_HAMBER_KELLY_2004.pdf.

Harris-Short, Sonia. "International Human Rights Law: Imperialist, Inept, and Ineffective? Cultural Relativism and the UN Convention on the Rights of the Child." *Human Rights Quarterly* 25, no. 1 (2003): 130–81.

Hart, Jason, ed. *Years of Conflict: Adolescence, Political Violence and Displacement*. New York: Berghahn Books, 2010. See esp. Hart's introduction, 1–20.

Hassall and Associates International. "Youth in Solomon Islands: A Participatory Study of Issues, Needs and Priorities." Final Report, 2003. https://www.youthpolicy.org/national/Solomon_Islands_2003_Youth_Study.pdf.

Hayner, Priscilla B. "Fifteen Truth Commissions—1974 to 1994: A Comparative Study." *Human Rights Quarterly* 16, no. 4 (1994): 597–655.

———. *Unspeakable Truths: Confronting State Terror and Atrocity*. New York: Routledge, 2002.

Hein, Karen. "Young People as Assets: A Foundational View." *Social Policy* 30, no. 1 (1999): 20–29.

Helsing, Jeff. "Young People's Activism and the Transition to Peace: Bosnia, Northern Ireland and Israel." With Namik Kirlic, Neil McMaster, and Nir Sonnenschein. In McEvoy-Levy, *Troublemakers or Peacemakers?*, 195–216.

Hendrick, Harry. "Constructions and Reconstructions of British Childhood: An Interpretive Survey, 1800 to the Present." In James and Prout, *Constructing and Reconstructing Childhood*, 2nd ed., 34–62.

———. "Constructions and Reconstructions of British Childhood: An Interpretive Survey, 1800 to the Present." In James and Prout, *Constructing and Reconstructing Childhood*, 3rd ed., 29–53.

Hendrixson, Anne. "Angry Young Men and Veiled Young Women: Constructing a New Population Threat." Corner House Briefing. The Corner House,

Dec. 2, 2004. http://www.thecornerhouse.org.uk/resource/angry-young-men-veiled-young-women.

Holzscheiter, Anna. *Children's Rights in International Politics: The Transformative Power of Discourse.* Basingstoke, UK: Palgrave Macmillan, 2010.

———. "Children as Agents in International Relations? Transnational Activism, International Norms, and the Politics of Age." In Beier, *Discovering Childhood in International Relations,* 65–87.

Huntington, Samuel P. *The Clash of Civilizations and the Remaking of World Order.* New Delhi: Penguin Books India, 1996.

———. *The Third Wave: Democratization in the Late Twentieth Century.* Norman: University of Oklahoma Press, 1991.

Huynh, Kim, Bina D'Costa, and Katrina Lee-Koo, eds. *Children and Global Conflict.* Cambridge: Cambridge University Press, 2015. See esp. Huynh, "Child Soldiers: Causes, Solutions and Cultures," 123–58; "Children and Agency: Caretakers, Free-Rangers and Everyday Life," 35–64.

Huyse, Luc. "Justice after Transition: On the Choices Successor Elites Make in Dealing with the Past." *Law and Social Inquiry* 20, no. 1 (1995): 51–78.

Ignatieff, Michael. *Human Rights as Politics and Idolatry.* Edited by Amy Gutmann. Princeton, NJ: Princeton University Press, 2001.

———. *The Warrior's Honor: Ethnic War and the Modern Conscience.* New York: Henry Holt, 1998.

International Labour Organization. "Decent Work Country Programme: Solomon Islands (2009–2012)." ILO, Aug. 19, 2009. http://www.ilo.org/wcmsp5/groups/public/—-asia/—-ro-bangkok/documents/publication/wcms_120555.pdf.

International Military Tribunal. *Trial of the Major War Criminals.* 42 vols. Nuremberg, 1947. Library of Congress. https://www.loc.gov/item/2011525338/.

Isaacs, Anita. "Truth and the Challenge of Reconciliation in Guatemala." In Quinn, *Reconciliation(s),* 116–46.

Jacob, Cecilia. *Child Security in Asia: The Impact of Armed Conflict in Cambodia and Myanmar.* London: Routledge, 2014.

James, Allison, and Alan Prout, eds. *Constructing and Reconstructing Childhood: Contemporary Issues in the Sociological Study of Childhood.* London: Falmer Press, 1990.

———. *Constructing and Reconstructing Childhood: Contemporary Issues in the Sociological Study of Childhood.* 2nd ed. New York: Routledge Falmer, 1997.

———. *Constructing and Reconstructing Childhood: Contemporary Issues in the Sociological Study of Childhood.* 3rd ed. London: Routledge, 2015.

James, Allison, Chris Jenks, and Alan Prout. *Theorizing Childhood.* Cambridge: Polity Press, 1998.

Jeffery, Renée. *Amnesties, Accountability, and Human Rights.* Philadelphia: University of Pennsylvania Press, 2014.

———. "The Forgiveness Dilemma: Emotions and Justice at the Khmer Rouge Tribunal." *Australian Journal of International Affairs* 69, no. 1 (2015): 35–52.
———, ed. *Transitional Justice in Practice*. New York: Palgrave Macmillan, 2017. See esp. "Transitional Justice and the Tensions," 1–36.
Jeffery, Renée, and Caitlin Mollica. "The Unfinished Business of the Solomon Islands TRC: Closing the Implementation Gap." *Pacific Review* 30, no. 4 (2017): 531–48.
Jeffery, Renée, and Hun Joon Kim. "Introduction: New Horizons; Transitional Justice in the Asia-Pacific." In *Transitional Justice in the Asia-Pacific*, edited by Renée Jeffery and Hun Joon Kim, 1–32. Cambridge: Cambridge University Press, 2014.
Jenks, Chris. *Childhood*. 2nd ed. London: Routledge, 2005.
———. "Decoding Childhood." In *Discourse and Reproduction: Essays in Honor of Basil Bernstein*, edited by Paul Atkinson, Brian Davies, and Sara Delamont, 173–90. Cresskill, NJ: Hampton Press, 1995.
Jourdan, Christine. "Masta Liu." In *Youth Cultures: A Cross-Cultural Perspective*, edited by Vered Amit-Talai and Helena Wulff, 202–22. London: Routledge, 1995.
Kaplan, Howard B. "Deviant Behavior and Self-Enhancement in Adolescence." *Journal of Youth and Adolescence* 7, no. 3 (1978): 253–77.
Kemper, Yvonne. "Youth in War-to-Peace Transitions: Approaches of International Organisations." Berghof Research Center for Constructive Conflict Management, Jan. 1, 2005. https://shorturl.at/aIPV4.
Kim, Hun Joon, and Renée Jeffery. Conclusion to *Transitional Justice in the Asia-Pacific*, 259–80.
Kiss, Elizabeth. "Moral Ambition Within and Beyond Political Constraints." In Rotberg and Thompson, *Truth v. Justice*, 68–98.
Kristeva, Julia. *Strangers to Ourselves*. New York: Columbia University Press, 1991.
Kritz, Neil J., ed. *Transitional Justice: How Emerging Democracies Reckon with Former Regimes*. 3 vols. Washington, DC: United States Institute of Peace Press, 1995.
Kuper, Jenny. *International Law Concerning Child Civilians in Armed Conflict*. Oxford: Clarendon Press, 1997.
Kwon, Soo Ah. "The Politics of Global Youth Participation." *Journal of Youth Studies* 22, no. 7 (Aug. 9, 2019): 926–40.
Ladisch, Virginie. "A Catalyst for Change: Engaging Youth in Transitional Justice." ICTJ Briefing. International Center for Transitional Justice, April 2018.
Ladisch, Virginie, and Joanna Rice. "Cote d'Ivoire Youth Find Voice Through Storytelling." International Center for Transitional Justice, Oct. 27, 2016. https://www.ictj.org/news/cote-divoire-youth-political-voice-stories-war.
Lambourne, Wendy. "Transitional Justice and Peacebuilding after Mass Violence." *International Journal of Transitional Justice* 3, no. 1 (2009): 28–48.

Lauren, Paul Gordon. *The Evolution of International Human Rights: Visions Seen.* 3rd ed. Philadelphia: University of Pennsylvania Press, 2011.
League of Nations. *Geneva Declaration of the Rights of the Child of 1924.* League of Nations, adopted Sept. 26, 1924. https://www.humanium.org/en/geneva-declaration/.
Lederach, John Paul. *Building Peace: Sustainable Reconciliation in Divided Societies.* Tokyo: United Nations University Press, 1994.
———. "Civil Society and Reconciliation." In *Turbulent Peace: The Challenges of Managing International Conflict,* edited by Chester A. Crocker, Fen Osler Hampson, and Pamela R. Aall, 841–54. Washington, DC: United States Institute of Peace Press, 2001.
———. *The Moral Imagination: The Art and Soul of Building Peace.* Oxford: Oxford University Press, 2005.
Lee, Nick. "The Challenges of Childhood: Distributions of Childhood's Ambiguity in Adult Institutions." *Childhood* 6, no. 4 (1999): 455–74.
———. *Childhood and Society: Growing Up in an Age of Uncertainty.* Buckingham, UK: Open University Press, 2001.
Lee-Koo, Katrina. "Children and Armed Conflict: Mapping the Terrain." In Huynh, D'Costa, and Lee-Koo, *Children and Global Conflict,* 9–34.
———. "Children and IR: Creating Spaces for Children." In Huynh, D'Costa, and Lee-Koo, *Children and Global Conflict,* 65–88.
———. "Children and Peacebuilding: Propagating Peace." In Huynh, D'Costa, and Lee-Koo, *Children and Global Conflict,* 185–211.
———. "Horror and Hope: (Re)Presenting Militarised Children in Global North–South Relations." *Third World Quarterly* 32, no. 4 (2011): 725–42.
Lutz, Ellen, and Kathryn Sikkink. "The Justice Cascade: The Evolution and Impact of Foreign Human Rights Trials in Latin America." *Chicago Journal of International Law* 2, no. 1 (2001): 1–33.
Macdonald, Alice. "'New Wars: Forgotten Warriors': Why Have Girl Fighters Been Excluded from Western Representations of Conflict in Sierra Leone?" *Africa Development* 33, no. 3 (2008): 135–45.
Machel, Graça. *Impact of Armed Conflict on Children.* UN Doc. A/51/306 (Aug. 26, 1996). https://undocs.org/A/51/306.
———. Truth and Reconciliation Commission. Testimony. Johannesburg Children's Hearing, Day 1, June 12, 1997. https://www.justice.gov.za/trc/special/children/machel.htm.
Macksoud, Mona S., and J. Lawrence Aber. "The War Experiences and Psychosocial Development of Children in Lebanon." *Child Development* 67, no. 1 (1996): 70–88.
Macksoud, Mona S., J. Lawrence Aber, and Ilene Cohn. "Assessing the Impact of War on Children." In *Minefields in Their Hearts: The Mental Health of Children in War and Communal Violence,* edited by Roberta J. Apfel and Bennett Simon, 218–30. New Haven, CT: Yale University Press, 1996.

Mahony, Chris, and Yasmin Sooka. "The Truth About the Truth: Insider Reflections on the Sierra Leonean Truth and Reconciliation Commission." In Ainley, Friedman, and Mahony, *Evaluating Transitional Justice*, 35–54.

Maiangwa, Benjamin, and Sean Byrne, "Peacebuilding and Reconciliation through Storytelling in Northern Ireland and the Border Counties of the Republic of Ireland." *Storytelling, Self, Society* 11, no. 1 (2015): 85–110.

Making Cents International. "Youth Microenterprise and Livelihoods: State of the Field." Lessons from the 2007 Global Youth Microenterprise Conference. Making Cents International, Jan. 2008. https://bettercarenetwork.org/sites/default/files/Youth%20Microenterprise%20and%20Livelihoods%20-%20State%20of%20the%20Field.pdf.

Mani, Rama. "Dilemmas of Expanding Transitional Justice or Forging the Nexus between Transitional Justice and Development." *International Journal of Transitional Justice* 2, no. 3 (2008): 253–65.

Mawson, Andrew. "Children, Impunity and Justice: Some Dilemmas from Northern Uganda." In Boyden and Berry, *Children and Youth on the Front Line*, 130–41.

McCabe, Kate. "Dreams of January." International Center for Transitional Justice, 2015. https://www.ictj.org/sites/default/files/subsites/dreams-january-tunisia/.

McDuie-Ra, Duncan. "Children and Civil Society in South Asia: Subjects, Participants and Political Agents." In D'Costa, *Children and Violence*, 46–61.

McEvoy, Kieran. "Beyond Legalism: Towards a Thicker Understanding of Transitional Justice." *Journal of Law and Society* 34, no. 4 (2007): 411–40.

McEvoy-Levy, Siobhán. "Children, Youth and Peacebuilding." In *Critical Issues in Peace and Conflict Studies: Theory, Practice and Pedagogy*, edited by Thomas Matyók, Jessica Senehi, and Sean Byrne, 159–76. Lanham, MD: Lexington Books, 2011.

———. "Human Rights Culture and Children Born of Wartime Rape." In *Born of War: Protecting Children of Sexual Violence Survivors in Conflict Zones*, edited by R. Charli Carpenter, 149–79. Bloomfield, CT: Kumarian Press, 2007.

———. *Peace and Resistance in Youth Cultures: Reading the Politics of Peacebuilding from Harry Potter to The Hunger Games*. London: Palgrave Macmillan, 2018.

———, ed. *Troublemakers or Peacemakers? Youth and Post-Accord Peacebuilding*. Notre Dame, IN: University of Notre Dame Press, 2006. See esp. "Introduction: Youth and the Post-Accord Environment," 1–26.

———. "Youth." In *Routledge Handbook of Peacebuilding*, edited by Roger MacGinty, 296–307. London: Taylor & Francis, 2013.

———. "Youth as Social and Political Agents: Issues in Post-Settlement Peace Building." Kroc Institute Occasional Paper. Joan B. Kroc Institute for International Peace Studies, University of Notre Dame, Notre Dame, IN, Dec. 2001.

McGillivray, Anne, ed. *Governing Childhood*. Aldershot, UK: Dartmouth, 1997.
Ministry of Women, Youth, and Children's Affairs. *Solomon Island National Youth Policy: 2010–2015*, Honiara: Solomon Islands Government, June 2010.
Ministry of Women, Youth, Children and Family Affairs. *Solomon Islands National Youth Policy 2017–2030*, Honiara: Solomon Islands Government, 2017.
Minow, Martha. *Between Vengeance and Forgiveness: Facing History After Genocide and Mass Violence*. Boston: Beacon Press, 1998.
Mollica, Caitlin. "The Diversity of Identity: Youth Participation at the Solomon Islands Truth and Reconciliation Commission." *Australian Journal of International Affairs* 71, no. 4 (2017): 371–88.
Moore, Clive. *Happy Isles in Crisis: The Historical Causes for a Failing State in Solomon Islands, 1998–2004*. Canberra, AU: Asia Pacific Press, 2004.
Munari, Alberto. "Jean Piaget." *Prospects* 24, no. 1 (1994): 311–27.
Murphy, Colleen. *A Moral Theory of Political Reconciliation*. Cambridge: Cambridge University Press, 2010.
Nagy, Rosemary. "Transitional Justice as Global Project: Critical Reflections." *Third World Quarterly* 29, no. 2 (2008): 275–89.
Ndlozi, George. Truth and Reconciliation Commission Testimony. Johannesburg Children's Hearing, Day 2, 1997, 6, 12. https://www.justice.gov.za/trc/special/children/ndlozi.htm.
Nelken, David. "Afterword: Choosing Rights for Children." In *Children's Rights and Traditional Values*, edited by Gillian Douglas and Leslie Sebba, 315–35. Aldershot, UK: Ashgate Publishing, 1998.
Newman, Edward. "The 'New Wars' Debate: A Historical Perspective Is Needed." *Security Dialogue* 35, no. 2 (June 2004): 173–89.
Nieuwenhuys, Olga. "Keep Asking: Why Childhood? Why Children? Why Global?" *Childhood* 17, no. 3 (Aug. 1, 2010): 291–96.
Nosworthy, David. "Children and Security Sector Reform in Post-Conflict Peacebuilding." Innocenti Working Paper 2010/09. Florence: UNICEF Innocenti Research Centre, June 2010. https://doi.org/10.18356/1bcc1d1d-en.
O'Kane, Claire, Clare Feinstein, and Annette Giertsen. "The Active Role of Children and Young People in Post-Conflict Peace." In Schnabel and Tabyshalieva, *Escaping Victimhood*, 32–66.
Office of the Secretary-General's Envoy on Youth. "Global Reactions to Security Council Resolution 2250 on Youth, Peace and Security." United Nations, Dec. 2015. https://www.un.org/youthenvoy/2015/12/global-reactions-to-security-council-resolution-2250-on-youth-peace-and-security/.
Oinas, Elina, Henri Onodera, and Leena Suurpää, eds. *What Politics? Youth and Political Engagement in Africa*. Leiden, NL: Brill, 2018.
Olsen, Tricia D., Leigh A. Payne, and Andrew G. Reiter. *Transitional Justice in Balance: Comparing Processes, Weighing Efficacy*. Washington, DC: United States Institute of Peace Press, 2010.

Orentlicher, Diane F. "Settling Accounts: The Duty to Prosecute Human Rights Violations of a Prior Regime." *Yale Law Journal* 100, no. 8 (1991): 2537–2615.
Ozcelik, Asli, Yulia Nesterova, Graeme Young, and Alex Maxwell. "Youth-Led Peace: The Role of Youth in Peace Processes." SSRN Scholarly Paper. Rochester, NY: Social Science Research Network, 2021. https://papers.ssrn.com/abstract=3853760.
Özerdem, Alpaslan, and Sukanya Podder. *Youth in Conflict and Peacebuilding: Mobilization, Reintegration and Reconciliation*. London: Palgrave Macmillan, 2015.
Parmar, Sharanjeet, Mindy Jane Roseman, Saudamini Siegrist, and Theo Sowa, eds. *Children and Transitional Justice: Truth-Telling, Accountability and Reconciliation*. Cambridge, MA: Human Rights Program, Harvard Law School, 2010.
Paulson, Julia. "Truth Commissions and National Curricula: The Case of Recordándonos in Peru." In Parmar et al., *Children and Transitional Justice*, 327–64.
Peters, Krijn. "Re-Examining Voluntarism: Youth Combatants in Sierra Leone." Pretoria, SA: Institute for Security Studies, April 1, 2004.
———. *War and the Crisis of Youth in Sierra Leone*. Cambridge: Cambridge University Press, 2011.
Peters, Krijn, and Paul Richards. "'Why We Fight': Voices of Youth Combatants in Sierra Leone." *Africa* 68, no. 2 (1998): 183–210.
Philpott, Daniel. "Beyond Politics as Usual: Is Reconciliation Compatible with Liberalism?" In *The Politics of Past Evil: Religion, Reconciliation, and the Dilemmas of Transitional Justice*, edited by Daniel Philpott, 11–44. Notre Dame, IN: University of Notre Dame Press, 2006.
———. "Reconciliation: An Ethic for Responding to Evil in Global Politics." In *Confronting Evil in International Relations: Ethical Responses to Problems of Moral Agency*, edited by Renée Jeffery, 115–49. New York: Palgrave Macmillan, 2008.
Pigou, Piers. "Children and the South African Truth and Reconciliation Commission." In Parmar et al., *Children and Transitional Justice*, 115–58.
Platt, Anthony M. *The Child Savers: The Invention of Delinquency*. Chicago: University of Chicago Press, 1969.
Postman, Neil. *The Disappearance of Childhood*. London: Vintage Books, 1994.
Prout, Alan. "Participation, Policy and the Changing Conditions of Childhood." In *Hearing the Voices of Children: Social Policy for a New Century*, edited by Christine Hallett and Alan Prout, 11–25. London: Routledge Falmer, 2003.
Prout, Alan, and Allison James. "A New Paradigm for the Sociology of Childhood? Provenance, Promise and Problems." In James and Prout, *Constructing and Reconstructing Childhood*, 3rd ed., 6–28.

Pruitt, Lesley J. "Gendering the Study of Children and Youth." *Peacebuilding* 3(2): 157–70.

———. "Rethinking Youth Bulge Theory in Policy and Scholarship: Incorporating Critical Gender Analysis." *International Affairs* 96, no. 3 (2020): 711–28.

———. *Youth Peacebuilding: Music, Gender, and Change*. Albany: State University of New York Press, 2013.

———. "Youth, Peace & Security: Gender Matters in Asia and the Pacific." *Global Change, Peace & Security* 33, no. 3 (2021): 241–57.

Pruitt, Lesley, Helen Berents, and Gayle Munro. "Gender and Age in the Construction of Male Youth in the European Migration 'Crisis.'" *Signs: Journal of Women in Culture and Society* 43, no. 3 (2018): 687–709.

Pupavac, Vanessa. "Misanthropy Without Borders: The International Children's Rights Regime." *Disasters* 25, no. 2 (2001): 95–112.

Quinn, Joanna R. *The Politics of Acknowledgement: Truth Commissions in Uganda and Haiti*. Law and Society Series. Vancouver: UBC Press, 2010.

———, ed. *Reconciliation(s): Transitional Justice in Postconflict Societies*. Montreal, QC: McGill-Queen's University Press, 2009. See esp. Quinn's introduction, 3–13.

———. "What of Reconciliation? Traditional Mechanisms of Acknowledgment in Uganda." In Quinn, *Reconciliation(s)*, 174–206.

Ramírez-Barat, Clara. "Engaging Children and Youth in Transitional Justice Processes: Guidance for Outreach Programs." New York: International Center for Transitional Justice, Nov. 2012. https://www.ictj.org/sites/default/files/ICTJ-Report-Children-Youth-Outreach-2012.pdf.

Rhedding-Jones, Jeanette. "Shifting Ethnicities: 'Native Informants' and Other Theories from/for Early Childhood Education." *Contemporary Issues in Early Childhood* 2, no. 2 (2001): 135–56.

Rogers, Carl M., and Lawrence S. Wrightsman. "Attitudes toward Children's Rights: Nurturance or Self-Determination?" *Journal of Social Issues* 34, no. 2 (1978): 59–68.

Roht-Arriaza, Naomi. "Civil Society in Processes of Accountability." In Bassiouni, *Post-Conflict Justice*, 97–98.

———. "State Responsibility to Investigate and Prosecute Grave Human Rights Violations in International Law." *California Law Review* 78, no. 2 (1990): 449–514.

———. "The New Landscape of Transitional Justice." In *Transitional Justice in the Twenty-First Century: Beyond Truth versus Justice*, edited by Javier Mariezcurrena and Naomi Roht-Arriaza, 1–16. Cambridge: Cambridge University Press, 2006.

Rosen, David M. *Armies of the Young: Child Soldiers in War and Terrorism*. New Brunswick, NJ: Rutgers University Press, 2005.

Rousseau, J. J. *Emile, or Education*. Translated by Barbara Foxley. London: J. M. Dent & Sons, 1911.

Schapiro, Tamar. "What Is a Child?" *Ethics* 109, no. 4 (1999): 715–38.
Scheper-Hughes, Nancy, and Carolyn Fishel Sargent. "Introduction: The Cultural Politics of Childhood." In *Small Wars: The Cultural Politics of Childhood*, edited by Nancy Scheper-Hughes and Carolyn Fishel Sargent, 1–16. Berkeley: University of California Press, 1998.
Schlegel, Alice. "A Cross-Cultural Approach to Adolescence." *Ethos* 23, no. 1 (1995): 15–32.
Schnabel, Albrecht, and Anara Tabyshalieva, eds. *Escaping Victimhood: Children, Youth and Post-Conflict Peacebuilding*. New York: United Nations University Press, 2013. See esp. "Opportunities Missed: Sidelining Children and Youth in Post-Conflict Recovery and Reform Efforts," 3–31.
Schwartz, Stephanie. *Youth and Post-Conflict Reconstruction: Agents of Change*. Washington, DC: United States Institute of Peace Press, 2010.
Segal, Lauren, Joy Pelo, and Pule Rampa. "Into the Heart of Darkness: Journeys of the Amagents in Crime, Violence and Death." In *Crime Wave: The South African Underworld and Its Foes*, edited by Jonny Steinberg, 94–114. Johannesburg, SA: Witwatersrand University Press, 2001.
Senehi, Jessica, and Sean Byrne. "From Violence Toward Peace: The Role of Storytelling for Youth Healing and Political Empowerment after Social Conflict." In McEvoy-Levy, *Troublemakers or Peacemakers?*, 235–58.
Sharp, Dustin N. "Beyond the Post-Conflict Checklist: Linking Peacebuilding and Transitional Justice Through the Lens of Critique." *Chicago Journal of International Law* 14, no. 1 (2013): 165–96.
———. "Development, Human Rights and Transitional Justice: Global Projects for Global Governance." *International Journal of Transitional Justice* 9, no. 3 (2015): 517–26.
———. "Interrogating the Peripheries: The Preoccupations of Fourth Generation Transitional Justice." *Harvard Human Rights Journal* 26 (2013): 149–78.
Shaw, Rosalind, and Lars Waldorf. "Introduction: Localizing Transitional Justice." In *Localizing Transitional Justice: Interventions and Priorities after Mass Violence*, edited by Rosalind Shaw, Lars Waldorf, and Pierre Hazan, 3–26. Stanford, CA: Stanford University Press, 2010.
Shepler, Susan. "The Rites of the Child: Global Discourses of Youth and Reintegrating Child Soldiers in Sierra Leone." *Journal of Human Rights* 4, no. 2 (2005): 197–211.
Sheppard, Ann. "Child Soldiers: Is the Optional Protocol Evidence of an Emerging 'Straight-18' Consensus." *International Journal of Children's Rights* 8, no. 1 (2000): 37–70.
Sierra Leone Government. "Sierra Leone National Youth Policy." June 30, 2003. https://www.youthpolicy.org/national/Sierra_Leone_2003_National_Youth_Policy.pdf.
Sikkink, Kathryn. *The Justice Cascade: How Human Rights Prosecutions Are Changing World Politics*. New York: W. W. Norton, 2011.

Sikkink, Kathryn, and Hun Joon Kim. "The Justice Cascade: The Origins and Effectiveness of Prosecutions of Human Rights Violations." *Annual Review of Law and Social Science* 9, no. 1 (2013): 269–85.
Simpson, Graeme. *The Missing Peace: Independent Progress Study on Youth, Peace and Security*. Progress Study on Youth, Peace and Security, New York: UN Peacebuilding Support Office, 2018. https://digitallibrary.un.org/record/3846611?ln=en.
Singer, P. W. *Children at War*. Berkeley: University of California Press, 2006.
———. "Talk Is Cheap: Getting Serious about Preventing Child Soldiers." *Cornell International Law Journal* 37, no. 3 (2004): 561–86.
Skelton, Ann. "Restorative Justice as a Framework for Juvenile Justice Reform: A South African Perspective." *British Journal of Criminology* 42 (2002): 496–513.
Smith, Alison. "Basic Assumptions of Transitional Justice and Children." In Parmar et al., *Children and Transitional Justice*, 31–66.
Snyder, Jack, and Leslie Vinjamuri. "Trials and Errors: Principle and Pragmatism in Strategies of International Justice." *International Security* 28, no. 3 (Winter 2003): 5–44.
Solomon Islands Government. "National Youth Policy 2010–2015." June 2010.
Solomon Islands Truth and Reconciliation Commission. *Solomon Islands Truth and Reconciliation Commission Final Report: Confronting the Truth for a Better Solomon Islands*. 5 vols. Honiara, Solomon Islands, 2012. https://catalogue.nla.gov.au/catalog/6613097.
Solomon, Richard H. Preface to Kritz, *Transitional Justice*, xiii.
Sommers, Marc. "In the Shadow of Genocide: Rwanda's Youth Challenge." In McEvoy-Levy, *Troublemakers or Peacemakers?*, 81–98.
Spalding, Savannah, Casey Odgers-Jewell, Hayley Payne, Caitlin Mollica, and Helen Berents. "Making Noise and Getting Things Done: Youth Inclusion and Advocacy for Peace: Lessons from Afghanistan, South Sudan and Myanmar." Queensland, AU: QUT Centre for Justice, 2012. https://research-repository.griffith.edu.au/bitstream/handle/10072/421260/Berents5114457-Accepted.pdf?sequence=2.
Squire, Corinne. "Experience-Centred and Culturally Oriented Approaches to Narrative." In *Doing Narrative Research*, edited by Molly Andrews, Corinne Squire, and Maria Tamboukou, 41–63. Los Angeles: SAGE, 2008.
Squire, Corinne, Molly Andrews, and Maria Tamboukou. "Introduction: What Is Narrative Research?" In *Doing Narrative Research*, edited by Molly Andrews, Corinne Squire, and Maria Tamboukou, 1–21. Los Angeles: SAGE, 2008.
Sriram, Chandra Lekha. "Revolutions in Accountability: New Approaches to Past Abuses." *American University International Law Review* 19, no. 2 (2003): 301–429.

Stanley, Liz. "Madness to the Method? Using a Narrative Methodology to Analyse Large-Scale Complex Social Phenomena." *Qualitative Research* 8, no. 3 (2008): 435–47.
Stone-Mediatore, Shari. *Reading Across Borders: Storytelling and Knowledges of Resistance*. New York: Springer, 2016.
Swaine, Aisling, and Thomas Feeny. "A Neglected Perspective: Adolescent Girls' Experiences of the Kosovo Conflict of 1999." In Boyden and Berry, *Children and Youth on the Front Line*, 63–84.
Tabak, Jane. "A Tale of a (Dis) Orderly International Society: Protecting Child-Soldiers, Saving the Child, Governing the Future." In Beier, *Discovering Childhood in International Relations*, 115–34.
Tabak, Jana, and Letícia Carvalho. "Responsibility to Protect the Future: Children on the Move and the Politics of Becoming." In *Children and the Responsibility to Protect*, edited by Bina D'Costa and Luke Glanville, 115–38. Leiden, NL: Brill Nijhoff, 2019.
Teitel, Ruti G. *Globalizing Transitional Justice: Contemporary Essays*. New York: Oxford University Press, 2014.
———. "Transitional Justice Genealogy." *Harvard Human Rights Journal* 16 (2003): 69–94.
Timor-Leste Commission for Reception, Truth, and Reconciliation (CAVR). *Chega! The Final Report of the Timor-Leste Commission for Reception, Truth, and Reconciliation*. Dili, Timor-Leste: CAVR, 2005. http://chegareport.org/Chega%20All%20Volumes.pdf.
Truth and Dignity Commission, Tunisia. "Final Comprehensive Report: Executive Summary" (English translation). Tunisia: Avocats Sans Frontières, May 2019. http://www.ivd.tn/rapport/doc/TDC_executive_summary_report.pdf.
Truth and Reconciliation Commission. *La Comisión de La Verdad y Reconciliación (CVR): Informe Final*. Peru, 2004. https://www.cverdad.org.pe/ifinal/.
———. "Political Party Submissions: ACDP Submission." Special Hearings Transcripts, Day 1, South Africa TRC, 19.8.9. Capetown, South Africa. https://www.justice.gov.za/trc/special/trc-spht.pdf.
———. *Report for the Children of Sierra Leone*. Freetown, Sierra Leone: UNICEF, 2004.
———. *Truth and Reconciliation Commission of South Africa Report*. 7 vols. Truth and Reconciliation Commission, 1998. https://www.justice.gov.za/trc/report/.
———. *Witness to Truth: Report of the Sierra Leone Truth and Reconciliation Commission*. 3 vols. Freetown, Sierra Leone: Sierra Leone Truth and Reconciliation Commission, 2004. http://www.sierraleonetrc.org/index.php/view-the-final-report/download-table-of-contents.
Truth and Reconciliation Commission of Canada. "Mandate for the Truth and Reconciliation Commission" Schedule N. Winnipeg, MB: Government of Canada. https://www.residentialschoolsettlement.ca/SCHEDULE_N.pdf.

Tutu, Desmond. *No Future Without Forgiveness*. New York: Random House, 2012.

———. "Foreword: The Voices of Our Children." In Chubb and van Dijk, *Between Anger and Hope*, i–x.

UN Children's Fund (UNICEF). "The Paris Principles: Principles and Guidelines on Children Associated with Armed Forces or Armed Groups." UN Children's Fund (UNICEF), Feb. 2007. https://www.refworld.org/docid/465198442.html.

UN Department of Economic and Social Affairs (UNDESA). "Definition of Youth." UNDESA, accessed June 4, 2021. https://www.un.org/esa/socdev/documents/youth/fact-sheets/youth-definition.pdf.

UN Development Programme. "UNDP Youth Strategy 2014–2017: Empowered Youth, Sustainable Future." UNDP, 2014.

UN General Assembly. Resolution 34/4. International Year of the Child. A/RES/34/4 (Oct. 18, 1979). https://undocs.org/A/RES/34/4.

———. Resolution 40/14. International Youth Year: Participation, Development, Peace. A/RES/40/14 (Nov. 18, 1985). https://undocs.org/A/RES/40/14.

———. Resolution 50/81. World Programme of Action for Youth to the Year 2000 and Beyond. A/RES/50/81 (Mar. 13, 1996). https://undocs.org/A/RES/50/81.

———. Resolution 56/117. Policies and Programmes Involving Youth. A/RES/50/81 (Jan. 18, 2002). https://undocs.org/A/RES/56/117.

UN Member States. "The Paris Commitments to Protect Children from Unlawful Recruitment or Use by Armed Forces or Armed Groups." UN Children's Fund (UNICEF), Feb. 2007. https://childrenandarmedconflict.un.org/publications/ParisCommitments_EN.pdf.

UN Secretary-General. *International Youth Year: Participation, Development, Peace.* UN Doc. A/40/256 (May 6, 1985). https://undocs.org/A/40/256.

———. *Policies and Programmes Involving Youth.* UN Doc. E/CN.5/2017/5 (Nov. 21, 2016). https://undocs.org/E/CN.5/2017/5.

———. *The Rule of Law and Transitional Justice in Conflict and Post-Conflict Societies.* UN Doc. S/2004/616 (Aug. 23, 2004). https://undocs.org/en/S/2004/616.

———. *Youth and Peace and Security.* UN Doc S/2020/167 (March 2, 2020). https://undocs.org/en/S/2020/167

UN Security Council. Resolution 2250 on Youth, Peace, and Security. S/RES/2250 (Dec. 9, 2015). https://undocs.org/en/S/RES/2250(2015).

UNICEF. "Cape Town Principles and Best Practices." UNICEF, April 27, 1997.

UNICEF Innocenti Research Centre and International Center for Transitional Justice. *Children and Truth Commissions.* Florence: UNICEF Innocenti Research Centre, 2010. https://www.unicef-irc.org/publications/pdf/truth_commissions_eng.pdf.

Urdal, Henrik. "A Clash of Generations? Youth Bulges and Political Violence." *International Studies Quarterly* 50, no. 3 (2006): 607–29.

———. "The Demographics of Political Violence: Youth Bulges, Insecurity and Conflict." In *Too Poor for Peace? Global Poverty, Conflict, and Security in the 21st Century*, edited by Lael Brainard and Derek Chollet, 90–100. Washington, DC: Brookings Institution Press, 2007.

US Agency for International Development (USAID). "Youth and Conflict: A Toolkit for Intervention." USAID, 2005. https://resourcecentre.savethechildren.net/document/youth-and-conflict-toolkit-intervention/.

Utas, Mats. "Fluid Research Fields: Studying Ex-Combatant Youth in the Aftermath of the Liberian Civil War." In Boyden and Berry, *Children and Youth on the Front Line*, 209–36.

Van Bueren, Geraldine. *The International Law on the Rights of the Child*. The Hague: Martinus Nijhoff, 1998.

Vella, Louise. "Documenting Women's Experiences of Conflict and Sexual Violence: On the Ground with the Solomon Islands Truth and Reconciliation Commission." In Jeffrey, *Transitional Justice in Practice*, 141–69.

———. "'What Will You Do with Our Stories?' Truth and Reconciliation in the Solomon Islands." *International Journal of Conflict and Violence* 8, no. 1 (2014): 92–103.

Villa-Vicencio, Charles. "Restorative Justice: Ambiguities and Limitations of a Theory." In *The Provocations of Amnesty: Memory, Justice, and Impunity*, edited by Charles Villa-Vicencio and Erik Doxtader, 30–50. Trenton, NJ: Africa World Press, 2003.

Wallis, Joanne, Renée Jeffery, and Lia Kent. "Political Reconciliation in Timor Leste, Solomon Islands and Bougainville: The Dark Side of Hybridity." *Australian Journal of International Affairs* 70, no. 2 (2016): 159–78.

Walsh, Pat, ed. *Chega! Book 1: What Happened and How to Stop It Happening Again*. Translated by Mayra Walsh. Dili, Timor-Leste: INSIST Press, 2015. http://www.chegareport.org/download-chega-products-2/.

Watson, Alison M. S. "Centralizing Childhood, Remaking the Discourse." In Beier, *Discovering Childhood in International Relations*, 243–61.

———. "Children and International Relations: A New Site of Knowledge?" *Review of International Studies* 32, no. 2 (2006): 237–50.

———. *The Child in International Political Economy: A Place at the Table*. London: Routledge, 2009.

Wells, Karen. *Childhood in a Global Perspective*. Cambridge: Polity Press, 2009.

Wessells, Michael. "Child Soldiers, Peace Education, and Postconflict Reconstruction for Peace." *Theory Into Practice* 44, no. 4 (2005): 363–69.

Wiebelhaus-Brahm, Eric. *Truth Commissions and Transitional Societies: The Impact on Human Rights and Democracy*. Abingdon, UK: Routledge, 2010.

World Youth Forum Delegates. *Dakar Youth Empowerment Strategy*. Transmitted by letter dated Oct. 4, 2001, from the Permanent Representative of Senegal to the United Nations to the Secretary-General. U.N. Doc. A/C.3/56/2 (Oct. 8, 2001). https://undocs.org/A/C.3/56/2.

Wyness, Michael. *Childhood and Society: An Introduction to the Sociology of Childhood*. Basingstoke, UK: Palgrave Macmillan, 2006.

Wyness, Michael, Lisa Harrison, and Ian Buchanan. "Childhood, Politics and Ambiguity: Towards an Agenda for Children's Political Inclusion." *Sociology* 38, no. 1 (2004): 81–99.

Young, Laura A., and Rosalyn Park. "Engaging Diasporas in Truth Commissions: Lessons from the Liberia Truth and Reconciliation Commission Diaspora Project." *International Journal of Transitional Justice* 3, no. 3 (2009): 341–61.

Zehr, Howard. "Restorative Justice: The Concept." *Corrections Today* 59, no. 7 (Dec. 1997): 68–70.

———. "Restorative Justice: When Justice and Healing Go Together." *Track Two: Constructive Approaches to Community and Political Conflict* 6, no. 3 (1997): 1–4.

Index

accountability, 5, 36–37, 136, 139, 201–202; for past violence, 6, 47; pursuit of, 17, 22, 37, 40–43, 53, 88, 216; through acknowledgement, 11, 28, 31, 140, 207; *see also* justice, transitional justice
adults, 20, 91; identities distinct from young people, 21, 57–59, 69, 207; mediating the participation of young people, 144, 149, 152, 187; perceptions of young people, 70, 96, 102, 119, 195; responsibility to protect children, 102, 112, 154; *see also* belonging, young people, youth, children
agency, 4, 17–19, 46; claim to, 11, 25–29, 42, 50, 155, 166, 214; definition of, 17–18; denial of, 29, 49, 34, 78, 106, 113, 129, 209; of young people, 20, 43–44, 208–211; over their stories, 5–6, 9, 47–48, 121–122, 172, 202; *see also* capacity, ownership, participation, subjecthood
Allen, Matthew, 32, 219n1

"big men," 3, 32, 165, 186–187
bystanders, 60, 81, 104

belonging: bestowed by adults, 60, 96; claimed by young people, 66, 71, 197; *see also* adults, agency, ownership
Berents, Helen, 73, 82, 128
Boyden, Jo, 63, 72

Canadian Truth and Reconciliation Commission (TRC), 204–205; *see also* transitional justice, truth and reconciliation commissions (TRCs)
capacity, 3–5, 65, 132–133, 140, 175, 258n8; as decision makers, 51, 54, 60, 98, 133, 199; of youth, 19, 55, 68, 183, 203; to meaningfully contribute, 65, 80, 116, 134, 146–150; *see also* agency, ownership, political will, subjecthood
Chega!, 22, 151–157, 223n63; *see also* Timor-Leste
child: Convention on the Rights of the, 17, 62, 119, 152, 170, 212; *see also* young people
child soldiers, 19–20, 64, 74, 103, 127–128, 187; experiences as, 64, 74–76, 113; stories of, 69, 114; *see also* deviance, victimhood, victim/perpetrator binary

283

childhood, 69–71, 91–95, 211; as socially constructed, 64, 72–74; conceptions of, 15–17, 19, 60–63, 71, 91; lost, 58, 74, 129, 138, 142, 193; *see also* young people, youthhood

children, 13–16, 62–63; experiences of, 9, 17, 57, 65–69, 90, 112, 123, 155, 185; rights, 19, 63–65, 89, 92–93, 97–100; *see also* young people, youth

citizenship, 45–48, 104, 127, 131, 145–146, 166, 197

conflict: causes of, 76–78, 143, 185; experiences of, 9, 20–21, 32–33, 47–50, 90, 106, 114, 127, 144–145, 155, 164, 186, 210; stories of, 6, 11, 22, 81, 118, 123, 138, 142–145, 154, 173–174, 195, 204; *see also* violence

D'Costa, Bina, 57, 99

deviance: as discourse, 123–124, 137; as narrative 140–148, 158; classification of young people, 115, 126, 141, 187, 212; role, 73, 122, 132; youth as, 75–78, 148–150; *see also* child soldiers

dialogue, 11–16, 18–19, 91, 105, 123, 129–133; as shared, 3, 11, 205; *see also* narrative, storytelling

embodiments of political agendas, 51, 70–71, 85, 90, 155, 204; *see also* representations

empowerment: as opportunity, 4–6, 7–9, 11, 22, 124, 136; restriction, 60, 114, 172; to participate, 10, 129–133, 163–164, 167, 206, 212, 216; *see also* ownership

future, the: aspirations of transitional communities, 11–12, 122, 126, 130–137, 146, 208; leaders, 67, 97, 145, 195, 204–205, 207; of young people, 69, 90, 107, 110–111, 155, 191, 197

gender considerations, 17, 78, 189, 216–127

Geneva Dialogue, 97–98, 241n34

Graça Machel Report, 18, 74, 103, 113

Gready, Paul, 58, 100, 105, 183

Greed-grievance model, 77–78, 142; *see also* youth bulge thesis, deviance

Guadalcanal Isatabu Freedom Movement (IFM), 184–186, 190

healing, 4, 11–12, 35, 46–47, 101, 163–164, 167, 193, 205

holistic approaches, 20–23, 35, 43, 45–46, 142, 153, 158, 162, 202–204; *see also* reconciliation, transitional justice

human rights: abuses, 11, 38–39, 40–43, 184, 204–205; as discourse, 36, 97; children's, 19, 63–65, 89, 92, 97–100, 109; holders, 13, 104; past violations, 4, 6, 13, 22, 31, 42, 86

institutional slippage between classifications of young people, 13, 33–34, 90, 121, 134, 156, 208; *see also* agency, representation

interpersonal relationships, 3–4, 11–12, 45, 154, 170–173, 202, 206; *see also* trust

Jacob, Cecilia, 72, 183

Jeffery, Renee, 37, 41, 49

justice: as inclusive practice, 2, 3, 170, 206; restorative, 24–25, 34, 41–44, 100, 134, 190, 214;

retributive, 6, 25, 35, 38–41, 159, 173; the pursuit of, 6, 40, 42–43, 49; *see also* accountability, transitional justice

Kastom, 184, 189; see also *Masta Liu*, Solomon Islands
Knowledge: local, 7, 15, 37, 53, 135–140, 147–149, 184–185; producers; 5, 12, 25–27, 34, 55, 73, 81–82, 108, 123–124, 139, 160, 202, 204, 213

Lee-Koo, Katrina, 57, 60, 68, 70, 95, 99

Malaita Eagle Force (MEF), 184–186, 190
McEvoy-Levy, Siobhan, 26, 57, 68, 79, 111, 177, 183
Masta Liu, 32, 180, 187–188, 225n5, 257n86; see also *Kastom*, Solomon Islands

narrative, 8–9; as methodology, 27–28; child soldier, 20; construction of, 10, 24–25, 45, 75, 133, 161, 170, 201; institutionalized, 7, 18, 109, 115, 134–135, 136, 158, 161, 169, 170–171, 191, 206; reconciliation, 20, 29, 57–58, 94, 104, 109, 117, 163–165, 181; *see also* storytelling
National Youth Policy, 32, 125, 136, 139–140, 145, 172; for the Solomon Islands, 175–178

ownership: claim to, 51, 121; denial of, 49, 111; opportunities for, 5, 12, 60, 89, 122, 165, 171–172; over their stories, 13, 33, 122, 202; *see also* agency, empowerment, political will

participation: as meaningful, 8, 48, 59, 65, 130, 136, 139, 172, 176, 202; as political, 18, 32, 62, 79, 96, 125, 165–166, 170–174; as substantive, 1–2, 7–10, 61, 77–78, 80–86, 104, 124, 129–133, 148, 203–205; capacity, 3, 8, 16, 50, 66, 88, 99, 106–111; of young people, 7, 21, 58, 62, 82, 90, 97, 124, 133, 204, 208; parameters, 8, 63, 66, 88, 96, 160, 215; *see also* agency, substantive inclusion
peace: formal architecture, 5, 10–13, 81; lasting, 5–6, 44, 143; recipients of, 75, 152–153; spoilers to, 20, 66, 76–77, 115, 150; sustainable, 11–12, 16, 24, 36, 64, 78, 88, 133–134, 144, 170, 173, 177, 192, 202–205, 208
peacebuilding, as discourse, 24, 214; 40, 59, 64, 180; contributions of youth to, 73, 80–81, 116, 130, 137, 177; *see also* transitional justice
Peruvian TRC, 88, 94, 111–119, 174
Philpott, Daniel, 44–45
policymakers, 18, 34, 73, 199, 209, 215; recommendations for, 214–216
political symbols, 67, 97, 155, 164, 198
political will, 6, 12, 51–52, 59, 69, 81, 98, 107–109, 131, 144–145, 150, 160, 172, 177, 182, 198, 205, 210; *see also* capacity, ownership
post-conflict: environments 47, 68, 73, 79–81; inclusion of young people, 6, 18, 29, 51, 60–62, 139, 205, 153; institutions, 8–10, 125–127, 150–151, 209, 211–213; needs of young people, 22, 10–13, 166, 177; practices, 55, 59, 81–82, 114, 137, 160; *see also* transitional justice

protection of children (perceived), 61, 75, 80, 92, 99–100, 104, 111, 118, 151, 207; see also young people, victimhood
protectionist strategies, 58, 60, 69, 71–72, 79, 87, 92, 97–99, 120, 154, 185; see also victim/perpetrator binary

Quinn, Joanna, 41, 46, 178

reconciliation, 10–13, 16–18, 44–49; as discourse, 19–20, 78, 87–90, 122, 206–207; goal of, 25, 54, 100, 181, 214; interpersonal, 2–4, 12, 36, 45, 47, 162, 167, 215; narrative, 9, 23, 26–28, 34, 57–58, 62, 90–91, 104, 109–112, 135, 143, 161, 174, 192–194, 207–212; political, 36, 45–47, 154, 214; processes, 15–17, 23, 46, 87, 119, 134, 158–160, 209 215; sites of agency, 10; see also truth and reconciliation commissions (TRCs), sustainable peace, transitional justice
reporting practices, 20, 33, 49, 86–87, 100, 118, 154, 167–168, 170; accessible, 22, 162; as limited, 109, 112–114, 125; as mandates, 160, 208–209; see also storytelling, truth and reconciliation commissions, truth-telling
representation: dominant, 56, 90, 108, 114, 116, 180; inclusive, 7, 166; institutional, 16, 29, 58, 64, 108, 111, 157, 184; narrow, 29, 32, 48, 54, 107, 115, 140, 209; of young people 55, 58, 62–64, 68–70, 78, 87–88, 92–95, 103; public, 23, 27, 33–34, 78, 121–123; tokenistic, 7, 216

Sierra Leone, 22, 16, 121–157, 211–213; see also truth and reconciliation commissions (TRCs)
silences, 38, 61, 75, 79, 103, 128, 132; institutional, 94, 107–108, 113, 154, 179; of young peoples' voices, 17, 62, 106, 109, 127, 186, 208–211
Solomon Islands: community, 1, 164, 169, 175, 179, 181, 188, 203; youth, 2–3, 32, 159–162, 167–170, 175–180; see also truth and reconciliation commissions (TRCs)
South Africa, 21, 88, 120, 142, 151, 153, 174, 211; TRC in, 40, 85–119; see also truth and reconciliation commissions (TRC)
storytelling, 2–4, 21, 25–27, 31–34, 41, 88, 132, 138, 148, 158, 163–164, 205–207; as process, 25, 47–48; see also narrative, truth and reconciliation commissions (TRCs), truth-telling
subjecthood, 52, 163–166, 171–173; see also agency, capacity
substantive inclusion, 7–10, 25, 34–36, 122, 139, 160, 204, 215; see also participation
sustainable peace 5–6, 16, 64, 88, 130–133, 144, 192, 202; see also reconciliation, transitional justice

Tensions, the, 1–3, 31–33, 161–166, 186–198, 219n1
Timor-Leste, 16, 21–22, 121–158, 174; see also *Chega!*, truth and reconciliation commissions (TRCs)
transitional justice: evolution, 36–38; institutions, 60, 121, 206; mechanisms, 7, 40–42, 96, 165, 206; practices, 4, 13, 23, 33–34,

40, 122, 128, 141, 155–157, 201, 206, 208, 215–216, 230n84; processes, 4, 16, 33–35, 51, 85, 162, 190, 202–203; scholarship, 31–53, 227n36; youth in, 55, 82, 90, 141, 156, 172, 191, 210, 214, 233n12; *see also* accountability, justice, reconciliation

trust: building, 12, 43, 47, 122, 150, 159, 168, 178, 190; restoration of, 6, 9, 45–46, 173, 202, 214; *see also* interpersonal relationships

truth and reconciliation commissions, 6, 14, 49–51, 206; as a process, 5, 8, 13, 24, 54, 114, 154, 166, 207–208; final reports of, 13, 21, 28, 38, 50, 57–58, 115, 129, 173–174, 207, 209; mandates, 29, 31–33, 48, 54, 100–102, 108, 122, 160, 199, 204–205; outcomes of, 33, 41, 94, 164; young people's engagement with, 8, 16–17, 21–24, 28, 30, 65, 160, 206; *see also* reconciliation, truth-telling; *see also* reporting practices, truth-telling

truth-telling, 25, 47, 205; as a process 25–26, 214; as practice 23, 124

Ubuntu, 100–101

United Nations: definition of youth, 66; General Assembly, 91, 129–131; Security Council Resolution 2250 on Youth, Peace and Security, 4–5, 206; World Programme of Action for Youth, 135; *see also* Convention on the Rights of the Child

victimhood: perceptions of, 64, 73, 79, 110–111, 128
victim/perpetrator binary, 9, 30, 55–59, 79, 119, 124–129, 137, 156–160, 175, 190–194, 209–213; *see also* protectionist strategies

violence: causes of, 11–12, 49, 107, 210; participation in 109–110; perpetrators of, 9, 20, 30, 47, 58 97, 143–144, 169, 175, 187, 191; propensity for, 77, 115; victims of, 111; *see also* conflict, victim/perpetrator binary

visibility: bestowed upon young people by adults, 48, 91; claimed, 24–25, 92; of young people, 28, 35, 49, 62, 87, 92, 99, 105–106, 116

voices: of children, 27, 97, 104, 107, 154; of youth, 14, 21, 26–27, 51, 59, 80, 88, 90–91, 111, 123, 132, 137, 158, 161–162, 190, 209; youth distinct from children, 59, 82, 90

Witness to Truth: Report of the Sierra Leone TRC, 22, 121; *see also* transitional justice, truth and reconciliation commissions, truth-telling

young people: agency of, 63, 91; definition of, 15, 65–67; as marginalized, 6, 18, 25, 127–128, 144, 154, 167–168, 206–208; as substantive participants 67, 131, 140, 165, 173; diverse experiences of, 90, 115, 156; engagement of, 72, 101, 111, 118–119, 211–212; representations of, 19–20, 27, 69–70, 95–103, 107–108, 119, 127, 149–152, 170, 183, 208

youth: as a development asset, 79, 103, 136–137, 177, 195; as agents of change, 56, 66–67, 80, 115–116, 131, 192; as a threat to security youth 58, 61–62, 80, 154, 190, 208; *see also* children, young people youthhood, 14, 60, 125, 134; *see also* childhood, young people

youth@work, 1–3, 173

youth bulge theory, 58, 74, 76–77, 142, 233n17, 238n86; *see also* deviance

www.ingramcontent.com/pod-product-compliance
Ingram Content Group UK Ltd.
Pitfield, Milton Keynes, MK11 3LW, UK
UKHW041916140426
5217IPUK00013B/179